Robert E. Williams
Gainesville, Fla. 32601

Y0-BYA-121

14

Digital Simulation
of Continuous Systems

Digital Simulation
of Continuous Systems

Yaohan Chu, *Professor*
University of Maryland

with the collaboration of
Frederick J. Sansom and
Harry E. Petersen

McGraw-Hill Book Company

New York   St. Louis   San Francisco   London
Sydney   Toronto   Mexico   Panama

Digital Simulation
of Continuous Systems

Dedicated to Paul F. Fuhrmeister of Langley Research Center, NASA, whose vision and pioneering effort have brought about probably the most advanced computer complex for the large-scale, all-digital, real-time simulation.

Preface

Since the advent of commercial electronic analog computers about two decades ago, analog computers have been widely used in schools and industries for the simulation of continuous systems. The analog computer has been proved to be an invaluable tool for simulation of continuous models and processes. It has also been found that the simulation makes one think in that he cannot simulate until he knows what to simulate. In recent years, hybrid computers have been added for iterative computations, parameter optimizations, Monte Carlo studies, adaptive or learning control simulations, and so forth. The use of simulation as a tool will undoubtedly become more popular in the future.

Digital simulation of continuous systems, or digital analog/hybrid simulation, is the use of a general-purpose digital computer to simulate continuous systems in a manner similar but not limited to the simulation on an analog or a hybrid computer. Digital simulation of continuous systems is not new, but it has become more and more accepted during recent years. Its wide usage appeared to begin when the digital computer was successfully used to give check solutions for analog simulations. This success had culminated in the use of the digital computer to generate details for setting up the analog computer. In the past decade, scientists and engineers have been developing digital-analog simulation languages to ease the programming effort on a digital computer. One language, MIMIC, which has been developed to succeed the MIDAS, is chosen as one of the simulation languages in this book. The original developers of the MIMIC language and processor, Frederick J. Sansom and Harry E. Petersen, collaborated on Chapters 2 and 6, respectively. Another language, DSL/90, which has also been widely accepted in the meantime, allows the joint use of DSL statements and FORTRAN statements; this gives a new approach to digital hybrid simulation. DSL/90 is thus chosen as another simulation language. In order to fully and effectively use the DSL, one should have knowledge in FORTRAN programming. FORTRAN is chosen as the third simulation language.

Many advantages in using the digital analog simulation are being recognized, among which are greater accuracy, no need of scaling, no hardware setup, easier maintenence, better machine utilization, rapid switching from one simulation to another, simpler storage of simulation programs for feasibility of function generation of two or more variables, and availability of mathematical functions in a digital computation facility. As a result of rapid advance in the computer technology, the cost per simulation is becoming lower and lower, and the latest super-speed digital computer has already made the large-scale, all-digital, real-time simulation a reality. And the spreading use of terminals for the on-line simulation is realizing the man-machine symbiosis, which so far has been available only on the analog computers.

This book is prepared with three objectives. The first is to teach digital simulation of continuous systems by MIMIC programming to those who have little or no programming background. The author's experience has shown that they can be instructed to simulate a model and obtain some results on the first day. This quick response reinforces the students' interest and convinces them that digital computer programming need not be a drudgery. To these students, Chapter 2 presents MIMIC programming in great detail and illustrates the syntax with examples. Those students who have had some programming background may find that the simulation by MIMIC (or MIMIC-like language) programming will reduce their programming time and effort. Since one can learn programming techniques by studying others' programs, Chapters 3 and 4 offer many examples in engineering and mathematical problems. Most of these examples include a short problem description, a brief introduction of the model, a set of numerical values for the simulation, the MIMIC program itself, and the result, mostly in plots. These examples may also serve as programming exercises. Some of these examples are selected from those commonly used to illustrate analog computer simulations; these examples enable some students to compare the results between the analog and digital computer simulations.

The second objective is to teach simulations by using three programming languages: the application-oriented languages of the MIMIC previously mentioned and the DSL/90 in Chapter 7, and the algorithmic language of FORTRAN IV in Chapter 5. These three languages are chosen because they have been the most widely accepted or used for digital simulation of continuous systems. MIMIC is the simplest to learn for digital analog simulations. DSL/90 offers a new approach for digital hybrid simulations. In order to use the DSL/90 effectively, one has to know FORTRAN programming (and the SIMIC processor in Chapter 6 is essentially a FORTRAN program). To compare these programming languages, the MIMIC programs in some examples are again shown in FORTRAN programs and DSL/90 programs from which their similarities and differences can be observed. Since the preparation of this manuscript began, there have appeared two new simulation languages, CSMP and CSSL. The CSMP (Continuous System Modeling Program) has become available for larger IBM/360 computer installations, while implementation of the CSSL (Continuous System Simulation Language) has just begun. Both languages evolved from and thus are similar to the DSL/90 and MIMIC. On the other hand, the simulation processors for the MIMIC and DSL/90 were both developed for the IBM 7090 family of computers, which are still widely used.

The third objective is to present the logic and construction of a simplified version of the MIMIC processor, called the SIMIC processor. This processor consists of less than 500 cards, and it is a working program. Chapter 6 describes the organization and the subroutines of this processor in great detail so that one may fully understand how a simulation processor functions. Such an understanding is just as important as the understanding of how an analog computer works, because the student may then be able to modify the language and change the processor. Indeed, Chapter 6 serves a more important purpose of demonstrating how one may construct a simulation processor for a MIMIC-like language to serve his particular profession.

This book is prepared for the engineers and scientists in the laboratories and industries who are interested in learning the subject and the programming of digital analog simulations. It is also written as a textbook for an undergraduate course on digital simulation of continuous systems or for an existing course on analog computers in which the subject of digital analog simulation is added. To teach digital analog simulation, the course may include the MIMIC language and programming in Chapters 1 through 4 in addition to adequate simulations on a large-scale general-purpose digital computer. For those digital computer installations where the MIMIC processor is not available, the SIMIC processor described in Chapter 6 may be implemented. To teach the students the digital hybrid simulation as well, FORTRAN programming in Chapter 5 and DSL/90 programming in Chapter 7 should be added. For a broader scope, the course may include Chapter 6 on the logic and construction of a simulation processor.

Much of the information for this book was taken from the available literature and the publications of the IBM Corporation, to which the author is indebted. The author wishes to acknowledge the review of Chapter 7 by W. M. Syn and D. K. Wyman of the IBM Corporation; the assistance by his students, particularly Hiroko Kobayashi, Howard Bloom, Herbert M. Ernst, I. L. Avrunin, and Binyork Ouyang; the services from the staff members of the Computer Science Center of the University of Maryland; and the typing of the manuscript by Pamela Pecknay of the Department of Electrical Engineering of the University of Maryland.

Yaohan Chu

Contents

Digital Simulation
of Continuous Systems

1
Introduction

Since general-purpose dc electronic analog computers became available soon after World War II, the analog computer has proved to be an invaluable tool for simulation of dynamic systems and solution of engineering problems. It has filled well the gap between exact analysis and physical intuition by providing a means for modeling. And modeling becomes a necessity where experimentation on actual hardware or testing on a prototype is too costly or too slow, or where danger exists to human operators. It has been said that "simulation makes people think." Indeed, one cannot simulate until he knows what to simulate; simulation thus offers a vehicle for learning and experimentation.

In this chapter, analog simulation of a simple continuous system to be modeled by a linear differential equation with constant coefficients is first introduced. Digital simulation of the same continuous system is then introduced. Since digital simulation of continuous systems requires the use of a simulation language, the development of simulation languages is reviewed; this review leads to the choice of the simulation languages to be presented in this book. Some remarks conclude this chapter.

1.1 ANALOG SIMULATION

Analog simulation [6, 9, 17, 36, 38]† means modeling of a physical system by using a general-purpose dc analog computer. Consider the classical linear mass-damper-spring system in Fig. 1.1. This system may be described by the following differential equation with constant coefficients:

$$M\ddot{x} + B\dot{x} + Kx = \sin(t) \tag{1.1}$$

where x = motion of mass
$\dot{x}$ = first derivative of x
$\ddot{x}$ = second derivative of x
M = mass
B = damping coefficient
K = spring constant

The forcing function of the system is a sinusoidal function of time t. It is obvious that the following two additional relations exist:

$$\dot{x} = \int_0^t \ddot{x}\, dt + \dot{x}(0) \tag{1.2}$$

$$x = \int_0^t \dot{x}\, dt + x(0) \tag{1.3}$$

where $\dot{x}(0)$ and $x(0)$ are initial conditions whose values are chosen to be 0 and A, respectively.

In using an analog computer to simulate the system, a block diagram is drawn, as shown in Fig. 1.2. Each block or circle represents a physically available element. The blocks with symbols ADD, MPY, DIV, and INT represent respectively the summer, multiplier, divider, and integrator. Blocks may have more than one input and/or more than one output. The circles symbolize generators. Those circles with

† Numbers in brackets are keyed to the References at the end of the chapter.

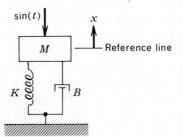

Fig. 1.1 A linear mass-damper-spring system.

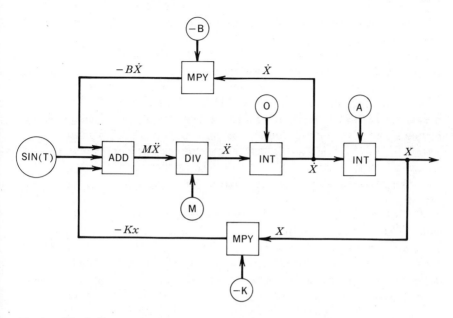

Fig. 1.2 Block diagram for the linear mass-damper-spring system.

symbols $-B$, O, A, M, and $-K$ generate constants, and that with $SIN(T)$ generates a sine function of T. Each circle has no input but may have more than one output. Each output from the block or the circle represents a variable or a constant, which physically is a voltage.

One can trace from the diagram that the upper MPY block output is $B\dot{x}$; the lower MPY block is $-Kx$; the DIV block output is $M\ddot{x}/M$; the ADD block output is $\sin(t) - B\dot{x} - Kx$; one INT block output is $\int_0^t \ddot{x}\,dt + \dot{x}(0)$, and the other INT block output is $\int_0^t \dot{x}\,dt + x(0)$. From the tracing, one may verify that the block diagram is constructed from the equation

$$M\ddot{x} = \sin(t) - B\dot{x} - Kx \qquad (1.4)$$

which is another form of Eq. (1.1). In this form, the term with the highest derivative is placed at the left side of the equation, and the remaining terms on the right side. The equality of Eq. (1.4) is implemented by the ADD block in Fig. 1.2. This is a very important technique in analog simulation, because it forms a computing loop by means of which an equation is solved.

The computer elements are connected according to the block diagram in Fig. 1.2. For this reason, it is commonly called a *setup diagram*.

A conventional setup diagram differs from that in Fig. 1.2 in employing blocks with many shapes (each representing a particular element) and in some cases with circuit schematics. The INT and ADD blocks in Fig. 1.2 differ from the actual elements slightly. The actual integrator and summer are made of operational amplifiers; each gives an output which is the negative of that of the ADD or INT block in Fig. 1.2. The multiplier with one of two inputs being a constant is a relatively simple element, called a potentiometer. A multiplier with both inputs being variables (or a divider) is a much more complex element; it may employ an instrument servo or many electronic components.

Magnitudes of problem variables (i.e., dependent variables) are represented on a general-purpose dc analog computer by voltages. For a 100-volt analog computer, the range of the voltages is -100 to $+100$ volts (-10 to $+10$ volts for a 10-volt computer). The scale factor of a program variable may be defined as the ratio of the maximum voltage (that is, 100 volts) to the maximum value of a program variable. *Magnitude scaling* is the task by which scale factors of all program variables are properly chosen so that none exceeds the maximum voltage. If a program variable exceeds the maximum voltage, then the corresponding amplifier becomes saturated and the result becomes erroneous. Magnitude scaling for a large simulation is frustrating and tedious, because there are many program variables and one usually does not know what would be the maximum values of these program variables. Trial runs with arbitrarily selected scale factors are necessary.

Time is the independent variable on an electronic analog computer. Similar to magnitude scaling, there is the task of *time scaling*, which is selecting the time scale factor of the independent variable for the simulation. The time scale factor may be defined as the ratio of computing time to problem time. There is a maximum computing time permissible on an analog computer because of consideration of accuracy of the result. If the time scale factor is 1, it is a real-time simulation. If the time scale factor is less or larger than 1, the simulation is respectively faster or slower than real time. Since there is only one time scale factor, the task of time scaling is much easier and simpler than the task of magnitude scaling.

After the setup diagram of a simulation is drawn, scale factors of all variables and constants are either determined or arbitrarily chosen. Voltages which represent input constants, initial conditions, values of potentiometer settings, and the like are determined. Next, the computer elements are connected on a patch board. The simulation is now ready for testing or checking out. Since solutions obtained from a general-purpose dc analog computer are in the form of voltages, instruments such as voltmeters, recorders, plotters, and cathode-ray-tube (CRT) displays are required for showing the results. These instruments are connected directly to those terminals of the computer whose values are to be shown. This direct access to and immediate display of computed results in an analog form is a very important advantage of analog simulation.

The accuracy of the result obtained from an electronic analog computer depends on the accuracies of the components of the computer. The accuracies of computer components vary from 0.005 to 3 percent of full scale. Therefore, a poor selection of scale factors could result in poor utilization of accurate range of the computer. When components require accuracies of better than about 0.2 percent, the costs of components increase rapidly. Because of limitation of component accuracies, an accuracy of 1 percent for a simulation with a modest complexity is considered excellent, though an accuracy of a few percent is more likely.

The limited accuracy of an analog computer cannot meet the need in simulating missiles and space vehicles. In these applications, the digital computer can give adequate accuracy for the trajectory computation, while the analog computer is fast enough for the vehicle dynamics. The combined use of analog and digital computers has led to the development of hybrid simulation. Hybrid simulations are now applied to Monte Carlo studies, parameter optimizations, iterative computations, and adaptive or learning control simulations. A hybrid computer facility is far more expensive than an analog-computer facility. And hybrid simulation requires both analog-computer programming and digital-computer programming. However, adequate speed of solutions necessary for certain applications and convenience of immediate access to the results are two most important benefits from an analog or a hybrid computer facility.

1.2 DIGITAL SIMULATION

Digital simulation of continuous systems, which is also referred to in this book as *digital analog simulation*, is the use of a general-purpose digital computer to simulate continuous systems in a manner similar but not limited to the simulation on an analog computer or a hybrid computer. Since digital simulation requires programming on a digital computer, it should have a suitable programming language. A programming language for digital simulation of continuous systems is called a simulation language. Since the block diagram (or setup diagram) is the language of analog simulation, the block diagram has been transformed into a block-oriented language which has become a part of a programming language for digital simulation of continuous systems.

As an example of digital simulation, consider the block diagram in Fig. 1.2, which represents the linear mass-damper-spring system in Fig. 1.1. For each block, one writes a "statement" to show the inputs, the output, and the function of the block. Thus, the two MPY blocks in Fig. 1.2 can be written as

$$\text{NEGBX} = \text{MPY(1DX,NEGB)} \qquad (1.5)$$
$$\text{NEBKX} = \text{MPY(X,NEGK)} \qquad (1.6)$$

where the inputs $\dot{x}$, $-B$, x, and $-K$ are represented, respectively, by 1DX, NEGB, X, and NEGK, and the outputs $-B\dot{x}$ and $-Kx$, respectively, by NEGBX and NEGKX. Similarly, the ADD and DIV blocks can be written as

$$\text{M2DX} = \text{ADD(NEGBX,NEGKX,SIN(T))} \qquad (1.7)$$
$$\text{2DX} \ \ = \text{DIV(M2DX,M)} \qquad (1.8)$$

where M, $\ddot{x}$, $M\ddot{x}$, and sin (t) are represented, respectively, by M, 2DX, M2DX, and SIN(T). T represents the independent variable t. And the two INT blocks are

$$\text{1DX} = \text{INT(2DX,0.)} \qquad (1.9)$$
$$\text{X} \ \ = \text{INT(1DX,A)} \qquad (1.10)$$

where $\dot{x}$ and x are represented, respectively, by 1DX and X, and **A** and 0 are the initial conditions.

The above six statements thus describe the linear mass-damper-spring system. In each of these statements, the output is at the left side of the equal sign, the inputs (as well as parameters such as initial conditions in the INT blocks) are enclosed by a pair of parentheses, and the function is represented by a symbolic name. Function names such as MPY and INT, as well as SIN and T, are so-called *reserved words;* they should not be used for other names.

Instead of using a block diagram, a modern simulation language may describe the system directly from the equation. For example, simulation of the above mass-damper-spring system may be described by the following statements:

$$\text{CON(M,B,K)} \qquad (1.11)$$
$$\text{PAR(A)} \qquad (1.12)$$
$$\text{2DX} = (-\text{B*1DX} - \text{K*X} + \text{SIN(T))/M} \qquad (1.13)$$
$$\text{1DX} = \text{INT(2DX,0.)} \qquad (1.14)$$
$$\text{X} \ \ = \text{INT(1DX,A)} \qquad (1.15)$$
$$\text{FIN(T,1.)} \qquad (1.16)$$
$$\text{OUT(T,X)} \qquad (1.17)$$
$$\text{PLO(T,X)} \qquad (1.18)$$
$$\text{END} \qquad (1.19)$$

where x, $\dot{x}$, and $\ddot{x}$ are represented by X, 1DX, and 2DX, respectively; M, B, K, and A by the same letters; and sin (t) and t by SIN(T) and T, respectively.

The above statement (1.13) describes Eq. (1.1), while statements (1.14) and (1.15) describe Eqs. (1.2) and (1.3). The CON statement specifies that coefficients M, B, and K are constants; their values are to be provided later. The PAR statement specifies that initial condition A is a parameter whose value is also to be provided later. A parameter is a constant, except that its value may be changed after each run (i.e., after each simulation of the system). In addition, there must be a FIN statement to specify the condition for terminating the simulation; statement (1.16) specifies the terminating condition to be T larger than 1. The OUT statement gives a tabular output with two columns: one column for the independent variable T and the other for the dependent variable X. The PLO statement gives a plot of X versus T. (It can be a plot on the printer or a plot on the plotter, or both) The END statement indicates the end of the program. Values of the constants and parameters follow this statement. This completes a digital simulation program written in a simulation language which is called MIMIC.

When the program for a digital simulation is written, it is punched into a deck of cards. This deck is added to control cards (normally required in a digital-computer facility) and then sent to the facility to be run. Should any error have been committed, such as punched-card error, control-card error, programming error, or modeling error, the result will not be correct. These errors have to be corrected, and the task of removing them is commonly known as "debugging." When the debugging task is over, the deck is ready to make one or many simulation runs.

In the above example, magnitude scaling and time scaling have not been mentioned. For a digital-computer facility suitable for digital analog simulation, the computer should have hardware in floating-point arithmetic. The number that a variable or a constant may represent in such a computer can be in an extremely large range. For example, the number in the IBM 7090 family of computers ranges approximately from -10^{38} to $+10^{38}$, except those very small numbers near zero (approximately between 0 and $\pm 10^{-38}$), and has a precision of eight decimal digits. Such a range and precision are far from what an analog computer can match. Therefore, no magnitude scaling is normally needed. Time scaling can also be eliminated for most cases since variable-step integration algorithms have become available. For those few cases where time scaling is needed, it can be simply done.

In a large-scale digital-computer facility normally operated for batch processing, the computer time for a simulation may be longer than the problem time, because a significant amount of time is required for output preparation (special plotting) and overhead processing of the computer system. However, it is now possible to simulate some systems on a real-time basis on so-called superspeed digital computers, and leave simulations faster than real time to hybrid computers.

The accuracy of the result obtained from an electronic digital computer depends on the model that is being simulated, the "numerical integrator," and the number of significant digits by which the number is represented in the digital computer. In general, the result from a digital simulation is more accurate than that from an analog simulation. On the other hand, the digital computer is a serial machine, while the analog computer is a parallel machine. A more complex model requires more time and memory capacity on the digital computer but more equipment on the analog computer. Nevertheless, it is common nowadays to use the result of a digital simulation as a check solution for a more complex analog simulation.

1.3 SIMULATION LANGUAGES

The development of digital analog simulation is that of simulation languages and simulators. The first digital analog simulator has been credited to Selfridge, who reported in 1955 [1] a digital computer program developed at the U.S. Naval Ordnance Test Station, Inyokern, California, to enable the digital computer to handle a larger problem and to achieve a greater accuracy than the available REAC (Reeves Electronic Analog Computer) could. Selfridge showed that the block organization of an analog computer could be adopted on a digital computer. The simulator was written on the IBM 701 computer. Simpson's rule was used for integration. Selfridge indicated that in a problem on aeroballistics one hour's work (including half an hour of computer time) was sufficient to add another equation to the digital-computer program, but about six hours was necessary on the analog computer. However, the IBM 701 computer was the first large-scale digital computer that IBM built; it has no hardware in floating-point arithmetic. And, in 1955, development of assemblers was in its early stage. Interpreters, compilers, monitors, and other software that are commonplace today had not been conceived and developed. Thus, Selfridge was a Charles Baggage, because computer technology and programming techniques were not ready.

Since then, a great number of simulation languages and simulators [16, 26] have been developed. In 1958, Lesh [2] extended Selfridge's work and developed, at the Jet Propulsion Laboratory of the California Institute of Technology, the DEPI (Differential Equations Pseudo-code Interpreter). The interpreter was written for the DATATRON 204 computer (a small-scale digital computer even at that time). The fourth-order Runge-Kutta method was used for integration. This work was not fully completed. In 1959, DEPI was rewritten for the IBM 704 computer by Hurley [5] and called DEPI 4. This effort led to the development at the University of Wisconsin in 1961 of a more significant

language called DYSAC (DigitallY Simulated Analog Computer).
DYSAC was written by Hurley and Skiles [11] for the CDC 1604 computer. Use of the fourth-order Runge-Kutta method for integration was
retained. Mathematical functions normally available in a digital-computer system, such as exponential, logarithmic, and transcendental functions, were made available in DYSAC. A set of 16 control statements
was provided to permit a series of runs for varying parameters or initial
conditions from run to run. Diagnostic messages for programming errors
or computational difficulties were provided; such messages are of great
help in debugging digital-computer programs. Mode-switching integrators were later added to DYSAC by Schaefer.

The development of DYSAC brought about in 1964 a series of
BLOC (BLock Oriented Compiler) languages at the University of Wisconsin and the University of Colorado: COBLOC, FORBLOC, HYBLOC,
and MADBLOC. COBLOC, developed by Janoski, Schaefer, and Skiles
[29], was written for the CDC 1604 and 3600 computers. It provides,
in addition to the usual blocks, mode-switching integrators and logical
building blocks such as gates and flip-flops. It generates check solutions for hybrid simulations and is a substitute for hybrid computers.
FORBLOC, developed by Vebber, translates a DYSAC language into a
FORTRAN program; this makes the simulator available on other digital
computers which have a suitable FORTRAN compiler. HYBLOC was
developed by Hurley; it is a hybrid computer simulator written for the
IBM 7090 family of computers. MADBLOC, developed by Rideout
and Tavernini [18], is also a hybrid simulator. It is written in the MAD
language (an algorithmic language developed at the University of
Michigan). FORBLOC and MADBLOC use trapezoidal formulas for
integration; HYBLOC employs fourth-order Runge-Kutta formula;
COBLOC offers a choice of fourth-order Runge-Kutta formula, fifth-
order Runge-Kutta formulas, or a fifth-order predictor-corrector.

In the meantime, Stein, Rose, and Parker [3] developed, in 1958,
ASTRAL (Analog Schematic Translator to Algebraic Language) for the
IBM 704 computer. In addition to being a significant advance in the
syntax of simulation language, ASTRAL was written as a compiler which
generated a FORTRAN program. Thus, FORTRAN was used as an
intermediate language. ASTRAL also permitted the use of FORTRAN
arithmetic statements in a certain specific manner. It introduced automatic sorting of the statements of a simulation program into a proper
order; this feature makes preparation of a simulation program similar to
wiring on the patch board of an analog computer.

In 1962, DAS (Digital Analog Simulator) was developed by Gaskill,
Harris, and McKnight [12] at the Martin Company, Orlando, Florida,
for the IBM 7090 computer. DAS was similar to DEPI and DYSAC,

but used a more basic set of blocks (or functions) and a simpler procedure for writing the simulation program. It was a compiler which translated a simulation program into an FAP (7090 symbolic assembly language) program. The outstanding feature was ease of programming and automatic checking of programming errors. It employed the simple Euler's formula for integration and provided no sorting. Harnett, Sansom, and Warshawsky [13], inspired by the work of DAS, developed in 1963 at Wright-Patterson Air Force Base an improved version of DAS, which was called MIDAS (Modified Integration Digital Analog Simulator). The simulator was written by Petersen [14]. MIDAS sparked acceptance by hundreds of large computer installations and met with an unprecedented success, which may be attributed to the following reasons. First, analog-computer users were looking for a simple way to obtain checking solutions for analog simulation and to determine optimum amplitude and time scalings. Second, the MIDAS simulator provides many useful features, including arbitrary function generation of single variable, an implicit function to handle algebraic loops, automatic sorting to ease the programming, and a variable-step fifth-order predictor-corrector for integration. The variable-step feature allows the step size in the MIDAS integration routine to adjust itself and thus relieves the programmer from the chore of time scaling, except for a few cases. This feature represents the basic departure of MIDAS from its predecessor, DAS. Third, MIDAS was written for the IBM 7090 family of computers, which was the most popular large-scale digital computer of the period. Thus, with the arrival of MIDAS, digital analog simulation reached a climax. One might add that Selfridge's dream came true. MIDAS was an interpreter; a compiler version was reported by Burgin [30] in 1966.

The outstanding success of MIDAS spurred a series of new developments during the succeeding years. Digital-computer manufacturers, who up to that time had paid little attention to this application of digital computers, now realized the market potential of digital analog simulation. Since then, some have offered software for their digital computers, while one has marketed an integrated system for the digital analog simulation. IBM sponsored a scientific computing symposium on digital simulation of continuous systems in June, 1966 [37]. In view of the important advantage of direct access and immediate display of computed results on an analog computer, on-line digital analog simulation by display consoles or remote terminals was experimented. A large-scale, real-time, all-digital simulation facility was seriously considered and later implemented by a research center instead of a hybrid simulation facility. In Italy, development of the SIOUX system and a block-oriented language for hybrid simulation was described by De Backer and van Wauwe [24]. In Australia, work on SIMTRAN was reported [25]; SIMTRAN allowed intermixing with FORTRAN on a subroutine basis and was being designed for on-line users. In Great Britain, Hughes and Brameller [32] developed SAM (Simulation of Analogue Methods), and Dineley and Preece [33] developed KALDAS (Kidsgrove ALgol Digital Analogue Simulation). Both simulated an analog computer. SAM was written in C.H.L.F.3 Mercury Autocode for Mercury computers, while KALDAS was written in ALGOL for English Electric Leo-Marconi KDF9 computers. And in Germany, work on ASIM for digital analog simulations was reported by Jentsch [43].

Sansom and Petersen, confident with the success of MIDAS, recognized that MIDAS could be much improved and, in 1965, presented MIMIC [20, 39], a successor to MIDAS, which also was written for the IBM 7090 family of computers. Since MIMIC, like its predecessor, is a block-oriented language, a simulation program can be prepared from a block diagram. But it allows FORTRAN-like algebraic expressions and nesting of functions (i.e., blocks); one may also write a simulation program with FORTRAN-like statements. This feature eliminates the necessity of drawing a block diagram and greatly reduces the number of statements. MIMIC features a logical control variable, permits subprograms written in MIMIC, employs a variable-step fourth-order Runge-Kutta method for integration, and provides hybrid and logical functions for hybrid simulations. While MIDAS was an interpreter, MIMIC is a compiler which translates a simulation program directly into a machine-language program; no further compilation or assembly is required. MIMIC is more efficient than MIDAS, and executes a program ten times faster than MIDAS. MIMIC has also been widely distributed and accepted. For these reasons, MIMIC is chosen as one of the simulation languages to be presented in this book.

About the time MIMIC was presented, DSL/90 was introduced by IBM Corporation for the IBM 7090 family of computers. It was developed by Syn and Wyman [21, 22, 34] and updated in late 1967 to become DSL/360 [40]. A special version, DSL/44, for the IBM System 360/44 was also available in 1967. DSL (Digital Simulation Language) is a block-oriented language with a large number of blocks. It allows a choice of six integration routines and sorts the statements of a DSL simulation program. Plot output is available on an IBM 1627 plotter. The DSL processor was written in FORTRAN IV (with some MAP coding). It first translates a simulation program into FORTRAN IV subroutines, which are then compiled. The compiled result is served as an input to the simulator. DSL combines features of simulation language MIDAS and algorithmic language FORTRAN. It permits intermixing of DSL statements and FORTRAN statements; this extends some FORTRAN capability to DSL programming. It also permits incorporation of a DSL program into a FORTRAN program; this extends DSL capability to FORTRAN programming. Thus, DSL gives a new approach to digital hybrid simulation. Because DSL has also been widely distributed and accepted, it is chosen as another simulation language to be presented in this book. In addition to DSL, IBM also offered System/360 CSMP (Continuous System Modeling Program) to the IBM 360 and 1130 computers. The CSMP is similar to the DSL/90, as the former was derived from the latter. In order to make fullest and most effective use of the DSL or CSMP, one should have knowledge in FORTRAN programming. For this reason, FORTRAN is chosen as the third simulation language.

The Simulation Software Committee [42] of the Simulation Council, Inc., which was formed in May, 1965, for proposing a standard language for continuous system simulation, published CSSL (Continuous System Simulation Language) in December, 1967. It was an impressive proposal. As stated in the proposal, CSSL is primarily a communication language for dynamic system simulation with little concern for problems of implementation. The MIMIC language was chosen as the starting point, but CSSL is heavily influenced by DSL/90, FORTRAN, and ALGOL. CSSL was designed with the objective of providing, on the one hand, an extremely simple and obvious programming tool for the novice user and, on the other hand, a great flexibility and power for the sophisticated programmer faced with a major programming task. It is also an objective that the language be flexible for expansion (particularly for input/output) in view of anticipated wide use of displays, terminals, and time-sharing systems.

Before leaving this survey of simulation languages, a number of interesting developments should be mentioned. In 1962, the development of APACHE (Analog Programming And CHEcking) by EURATOM in Ispra, Italy, was reported [8]. APACHE was to produce a detailed list of instructions for setting up a simulation for a particular but popular analog computer, PACE/231R. However, it was not fully ready until the release of version IV in July, 1965 [27]. This approach of using a digital computer can reduce programming time on an analog computer, but it does not make full use of the capability of a digital computer in simulating a model in comparison with the approach by digital analog simulation.

DES-1 (Differential Equation Solver), conceived and developed by Palevsky, Howell, and Levine in 1963 [10, 19], consists of an SDC 9300 computer, with hardware floating-point arithmetic, a special set of software accepting a block-oriented language, and a control console to aid the operator in program debugging and in simulation control. It was designed to be operated like an analog computer. It is unique in that an integrated system is made commercially available for digital analog simulation; this may not be too surprising in view of Palevsky's long interest in digital differential analyzers.

PACTOLUS was introduced in 1964 by Brennan and Sano [15] of IBM San José as an attempt to make a small-scale general-purpose digital computer act like an analog computer. It was written in FORTRAN II-D for the IBM 1620 computer with the 1627 plotter and a card read-punch. This work was significant in two respects. It provided the 1620 computer users a possibility of using digital analog simulation. More significantly, it demonstrated the potential of on-line digital analog simulation, as remote terminals, visual displays, and multiprogramming were just over the horizon. Green [35] reported in 1966 the development of OLDAS (On-Line DAS) at the Naval Weapons Laboratory, Dahlgren, Virginia. It was written for the IBM 360/50 computer with 2250 display console. Schlesinger and Sashkin [28, 37] also reported in 1966 the development of EASL (Engineering Analysis and Simulation Language) for the IBM 7094 computer. It allows intermixing with FORTRAN statements. The EASL is implemented with two consoles: a CRT console for on-line display and a typewriter/plotter console for on-line plotting and data entry.

The above simulation languages are used for simulating continuous systems. A language for simulating sampled-data systems, called BLODI (BLOck DIagram compiler), was first adopted for use at Bell Laboratories in 1959 [7]. It is a block-oriented language with different kinds of blocks, such as amplifier, clipper, rectifier, and filter. BLODI was later improved and called BLODIB. BLODIB, reported by Karafin in 1965 [23, 37], was written for the IBM 7094II computer. It is used mainly for processing a relatively smooth signal. An example of using BLODIB for simulating a vocoder system was reported by Golden [31].

While digital simulations of continuous systems which model after ordinary differential equations were being developed, automation of the solutions of partial differential equations was being pursued. Forsythe and Wasow [44] reported that in 1957 an association of the IBM 704 computer users called SPADE started project SCOPE. The goal of this project was to handle problems involving systems of up to 10 simultaneous partial differential equations in one or two space variables, plus possibly a timelike variable. The equations and the boundary conditions are permitted to be nonlinear, but the user must provide his own numerical analysis. It was learned recently that the SPADE/SCOPE work has not progressed very far since 1960.

In 1962, Engeli reported the development of the ELLIPTIC language and processor [46, 47] for computing the finite-difference stars in rectangular grids over arbitrary domains and for solving the resulting matrix problem by the Gauss-Jordan elimination method. Since 1964, a limited effort under Dr. Elizabeth Cuthill's direction has been spent in exploring semianalytic methods and in solving boundary- and initial-value partial differential equation problems. This effort makes use of the available FORMAC language and processor [49]. A research program [50] under Prof. R. Kohr's direction at the school of mechanical engineering of Purdue University explores the use of a hybrid computer facility for developing semianalytic solutions to partial differential equations by the so-called method of weighted residuals [51]. Since 1967, H. M. Ernst at the department of electrical engineering of the University of Maryland has undertaken a research program in developing a MIMIC-like language and processor for several classes of partial differential equations, integral equations, and integrodifferential equations by means of semianalytic methods [51].

The most advanced and comprehensive work published to date is the SALEM [52], which was a doctoral dissertation by S. M. Morris under Prof. W. E. Schiesser's supervision at Lehigh University in 1967. SALEM is a digital simulation language and processor for solving partial differential equations. It accepts 17 different types of elliptic, parabolic, and hyperbolic partial differential equations of the second order. Constant or variable coefficients, linear or nonlinear, are allowed. General boundary and/or initial conditions can be expressed. Rectangular, cylindrical, and spherical coordinates may be used. A contribution is the automatic interval adjustment to maintain truncation-error bounds. However, until recently, the processor had not been released.

1.4 DIGITAL SIMULATION PROCESSOR

A digital computer executes the program only when it is in *machine language*. Machine language today constitutes only 1s and 0s and, in some machines, coded characters. A simulation program (i.e., a program written in a simulation language) must first be translated into a machine language before it can be executed. A specially written program which performs these and other functions for digital simulation of continuous systems is called here a *digital simulation processor*.

A processor can be an interpreter or a compiler. If a processor completes translation of the simulation program before simulation begins, it is called a *compiler*. Once a simulation program is compiled, it can be used for many runs without further compilation unless changes in the simulation program are to be made. If a processor translates one statement of the simulation program and then executes it before it translates the others, it is called an *interpreter*. For more than one run, an interpreter requires more computer time, because interpretation is required for each run. But it can offer flexibility for program changes during or after a run.

What are the functions of a digital simulation processor?   The first function is translation.   It translates a simulation program to one in an intermediate language.   This intermediate language can be a block-oriented language similar to the original simulation language, or it can be a known programming language.   The former approach gives simplicity and needs less computer time.   An example is the function language in the MIMIC processor; the function language is essentially a block-oriented language in a tabular form.   The latter approach may extend the capability of the programming language to the original simulation language.   Another example is the FORTRAN IV language, which is the intermediate language for the DSL processor.   The program in the intermediate language is then translated into one in machine language either directly or through another translation.   In the case of the DSL processor, the program in FORTRAN IV is translated into one in MAP (an assembly language), which is then translated to the machine language of the 7090 computers.

The second function of a digital simulation processor is sorting, which sequences the statements in the simulation program or in the program in the intermediate language into a proper order.   The sorting logic was presented by Stein and Rose [4].   Briefly, a block (or a function) is in a proper order if the values of the inputs to the block are known when the operation of the block is to be computed.   Constants, parameters, and initial conditions are all known quantities.   Provision of sorting makes the simulation language nonprocedural.   The third function is simulation.   The processor initializes the simulation, computes the model, calls the integration routine, iterates the computation cycle, tests for termination of a simulation run, and determines additional simulation runs.   A fourth function is integration, which may be regarded as the heart of digital simulation.   There are many integration formulas; their choice affects accuracy of the result and the amount of the computer time. In case of using variable step size, the choice of error criterion is important.   The choice of absolute or relative error and the choice of the amount of error limit are sensitive to accuracy and speed of the integration routine.   The fifth function is to handle inputs and outputs. Before the simulation starts, values of constants, parameters, and initial conditions have to be read in.   At an appropriate time during a simulation run, the simulated result must be outputted.   The output can be a table from the printer, a plot from the plotter, or a display on the CRT console. These outputs can be off-line or on-line operations.   The sixth function is to provide a library of special routines such as the time-delay routine, function-generation routine, and random-number-generation routines. The processor does not have to keep those routines (such as mathematical routines) which are already in the library of the computer system.

   The MIMIC processor is now used as an example of a digital simulation processor. In describing the sequential operations of a digital-computer program, one often resorts to a diagram known as a flowchart. Figure 1.3 shows the flowchart of a greatly simplified digital simulation processor for MIMIC language programs. In the translation phase as shown in Fig. 1.3, the processor, after the initialization, translates a MIMIC simulation program into a program in an intermediate language, called a function language. This function-language program, which is in a tabular form, is next sorted into a proper sequence. For the MIMIC program in statements (1.11) to (1.19), the sorted function-language program is shown in Table 1.1. The function names in the second column of Table 1.1 can be regarded as block names. The inputs or initial conditions are in the third to sixth columns, and the output is in the first column. If the first two and the last four functions are ignored, the middle nine functions can be drawn into a block diagram almost identical to that in Fig. 1.2, except that a NEG (negative) block and a SUB (subtract) block are used instead of negative values of B and K being used in Fig. 1.2. Thus, MIMIC is basically a block-oriented language.

   The processor next translates the function-language program into a machine-language program. This program represents the model to be simulated, and is to be called later by the integration routine for computing the derivatives. The direct translation to machine language in the MIMIC processor is unique. This approach eliminates further compilation or assembly, and thus reduces the computer time. At this point, the translation phase is completed.

   The processor now enters the simulation phase. After initializing the simulation phase, it reads input data, writes headings for the outputs, and then stores the printer output and the plot output on separate magnetic tapes. The termination condition of the run is tested. If the condition is not met, the processor calls in the integration routine, which, in this case, performs numerical integration and computes the derivatives. (The statements which are involved in the derivative computation represent the model.) The numerical integration and derivative computation are alternated until the time is reached to give the next output. This forms a computing loop, as shown in the flowchart of Fig. 1.3. When the termination condition for the run is met, the termination condition for the simulation is tested. If another run is required, the processor reads input data for the next run. This forms another loop, as shown in the flowchart of Fig. 1.3. If there is no more run, the PRINT data stored on a magnetic tape are ready for an off-line printing. Furthermore, the PLOT routine is called in and the PLOT data previously stored on the magnetic tape are processed for an off-line plotting. The digital simulation is now completed.

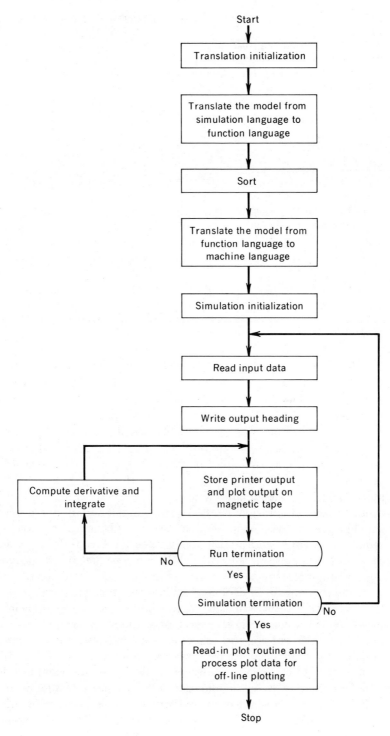

Fig. 1.3 Flowchart of a digital simulation processor.

Table 1.1   An example function-language program

Function output	Function name	Function input	Function input	Function input	Initial condition
	CON	M	B	K	
	PAR	A			
102	SIN	T			
103	MPY	B	1DX		
104	MPY	K	X		
002	NEG	103			
105	SUB	002	104		
106	ADD	105	102		
2DX	DIV	106	M		
1DX	INT	2DX			O
X	INT	1DX			A
	FIN	T	1.		
	OUT	T	X		
	PLO	T	X		
	END				

1.5 REMARKS

A general-purpose digital computer for digital simulation of continuous systems has a number of requirements. It should have hardware floating point arithmetic in order to eliminate magnitude scaling, a long word length to reduce round-off error, and a random-access memory sufficient for handling large-scale simulation. It should have a speed of operation adequate for compilation and computation of simulation programs. The integration routine should be able to vary the step size automatically so as to practically eliminate time scaling, should employ a sufficiently sophisticated integration method for giving a required accuracy, and should have provision to handle discontinuities. Terminals for the remote data entry and plotting, as well as CRT consoles for visual displays, are becoming more available, though they are still expensive. The digital computer should be capable of multiprogramming or time sharing if the on-line operation of these terminals is practical.

Many advantages in using digital analog simulation are being recognized, among which are greater accuracy, almost no need of scaling, trading of one element for the other (e.g., a multiplier for an integrator), possible function generation of two or more variables, availability of mathematical functions normally available in a digital-computer facility, and feasibility of hybrid simulation. Additional advantages are rapid switching from one simulation to another; simpler storage of simulation programs for reuse, as no patch boards are involved; easier maintenance, as there are no accuracy tests and no calibration; and better machine utilization because the computer system can be immediately switched for other applications. As a result of the rapid advance in computer technology, the cost per computation (or simulation) is becoming even lower, and the latest superspeed digital computers make the real-time digital analog simulation already feasible in many instances.

PROBLEMS

1.1. Given a model described by the set of equations

$$(\dot{x} - y)z = xw$$
$$(\dot{y} + x)z = yw$$
$$z^2 = x^2 + y^2$$
$$w = 1 - x^2 - y^2$$

and given the initial conditions

$$x(0) = 0.5 \qquad y(0) = 0$$

use the blocks ADD, SUB, MPY, DIV, INT, and SQR (square root) to draw a block diagram for simulating the model.

1.2. Given a model described by the set of equations

$$M_1\ddot{x} + B_1\dot{x} + K_1x = C_1y$$
$$M_2\ddot{y} + B_2\dot{y} + K_2y = C_2x$$

and given the initial conditions

$$\dot{x}_0 = 0 \qquad x_0 = A$$
$$\dot{y}_0 = 0 \qquad y_0 = 1$$

draw a block diagram for simulating the model. The following are the constants and their values:

$$M_1 = 0.5 \qquad M_2 = 1$$
$$B_1 = 1 \qquad B_2 = 4.89$$
$$K_1 = 1.3 \qquad K_2 = 12.643$$

The following are the parameters and the values for two cases:

(a) $C_1 = 0.1 \qquad C_2 = 0.16 \qquad A = 0$
(b) $C_1 = 0.5 \qquad C_2 = 0.20 \qquad A = 0$

1.3. A mechanical system, shown in Fig. 1.4, transmits a rotational motion from a power source to a driven shaft. It is a three-degree-of-freedom torsional vibration system, described by the following set of equations:

$$\ddot{A}_0 + M_1\dot{A}_0 + M_2\dot{A}_1 + M_3A_0 + M_4A_1 = 0$$
$$\ddot{A}_1 + M_5\dot{A}_1 + M_6\dot{A}_2 + M_7A_0 + M_8A_1 + M_9A_0 + M_{10}A_2 = 0$$
$$\ddot{A}_2 + M_{11}\dot{A}_2 + M_{12}\dot{A}_1 + M_{13}A_2 + M_{14}A_1 = 0$$

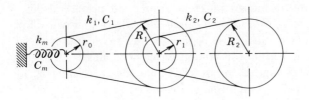

Fig. 1.4 A three-degree-of-freedom torsional vibration system.

where
$$M_1 = (C_m + 2C_1 r_0^2)/I_0 \qquad = 1 \ \text{sec}^{-1}$$
$$M_2 = -2C_1 R_1 r_0/I_0 \qquad = -2 \ \text{sec}^{-1}$$
$$M_3 = (k_m + 2k_1 r_0^2)/I_0 \qquad = 10 \ \text{sec}^{-2}$$
$$M_4 = -2k_1 R_1 r_0/I_0 \qquad = -20 \ \text{sec}^{-2}$$
$$M_5 = (2C_1 R_1^2 + 2C_2 r_1^2)/I_1 = 2.25 \ \text{sec}^{-1}$$
$$M_6 = -2C_2 R_2 r_1/I_1 \qquad = -1 \ \text{sec}^{-1}$$
$$M_7 = -2C_1 R_1 r_0/I_1 \qquad = -0.5 \ \text{sec}^{-1}$$
$$M_8 = (2k_1 R_1^2 + 2k_2 r_1^2)I_1 = 22.5 \ \text{sec}^{-2}$$
$$M_9 = -2k_1 R_1 r_0/I_1 \qquad = -5 \ \text{sec}^{-2}$$
$$M_{10} = -2k_2 R_2 r_1/I_1 \qquad = -10 \ \text{sec}^{-2}$$
$$M_{11} = 2C_2 R_2^2/I_2 \qquad = 5.3 \ \text{sec}^{-1}$$
$$M_{12} = -2C_2 R_2 r_1/I_2 \qquad = -1.3 \ \text{sec}^{-1}$$
$$M_{13} = 2k_2 R_2^2/I_2 \qquad = 53.3 \ \text{sec}^{-2}$$
$$M_{14} = -2k_2 R_2 r_1/I_2 \qquad = -13.3 \ \text{sec}^{-2}$$

For the above, r_0, r_1, R_1, and R_2 are the pulley radii; k_1 and k_2 are the belt spring constants, k_m is the torsional spring constant; C_1 and C_2 are the belt damping constants, C_m is the torsional damping constant; I_0, I_1, and I_2 are the pulley inertias. The initial conditions are given as below:

$$A_0(0) = 0.0146 \ \text{rad}$$
$$A_1(0) = 0.0112 \ \text{rad}$$
$$A_2(0) = 0.0174 \ \text{rad}$$
$$\dot{A}_0(0) = \dot{A}_1(0) = \dot{A}_2(0) = 0$$

1.4. Write a sequence of statements similar to (1.11) through (1.19) for the following cases:

(a) The set of equations in Prob. 1.1
(b) The set of equations in Prob. 1.2
(c) The set of equations in Prob. 1.3

The termination conditions are:

(a) T = 2   (b) T = 3.5   (c) T = 5

1.5. Table 1.2 is a function-language program which is translated from a simulation program.

(a) Draw a block diagram, using the needed blocks (i.e., functions) from Table 1.2.

(b) Write a sequence of statements similar to (1.11) through (1.19) from the function program in Table 1.2.

Table 1.2 A function-language program

Function output	Function name	Function input	Function input	Function input	Initial condition
	CON	B			
	PAR	A	XO	1DXO	
102	MPY	A	1DX		
104	MPY	A	1DX	X	
105	MPY	104	X		
106	MPY	B	X		
107	SUB	102	105		
2DX	SUB	107	106		
1DX	INT	2DX			1DXO
X	INT	1DX			XO
	FIN	T	5.		
	OUT	T	X		
	END				

REFERENCES

1. Selfridge, R. G.: Coding a General Purpose Digital Computer to Operate as a Differential Analyzer, *Proc. Western Joint Computer Conf.*, 1955, pp. 82–84.
2. Lesh, F.: Methods of Simulating a Differential Analyzer on a Digital Computer, *J. ACM*, July, 1958, pp. 281–288.
3. Stein, M. L., J. Rose, and D. B. Parker: A Compiler with an Analog-oriented Input Language, *Proc. Western Joint Computer Conf.*, 1959, pp. 92–102.
4. Stein, M. L., and J. Rose: Changing from Analog to Digital Programming by Digital Techniques, *J. ACM*, January, 1960, pp. 10–23.
5. Hurley, J. R.: DEPI 4 (Differential Equations Pseudo-code Interpreter): An Analog Computer Simulator for the IBM 704, internal memorandum, Allis Chalmers Mfg. Co., Jan. 6, 1960.
6. Rogers, A. E., and T. W. Connolly: "Analog Computation in Engineering Design," McGraw-Hill Book Company, New York, 1960.
7. Kelly, J. L., Jr., C. Lochbaum, and V. A. Vyssotsky: A Block Diagram Compiler, *Bell System Tech. J.*, May, 1961, pp. 669–676.
8. Green, C., H. D. Hoop, and A. Debroux: APACHE: A Breakthrough in Analog Computing, *IRE Trans. Electron. Computers*, October, 1962, pp. 699–706.
9. Johnson, C. L.: "Analog Computer Techniques," 2d ed., McGraw-Hill Book Company, New York, 1963.
10. Palevsky, M., and J. V. Howell: The DES-1: A Real-time Digital Simulation Computer, *Proc. Fall Joint Computer Conf.*, 1963, pp. 459–472.
11. Hurley, J. R., and J. J. Skiles: Dysac, A Digitally Simulated Analog Computer, *Proc. Spring Joint Computer Conf.*, 1963, pp. 69–82.
12. Gaskill, R. A., J. W. Harris, and A. L. McKnight: DAS: A Digital Analog Simulator, *Proc. Spring Joint Computer Conf.*, 1963, pp. 83–90.
13. Harnett, R. T., F. J. Sansom, and L. W. Warshawsky: MIDAS Programming Guide, *Tech. Rept.* SEG-TDR-64-1, Wright-Patterson Air Force Base, January, 1964.
14. Petersen, H. E., F. J. Sansom, R. T. Harnett, and L. M. Warshawsky: Midas:

How It Works and How It's Worked, *Proc. Fall Joint Computer Conf.*, 1964, pp. 313–324.

15. Brennan, R. D., and H. Sano: Pactolus: A Digital Analog Simulator Program for IBM 1620, *Proc. Fall Joint Computer Conf.*, 1964, pp. 299–312.

16. Brennan, R. D., and R. N. Linebarger: A Survey of Digital Simulation: Digital Analog Simulator Programs, *Simulation*, vol. 3, no. 6, pp. 22–36, December, 1964.

17. Korn, G. A., and T. M. Korn: "Electronic Analog and Hybrid Computers," McGraw-Hill Book Company, New York, 1964.

18. Rideout, V. C., and L. Tavernini: Madbloc, A Program for Digital Simulation of Hybrid Computers, *Simulation*, January, 1965, pp. 20–24.

19. Levine, L.: The DES-1, A New Digital Computer for Solving Differential Equations, *Simulation*, April, 1965, pp. 264–276.

20. Sansom, F. J.: MIMIC: Successor to MIDAS, *Conf. Paper, Joint Meeting Central Midwestern Simulation Councils*, May, 1965.

21. Syn, W. M., and D. G. Wyman: DSL/90 Digital Simulation Language User's Guide, *Tech. Rept.* TR 02.355, IBM Corporation, San José, Calif., July 1, 1965.

22. Syn, W. M., and D. G. Wyman: DSL/90 Digital Simulation Language Systems Guide, IBM Corporation, San José, Calif., July 15, 1965.

23. Karafin, B. J.: The New Block Diagram Compiler for Simulation of Sampled-data Systems, *Proc. Fall Joint Computer Conf.*, Pt. I, 1965, pp. 55–61.

24. De Backer, W., and A. van Wauwe: The Sioux System and Hybrid Block Diagram, *Simulation*, July, 1965, pp. 32–35.

25. Benyon, P. R., and W. J. Henry: SIMTRAN in Australia, *Simulation*, September, 1965, pp. 158–159.

26. Clancy, J. J., and M. S. Fineberg: Digital Simulation Languages: A Critique and a Guide, *Proc. Fall Joint Computer Conf.*, 1965, pp. 23–36.

27. Burgin, G. H.: APACHE: Some Encouraging Experiences, *Simulation*, January, 1966, pp. 16–19.

28. Schlesinger, S. I., and L. Sashkin: EASL, *Simulation*, February, 1966, pp. 110–119.

29. Janoski, R. M., R. L. Schaefer, and J. J. Skiles: COBLOC: A Program for All Digital Simulation of a Hybrid Computer, *IEEE Trans. Electron. Computers*, February, 1966, pp. 74–82.

30. Burgin, G. H.: MIDAS III: A Compiler Version of MIDAS, *Simulation*, Simulation Council, Inc., March 1966, pp. 160–168.

31. Golden, R. M.: Digital Computer Simulation of Sampled-data Communication Systems Using the Block Diagram Compiler: BLODIB, *Bell System Tech. J.*, March, 1966, pp. 345–358.

32. Hughes, F. M., and A. Brameller: Digital Simulation of Analogue Methods, *Computer J.*, May, 1966, pp. 35–44.

33. Dineley, J. L., and C. Preece: KALDAS, An Algorithmically Based Digital Simulation of Analogue Computation, *Computer J.*, August, 1966, pp. 181–187.

34. Syn, W. M., and R. N. Linebarger, DSL/90: A Digital Simulation Program for Continuous System Modeling, *Proc. Spring Joint Computer Conf.*, 1966, pp. 165–187.

35. Green, D. T.: OLDAS: An On-line Simulation Language, Naval Weapons Laboratory, Dahlgren, Va., 1966.

36. James, M. L., G. M. Smith, and J. C. Wolford: "Analog-computer Simulation of Engineering Systems," International Textbook Company, Scranton, Pa., 1966.

37. Digital Simulation of Continuous Systems, *Proc. IBM Sci. Computing Symp.*, IBM Corporation, 1967.

38. Peterson, G. R.: "Basic Analog Computation," The Macmillan Company, New York, 1967.
39. Sansom, F. J.: MIMIC Programming Manual, *Tech. Rept.* SEG-TR-67-31, Wright-Patterson Air Force Base, Ohio, July, 1967.
40. Syn, W. M., and N. N. Turner: DSL/360 User's Manual, Notes, IBM Corporation, October, 1967.
41. System/360 Continuous System Modeling Program (360A-CX-16X): User's Manual, H20-0367-0, IBM Corporation, 1967.
42. The SCI Simulation Software Committee, The SCI Continuous System Simulation Language (CSSL), *Simulation*, December, 1967, pp. 281–303.
43. Jentsch, W.: "ASIM, ein Programmsystem für die Analogsimulation mittels Digitalrechner, "Elektronische Datenverarbeitung," vols. 4 and 5, 1967, pp. 173–179, 191–198.
44. Forsythe, G. E., and W. R. Wasow: "Finite-difference Methods for Partial Differential Equations," John Wiley & Sons, Inc., New York, 1960.
45. Private communication from D. M. Young to H. M. Ernst, Nov. 3, 1967.
46. Engeli, M.: "Automatisierte Behandlung elliptischer Randwetprobleme," doctoral dissertation, Eidgenossischen Technischen Hochschule, Zurich, Switzerland, 1962.
47. Engeli, M., and P. Lauechli: Automatic Calculation and Programming of Difference Equations for Elliptic Boundary Value Problems, *Proc. IFIP Congr., Munich, Germany*, 1962.
48. Cuthill, E.: Unpublished notes, Naval Ship Research and Development Center, U.S. Navy, AML, 1966.
49. Bond, E., et al.: FORMAC: An Experimental Formula Manipulation Compiler, *Proc. 19th Natl. Conf.*, ACM, August, 1964.
50. Kohr, R., and D. E. Abbott: Unpublished notes on approximation methods for solving engineering problems, Purdue University, July, 1968.
51. Crandall, S. H.: "Engineering Analysis," McGraw-Hill Book Company, New York, 1956.
52. Morris, S. M.: "SALEM: A Programming System for the Simulation of Systems Described by Partial Differential Equations," doctoral dissertation, Department of Chemical Engineering, Lehigh University, Bethlehem, Pa., 1967.

2
MIMIC Programming

As mentioned previously, the MIMIC language and processor were developed by Petersen and Sansom for the IBM 7090 family of computers. Since MIMIC became available in 1965, it has been translated for use in many other computers, among which are the UNIVAC 1107 and 1108 computers and the CDC 3000 and CDC 6000 families of computers. A program written in the MIMIC language by a user for simulating a model is called a *MIMIC program*. After the MIMIC program is written, it is compiled, sorted, assembled, and executed by the MIMIC processor. This chapter describes MIMIC programming. Applications of MIMIC programming are presented in the next two chapters. A simplified version of the MIMIC processor is presented in Chap. 6.

2.1 MIMIC CARDS

A MIMIC program consists of MIMIC statements and data. Each statement performs a step of computation, simulation, or control and is punched on one card. The data which provide the numerical values for a

1	2	10	19	73
	LCV name field	Result name field	Expression field	

(a)

1	13	25	37	49	61	73

(b)

Fig. 2.1 Card formats for MIMIC statements and data: (a) statement card format; (b) data card format.

simulation are grouped and punched on one or more cards. The card formats and the order of these cards in forming a MIMIC program are now described.

2.1.1 CARD FORMATS

Figure 2.1a shows the format for the statement card. If there is a symbol in column 1, the card is a *comment card*, which is provided for better readability of the program and has no effect on the simulation. However, if there is a dollar sign $ in column 1, followed immediately by one of the words DELETE, LIST, or ABSERR in succeeding columns, the card is a MIMIC processor control card. Table 2.1 describes the functions of these three control cards.

MIMIC cards use fixed formats. There are four fields on each

Table 2.1   MIMIC processor control cards

Card	Description
$DELETE	Causes the function-language program not to be printed.
$LIST	Causes the listing of the location, name, and final values of all MIMIC variables at the end of each run.
$ABSERR	Causes the change of the error criterion in the integration routine from a relative to an absolute basis.

Table 2.2 Card format for MIMIC statements

Column	Description
1	(a) Any symbol in this column indicates this is a comment card. (b) A $ followed by one of words DELETE, LIST, or ABSERR (see Table 2.1).
2–7	Logical control variable name.
8–9	Not used.
10–15	Result name.
16–18	Not used.
19–72	Expression.
73–80	Identification.

statement card: the field of columns 2 to 7 for a *logical control variable (LCV) name*, the field of columns 10 to 15 for a *result name*, the field of columns 19 to 72 for an *expression*, and the field of columns 73 to 80 for *identification*. Columns 8 to 9 and 16 to 18 are not used. However, an equal-sign may be placed in column 16, 17, or 18 whenever desirable for better readability. The LCV name must start at column 2, the result name at column 10, and the expression at column 19. The statement format is summarized in Table 2.2.

The format for the data card is shown in Fig. 2.1b. Columns 1 to 72 of a data card are divided into six 12-column fields. Each field accommodates one decimal number; thus up to six numbers can be entered on each data card. Columns 73 to 80 may be used for identification.

2.1.2 CARD ORDER

With several exceptions, the statements in a MIMIC program can be placed in any order, because the MIMIC processor sorts the statements into a proper order. The exceptions are stated below:

1. Comment and processor control cards can be placed anywhere but must be before the END card.
2. All CON and CFN statement cards must precede any PAR or PFN statement cards.
3. The data cards for the CON, PAR, CFN, and PFN statements must have the same order as the CON, PAR, CFN, and PFN statement cards.
4. The END card must be the last statement card.
5. Data cards follow the END card.
6. The HDR cards should precede the OUT cards.

7. The cards for optional statements associated with the PLO card must occur after the PLO card to which they refer but before the next PLO card.

2.1.3 AN EXAMPLE

To illustrate the card formats and card order, the MIMIC program which consists of statements (1.11) to (1.19) is used as an example. This program is shown in the proper format together with a chosen set of data in Fig. 2.2. Notice that the comment cards begin at column 1, the result names at column 10, and the expressions at column 19. Also notice the two processor control cards, the locations of CON and PAR cards with respect to each other and to other cards, and the location of the END card with respect to data cards. No comment card is allowed between the END card and data cards. There are three decimal numbers on the first data card, which provides the values for constants M, B, and K. These three numbers are in columns 1 to 12, 13 to 24, and 25 to 36, respectively. There is one decimal number on the second, third, and fourth cards, each of which provides the value of parameter A for the first, second, and third run, respectively. When the deck of cards is prepared and sent to a digital computer installation for batch processing, system control cards required by the installation should be added.

2.2 BASIC LANGUAGE ELEMENTS

A MIMIC program consists of a sequence of statements. The statements are composed of basic language elements of constants, parameters, variables, operators, expressions, and functions. These language elements are presented here.

2.2.1 CONSTANTS

Constants are quantities of fixed values. In MIMIC, constants can be either numerical or logical. A numerical constant must have a decimal point. The range of the numerical constant is approximately from -10^{38} to -10^{-38}, from $+10^{-38}$ to $+10^{38}$ and 0 (these are the ranges of a floating-point number in the 7090 family of computers). A numerical constant can be expressed in the normal form or in the exponent form. Examples of a numerical constant in the normal form are

    0.
    0.0
    .0
    21.4567
    −.203
    +8.006789

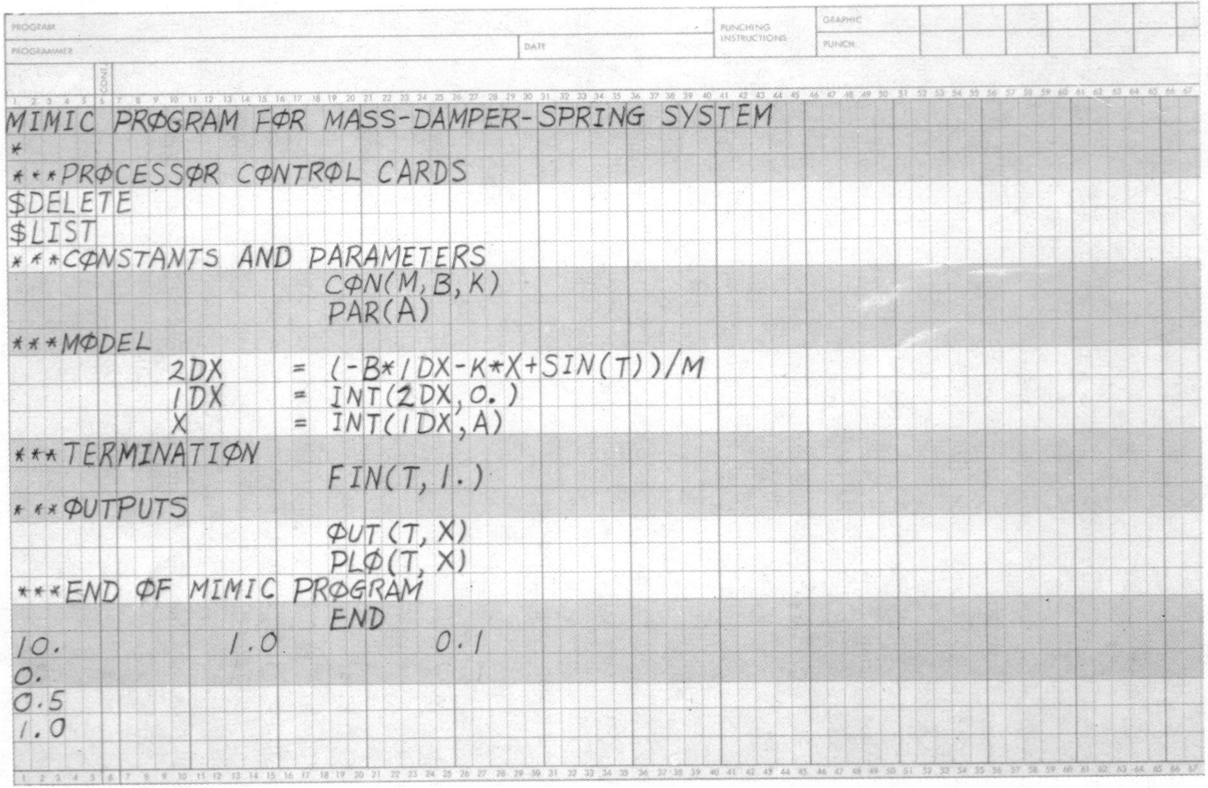

```
MIMIC PROGRAM FOR MASS-DAMPER-SPRING SYSTEM
*
*** PROCESSOR CONTROL CARDS
$DELETE
$LIST
*** CONSTANTS AND PARAMETERS
              CON(M,B,K)
              PAR(A)
*** MODEL
       2DX  = (-B*1DX-K*X+SIN(T))/M
       1DX  = INT(2DX,0.)
       X    = INT(1DX,A)
*** TERMINATION
              FIN(T,1.)
*** OUTPUTS
              OUT(T,X)
              PLO(T,X)
*** END OF MIMIC PROGRAM
              END
10.     1.0       END      0.1
0.5
1.0
```

Fig. 2.2 MIMIC program in correct card formats.

In the normal form, the constant may have up to nine significant digits. Examples of a numerical constant in the exponent form are

0.E0	(0)
3.56E−4	(3.56×10^{-4})
−.92E+2	($-.92 \times 10^{2}$)
2.5E2	(2.5×10^{2})

In the exponent form, the exponent, which is the right side of E, must be an integer, and the fraction, which is the left side of E, must have a decimal point. When a constant is entered in a field of the data card, a numerical constant in the exponent form must be *right-justified*, but a numerical constant in the normal form requires no left or right justification.

If a numerical constant has six or fewer symbols (decimal digit, positive or negative sign, or a decimal point), it is called in MIMIC a *literal*. Examples of literals are

3.21
−.2134
+.0245
12345.

A literal can be entered into a MIMIC program without using a CON statement. For example, constant M in the MIMIC program in Fig. 2.2 can be entered by the statement

M = 10.0

instead of using the CON statement in Fig. 2.2. However, if the value of M is 10.0001 (more than six symbols) instead of 10.0, then a CON statement (or a statement M = 10.+.0001) is used.

A logical constant has only two values: TRUE and FALSE. The representation of FALSE in the MIMIC processor is a zero, and that of TRUE is any nonzero number. Interpretation of a nonzero value of a real variable as a logical constant may sometimes be utilized to simplify MIMIC statements, as will be further discussed.

2.2.2 PARAMETERS

Parameters are also constants. A constant remains unchanged during a simulation study, while a parameter may change from run to run (but not during a run). The above discussion on constants applies also to parameters, except that there is no literal for a parameter.

2.2.3 VARIABLES

Variables are symbolic representations of quantities whose values vary during a run. These representations are called variable names. A *vari-*

able name contains from one to six digits or alphameric characters
(0, . . . , 9, A, B, . . . Z).   Examples of valid variable names are

> A
> 1DX
> 2DX1
> XDOT
> 15

Notice that the first character can be a digit (different from FORTRAN)
and that an integer constant (i.e., no decimal point) is a name, not a
constant.   Examples of invalid variable names are:

> A(1)
> A X
> A,X
> XYZ.
> DD15DOT

These names are invalid because parentheses, blank, comma, and period
are not alphameric characters or because the name exceeds six characters.

   Like constants and parameters, a variable can be a real variable or a
logical variable.   A real variable represents a numerical quantity, while
a logical variable represents a logical quantity.   The variable in columns
2 to 7 of a statement (see Fig. 2.1*a*) is a logical variable which is given a
special name: *logical control variable,* or LCV.   As will be discussed, the
presence of a logical control variable makes the statement a conditional
one.

2.2.4 RESERVED NAMES

Reserved names are variable names which carry special meanings to the
MIMIC processor.   There are six reserved names, as described below:

1. *T*   This name represents the independent variable.
2. *DT*   This name represents the amount by which T changes between
   printouts.
3. *DTMAX*   This name represents the maximum step size that is
   allowed during integration.
4. *DTMIN*   This name represents the minimum step size that is allowed
   during integration.
5. *TRUE*   This name represents the TRUE value of a logical constant.
6. *FALSE*   This name represents the FALSE value of a logical constant.

   The above names should not be used in a MIMIC program to represent other quantities.   Since they occur most often, the user should
memorize them.

Table 2.3   **MIMIC operators**

Symbol	Operation
+	Addition
−	Subtraction, negation
*	Multiplication
/	Division
(	Grouping
)	Grouping
,	Separation
=	Equality

2.2.5 OPERATORS

Operators denote arithmetic and other operations. The MIMIC operators are shown in Table 2.3. There are four arithmetical operators: addition, subtraction, multiplication, and division. No arithmetic operator should immediately follow another arithmetic operator. The parentheses are used to indicate the order in which arithmetic operations of an expression are to be performed. The comma is used as a separator of function arguments. The equal-sign indicates the usual meaning of equality (not the FORTRAN meaning of replacement).

2.2.6 FUNCTIONS

Like a block, a function denotes an operation performed on the given inputs to produce an output. There are 57 MIMIC functions, which,

Table 2.4   **Mathematical functions**

Name	General form†	Function description
ADDITION	R = ADD(A,B(,C,D,E,F))	R = A+B(+C+D+E+F)
SUBTRACTION	R = SUB(A,B)	R = A−B
MULTIPLICATION	R = MPY(A,B(,C,D,E,F))	R = A*B(*C*D*E*F)
DIVIDE	R = DIV(A,B)	R = A/B
MULTIPLY AND ADD	R = MAD(A,B,C(,D,E,F))	R = A*B+C(*D+E*F)
NEGATION	R = NEG(A)	R = −A
EQUALITY	R = EQL(A)	R = A
ABSOLUTE VALUE	R = ABS(A)	R = |A|
SQUARE ROOT	R = SQR(A) for A ≥ 0	R = $\sqrt{A}$
SINE	R = SIN(A), A in radians	R = sin(A)
COSINE	R = COS(A), A in radians	R = cos(A)
ARCTANGENT	R = ATN(A(,B))	R = $\tan^{-1}(A/B)$, B = 1 if not specified
EXPONENTIAL	R = EXP(A(,B)) for B > 0	R = B^A, B = e if not specified
LOGARITHM	R = LOG(A(,B))	R = $\log_B A$, B = e if not specified

† Operands enclosed inside the inner pair of parentheses need not be specified.

together with the previously described arithmetic operations, are the operations that are provided by the MIMIC processor. A MIMIC function is denoted by a three-letter mnemonic name, followed by up to six arguments which are enclosed in parentheses and separated by commas. These arguments, sometimes called operands, are inputs to or initial conditions of a function.

MIMIC functions may be divided into six groups: mathematical functions; logical and control functions; integration, derivative, and implicit functions; input-output functions; special functions; and hybrid functions. The names, general forms, and descriptions of these functions are shown in Tables 2.4 through 2.10. In these tables, R and S represent the output of a function, and A through F and U through Z represent the arguments. A through F and R are real variables, while U through Z and S are logical variables. As will be shown, the real variable may be an arithmetic expression or a functional expression.

There are 14 mathematical functions in Table 2.4. The first seven functions commonly are not used; an arithmetic expression is used instead. It is difficult, if not impossible, to implement functions such as divide, sine (not necessarily sine of time), square-root, and arctangent in an

Table 2.5   Logical and control functions

Name	General form†	Function description	
AND	S = AND(U,V(,W,X,Y,X))	R = U∩V(∩W∩X∩Y∩Z)	
EXCLUSIVE OR	S = EOR(X,Y)	R = (X∩Y')∪(X'∩Y)	
INCLUSIVE OR	S = IOR(U,V(,W,X,Y,Z))	R = U∪V(∪W∪X∪Y∪Z)	
COMPLEMENT	S = COM(X), or NOT(X)	R = X'	
FUNCTION SWITCH	S = FSW(A,X,Y,Z)	S = X	A < 0
		S = Y	A = 0
		S = Z	A > 0
	R = FSW(A,B,C,D)	R = B	A < 0
		R = C	A = 0
		R = D	A > 0
LOGICAL SWITCH	R = LSW(X,B,C)	R = B	if X TRUE
		R = C	if X FALSE
TERMINATION	S = FIN(A,B)	S = TRUE	if A > B
		S = FALSE	otherwise
		This run is terminated when A > B.	
END OF PROGRAM	END	Signifies end of MIMIC program and beginning of MIMIC data.	

† Operands enclosed inside the inner pair of parentheses may not be specified.

Table 2.6 Integration, derivative, and implicit functions

Name	General form†	Function description
INTEGRATOR	R = INT(A,B(,C,D))	$R = B + \int A \, dt$ B is the initial condition.‡
INTEGRATOR LIMITER	R = LIN(A,B,C,D)	$R = 0 \quad B < C$ $R = A \quad C \leq B \leq D$ $R = 0 \quad B > D$
FIRST ORDER FUNCTION	R = FTR(A,B)	$B\dot{R} + R = A$ where A is the input and B the time constant.
DERIVATIVE FUNCTION	R = DER(A,B,C)	$R = C \quad$ at $t = 0$ $R = dB/dA$
IMPLICIT FUNCTION	R = IMP(A,B)§	$R = A$ where $|A - B(A)| \leq 5 \times 10^{-6} |A|$

† Operands enclosed inside the inner pair of parentheses need not be specified.
‡ When both C and D are TRUE or FALSE, the integrator is in OPERATE mode. When C is TRUE and D is FALSE, it is in RESET mode. When C is FALSE and D is TRUE, it is in HOLD mode.
§ Use of implicit function requires the use of a PAR statement.

analog computer. In Table 2.5, there are four logical functions, AND, EOR, IOR, and NOT; four control functions, FSW, LSW, FIN, and END. In Table 2.6, there are two functions involving integration, INT and FTR; one function for integration limiting, LIN; one derivative function, DER; and one implicit function, IMP. In Table 2.7, there are four input functions, CON, PAR, CFN, and PFN; two printer table-output functions, HDR and OUT; and seven printer (and/or plotter) plot-output functions, PLO, SCA, ZER, TTP, TTX, TTY, and OPT. In Table 2.9, there are two selection functions, MAX and MIN; two nonlinear functions, DSP and LIM; a delay function, TDL; four generating functions, FUN for one variable, FUN for two variables, RNG, and RNU; and four functions for defining or calling a subprogram written in MIMIC language, BSP, ESP, CSP, and RSP. In Table 2.10, there are four hybrid functions, MMV, TAS, FLF, and ZOH. The use of these functions will be subsequently described and illustrated.

2.2.7 EXPRESSIONS

An expression is a string of variables, parameters, literals, and functions separated by arithmetic operators, commas, and parentheses. An expression can be arithmetic, functional, or combined. An arithmetic expression is one with arithmetic operations but no functions. Examples of

Table 2.7   Input-output functions

Name	General form†	Function description
NAME CONSTANTS	CON(A(,B,C,D,E,F))	Enters constant names.
NAME PARAMETERS	PAR(A(,B,C,D,E,F))	Enters parameter names.
NAME FUNCTION (Constant)	R = CFN(A)	R is name of array. A is number of pairs or triples of points.
NAME FUNCTION (Parameter)	R = PFN(A)	R is name of array. A is number of pairs or triples of points.
PRINT OUTPUT	OUT(A(,B,C,D,E,F))	Prints A, B, C, D, E, F every DT units of T.
PRINT HEADERS	HDR(A(,B,C,D,E,F))	Prints heading names given in A, B, C, D, E, F.
PLOT	PLO(A,B(,C,D,E,F))	Plots B versus A, C versus A, etc., on printer and/or plotter.
SCALE	SCA(A,B(,C,D,E,F))	Specifies scale in units per division for plot variables.
ZERO	ZER(A,B(,C,D,E,F))	Specifies zero for plot variables.
PAGE TITLE	TTP, up to 36 characters	Titles page of a plot.
X-AXIS TITLE	TTX, up to 36 characters	Titles x axis of plot.
Y-AXIS TITLE	TTY, up to 36 characters	Titles y axis of plot.
OPTIONS	OPT(A,B,C,D,E,F)	See Table 2.8.

† Operands enclosed inside the inner pair of parentheses may not be specified.

arithmetic expressions are

$$A+B-C/D \qquad (2.1)$$
$$C*(D/100.)+B \qquad (2.2)$$
$$(A*(B-C)+D)/E+F \qquad (2.3)$$

The parentheses in the above expressions are used to specify the order in which the operations in an expression are to be performed. Where parentheses are omitted, the order of operations in an arithmetic expression follows the precedence in Table 2.11. A functional expression is one with functions but no arithmetic operations. Examples of functional expressions are

$$SQR(A) \qquad (2.4)$$
$$INT(A,B) \qquad (2.5)$$
$$FLF(X,Y,Z) \qquad (2.6)$$
$$IOR(X,Y,Z) \qquad (2.7)$$

Additional functional expressions are shown in Tables 2.4 through 2.10.
An argument of a functional expression may be another expression.   For
example, we have

$$IOR(AND(U,V), AND(X,Y)) \tag{2.8}$$
$$LSW(AND(X,Y),B,C) \tag{2.9}$$
$$INT(ABS(A), ZERO) \tag{2.10}$$

In other words, MIMIC allows nesting of functions.   A combined expression is one where there are both arithmetic operations and functions.
Examples of combined expressions are

$$SQR(A*A+B*B) \tag{2.11}$$
$$INT(SIN(A/(A+1.)),0.) \tag{2.12}$$
$$FSW(I*J+K,B,C,D) \tag{2.13}$$
$$INT(INT(-SIN(SQR(I*J+K)),1.),0.) \tag{2.14}$$

Table 2.8   Interpretation of the arguments of OPT statement†

Argument	Interpretation
A = 1.	Two printer pages are used for the plot.
A = K	2*K printer pages are used for the plot. The scale and zero are still selected on the basis of a 100 by 100 grid.
B = 1.	Each variable in the PLO statement is individually scaled.
B = 2.	The second through sixth variables use the *same* scale and zero. The scale and zero are picked to accommodate all the variables.
C = 1.	The plot generated by each PLO statement starts a new page.
C = 2.	The plot generated by the preceding PLO statement is printed a second time, and the plot generated by the next following PLO statement is superimposed upon the second printing.
D = 1.	Printer-plot only.
D = 2.	Off-line only.
D = 3.	Both.
E = 1.	Plot points and connecting lines.
E = 2.	Plot points only.
F = 1.	Use linear scales on both axes.
F = 2.	Use log scales for x, linear scales for y.
F = 3.	Use linear scales for x, log scales for y.
F = 4.	Use log scales on both axes.

† The options for arguments D, E, and F refer to off-line plots.   The values
and interpretation are merely a proposal.

Table 2.9   Special functions

Name	General form†	Function description
MAXIMUM	R = MAX(A,B(,C,D,E,F))	R = max(A,B(,C,D,E,F))
MINIMUM	R = MIN(A,B(,C,D,E,F))	R = min(A,B(,C,D,E,F))
DEAD SPACE	R = DSP(A,B,C)	R = A − B A < B R = 0 B ≤ A ≤ C R = A − C A > C
LIMITER	R = LIM(A,B,C)	R = B A < B R = A B ≤ A ≤ C R = C A > C
TIME DELAY	R = TDL(A,B,C)	R = A(t − B) for t > B where B may be a variable.‡
FUNCTION (one variable)	R = FUN(A,B)	R = A(B)
FUNCTION (two variables)	R = FUN(A,B,C)	R = A(B,C)
RANDOM NUMBER GENERATOR (gaussian)	R = RNG(A,B,C)	R = random sample from a gaussian distribution with mean A and standard deviation B. C is a starting number.
RANDOM NUMBER GENERATOR (uniform)	R = RNU(A,B,C)	R = random sample from a uniform distribution with lower limit A and upper limit B. C is a starting number.
BEGIN SUBPROGRAM	BSP(A(,B,C,D,E,F))	§
END SUBPROGRAM	ESP(A(,B,C,D,E,F))	
CALL SUBPROGRAM	CSP(A(,B,C,D,E,F))	¶
RETURN SUBPROGRAM	RSP(A(,B,C,D,E,F))	

† Operands enclosed inside the inner pair of parentheses may not be specified.
‡ C, the number of points of A to be stored, must be specified. A value of 100 is suggested. B may be a variable.
§ The subprogram name appears in the result column of the BSP and ESP cards. The inputs are named on the BSP card and the outputs on the ESP card.
¶ The name of the called subprogram is given in the result field of the CSP card. The RSP card must immediately follow the CSP card.

In the above, (A*A+B*B), (A/(A+1.)), and (I*J+K) are arithmetic expressions which serve as arguments of functions.

    An expression may also be classified as a numerical expression or a logical expression. If evaluation of an expression gives a numerical value, the expression is a numerical expression. Expressions (2.1)

Table 2.10   Hybrid functions

Name	General form	Function description
MONOSTABLE MULTIVIBRATOR	S = MMV(X,B)	S = X at t = 0 S is set TRUE when X is TRUE. R stays TRUE for B sec after X goes FALSE.
TRACK AND STORE	R = TAS(A,X,C)	R = C at t = 0 R = A when X TRUE R = R when X FALSE
FLIP-FLOP	S = FLF(X,Y,Z)	S = Z at t = 0 $S(t) = X \cup (Y' \cap S)$ where Y' = complement of Y $\quad$ S(t) = value of S at t sec later
ZERO ORDER HOLD	R = ZOH(A,B)	R = A where A is sampled every B sec

through (2.5) and (2.9) through (2.14) are numerical expressions. If evaluation of an expression results in a logical value, the expression is a logical expression.   Expressions (2.6) through (2.8) are logical expressions.

2.3 STATEMENTS

A MIMIC program is a sequence of statements.   The statement format has been shown in Fig. 2.1a.   Except the comment statement, which is one with any character in column 1, a MIMIC statement contains three fields: LCV (logical control variable), result, and expression.   There are four general forms of MIMIC statements which differ in the choice of these fields.   The first form of MIMIC statements consists of an expression only, mostly a functional expression; examples are shown in Fig. 2.3. The second form consists of a result name and an expression; most MIMIC statements are of this form, as shown in Fig. 2.4.   The third form consists of an LCV name and an expression; this form is a conditional version of the first form.   Examples of this form are shown in Fig. 2.5.   The fourth

Table 2.11   Precedence of operations

Operation	Precedence
Function evaluation	1 (highest)
*, /	2
+, −	3
=	4

1	2	10	19		73
			HDR		
			PAR(N,W)		
			HDR(T,AO)		
			CON(2PI)		
			OUT(,ERROR1,ERROR2)		
			PLO(X,1DX)		
			END		
			OUT(T,A,B)		
			FIN(A*T,5.)		
			RSP(V1,V2)		
			SCA(2.,5.,.5)		
			ZER(0.,10.,−1000.)		
			OPT(A,B,C,D,E,F)		
			SR2(X,Y,Z)		

Fig. 2.3 Examples of the first form of MIMIC statements.

1	2	10	19		73
		P	=	1.	
		Z	=	K/(C*P*DELTAX*DELTAX)	
		F2	=	F1 + A2*COS(2.*X)	
		NEONE	=	FSW(N − 1.,TRUE,TRUE,FALSE)	
		A	=	INT(F*COS(N*X),0.)*4./P	
		L2	=	AND(NOT(L1),NOT(L2))	
		PHASE	=	ATN(B/A)*DEGPR	
		YP	=	INT(2.*X*YP − N*(N + 1.)*Y,YPO)	
		DELTAE	=	DELTAE = DELTA + FSW(TIME,0.,.1,.1)	
		DTMAX	=	DTMIN	
		SAMPLE	=	BSP(X,Y,Z)	
		X	=	IMP(X,SIN(X) + Y)	
		F	=	CFN(5.)	
		DT	=	P/40.	
		TEST	=	FIN(A,B)	
		X	=	SRI(T − 5.,Y + Z*SIN(W),0.)	

Fig. 2.4 Examples of the second form of MIMIC statements.

1	2	10	19		72
	NEONE		HDR(T,AO)		
	S		OUT(T,VEXACT,X,V,W)		
	READ		PAR(A,PHI)		
	TEST		FIN(X*Y,DOD)		

Fig. 2.5 Examples of the third form of MIMIC statements.

1	2	10	19	}	72
	NEONE	AO	=	INT(F,O.)*2.1*P		
	L1	ERROR1	=	F1 − COS(X)		
	S	W	=	(W2 + W1 + 6.*Y3)*4.*PI/20.		
	D1	DT	=	.1		

Fig. 2.6 Examples of the fourth form of MIMIC statements.

form consists of an LCV name, a result name, and an expression; this is a conditional version of the second form. Examples of this form are shown in Fig. 2.6. Note that the result name is a real variable name or a logical variable name, but the LCV name must be a logical variable name.

2.3.1 LOGICAL CONTROL VARIABLE

As mentioned earlier, the presence of a logical control variable makes the statement a conditional one. To be specific, if the logical value of the LCV in a statement is TRUE, the statement associated with that LCV will be evaluated. If the value is FALSE, the statement will not be evaluated. By means of LCV, it is possible under program control to select the statements that should be evaluated.

As an example, assume that the following equations are to be evaluated as a part of a larger problem:

$$v = \begin{cases} \sin x & \text{for } t \leq 3.1416 \\ t - 3.1416 & \text{for } t > 3.1416 \end{cases} \tag{2.15}$$

The MIMIC statements in Fig. 2.7 will evaluate the above equations. In Fig. 2.7, TLEPI (T Less than or Equal to PI) and TGTPI (T Greater Than PI) are logical variables. The first FSW statement sets TLEPI equal to FALSE or TRUE, depending on whether the value of (T − 3.1416) is greater than zero or not. The second statement defines TGTPI to be the complement of TLEPI. These two logical control variables then select the third or fourth statement for computing the value of V.

Instead of using four statements, the above calculation can be pre-

1	2	10	19	}	72
		TLEPI	=	FSW(T − 3.1416,TRUE,TRUE,FALSE)		
		TGTPI	=	NOT(TLEPI)		
	TLEPI	V	=	SIN(X)		
	TGTPI	V	=	T − 3.1416		

Fig. 2.7 MIMIC statements for computing Eq. (2.15).

scribed by one MIMIC statement as follows:

$$V = \text{FSW}(T-3.1416, \text{SIN}(X), \text{SIN}(X), T-3.1416)$$

The above FSW function sets V equal to the second, third, or fourth argument, depending on whether the first argument is negative, zero, or positive.

The above FSW statement and the one in Fig. 2.7 also illustrate the important point that the second, third, and fourth arguments of an FSW statement can be either real quantities or logical quantities.

When LCV is present in the INT and FTR statements, one should note that these two functions are not initialized unless the LCV is TRUE at T equal to 0.

2.3.2 ARITHMETIC STATEMENTS

An arithmetic statement is a MIMIC statement of the second or fourth form whose expression is an arithmetic expression. The first, second, tenth, and fourteenth statements in Fig. 2.4, as well as the third and fourth statements in Fig. 2.6, are examples of arithmetic statements. The use of arithmetic operators in an arithmetic expression eliminates the need of the first seven functions in Table 2.4.

2.3.3 INPUT STATEMENTS AND FUNCTION GENERATION

There are four input statements: CON, PAR, CFN, and PFN. The general forms of these functions are shown in Table 2.7.

2.3.3.1 CON and PAR statements The CON and PAR statements provide a means for entering single values into a MIMIC program. Their arguments must be names, not expressions, because they are used to name constants and parameters. The use of these two statements in a MIMIC program has been shown in the example of Fig. 2.2. When there are more than one CON and/or PAR statements in a MIMIC program, they must be assembled in the correct order. All CON statements must precede the first PAR statement, and all data cards must have the same order as the statements to which they refer.

2.3.3.2 CFN and PFN statements The CFN and PFN statements provide a means for entering a table of data into a MIMIC program. To look up a value from the table, a FUN statement is required. The combination of CFN (or PFN) and FUN statements performs the function of arbitrary function generation. If the table of values does not change from run to run, a CFN statement is used; otherwise, a PFN statement is used. The following discussion on CFN applies to PFN. The order

Table 2.12 A table of
values for $y = f(x)$

x	y
−1.2	−4.2
0	−1.1
4.2	2.23
6.9	4.69
9.8	6.74

in which the input statements CON, PAR, CFN, and PFN must be followed in a MIMIC program has been described in Sec. 2.1.2 on card order.

2.3.3.3 Function generation of one variable The table of values can be a function of one variable or a function of two variables. Consider the case of a function of one variable. Let y be a function of x, or

$$y = f(x)$$

A table of values of function y is shown as an example in Table 2.12, where x and y may be called the input and output of the table, respectively. The input values do not have to be equally spaced, but they have to be in an algebraically increasing order. To enter this table into a MIMIC program, a CFN statement is required to specify the name of the table and the number of entries. Let the name of the table be F, and Table 2.12 has five entries. The CFN statement is shown in Fig. 2.8a,

1 2	10	19		72
	F	=	CFN(5.)	

(a)

1	13	25	37	72
− 1.2	− 4.2			
0.	− 1.1			
4.2	2.23			
6.9	4.69			
9.8	6.74			

(b)

Fig. 2.8 A CFN statement and its data cards. *(a)* A CFN statement; *(b)* data cards for a CFN statement.

and the data cards for this statement are shown in Fig. 2.8b.   There is
one pair of points per card, and the cards are placed in the proper order.
The values of x are in columns 1 to 12 and those of y in columns 13 to
24.   To look up a value from the table, the following FUN statement
(see Table 2.9) is required:

$$FX = FUN(F,X)$$

where the two arguments are the name of the table F and the name of the
input X, and FX is the chosen name of the output from the table.   If the
input is Z, then the FUN statement is

$$FZ = FUN(F,Z)$$

where FZ is the chosen name of the output from the table.   Thus, this
table can be used for more than one input (which is difficult to do for a
function generator in an analog computer).

Function FUN(F,X) utilizes linear interpolation.   Given (x_1,f_1),
(x_2,f_2), . . . , (x_n,f_n), where $x_1 < x_2 < \cdots < x_n$, then for an arbitrary
x the result R is determined by

$$R = \begin{cases} f_1 & \text{for } x \leq x_1 \\ f_n & \text{for } x \geq x_n \\ f_i + p_i(x - x_i) & \text{for } x_i \leq x \leq x_{i+1} \end{cases}$$

where

$$p_i = \frac{f_{i+1} - f_i}{x_{i+1} - x_i}$$

2.3.3.4   Function generation of two variables   Consider the case of a function of two variables.   Let z be a function of x and y, or

$$z = f(x,y)$$

A table of values of function z is shown as an example in Table 2.13, where
x and y may be called the inputs of the table and z the output.   To
enter this table into a MIMIC program, a CFN statement is required to
specify the name of the table and the number of entries.   Again, let F
be the name of the table, and Table 2.13 has 12 entries.   The CFN
statement is

$$F = CFN(12.)$$

Associated with this CFN statement are 12 data cards with a triple of
points per card.   The cards are arranged so that the values of x (the
first input) form an algebraically increasing sequence.   At each value of
x, the values of the y (the second input) must again form an algebraically

Table 2.13 A table of values for
$z = f(x,y)$

x	y	z
-2	1.5	2.1
-2	2.9	7.8
-2	3.8	6.4
0	-1.0	10.0
0	2.0	5.0
0	4.0	2.5
0	8.0	1.25
3	1.0	-1.0
3	2.5	-5.0
4	1.0	-1.0
4	2.5	2.5
4	4.5	6.5

increasing sequence. To look up a value from the table, the following FUN statement (see Table 2.9) is required:

$$FZ = FUN(F,X,Y)$$

where FZ is the chosen name of the output from the table F.

If the value of a table input is between two adjacent entries, linear interpolation is provided by the MIMIC processor. For functions of one variable, the function is given a zero slope for all values outside the tabulated range. For functions of two variables, the function is not defined outside the range of the input. Consequently, the user must ensure that the values of the input fall inside the tabulated values. This may be done by limiting the value of the input before looking up the function, or by extending the range of the function to cover all possible input values.

The number of tables, as well as the number of entries in each table, is limited by the capacity of the digital computer memory.

2.3.4 OUTPUT STATEMENTS

There are nine output statements: two for the output of a table, OUT and HDR, and seven for the output of a plot, PLO, SCA, ZER, TTP, TTX, TTY, and OPT. The general forms of these functions are shown in Tables 2.7 and 2.8.

2.3.4.1 OUT statement The OUT statement enables the user to print any variable name in the MIMIC program by specifying the variable name on an OUT statement. No more than six variable names may be included on any one OUT statement, but as many OUT statements as

1	2	10	19		72
			OUT(A,B,C,D,E,F)		
			OUT(,G,H,I,J,K)		
			OUT		

Fig. 2.9 Examples of OUT statements.

desired may be used in the program.   An example is shown in the first statement of Fig. 2.9.   The name PRI may be substituted for the name OUT.

The format of the table output is fixed.   It consists of six evenly spaced columns of numbers of the form

$$+x.xxxxxE+xx$$

Although the format is fixed, any column of the output table may be left blank by leaving an argument blank.   An example is shown in the second statement of Fig. 2.9.   Any line in the output table may be left blank by inserting a blank OUT statement.   An example is shown in the third statement of Fig. 2.9, which gives as the output a table with one blank line between every two lines of printing.

An expression may be used as an argument of an OUT statement. For example, the following statement is valid:

$$OUT(T,X,Y,SQR(X*X+Y*Y))$$

Printing of the output table occurs at specified intervals of the independent variable T (a reserved name).   The interval is determined by assigning a value to DT (a reserved name) either on a CON (or PAR) card or in an arithmetic statement.   If the value of DT is not specified, a value of 0.1 is chosen by the MIMIC processor.

2.3.4.2   HDR statement   The HDR statement enables the user to identify the columns of the output table.   Each HDR statement may have up to six names as headings, and each name may consist of no more than six *alphameric* characters.   An example is shown in the first statement of Fig. 2.10a.   The name HEA may be substituted for the name HDR. The HDR statement must precede the OUT statements, and the names on the HDR statements must line up horizontally and vertically with the variables they are identifying on the OUT statements.   The names are printed at the beginning of each run.   A blank column heading can be obtained by using an HDR statement with the corresponding argument of the HDR statement blank.   An example is shown in the second statement of Fig. 2.10a.   A blank line below the heading can be obtained by

1	2	10	19	73
			HDR(TIME,X,XDOT,Y,YDOT,ERROR) HDR(,U,V,W,R,S) HDR	

$$(a)$$

```
TIME  X  XDOT  Y  YDOT  ERROR
      U  V     W  R     S
```

$$(b)$$

Fig. 2.10 Examples of HDR statements. (a) HDR statements; (b) legends produced by the HDR statements in (a).

using an HDR statement with no arguments. An example is shown in the third statement of Fig. 2.10a. The HDR statements in Fig. 2.10a result in the legends shown in Fig. 2.10b. The legend appears at the start of each run. The blank HDR statement leaves a line between the legend and the first line of the table output.

If no HDR statements are used, the names used on the OUT statements are printed to the left of the variable at every PRINT interval. Figure 2.11 shows the table output of the MIMIC program in Fig. 2.2, which has no HDR card. The output in Fig. 2.11 is in an equation form (with equal-signs not shown).

2.3.4.3 PLOT statements The PLOT statements described here produce plots on the line printer at the termination of each run. They may also be made to produce plots on a digital plotter. As mentioned, there are

```
                A
          5.00000E-01

     T   0.                X   5.00000E-01
     T   1.00000E-01       X   4.99992E-01
     T   2.00000E-01       X   5.00033E-01
     T   3.00000E-01       X   5.00222E-01
     T   4.00000E-01       X   5.00653E-01
     T   5.00000E-01       X   5.01417E-01
     T   6.00000E-01       X   5.02600E-01
     T   7.00000E-01       X   5.04283E-01
     T   8.00000E-01       X   5.06540E-01
     T   9.00000E-01       X   5.09437E-01
     T   1.00000E 00       X   5.13033E-01
```

Fig. 2.11 Table output of a MIMIC program with no HDR card.

seven PLOT statements, as shown in Table 2.7. The PLO statement may have two to six arguments. The first argument is the independent variable of the plot, and the remaining arguments are plotted against this first argument, all on the same sheet. An example of a PLO statement is shown below:

PLO(X,Y,Z)

This statement results in a plot of y versus x superimposed upon a plot of z versus x. The points on the former curve are identified by letter A, and those on the latter by letter B.

The PLO statement† is all that is required to produce a plot. No more than 10 PLO statements may be used in any one program. If no other information is given, the MIMIC processor selects and labels the scales and identifies the plots. If a constant name or a literal name is used as an argument, it will not be plotted. Instead, its name and value will be printed at the top of each page of the plot. This feature can be used to identify plots by the parameter value used to obtain them. Any argument of a PLO statement may be an expression. Since the PLOT routine uses the argument name to identify the plots, it is more convenient to use only result names as arguments.

The SCA, ZER, TTP, TTX, TTY, and OPT statements are optional PLOT statements. They are provided to allow the user to exercise control over the plotted output. If they are used, they must be situated after the PLO statement to which they refer and before the next PLO statement.

The ZER and SCA (zero and scale) statements are used to impose user-selected scaling. The zero and scale are selected by assuming that plotting is to be done on a 100 by 100 grid. ZER is used to specify the location of the zero of the plot in terms of divisions from the bottom (or left) of the grid. SCA is used to specify the number of units per division. For example, assume that y and z are to be plotted versus x and have the following ranges:

$$0 \le x \le 200$$
$$-20 \le y \le 450$$
$$500 \le z \le 530$$

For x, it would be reasonable to have zero at the left and full scale equal to 200 units (2 units per division); for y, a full scale of 500 units (5 units per division) and a zero 10 divisions from the bottom. For z, it would be desirable to suppress the zero and let the bottom of the graph represent 500 units. To do this, select the scale, in this case 0.5 unit per division, and compute the zero by dividing the value required at the bottom of the

---

† The PLO statements in the MIMIC programs in Chaps. 3 and 4 are arranged to generate off-line plots by a digital plotter.

1	2	10	19		73
			PLO(X,Y,Z) SCA(2.,5.,.5) ZER(0.,10.,−1000.)		

Fig. 2.12 An example of SCA and ZER statements.

graph by the selected scale (that is, 500/0.5 = 1,000).   The required
zero is then the negative of this number.   The statements needed to use
these scales are shown in Fig. 2.12.

The TTP, TTX, and TTY statements provide titles, respectively, for
the page, the x axis, and the y axis of a plot.   Each title may contain up
to 36 characters.   The OPT statement shown in Table 2.7 provides the
options according to the values of the arguments.   The interpretation of
these arguments is shown in Table 2.8.

2.3.5 LOGICAL STATEMENTS

There are four logical functions: AND, IOR, EOR, and NOT (or COM),
as shown in Table 2.5.   The result R of an AND statement is TRUE if
all the arguments are TRUE.   The result R of an IOR statement is TRUE
if any of the arguments is TRUE.   These two statements may have two
to six arguments.   The EOR statement has two arguments X and Y;
the result R is TRUE if either X or Y is TRUE (but not both X and Y are
TRUE).   The NOT statement has only one argument; the result is the
complement of the argument.

2.3.6 CONTROL STATEMENTS

There are four control functions: FSW, LSW, FIN, and END, as shown
in Table 2.5.   The FSW statement allows conversion of a real variable
into a logical one for use as an LCV.   The LSW statement allows conversion of a logical variable into a real one.   The FSW statement

$$S = FSW(A,X,Y,Z)$$

selects X, Y, or Z as result S.   This selection depends on whether the
real value of A is less than, equal to, or larger than zero, where S, X, Y, and
Z are logical quantities.   The LSW statement

$$R = LSW(X,B,C)$$

selects B or C as result R according to whether the logical value of X is
TRUE or FALSE, respectively, where R, B, and C are real quantities.
As indicated in Table 2.5, the arguments of an FSW or an LSW state-
ment can be real or logical.   Thus, the FSW and LSW statements are not

limited to conversions between real and logical quantities.   For example,
interpretation of a nonzero value of a real variable as a logical one and
vice versa are sometimes conveniently utilized.

The FIN statement

FIN(A,B)

where A and B are any MIMIC expressions, controls the termination of
one run and the start of the next run.   When A is greater than B, the
current run is terminated, and the next set of parameters will be read
in and the next run will be started.   When the data cards are exhausted,
the simulation will terminate.

As shown in Table 2.5, the FIN statement defines a logical variable S
which is TRUE when A is equal to or greater than B and is FALSE
otherwise.   This feature can be used to control end-of-run computations
and provides a method for performing iterative computation.

The END statement is used to denote the end of the program and the
beginning of data.   Every MIMIC program must have one and only one
END statement.   If the END statement is omitted, the MIMIC processor will list all the cards of the MIMIC program and terminate.

The combination of logical control variable and FIN function provides a means of automatically changing parameters between runs.   As a
simple example, consider

$$x = \int_0^{10} e^{-at} \sin(\omega t + \phi) \tag{2.16}$$

which is to be evaluated for a equal to 0 to a equal to 10 at an increment of
0.1 and for ϕ equal to 0 to ϕ equal to 90 at an increment of 1.   A MIMIC
program for this evaluation is shown in Fig. 2.13.   In this program, a
and ϕ are parameters and their values are stored on 1,001 data cards (one
for each pair of the values of a and ϕ).

Instead of using many data cards for changing the values of parameters between the runs, automatic changing of the parameter values for
the program in Fig. 2.13 can be achieved by using a combination of an

1	2	10	19	73
			CON(W)	
			PAR(A,PHI)	
		X =	INT(EXP(−A*T)*SIN(W*T + PHI),0.)	
			FIN(T,10.)	
			OUT(T,X)	
			END	

Fig. 2.13   MIMIC program for evaluating integral (2.16).

1	2	10	19		73
			CON(W,READ)		1
	READ		PAR(A,PHI)		2
		X =	INT(EXP(−A*T)*SIN(W*T+PHI),0.)		3
		UPDATE =	FIN(T,10.)		4
	UPDATE	PHI =	PHI+1.		5
	UPDATE	READ =	FSW(PHI−90.5,FALSE,TRUE,TRUE)		6
			OUT(T,X)		7
			END		8

1	13		
Value of W	1.		
0.	0.		
.1	0.		
.2	0.		
.3	0.		
.4	0.		
.5	0.		
.6	0.		
.7	0.		
.8	0.		
.9	0.		
1.	0.		

Fig. 2.14 MIMIC program for evaluating integral (2.16).

LCV and a FIN statement, as shown in the MIMIC program of Fig. 2.14. In this program, READ and UPDATE are two logical variables. UPDATE becomes TRUE (a nonzero value) when T is equal to or greater than 10 (i.e., at the end of a run), and READ is TRUE when PHI is equal to or greater than 90.5. The first data card gives READ a value of TRUE, which causes the first set of values of parameters A and PHI to be read in. This set gives both A and PHI a value of 0. The computation now proceeds in a normal way until T becomes 10, the end of the run. At this time, UPDATE is set TRUE and statements 5 and 6 are executed for the first time, setting PHI equal to 1 and READ to FALSE. Since this is the end of the run, the processor sets T equal to 0, restores the initial conditions, and prepares to read in new values of A and PHI. But READ is FALSE, so that the PAR statement is not executed and the second run is made with A equal to 0 and PHI equal to 1. This process continues until PHI reaches 91, at which time READ is set TRUE by statement 6. When this happens, the second set of parameter values (third data card) is read in. This process continues until all the parameter cards have been exhausted. If only the final value of the integral (2.16) (i.e., at $t = 10$) had been required, UPDATE could also have been entered as the LCV of the OUT statement.

The MIMIC program in Fig. 2.14 increments the value of PHI by an arithmetic statement. The value of A can be incremented similarly by an arithmetic statement, resulting in only one data card for the parameter values.

2.3.7 INTEGRATION STATEMENTS

There are two integration statements, INT and FTR, and one LIN statement for limiting the output of an integration function. These three functions are shown in Table 2.6.

An INT function may be called an integrator, reminiscent of the integrator in an analog computer. There are four arguments, A, B, C, and D. Argument A is the integrand, B is the initial value, and C and D give the codes for mode control of the integrator. By these codes, the mode of each integrator can be individually controlled. These codes are shown in Table 2.14, where there are three modes, RESET, OPERATE, and HOLD. In the RESET mode, the output of the integrator is set to the initial value (that is, B), and no integration takes place. In the OPERATE mode, the integrator is updated by the integration routine; this is the normal mode. In the HOLD mode, the input to the integrator is removed and the output holds to the last value. The use of arguments C and D is optional. If these two arguments are not specified, the integrator is in the OPERATE mode.

In simulating a physical model where limiting the output of an integrator is involved, a special limiting function may be required. This limiting can best be described by using the mass-damper-spring system described by the equation

$$M\ddot{x} + B\dot{x} + Kx = f(t)$$

with the initial conditions

$$\dot{x}(0) = A \qquad \text{and} \qquad x(0) = x_0$$

where M = mass
B = damping coefficient
K = spring constant

There are physical stops which constrain the mass M to move only

Table 2.14   Integrator mode codes

C	D	Mode
FALSE	FALSE	OPERATE
FALSE	TRUE	HOLD
TRUE	FALSE	RESET
TRUE	TRUE	OPERATE

1 2	10	19	73
	2DX	1./M*(−B*1DXL−K*X+FT)	
	1DX	INT(2DX,A)	
	1DXL	LIN(1DX,X,XL,XU)	
	X	INT(1DXL,XO)	

Fig. 2.15 MIMIC statements illustrating a LIN statement.

between x_1 and x_2, or

$$x_1 \leq x \leq x_2$$

When the displacement x of mass M reaches the stop, the mass M must stop, implying that the velocity $\dot{x}$ is zero. This means that the input to the displacement integrator must be zero. This type of limiting function is performed by the LIN statement. For the above physical stops, we have

$$R = LIN(XDOT,X,X1,X2)$$

In the above LIN statement, R is equal to XDOT (that is, $\dot{x}$) for X1 $\leq$ X $\leq$ X2, but it is set to zero for X < X1 or for X > X2 until the derivative of XDOT (i.e., acceleration) changes sign. The MIMIC statements describing the above simulation are shown in Fig. 2.15. Note that the variable 1DXL in Fig. 2.15 is the limited x which is the input to the displacement integrator (i.e., last statement).

The FTR function performs the simple-lag transfer function

$$\frac{e_0}{e_1} = \frac{1}{\tau_s + 1}$$

which is described by the following FTR statement:

$$EO = FTR(EI,TAU)$$

The MIMIC processor generates computer instructions equivalent to those which would have resulted had the user written the transfer function in the differential form

$$\tau \dot{e}_0 + e_0 = e_1$$

which can be described by the following INT statement:

$$EO = INT((EI−EO)/TAU,0.)$$

All integrations specified by integration functions are performed by a centralized integration routine in the MIMIC processor. The routine employs a variable-step fourth-order Runge-Kutta method. (As an illus-

tration, a variable-step integration subroutine is shown in Chap. 5.)   The
step size h of the integration is limited by the range

$$\text{DTMIN} \leq h \leq \text{DTMAX} \leq \text{DT} \tag{2.17}$$

where DT, DTMAX, and DTMIN are previously mentioned reserved
names.   Examples of specifying the values of DT, DTMAX, and
DTMIN by arithmetic statements are shown in Fig. 2.16.   When the
statement

$$\text{DTMAX} = \text{DTMIN} \tag{2.18}$$

is used, the integration is carried out in a fixed step size.   If the value of
DT is not specified, it is set to 0.1.   If the value of DTMAX is not
specified, it is set to the value of DT.   The step size is automatically
changed by the integration routine to keep the relative error at in each
step below the absolute value of 5×10^{-6}.   (The error is computed by
comparing the value of y_{n+1} obtained by computing with two half-steps
and the value obtained by computing with one full step.)   The error
criterion can be changed from a relative to an absolute basis by using
a processor control card $ABSERR, shown in Table 2.2.

2.3.8 IMPLICIT STATEMENT

An equation of the form

$$x = f(x,y) \tag{2.19}$$

where unknown x appears on both sides of the equation and function f has
neither derivative nor integral, usually requires an iterative method of
solution, which can be specified by an IMP statement.   When an IMP
statement is used, a PAR statement is required to identify the unknown of
the equation and to provide the initial guess of the unknown.

As an example, consider the following equation:

$$x = \sin x + y \tag{2.20}$$

Variable y is assumed available elsewhere in the MIMIC program.
MIMIC statements for solving this equation are shown in Fig. 2.17,

1	2	10	19			73
		DTMAX =	0.01			
		DTMIN =	0.0001			
		DTMAX =	DTMIN			
		DTMAX =	DT			
		DT =	0.01			

Fig. 2.16 Examples of specifying the values of DT, DTMAX, and DTMIN.

1	2	10	19		73
			PAR(X)		
		X	IMP(X,SIN(X)+Y)		

Fig. 2.17 An example of using an IMP statement.

where the unknown X is identified by the PAR statement. There will be a data card for the PAR statement, though not shown in Fig. 2.17.

In the MIMIC processor, the implicit function employs the following iterative method for solving Eq. (2.19):

$$x_{n+1} = \frac{f_n - C_n X_n}{1 - C_n}$$

$$c_n = \frac{f_n - f_{n-1}}{X_n - X_{n-1}} \tag{2.21}$$

where

$$f_n = f(x_n, y)$$

The MIMIC processor does not increment the independent variable T of a MIMIC program until the computation of a sequence of x_n's reaches the following condition:

$$|x_n - f_n| \le 5 \times 10^{-6}|x_n| \tag{2.22}$$

The value of x_n at this time is taken as the solution of Eq. (2.19). When this value is obtained, the MIMIC processor advances the independent variable T and continues the computation.

The above iteration required by an implicit statement can be quite time-consuming. The following is an example, showing that in some cases implicit statements can be avoided. Consider the equations

$$x = y + z$$

$$y = -0.5x + \sqrt{u^2 + v^2} \tag{2.23}$$

MIMIC statements for finding unknown x are shown in Fig. 2.18. Although x was chosen as the unknown, y could have been used equally

1	2	10	19		73
			PAR(X)		
		Y	−.5*X+SQR(U*U+V*V)		
		X	IMP(X,Y+Z)		

Fig. 2.18 An example of using an IMP statement.

1	2	10	19		73
		X	Y + Z		
		Y	−.5*X + SQR(U*U + V*V)		

Fig. 2.19   An example of not using an IMP statement.

well. However, manipulation of these two equations gives the two equations

$$x = \frac{1}{1.5}\left(\sqrt{u^2 + v^2} + z\right)$$

$$y = -0.5x + \sqrt{u^2 + v^2}$$

(2.24)

which eliminates the use of an IMP statement.

It may happen that there exists in a simulation an implicit relation of which the programmer is not aware. In this case, the MIMIC processor will print an error message and delete the execution of the MIMIC program. For example, if Eq. (2.23) is to be solved without the use of an IMP statement, the MIMIC statements are shown in Fig. 2.19. The function-language program generated by the MIMIC processor for these statements is shown in Fig. 2.20, and the error message in Fig. 2.21. Notice that the message is written in terms of the function language, and all unaffected statements are replaced by asterisks.

2.3.9 HYBRID STATEMENTS

There are four hybrid functions, MMV, TAS, FLF, and ZOH, as shown in Table 2.10. (MMV actually represents a digital element, and FLF, a logic element.) The MMV statement represents a monostable multivibrator, whose output S is initially equal to X. Output S is set TRUE when X is TRUE and remains TRUE for B sec after X becomes FALSE. The TAS statement represents a track-and-hold circuit, where output R follows input A when input X is TRUE but holds its value when X becomes FALSE. The FLF statement represents an RS flip-flop, where

```
X       ADD     Y       Z
(101)   MPY     U       U
(102)   MPY     V       V
(103)   ADD     (101)   (102)
(104)   SQR     (103)
(105)   NEG     .5
(106)   MPY     (105)   X
Y       ADD     (106)   (104)
```

Fig. 2.20   A generated function-language program.

THE FOLLOWING LIST CONTAINS ONE OR MORE CLOSED LOOPS:

X	ADD	Y	******
(106)	MPY	******	X
Y	ADD	(106)	******

Fig. 2.21 An error message.

inputs X and Y are SET and RESET inputs, respectively.   Input Z is the initial status of the flip-flop.   The ZOH statement represents a sample-and-hold circuit, which samples input A every B sec and in the meantime holds the sampled value.

When any of these hybrid statements is used in a MIMIC program, integration in a fixed step size should be used.   This can be specified by using statement (2.18).

2.3.10 OTHER STATEMENTS

There is a derivative function DER(A,B,C) in Table 2.6.   The output of a DER statement is the derivative of input B with respect to argument A, while argument C is the initial value of the derivative.

There are two selection statements, MAX and MIN, as shown in Table 2.9.   The MAX statement selects the largest input as the output, while the MIN statement selects the smallest.   The number of inputs can be two to six.

There are two functions for generating random numbers, RNU(A,B,C) and RNG(A,B,C), as shown in Table 2.9.   An RNU function generates a sequence r_n of fixed-point numbers from the following relation, given starting value $r_0 = C$:

$$r_n = (5^{15} - 1)r_{n-1}(\text{mod } 2^{35})$$

where mod denotes modulo.   The result r_n is packed into a floating-point number R_n in the range $(0,1)$.   The final result R in the range (A,B) is obtained from the relationship

$$R = A + (B - A)R_n$$

An RNG function first generates the above sequence R_n.   Then the value of R_n is used as an input to a subroutine which generates the sequence S_n with the gaussian distribution.   The final result is

$$R = A + BS_n$$

where A is the mean A and B is the standard deviation.

Also in Table 2.9, there is a DELAY statement, TDL, which gives an output equal to input A after a time delay of B.   Input B may be a variable. The number of points of input A to be stored are specified by input C; a value of 100 for C is suggested. Function TDL uses the same linear interpolation algorithm as that for function FUN(F,X) shown earlier.

There are two nonlinear statements, DSP and LIM, in Table 2.9. The DSP statement represents a dead-space element, which gives no output when the value of A is between the values of arguments B and C. It gives an output equal to $(A-B)$ when input A is less than B and an output equal to $(A-C)$ when input A is larger than C. The LIM statement represents a limiter, which gives an output equal to input A when the value of input A is between the values of arguments B and C. The output is limited to argument C when input A is larger than C, and limited to argument B when input A is smaller than B. Notice the difference between the LIM and LIN statements.

2.4 USER'S OPTIONS

In order to extend the available functions, MIMIC allows the user to provide his own functions. For this purpose, the user may choose the use of subprograms in MIMIC language or subroutines in FORTRAN language.

2.4.1 MIMIC LANGUAGE SUBPROGRAM

Subprograms in MIMIC language with multiple outputs are allowed in a MIMIC program. There are four statements, BSP, ESP, CSP, and RSP, involved with a MIMIC language subprogram. These functions are shown in Table 2.9.

A subprogram is defined as those MIMIC statements between a BSP (BEGIN SUBPROGRAM) statement and an ESP (END SUB-PROGRAM) statement. The name of the subprogram is located in the result name field of the BSP and ESP statements. The inputs of the subprogram are specified as arguments of the BSP function and the outputs as arguments of the ESP function. After the subprogram is defined, it can be called by a pair of CSP (CALL SUBPROGRAM) and RSP (RETURN SUBPROGRAM) statements more than once in the MIMIC program. When a subprogram is called, the inputs to the subprogram are listed as arguments of the CSP function, and the outputs as those of the RSP function. The following five rules should be observed in writing or calling a subprogram:

1. The MIMIC statements in a subprogram must be in a proper order, as the MIMIC processor does not sort the statements in the subprogram. To be in a proper order, a variable in a statement in the

1 2	10	19	73
	SAMPLE	BSP(X,Y,Z)	
	X1	X*COS(Z)+Y*SIN(Z)	
	Y1	−X*SIN(Z)+Y*COS(Z)	
	SAMPLE	ESP(X1,Y1)	

Fig. 2.22 A MIMIC language subprogram.

subprogram must be an input of the subprogram, a previous result in the subprogram, or a variable in the MIMIC program whose value has been defined.
2. If a variable in a subprogram has the same name as a variable in the MIMIC program, these two variables are considered as the same variable. Therefore, the variables in the MIMIC program can be used in the subprogram without being further defined.
3. The RSP statement must follow immediately the CSP statement.
4. Functions INT and FTR should not be used in the subprogram.
5. The arguments of the CSP statement may themselves be expressions.

As an example, write a subprogram in MIMIC language for computing the coordinates after rotating a two-dimensional vector through an angle. The equations are

$$x_1 = x \cos z + y \sin z$$
$$y_1 = -x \sin z + y \cos z$$
(2.25)

The inputs to the subprogram are x, y, and z, and the outputs are x_1 and y_1. The subprogram is named SAMPLE and is shown in Fig. 2.22. Now, if the two sets of equations

$$v_1 = u_1 \cos u_3 + u_2 \sin u_3$$
$$v_2 = -u_1 \sin u_3 + u_2 \cos u_3$$
(2.26)

and

$$p_1 = \omega_1 \cos \omega_3 + \omega_2 \sin \omega_3$$
$$p_2 = -\omega_1 \sin \omega_3 + \omega_2 \cos \omega_3$$
(2.27)

1 2	10	19	73
	SAMPLE	CSP(U1,U2,U3)	
		RSP(V1,V2)	
	SAMPLE	CSP(W1,W2,W3)	
		RSP(P1,P2,)	

Fig. 2.23 Examples of calling a MIMIC subprogram.

```
SUBROUTINE SR1(A,B,C,D,E,F,G)
G = B
IF(A.GT.0.)   G = C
RETURN
END
```

Fig. 2.24 A FORTRAN language subprogram.

are to be computed, subprogram SAMPLE is called to perform the computation, instead of writing these similar statements twice. Each call of the subprogram SAMPLE consists of two statements, and four CALL statements are shown in Fig. 2.23.

2.4.2 FORTRAN LANGUAGE SUBPROGRAM†

In the MIMIC processor, subroutines with names SR1, SR2, SR3, SR4, and SR5 are dummy subroutines which are to be replaced by the user's FORTRAN subroutines. Each of these subroutines can have up to seven arguments: six inputs and one output.

As an example, write a FORTRAN subprogram to represent a logical switch (assume that the LSW function in Table 2.5 is not available) for computing the following equations:

$$x = \begin{cases} y + z \sin \omega & \text{for } t \leq 5 \\ 0 & \text{for } t > 5 \end{cases} \tag{2.28}$$

The FORTRAN subprogram is shown in Fig. 2.24. Note that seven arguments are required in the first statement, even though only four arguments (three inputs and one output) are needed. And the result must always be represented by the seventh argument. If this FORTRAN subprogram is now called to compute Eq. (2.28), a CALL statement is required, as shown in Fig. 2.25.

† This section may be deferred until FORTRAN programming is presented in a later chapter.

1	2	10	19		73
		X	SRI(T−5.,Y+Z*SIN(W),0.)		

Fig. 2.25 An example of calling a FORTRAN subprogram.

```
      SUBROUTINE SR1(A,B,C,D,E,F,G)
      IF(D.EQ.2.) GO TO 10
      G = A*COS(C)+B*SIN(C)
      RETURN
10    G = -A*SIN(C)+B*COS(C)
      RETURN
      END
```

Fig. 2.26 A FORTRAN language subprogram.

1 2	10	19	73
	X1 Y1	SR1(X,Y,Z,1.) SR1(X,Y,Z,2.)	

Fig. 2.27 Examples of calling a FORTRAN subprogram.

That there can be only one argument as the output is a limitation of a FORTRAN language subprogram.   However, this can be overcome by use of multiple calls.   As an example, Eqs. (2.25), which describe the rotation of a two-dimensional vector through an angle, are again chosen. The FORTRAN subprogram is shown in Fig. 2.26, where arguments A, B, and C are inputs, G is the output, and D is a switch for selecting one from two arithmetic statements.   If the FORTRAN subprogram is now called to compute Eqs. (2.25), two CALL statements are required, as shown in Fig. 2.27.

2.5 TEST PROGRAMS AND PROGRAM DEBUGGING

In learning to use a new programming language, a user is liable to make errors in writing programs because of his unfamiliarity with the syntax and programming technique of that language.   One approach to shorten the learning time is to write programs for the purpose of testing those statements which are unfamiliar to the user.   After a program is written, the user begins to find the errors.   The process of finding the errors and removing them from the program is commonly referred to as "debugging."   This section presents the idea of writing test programs and discusses the problem of program debugging.

.5.1 TEST PROGRAMS

It may happen that the syntactical description of a statement is not clear or that the programming manual is actually in error.   Whenever such a

```
              TEST OF ARCTANGENT FUNCTION
              *
                                  PAR(A,B)
                            F     = ATN(A,B)
                            X     = F*180./3.1416
                                  FIN(T,0.)
                                  HDR(ARCTAN)
                                  OUT(X)
                                  END
                  +1.              +2.
                  -2.              +1.
                  -2.0             -1.
                  +1.              -2.
```

Fig. 2.28 MIMIC program for testing the ATN function.

```
TEST FSW AND LSW FUNCTIONS
*
           DT      = 2.0
           PHI     = T*3.1416/180.
           A       = SIN(PHI)
           B       = -A
           F       = FSW(T-180.,A,0.,B)
           G       = FSW(T-90.,A,0.,0.)
*
           L       = FSW(T-180.,TRUE,TRUE,FALSE)
           H       = LSW(L,A,B)
*
                     FIN(T,360.)
                     HDR(DEGREE,G,F,H,L)
                     HDR
                     OUT(T,G,F,H,L)
                     END
```

Fig. 2.29 MIMIC program for testing FSW and LSW statements.

```
TEST DERIVATIVE FUNCTION
*
                     PAR(DTMAX)
*
           DT      = .02
           A       = 1.0
*
           FIRST   = SIN(A*T)
           TEST1   = DER(T,FIRST,A)/A
*
           SECOND  = COS(A*T)
           TEST2   = -DER(T,SECOND,0.)/A
*
           THIRD   = A*T
           TEST3   = DER(T,THIRD,A)
*
           FOURTH  = EXP(T)
           TEST4   = DER(T,FOURTH,1.)
*
                     FIN(T,2.)
                     HDR(T,FIRST,SECOND,THIRD,FOURTH)
                     HDR(, TEST2,TEST1,,TEST3,TEST4)
                     HDR
                     OUT(T,FIRST,SECOND,THIRD,,FOURTH)
                     OUT(, TEST2,TEST1,,TEST3,TEST4)
                     OUT
                     END
     .5
     .1
     .02
```

Fig. 2.30 MIMIC program for testing the DER statement.

```
TEST ZOH AND TAS FUNCTIONS
*
                PAR(N)
        DT      = .1
        A       = EXP(-T)
        B       = ZOH(A,N)
*
        TRACK   = FSW(T-.8,TRUE,TRUE,FALSE)
        R       = TAS(A,TRACK,0.)
*
                FIN(T,4.)
                HDR(TIME,A,B,R)
                HDR
                OUT(T,A,B,R)
                END
.1
.2
.05
```

Fig. 2.31 MIMIC program for testing ZOH and TAS statements.

difficulty arises, one may resolve it quickly by writing a test program. For example, Fig. 2.28 shows a program for testing whether the sign of the ATN function is correct in the four quadrants. Whenever there is a discrepancy between what is stated in the programming manual and what is obtained from the computer (assume that the program has been debugged), it is the computer which is right. One may assume that it is the computer (together with its software) which speaks the "native language."

```
TEST OF TDL, MAX,   AND MIN FUNCTIONS
*
        DTMIN   = DTMAX
        DTMAX   = 1.0
        DT      = 1.0
*
        A       = T
        B       = TDL(A,1.)
        C       = 2.*B
        D       = TDL(C,2.)
        E       = MAX(A,B,C,D)
        F       = MIN(A,B,C,D)
*
                FIN(T,10.)
                HDR(TIME,A,B,D,E,F)
                HDR
                OUT(T,A,B,D,E,F)
                END
```

Fig. 2.32 MIMIC program for testing TDL, MAX, and MIN statements.

```
GENERATION OF RANDOM NUMBERS
*
                   PAR(P)
         DTMIN  =  DTMAX
         DTMAX  =  1.
         DT     =  .1
*
         A      =  RNG(0.,.3,P)
         B      =  RNU(0.,1.,P)
*
                   FIN(T,9.)
                   HDR(TIME,A,B)
                   HDR
                   OUT(T,A,B)
                   END
• 1
• 2
• 3                                    Fig. 2.33  MIMIC program for test-
• 4                                    ing RNG and RNU statements.
```

Figures 2.29 through 2.33 show additional test programs.   The program in Fig. 2.29 tests the FSW and LSW statements; that in Fig. 2.30 tests the DER statement; that in Fig. 31 tests the ZOH and TAS statements; that in Fig. 2.32 tests the TDL, MAX, and MIN statements; and that in Fig. 2.33 tests the RNG and RNU statements.

2.5.2 PROGRAM DEBUGGING

It is common to find errors after a program is written.   Successful execution of the program cannot be achieved until these errors are removed. There are four types: key-punch error, control-card error, programming error, and simulation error.   The key-punch error is due to incorrect key punching; it is probably the most common.   A listing of the program deck is very helpful, as the user may readily detect key-punch errors by scanning over the listing.   Once found, these errors can be easily removed by punching correct cards.

The control-card error is due to wrong card format, misspelled system code, incorrect identification data, missing control card, or incorrect order of control cards.   With a control-card error, processing of the program may not even start; or if processing is started, it may not be completed.   Even if there is no control-card error, the processing may be stopped due to such a cause as an underestimate in the computer time or in the number of printed pages.   Control-card errors often happen to beginning users or at a new computer facility.   A careful reading of the proper manual or advice by a system programmer removes most of this kind of error.

The programming error is caused by violations of the syntax of the language, such as improper variable or constant name, incorrect card format, missing symbols, incorrect order of statements, and the like. The processor often provides error messages to assist the user to debug his program. The MIMIC processor detects and identifies errors due to undefined variable and constant names, use of a function which is not available in the list of MIMIC functions, and multiple definition of a result name. It also detects a BSP statement not followed by an ESP statement or a CSP statement not immediately followed by an RSP statement. It can also detect algebraic loops where implicit statements should be used. An example of an error message for a closed loop is shown in Fig. 2.21.

A simulation error is an error in the original model of which the user may be unaware. These errors can be improper representation of the physical system, wrong values of constants, inconsistent use of physical units, and the like. The MIMIC processor generates a function-language program, which is illustrated in Table 1.1 and in Fig. 2.20. By using this generated program, the user can construct a block diagram from which simulation error may be detected.

PROBLEMS

2.1. Identify and explain the function of each statement
    (a) In Fig. 2.3   (b) In Fig. 2.4
    (c) In Fig. 2.5   (d) In Fig. 2.6

2.2. Insert an HDR statement in the MIMIC program in Fig. 2.2 and run the program.

2.3. Run the MIMIC program in Fig. 2.2 after changing the data cards into the following forms:
    (a) The exponent form, right-justified in their respective numerical fields
    (b) The normal form, right-justified in their respective numerical fields
    (c) The normal form, neither right- nor left-justified in their respective numerical fields

2.4. Run the MIMIC program in Fig. 2.28 and determine whether the sign is correct.

2.5. What waveforms are produced by variables F, G, and H in the MIMIC program in Fig. 2.29?

2.6. For the MIMIC program in Fig. 2.30:
    (a) How close are the values between the values represented by FIRST and TEST2, between SECOND and TEST1, and between FOURTH and TEST4?
    (b) What is the value represented by TEST3?
    (c) What is the effect to the answers in part a due to different values of DT?

2.7. For the MIMIC program in Fig. 2.31:
    (a) Compare the values represented by variables A and B.
    (b) What is the response represented by variable R?

2.8. For the MIMIC program in Fig. 2.32:
    (a) What is the purpose of the first three arithmetic statements?
    (b) What are the sequences of the generated numbers represented by variables B, C, and D?
    (c) What is the maximum value selected by the MAX statement?
    (d) What is the minimum value selected by the MIN statement?

2.9. Test the MIMIC program in Fig. 2.33 and plot the values of A and B.

2.10. Use the IMPLICIT statement to compute the solution of the following equations:

    (a) $x - \cos x = 0$ *Ans.:* $x = 0.739$

    (b) $\phi \tan \phi - 1 = 0$ *Ans.:* $\phi = 0.86$

    (c) $y^2 - \sin y = 0$ *Ans.:* $y = 0.8767$

2.11. Write MIMIC programs to compute the following integrals:

    (a) $\displaystyle\int_0^\pi \sin^2 x \, dx$ *Ans.:* $\pi/2$

    (b) $\displaystyle\int_0^1 \frac{1 + x^2}{1 + x^4} \, dx$ *Ans.:* $\sqrt{2}\pi/4$

    (c) $\displaystyle\int_0^\infty x e^{-x} \sin x \, dx$ *Ans.:* $\frac{1}{2}$

REFERENCES

1. Sansom, F. J., and H. E. Petersen: Mimic Programming Manual, *Tech. Rept.* SEG-TR-67-31, Wright-Patterson Air Force Base, Ohio, July, 1967.

2. Chu, Y.: Digital Analog Simulation Techniques, *Proc. Fifth Congr. Intern. Assoc. Analogue Computation, Lausanne, Switzerland,* 1967.

3. Petersen, H. E., and F. J. Sansom: Further Developments in the Handling of Implicit Functions, *Simulation,* January, 1966, Simulation Council, Inc., p. 15.

4. Hastings, C., Jr.: "Approximations for Digital Computers," Princeton University Press, Princeton, N.J., 1955.

3
Engineering Applications

MIMIC programming has been shown in Chap. 2. Engineering applications of MIMIC programming are presented in this chapter, while mathematical applications are discussed in the next chapter. Most of the examples in these chapters include a short problem description, a brief introduction of the model, a set of numerical values for the simulation, the MIMIC program which has been debugged, and the result, mostly in plots. The PLO statements in these MIMIC programs are arranged to generate off-line plots by a digital plotter.

3.1 GENERATION OF FUNCTIONS AND FIGURES

As shown in the last chapter, the independent variable in a MIMIC program is represented by reserved word T. One may look upon T as a counter whose contents, initially set to zero, are incremented automatically by an amount specified by reserved word DT. The consecutive values of T may be used as an ordered series of arguments. In addition,

```
*****GENERATION OF TABLES OF FUNCTIONS
*
         DT        = 1.0
*
         M         = T+1.
         A         = SQR(T)
         B         = EXP(-T)
         C         = LOG(M)
*
                     FIN(T,50.)
                     HDR(N,SQRN,EXPN,M,LOGM)
                     HDR
                     OUT(T,A,B,M,C)
                     PLO(T,A,B,M,C)
                     END
```

Fig. 3.1 MIMIC program for the generation of three functions.

the contents of the counter may be used as a convenient condition for terminating computation by a FIN statement. These and other features of MIMIC make convenient the generation of some functions and figures.

3.1.1 ELEMENTARY FUNCTIONS

As examples of generating a table of values of a function, the following statements may be used to generate a table of square-root function A, exponential function B, and logarithmic function C:

$$A = SQR(T)$$
$$B = EXP(-T) \qquad\qquad (3.1)$$
$$C = LOG(M)$$

where $M = T+1$. The above statement for function C is not $LOG(T)$ but $LOG(M)$; this is so written in order to avoid $LOG(0)$ when variable T equals 0. The new variable M is formed by linearly shifting variable T one unit.

A MIMIC program for generating these three functions is shown in

N	SQRN	EXPN	M	LOGM
0.	0.	1.00000E 00	1.00000E 00	0.
1.00000E 00	1.00000E 00	3.67879E-01	2.00000E 00	6.93147E-01
2.00000E 00	1.41421E 00	1.35335E-01	3.00000E 00	1.09861E 00
3.00000E 00	1.73205E 00	4.97871E-02	4.00000E 00	1.38629E 00
4.00000E 00	2.00000E 00	1.83156E-02	5.00000E 00	1.60944E 00
5.00000E 00	2.23607E 00	6.73795E-03	6.00000E 00	1.79176E 00
6.00000E 00	2.44949E 00	2.47875E-03	7.00000E 00	1.94591E 00
7.00000E 00	2.64575E 00	9.11882E-04	8.00000E 00	2.07944E 00
8.00000E 00	2.82843E 00	3.35463E-04	9.00000E 00	2.19722E 00
9.00000E 00	3.00000E 00	1.23410E-04	1.00000E 01	2.30259E 00
1.00000E 01	3.16228E 00	4.53999E-05	1.10000E 01	2.39790E 00

Fig. 3.2 Table output from the MIMIC program in Fig. 3.1.

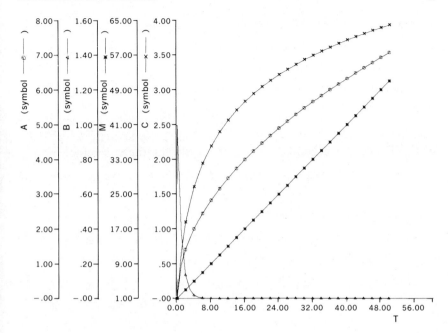

Fig. 3.3 Plot of four elementary functions.

Fig. 3.1, where DT is chosen to be 1.   The table is given by an OUT statement, and the plot by a PLO statement.   The table and the plot are
shown in Figs. 3.2 and 3.3, respectively.

SIN, COS, and TAN statements are available; these statements may
be used to generate sine, cosine, tangent, and other trigonometric
functions.

3.1.2 GEOMETRICAL FIGURES

It is more convenient to use equations in parametric form to generate
geometric figures by MIMIC programming, and variable T is used as the
parameter.   For example, in rectangular coordinates, a circle of radius R
can be generated by the following equations:

$$X = R \cos \phi \qquad Y = R \sin \phi$$
$$\phi = \frac{\pi T}{180} \tag{3.2}$$

where T is in degrees.   An ellipse can be generated by the following pair:

$$X = 4R \cos \phi \qquad Y = 2R \sin \phi \tag{3.3}$$

A cycloid can be generated by the pair

$$X = R(\phi - \sin \phi) \qquad Y = R(1 - \cos \phi) \tag{3.4}$$

and an Archimedean spiral by the pair

$$X = R\,\phi\cos\phi \qquad Y = R\,\phi\sin\phi \tag{3.5}$$

A MIMIC program using the above parametric equations to generate these figures is shown in Fig. 3.4. For a series of values of R, families of these geometrical figures can be generated.

Geometric figures can also be generated by using a pair of time derivatives $\dot{X}$ and $\dot{Y}$, where X and Y represent, respectively, the abscissa and ordinate of rectangular coordinates. For example, the pair

$$\dot{X} = C_1 \qquad \dot{Y} = C_2 \tag{3.6}$$

```
*****GENERATION OF GEOMETRIC CURVES
*
                    CON(PI)
*
        DT       = 5.0
        PHI      = T*PI/180.
*
*CIRCLE
        R        = 1.
        X1       = R*COS(PHI)
        Y1       = R*SIN(PHI)
*
*ELLIPSE
        A        = 4.
        B        = 2.
        X2       = A*COS(PHI)
        Y2       = B*SIN(PHI)
*
*CYCCOID
        X3       = R*(PHI-SIN(PHI))
        Y3       = B*(1.0-COS(PHI))
*
*SPIRAL
        K        =R*PHI
        X4       = K*COS(PHI)
        Y4       = K*SIN(PHI)
*
                    FIN(T,720.)
                    HDR(T,X1,Y1,X2,Y2)
                    HDR( ,X3,Y3,X4,Y4)
                    HDR
                    OUT(T,X1,Y1,X2,Y2)
                    HDR( ,X3,Y3,X4,Y4)
                    PLO(X1,Y1)
                    PLO(X2,Y2)
                    PLO(X3,Y3)
                    PLO(X4,Y4)
                    END
  3.1415936536
```

Fig. 3.4 MIMIC program for the generation of geometric curves.

gives a line whose slope is determined by the ratio C_2/C_1, and whose starting location is determined by the initial values of X and Y. If C_1 is zero but C_2 is not, the line is vertical; if C_2 is zero but C_1 is not, the line is horizontal.

As another example, the following pair generates a circle:

$$\dot{X} = C_3 \sin \omega t \qquad \dot{Y} = C_3 \cos \omega t \tag{3.7}$$

where constants C_3 and ω determine the radius, and initial conditions determine the starting location. The starting time t_1 at which the relations begin to hold can be represented as below:

$$\begin{aligned} \dot{X} &= C_3 \sin \omega(t - t_1) \\ \dot{Y} &= C_3 \cos \omega(t - t_1) \end{aligned} \quad \text{for } t \geq t_1 \tag{3.8}$$

The above figures, which are generated by integration, may be rotated when the following pair of transformation equations is used:

$$\begin{aligned} \dot{X}_{\text{new}} &= \dot{X} \cos \phi - \dot{Y} \sin \phi \\ \dot{Y}_{\text{new}} &= \dot{X} \sin \phi + \dot{Y} \cos \phi \end{aligned} \tag{3.9}$$

where ϕ is the amount of the angle rotated about the starting location X_0 and Y_0. The figures can also be linearly transformed by the following pair of transformation equations:

$$\dot{X}_{\text{new}} = A\dot{X} \qquad \dot{Y}_{\text{new}} = B\dot{Y} \tag{3.10}$$

where A and B are constants. If A and B are equal, the figure is shrinking if A and B are positive but less than 1, or enlarging if A and B are positive but larger than 1. If A is not equal to B but they are positive, the figure stretches or compresses. If either A or B, or both, are negative, mirror images about the respective axes can be produced.

Interesting figures may also be generated by using the following pair of linear differential equations with constant coefficients:

$$\begin{aligned} \ddot{X} &= -2\zeta_x\omega_{nx}\dot{X} - \omega_{nx}^2 X + \omega_{nx}^2 F_1(t) \\ \ddot{Y} &= -2\zeta_y\omega_{ny}\dot{Y} - \omega_{ny}^2 Y + \omega_{ny}^2 F_2(t) \end{aligned} \tag{3.11}$$

where X and Y represent the abscissa and ordinate of the rectangular coordinates. ω_{nx}, ω_{ny}, ζ_x, and ζ_y are constants. ω_n's are sometimes called undamped natural frequencies, and ζ's are called damping coefficients. F's are forcing functions. If F's and ζ's are zero, then Eqs. (3.11) become

$$\ddot{X} = -\omega_{nx}^2 X \qquad \ddot{Y} = -\omega_{ny}^2 Y \tag{3.12}$$

Equations (3.12) give the known Lissajous figures when ω_{nx}/ω_{ny} or ω_{ny}/ω_{nx} is an integer. If only F's are zero, Eqs. (3.11) become

$$\begin{aligned} \ddot{X} &= -2\zeta_x\omega_{nx}\dot{X} - \omega_{nx}^2 X \\ \ddot{Y} &= -2\zeta_y\omega_{ny}\dot{Y} - \omega_{ny}^2 Y \end{aligned} \tag{3.13}$$

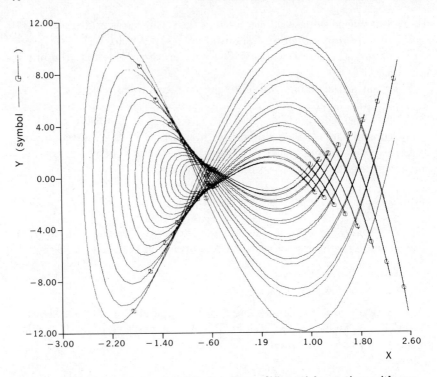

Fig. 3.5 Plot of a figure generated by two linear differential equations with constant coefficients.

Figure 3.5 shows a figure generated by Eqs. (3.13) with constants ζ_x, ω_{nx}, ζ_y, and ω_{ny} equal to -0.01, 1, -0.01, and 2.5, respectively. The initial conditions are 1 for both X_0 and Y_0 and are 0 for both $\dot{X}_0$ and $\dot{Y}_0$. (The plot routine generates six symbols such as circle, triangle, cross, star, etc., to identify up to six curves on a plot (as a example, see Fig. 3.3.) Though not needed, the small circles in Fig. 3.5 and other figures remain even when there is only one curve.)

3.2 GENERATION OF WAVEFORMS

MIMIC programming may also be used to generate waveforms. Here are shown the generations of modulated waveforms, pulse waveforms, and periodic waveforms.

3.2.1 MODULATED WAVEFORMS

The modulated wave in a communication or an instrumentation system consists of a *carrier* $F_c(t)$, or

$$F_c(t) = V \cos \omega_c t \tag{3.14}$$

where V is the carrier amplitude and ω_c the carrier frequency, and a signal or *modulating wave* $F_m(t)$. If the modulating wave modulates the amplitude of the carrier, it is called *amplitude modulation* (AM). The amplitude-modulated wave is described by the expression

$$F_{AM}(t) = V[1 + cF_m(t)] \cos \omega_c t \qquad (3.15)$$

where c is a constant. If modulating wave F_m is sinusoidal with a modulating frequency ω_m, we then have

$$F_{AM}(t) = V(1 + m_a \cos \omega_m t) \cos \omega_c t \qquad (3.16)$$

where m_a is the modulation factor. An amplitude-modulated wave represented by Eq. (3.16) is shown in Fig. 3.6, where the ratio of ω_c/ω_m is 20.

Equation (3.16) can be rewritten into the following form:

$$F_{AM}(t) = V \left\{ \cos \omega_c t + \frac{m}{2} \left[\cos (\omega_c + \omega_m)t + \cos (\omega_c - \omega_m)t \right] \right\} \qquad (3.17)$$

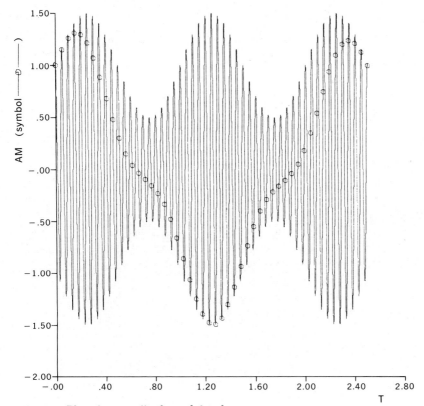

Fig. 3.6 Plot of an amplitude-modulated wave.

As shown, the modulation of a sinusoidal carrier with frequency ω_c by a sinusoidal signal with frequency ω_m gives rise to three frequencies. The two new frequencies $(\omega_c + \omega_m)$ and $(\omega_c - \omega_m)$ are called *sidebands* because they lie at the two sides of the carrier frequency on a spectrum diagram. The word *sideband* becomes more meaningful when the modulating wave is composed of a frequency band instead of a single frequency.

Because the carrier component of an amplitude-modulated wave contains 50 percent of power but no information, the carrier in an AM wave is filtered out before transmission. The resulting modulated wave, called *double sideband* (DSB), is

$$F_{\mathrm{DSB}}(t) = CF_m(t) \cos \omega_c t \tag{3.18}$$

where C is a constant. A DSB wave is shown in Fig. 3.7, which is the AM wave in Fig. 3.6 with the carrier component removed. Should one of the two frequencies (or frequency bands) be additionally filtered out before transmission, the resulting modulated wave is called *single sideband* (SSB).

Instead of the amplitude, the phase of a carrier can be modulated; this is called *phase modulation* (PM). The resulting modulated wave is

$$F_{\mathrm{PM}}(t) = V \cos [\omega_c t + CF_m(t)] \tag{3.19}$$

where C is a constant; in the case of a sinusoidal modulating wave, we have

$$F_{\mathrm{PM}}(t) = V \cos (\omega_c t + m_p \cos \omega_m t) \tag{3.20}$$

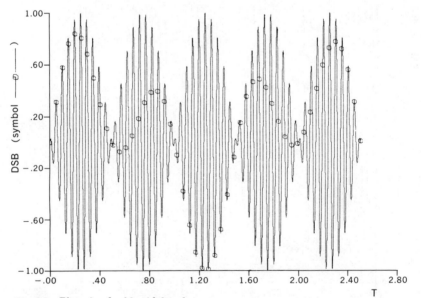

Fig. 3.7 Plot of a double-sideband wave.

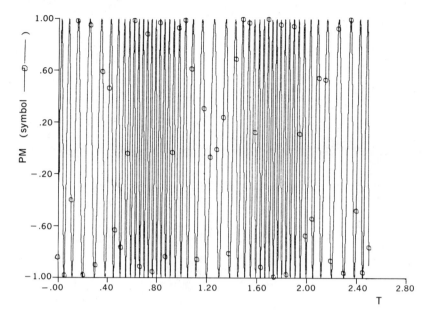

Fig. 3.8 Plot of a phase-modulated wave.

where m_p is the *modulation index*. A PM wave represented by Eq. (3.20) is shown in Fig. 3.8 with m_p equal to 10.

Since the time derivative of phase gives the frequency, modulating the carrier gives *frequency modulation* (FM), and the resulting modulated wave is

$$F_{\text{FM}}(t) = V \cos [\omega_c t + C \int F_m(t) \, dt] \tag{3.21}$$

where C is a constant; in the case of a sinusoidal modulating wave, we have

$$F_m(t) = V \cos (\omega_c t + m_f \sin \omega_m t) \tag{3.22}$$

where m_f is the *modulation index*. An FM wave represented by Eq. (3.22) is shown in Fig. 3.9 with m_f equal to 10.

The MIMIC program which produces the modulated waveforms in Figs. 3.6 through 3.9 is shown in Fig. 3.10. Because of very large values of the frequencies employed in communication systems, it is necessary to use time scaling to generate these waveforms.

3.2.2 PULSE WAVEFORMS

A single pulse can be generated by using two FSW statements as follows:

$$\begin{aligned} &\text{L} = \text{FSW}(\text{T}-1.,0.,1.,1.) \\ &\text{P} = \text{FSW}(\text{T}-3.,\text{L},0.,0.) \end{aligned} \tag{3.23}$$

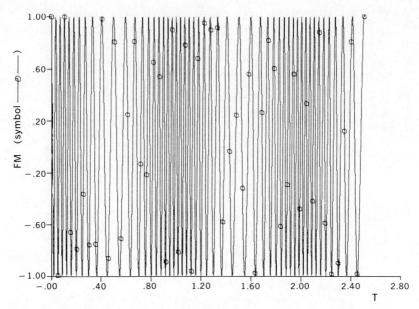

Fig. 3.9 Plot of a frequency-modulated wave.

```
*****GENERATION OF MODULATED SIGNALS
*
                    CON(2PI)
*
          DT        = .001
          WC        = 2PI*20.0
          WM        = 2PI*1.0
          M         = 10.
*
          AM        = (1.+0.50*SIN(WM*T))*COS(WC*T)
          DSB       = SIN(WM*T)*COS(WC*T)
          FM        = COS(WC*T+M*SIN(WM*T))
          PM        = COS(WC*T+M*COS(WM*T))
*
                    FIN(T,2.5)
                    HDR(T,FM,PM)
                    HDR(T,AM,DSB)
                    HDR
                    PLO(T,AM)
                    PLO(T,DSB)
                    PLO(T,FM)
                    PLO(T,PM)
                    END
6.28319
10.
```

Fig. 3.10 MIMIC program for the generation of modulated waves.

The first statement states that L is 0 until T is equal to or greater than 1, when L becomes 1. The second statement states that P is equal to L until T is equal to or greater than 3, when P becomes 0. Thus, the first statement generates the leading edge at T equal to 1, and the second statement the trailing edge at T equal to 3.

Numbers 0 and 1 are used here instead of alphameric constants FALSE and TRUE in the FSW statement. This is possible because FALSE in the MIMIC compiler is represented by a 36-bit binary number with all bits being 0, while TRUE is represented by any other binary number. This representation of TRUE and FALSE is desirable in this case, because output L of the first statement can then be used as the input of the second statement to obtain the desired pulse duration. To generate a train of pulses in this manner requires two FSW statements for each pulse, although each pulse duration can be different from the others. An example of a MIMIC program which generates a pulse train of four pulses is shown in Fig. 3.11. An IOR statement combines the pulses into a train. The plotted pulse train is shown in Fig. 3.12.

If the pulses in a train are very narrow, they can be used to produce sampled waveforms. Figure 3.13 shows a MIMIC program which causes generation of a train of six pulses, each of 0.1 duration. This train of

```
*****GENERATION OF A PULSE TRAIN
*
          DT      = 0.01
*
          L1      = FSW(T-  1.0,0.,1.,1.)
          P1      =FSW(T-  1.5,L1,0.,,0.)
*
          L2      = FSW(T-  4.0,0.,1.,1.)
          P2      = FSW(T-  4.5,L2,0.,,0.)
*
          L3      = FSW(T-  7.0,0.,1.,1.)
          P3      = FSW(T-  7.5,L3,0.,,0.)
*
          L4      = FSW(T-10.0,0.,1.,1.)
          P4      = FSW(T-10.5,L4,0.,,0.)
*
          PULSE   = IOR(P1,P2,P3,P4)
*
                    FIN(T,12.0)
                    HDR(T,PULSE)
                    HDR
                    OUT(T,PULSE)
                    PLO(T,PULSE)
                    END
```

Fig. 3.11 MIMIC program for the generation of a pulse train.

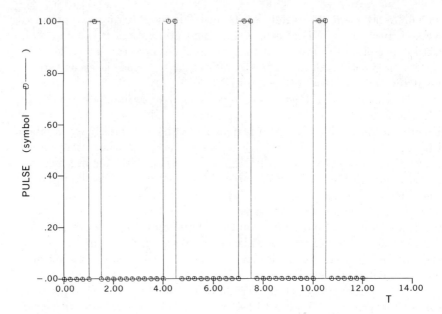

Fig. 3.12 Plot of a pulse train.

narrow pulses then samples an exponential waveform; the sampled waveform is shown in Fig. 3.14. Note that the pulses are combined into a train by five additions, while the sampling of the exponential function by the pulse train is obtained by a multiplication.

A train of pulses can also be used to produce pulse-modulated waveforms. As an example, let $F(t)$ be a sinusoidal function

$$F(t) = \sin\left(\frac{2\pi t}{P}\right) \tag{3.24}$$

where P is the period. A pulse train is required to modulate $F(t)$ to produce a pulsed sine wave (or tone-burst signal). Figure 3.15 shows a MIMIC program which causes generation of a train of pulsed sine waves. (LP in the program represents the period of the pulse train.) Variables P1, P2, and P3 in Fig. 3.15 represent the pulses which occur at T equal to 0, 3, and 6. These pulses are used as logical control variables to control the execution of three SIN statements; this gives a train of pulsed sine waves, as shown in Fig. 3.16.

Instead of being used as logical control variables, variables P1, P2, and P3 can be used to modulate sine waves by multiplication. Figure 3.17 shows a MIMIC program where P1, P2, and P3 are regarded as numbers and are multiplied by the respective SIN statements to give

```
*****SAMPLED OUTPUT OF AN EXPONENTIAL FUNCTION
*
            DT        = 0.01
*
            L1        = FSW(T- 1.0,0.,1.,1.)
            P1        = FSW(T- 1.1,L1,0.,,0.)
*
            L2        = FSW(T- 4.0,0.,1.,1.)
            P2        = FSW(T- 4.1,L2,0.,,0.)
*
            L3        = FSW(T- 7.0,0.,1.,1.)
            P3        = FSW(T- 7.1,L3,0.,,0.)
*
            L4        = FSW(T-10.0,0.,1.,1.)
            P4        = FSW(T-10.1,L4,0.,,0.)
*
            L5        = FSW(T-13.0,0.,'.,1.)
            P5        = FSW(T-13.1,L5,0.,,0.)
*
            P6        = FSW(T-16.1,L6,0.,,0.)
            L6        = FSW(T-16.0,0.,1.,1.)
*
            Y         = EXP(-T/8.0)*(P1+P2+P3+P4+P5+P6)
*
                      FIN(T,18.0)
                      HDR(T,Y)
                      HDR
                      OUT(T,Y)
                      PLO(T,Y)
                      END
```

Fig. 3.13 MIMIC program for the generation of the sampled waveform of an exponential function.

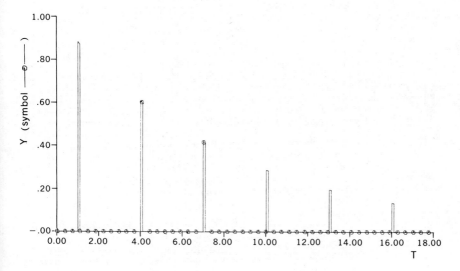

Fig. 3.14 Plot of a sampled wave of the exponential function.

```
*****GENERATION OF A PULSED SINE WAVE            VERSION A
*
                    CON(2PI)
*
          DT       = .002
          P        = .25
          LP       = 12.*P
*
PI        F        = SIN(2PI*T/P)
P2        F        = SIN(2PI*(T-LP)/P)
P3        F        = SIN(2PI*(T-2.*LP)/P)
*
          L1       = FSW(T,     0.,1.,1.)
          P1       = FSW(T-1.,L1,0.,0.)
*
          L2       = FSW(T-3.,0.,1.,1.)
          P2       = FSW(T-4.,L2,0.,0.)
*
          L3       = FSW(T-6.,0.,1.,1.)
          P3       = FSW(T-7.,L3,0.,0.),
*
                    FIN(T,6.0)
                    HDR(T,F)
                    HDR
                    OUT(T,F)
                    PLO(T,F)
                    END
```

Fig. 3.15 MIMIC program for the generation of a pulsed sine wave.

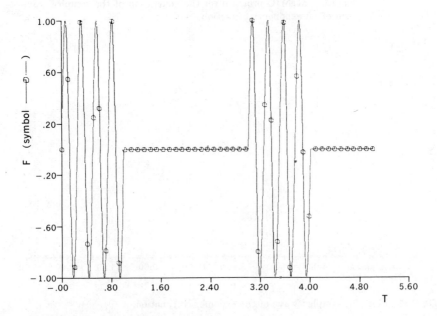

Fig. 3.16 Plot of a pulsed sine wave.

```
*****GENERATION OF A PULSED SINE WAVE          VERSION B
*
                   CON(2PI)
*
         DT    = .002
         P     = .25
         LP    = 12.*P
*
         F1    = SIN(2PI*T/P)*P1
         F2    = SIN(2PI*(T-LP)/P)*P2
         F3    = SIN(2PI*(T-2.*LP)/P)*P3
         F     = F1+F2+F3
*
         L1    = FSW(T,    0.,1.,1.)
         P1    = FSW(T-1.,L1,0.,0.)
*
         L2    = FSW(T-3.,0.,1.,1.)
         P2    = FSW(T-4.,L2,0.,0.)
*
         L3    = FSW(T-6.,0.,1.,1.)
         P3    = FSW(T-7.,L3,0.,0.)
*
                   FIN(T,5.0)
                   HDR(T,F)
                   HDR
                   PLO(T,F)
                   END
  6.28319
```

Fig. 3.17 Another MIMIC program for the generation of a pulsed sine wave.

respective modulated sine waves.   These sine waves are then combined by addition to give a train of pulsed sine waves.

3.2.3 PERIODIC WAVEFORMS

Periodic waveforms may be generated by generating individual waveforms in each period and then combining these waveforms into a periodic one.   Three periodic waveforms are shown in Figs. 3.18 through 3.20. Consider the generation of the periodic sawtooth wave in Fig. 3.18.   The sawtooth waveforms during the first four periods are described by the following relations:

$$
\begin{aligned}
Y &= T & &\text{for B1 being true} \\
Y &= T-1. & &\text{for B2 being true} \\
Y &= T-2. & &\text{for B3 being true} \\
Y &= T-3. & &\text{for B4 being true}
\end{aligned}
\qquad (3.25)
$$

where B1 is true if $0 \leq t < 1$
    B2 is true if $1 \leq t < 2$
    B3 is true if $2 \leq t < 3$
    B4 is true if $3 \leq t < 4$

It is apparent that B's can represent the pulses of a pulse train.

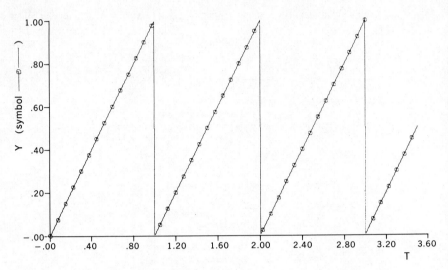

Fig. 3.18 Plot of a periodic sawtooth waveform.

A MIMIC program which generates the periodic sawtooth waveform in Fig. 3.18 is shown in Fig. 3.21. The B's are generated as though they were pulses; thus, FSW statements are used in a manner similar to those in Figs. 3.11, 3.13, 3.15, and 3.17. These pulses have a period of 1 and occur at T equal to 0, 1, 2, or 3. These B's are then used as logical control variables to sequence the execution of the individual waveforms.

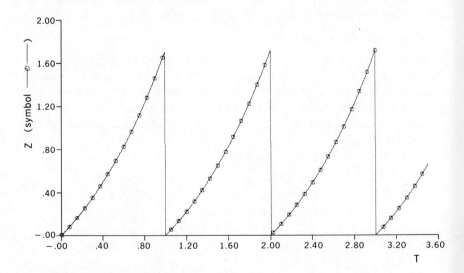

Fig. 3.19 Plot of a periodic exponential waveform.

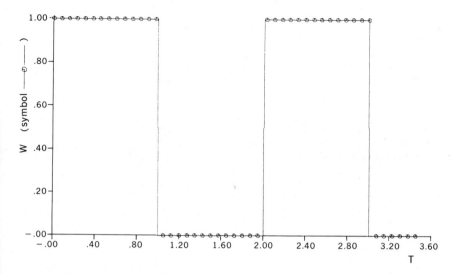

Fig. 3.20 Plot of a periodic square waveform.

The program in Fig. 3.21 also generates a periodic exponential waveform and a periodic square waveform; these waveforms are shown in Figs. 3.19 and 3.20, respectively.

Logical control variables B1, B2, B3, and B4 can alternatively be obtained by using FSW, AND, and NOT statements. A MIMIC program which makes use of these statements to generate a sawtooth waveform such as the one in Fig. 3.18 is shown in Fig. 3.22. In Fig. 3.22, A1, A2, A3, and A4 represent four pulses with four different durations; their leading edges all occur at T equal to 0, while the trailing edges occur at T equal to 1, 2, 3, and 4, respectively. The AND statements change the occurrences of the leading edges to their respective desired times.

Another alternative way to generate a periodic waveform is to use TDL statements, which are time-delay elements. Let the waveform in the first period be

$$Y1 = T \tag{3.26}$$

When Y1 passes through a delay element with a delay equal to 1, we have output Y2:

$$Y2 = TDL(Y1, 1.) \tag{3.27}$$

Y2 is the waveform in the second period. The waveforms in other periods

```
*****GENERATION OF PERIODIC WAVEFORMS
             DT      = 0.005
             X       = T
*
*****EQUATIONS TO GENERATE A SAWTOOTH WAVEFORM
*
  B1        Y       = X
  B2        Y       = X-1.
  B3        Y       = X-2.
  B4        Y       = X-3.
*
*****EQUATIONS TO GENERATE AN EXPONENTIAL WAVEFORM
*
  B1        Z       = EXP(X)    -1.
  B2        Z       = EXP(X-1.)-1.
  B3        Z       = EXP(X-2.)-1.
  B4        Z       = EXP(X-3.)-1.
*
*****EQUATIONS TO GENERATE A SQUARE WAVEFORM
*
  B1        W       = 1.0
  B2        W       = 0.0
  B3        W       = 1.0
  B4        W       = 0.0
*
*GENERATION OF LCV FOR THE 1ST PERIOD
             A1      = FSW(X,    0.,1.,1.)
             B1      = FSW(X-1.,A1,0.,0.)
*
*GENERATION OF LCV FOR THE 2ND PERIOD
             A2      = FSW(X-1.,0.,1.,1.)
             B2      = FSW(X-2.,A2,0.,0.)
*
*GENERATION OF LCV FOR THE 3RD PERIOD
             A3      = FSW(X-2.,0.,1.,1.)
             B3      = FSW(X-3.,A3,0.,0.)
*
*GENERATION OF LCV FOR THE 4TH PERIOD
             A4      = FSW(X-3.,0.,1.,1.)
             B4      = FSW(X-4.,A4,0.,0.)
*
*TERMINATION AND OUTPUTS
             FIN(T,3.5)
             HDR(T,Y,Z,W)
             HDR
             OUT(T,Y,Z,W)
             PLO(T,Y)
             PLO(T,Z)
             PLO(T,W)
             END
```

Fig. 3.21 MIMIC program for the generation of periodic waveforms.

are similarly generated,

$$Y3 = TDL(Y2, 1.)$$
$$Y4 = TDL(Y3, 1.)$$

(3.28)

and the following ADDITION statement combines these waveforms to give the periodic wave:

$$Y = Y1 + Y2 + Y3 + Y4$$

(3.29)

A MIMIC program which generates a sawtooth waveform by using TDL statements is shown in Fig. 3.23, where logical control variable L controls the trailing edge of the sawtooth. This logical control variable can be avoided if the following FSW statement is employed:

$$Y1 = FSW(T-1.,T,0.,0.)$$

(3.30)

Note that T in the above FSW statement forms the sawtooth with its trailing edge controlled by the 0s in the above FSW statement.

If a periodic sawtooth wave such as that in Fig. 3.18 but having the sawteeth in the odd periods only is to be generated, it can be obtained by merely using a proper amount of delay. If, for example, the even

```
*****GENFRATION OF A SAWTOOTH WAVEFORM     VERSION B
*
            DT      = 0.01
            X       = T
*
   R1       Y       = X
   R2       Y       = X-1.
   R3       Y       = X-2.
   R4       Y       = X-3.
*
            A1      = FSW(X-1.,1.,0.,0.)
            A2      = FSW(X-2.,1.,0.,0.)
            A3      = FSW(X-3.,1.,0.,0.)
            A4      = FSW(X-4.,1.,0.,0.)
*
            R1      = A1
            R2      = AND(A2,NOT(A1))
            R3      = AND(A3,NOT(A2))
            R4      = AND(A4,NOT(A3))
*
            FIN(T,4.)
            HDR(T,Y)
            HDR
            OUT(T,Y)
            PLO(T,Y)
            END
```

Fig. 3.22 MIMIC program for the generation of a sawtooth waveform.

periods of Fig. 3.18 should be zero, the following statements generate a periodic wave with four sawteeth in the odd periods:

$$
\begin{aligned}
Y1 &= FSW(T-1.,T,0.,0.) \\
Y2 &= TDL(Y1,2.) \\
Y3 &= TDL(Y2,2.) \\
Y4 &= TDL(Y3,2.) \\
Y &= Y1 + Y2 + Y3 + Y4
\end{aligned}
\tag{3.31}
$$

Notice that the above TDL statements have a delay of 2 instead of 1.

The use of TDL statements gives two restrictions. First, each TDL statement requires at least 100 memory locations; thus its use limits the maximum size of a MIMIC program. Second, the selection of DT has to observe the following condition:

$$
\text{Delay} \geq N \cdot DT
\tag{3.32}
$$

where N denotes the number of memory locations for the TDL statement which can be specified if more than 100 are required. For a chosen delay of a TDL statement, there is a minimum DT. This minimum DT may be too large for the desired plot, but this situation can sometimes be remedied by using a larger N if sufficient memory locations are available.

Another alternative way to generate a periodic waveform is to make use of electronic circuit techniques. Consider the case of generating a periodic triangular wave. A SIN statement is used to generate a sinusoidal wave. An FSW statement is next used to convert the sinusoidal wave into a periodic rectangular wave. An INT statement is finally used to integrate the square wave into a periodic triangular wave. Such a MIMIC program is shown in Fig. 3.24, where Z represents the sinusoidal wave and Y, the generated triangular wave. The generated rec-

```
*****GENERATION OF A PERIODIC SAWTOOTH WAVE USING TDL STATEMENTS
*
          L        = FSW(T-1.,1.,0.,0.)
*
   L      Y1       = T
          Y2       = TDL(Y1,1.)
          Y3       = TDL(Y2,1.)
          Y4       = TDL(Y3,1.)
          Y        = Y1+Y2+Y3+Y4
*
                   FIN(T,4.)
                   HDR(T,Y)
                   OUT(T,Y)
                   PLO(T,Y)
                   END
```

Fig. 3.23 MIMIC program for the generation of a periodic sawtooth wave by TDL statements.

```
*****GENERATION OF PERIODIC WAVEFORMS BY CIRCUIT TECHNIQUE
*
                    CON(2PI)
         P        = 1.0
         DT       = 0.01
*
         Z        = SIN(2PI*T/P)
*
         X        = FSW(Z,-1.,0.,+1.)
         Y        = INT(X,0.)
*
         A        = Z-0.3
         B        = FSW(A,-1.,0.,+1.)
*
                    FIN(T,2.)
                    HDR(T,Z,X,Y,A,B)
                    OUT(T,Z,X,Y,A,B)
                    PLO(T,Z)
                    PLO(T,X,Y)
                    PLO(T,A,B)
                    END
 6.28318531
```

Fig. 3.24 MIMIC program for the generation of a periodic waveform by circuit technique.

tangular and triangular waves are shown in Fig. 3.25. Also specified in the program of Fig. 3.24 is the generation of a nonsymmetric square wave, which is represented by B in the program. Notice that the nonsymmetry is obtained by biasing the sine wave to a proper amount.

Finally, a concise way which requires only one FSW statement per period to generate a periodic sawtooth wave is shown in the MIMIC program in Fig. 3.26, where there are four sawteeth during the 4-sec time interval. The FSW statement in Fig. 3.26,

$$P3 = FSW(T-4.,T-3.,0.,0.)$$

generates the fourth sawtooth which occurs during the time interval from T equal to 3 to T equal to 4. The FSW statement

$$P2 = FSW(T-3.,T-2.,P3,P3)$$

generates the third and the fourth sawteeth occurring during the time interval from T equal to 2 to T equal to 4. The FSW statement

$$P1 = FSW(T-2.,T-1.,P2,P2)$$

generates the second, third, and fourth sawteeth occurring during the time interval from T equal to 1 to T equal to 4. And finally, the FSW statement

$$P0 = FSW(T-1.,T,P1,P1)$$

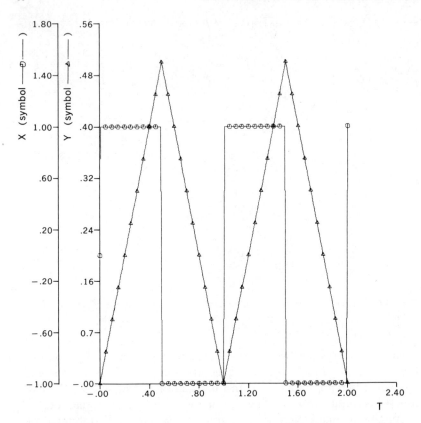

Fig. 3.25 Plot of periodic waveforms generated by the MIMIC program in Fig. 3.24.

generates the four sawteeth occurring during the time interval from T equal to 0 to T equal to 4. In this program, each FSW statement not only generates a sawtooth but also sequences it consecutively into the desired periodic sawtooth waveform.

3.3 ENGINEERING ANALYSIS AND DESIGN

3.3.1 PILOT–EJECTION SYSTEM

A system is devised to eject a pilot from a fighter aircraft. When being ejected, the pilot and his seat, as shown in Fig. 3.27, are caused to travel along the rails and exit at a velocity V_e from the rail and at an angle θ_e backward from the vertical.

It is necessary to determine the trajectory of the ejected pilot in order to ascertain whether he would strike the vertical stabilizer of the

```
$EXECUTE          IBJOB
$ID    CHU   *305/65/020*3M*
$IBJOB            FIOCS
$IBLDR MIMIC  LIBE
$DATA
*****GENERATION OF A PERIODIC SAWTOOTH WAVEFORM
*****      USING ONE FSW STATEMENT PER PERIOD
*
        DT       = .02
*
        P3       = FSW(T-4.,T-3.,0.,0.)
        P2       = FSW(T-3.,T-2.,P3,P3)
        P1       = FSW(T-2.,T-1.,P2,P2)
        P0       = FSW(T-1.,T,P1,P1)
                   FIN(T,4.5)
                   HDR(T,P0,P1,P2,P3)
                   OUT(T,P0,P1,P2,P3)
                   PLO(T,P0,P1,P2,P3)
                   END
'
$EXECUTE          IBJOB
$ID    CHU   *305/65/020*3M
$IBJOB            GO,NOSOURCE,FIOCS
$IBLDR MMPLOT LIBE
```

Fig. 3.26 MIMIC program for the generation of a periodic sawtooth wave by one FSW statement per period.

aircraft.   The trajectory is to be determined under various combinations
of aircraft speed and altitude, as the drag on the pilot, which causes his
relative motion with respect to the aircraft, is a function of air density
and velocity.

Let X and Y be the rectangular coordinates, fixed with respect to
the airframe.   The pilot-and-seat combination becomes disengaged from
the rails when the combination travels a distance Y_1 along the Y direction.

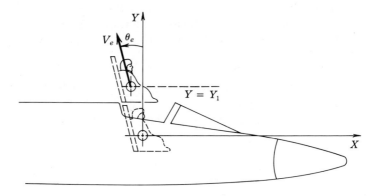

Fig. 3.27 Geometry of pilot ejection from the aircraft.

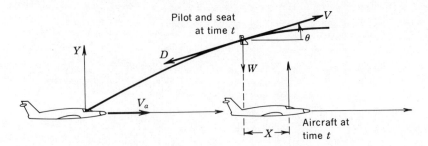

Fig. 3.28   Motion of the pilot and aircraft after the ejection.

Before disengaging, the combination receives no acceleration with respect to the airframe.   After disengaging, the combination as shown in Fig. 3.28 experiences a drag along the velocity direction and the gravity; it thus follows a ballistic trajectory.   Assume that the aircraft is flying level at a constant speed.   The acceleration and angular rate of the combination before and after the disengaging are

$$\dot{V} = \begin{cases} 0 & 0 \leq Y < Y_1 \\ -\dfrac{D}{m} - g \sin \theta & Y \geq Y_1 \end{cases} \tag{3.33}$$

$$\dot{\theta} = \begin{cases} 0 & 0 \leq Y < Y_1 \\ \dfrac{-(g \cos \theta)}{V} & Y \geq Y_1 \end{cases} \tag{3.34}$$

where

$$D = \tfrac{1}{2}\rho C_d S V^2 \tag{3.35}$$

D is the aerodynamic drag on the combination. V and m are the velocity and mass of the combination, respectively, g is the gravity constant, and θ is the angle which the velocity V makes with the X axis.   The trajectory of the relative motion of the combination with respect to the aircraft can be described by the following two differential equations:

$$\dot{X} = V \cos \theta - V_a \qquad \dot{Y} = V \sin \theta \tag{3.36}$$

where V_a is the velocity of the aircraft.   In solving the above set of equations, the initial values of V and θ are determined from the initial-velocity vector at the moment when the combination leaves the rails. These values are given by

$$V(0) = \sqrt{(V_a - V_e \sin \theta_e)^2 + (V_e \cos \theta_e)^2}$$
$$\theta(0) = \tan^{-1} \frac{V_e \cos \theta_e}{V_a - V_e \sin \theta_e} \tag{3.37}$$
$$X(0) = Y(0) = 0$$

where V_e is exit velocity and θ_e the exit angle of the pilot-and-seat combination. The conditions for determining whether an ejection is successful or not are:

1. When the pilot is beyond the vertical stabilizer or -60 ft along the X axis
2. When the pilot is well above the rail or 30 ft along the Y axis
3. When the pilot-and-seat combination has disengaged the rails for 4 sec

A MIMIC program for computing the ejection trajectories is shown in Fig. 3.29. Equivalent symbols and computation data are shown in Table 3.1. Four cases are to be computed: aircraft velocity at 500 or 900 fps and each at sea level or at 60,000 ft. In the program, initial values need to be computed only once when T is zero; this is controlled by logical control variable TEQ0 (time equal to 0). The conditions that Y is less than Y_1 and that Y is equal to or greater than Y_1 are expressed by logical control variables YLTY1 and YGEY1. The computed initial value $V(0)$ is 491.17 fps. The results for the case of V_a equal to 500 fps and ρ equal to 0.0002238 slug-ft³ (at 60,000 ft) are shown in the plots in Figs. 3.30 through 3.32. Figure 3.30 shows the trajectory of the pilot-and-seat combination with respect to the aircraft. Figure 3.31 shows the

Table 3.1   Equivalent symbols and computation data for pilot ejection system

Program symbol	Equation symbol	Value
X, 1DX	$X, \dot{X}$	
Y, 1DY	$Y, \dot{Y}$	
V, 1DV	$V, \dot{V}$	
TH, 1DTH	$\theta, \dot{\theta}$	
THE	θ_e	15/57.3 rad
THED	θ_{ed}	15°
VO	$V(0)$	To be computed
THO	$\theta(0)$	To be computed
	$X(0)$	0
	$Y(0)$	0
VE	V_e	40 fps
VA	V_a	900 or 500 fps
RHO	ρ	0.0023769 or 0.0002238 slug-ft³
Y1	Y_1	4 ft
M	m	7 slugs
G	g	32.2 ft/sec²
CD	C_d	1
S	S	10 ft²

```
*****PILOT EJECTION SYSTEM
                   PAR(VA, RHO)
            DT      = 0.02
            M       = 7.
            G       = 32.2
            CD      = 1.
            S       = 10.
            Y1      = 4.
            VE      = 40.
            THED    = 15.
PRECOMPUTE CONSTANTS
            TEQO        FSW(T, FALSE, TRUE, FALSE)
    TEQO    THE         THED/57.3
    TEQO    VX          VA-VE*SIN(THE)
    TEQO    VY          VE*COS(THE)
    TEQO    VO          SQR(VX*VX+VY*VY)
    TEQO    THO         ATN(VY, VX)
    TEQO    PD          .5*RHO*CD*S
SOLVE EQUATIONS
            X           INT(V*COS(TH) - VA, 0.)
            Y           INT(V*SIN(TH), 0.)
            YLTY1       FSW(Y-Y1, TRUE, FALSE, FALSE)
            YGEY1       NOT(YLTY1)
    YLTY1   1DV         EQL(0.)
    YGEY1   1DV         -D/M - G*SIN(TH)
    YGEY1   D           PD*V*V
            V           INT(1DV, VO)
    YLTY1   1DTH        EQL(0.)
    YGEY1   1DTH        -G*COS(TH)/V
            TH          INT(1DTH, THO)
            THD     = TH*57.296
            THOD    = THO*57.296
*THD IS IN DEGREES
*COORDINATE CONVERSION
            XA      = X+VA*T
            YA      = Y
FINISH STATEMENTS
                        FIN(-60., X)
                        FIN(Y, 30.)
                        FIN(T, 4.)
HEADER
    TEQO                HDR(VO,THOD)
                        HDR(T,X,Y,THD,V)
                        HDR
OUTPUT
    TEQO                OUT(VO,THOD)
                        OUT(T,X,Y,THD,V)
                        PLO(X,Y)
                        PLO(XA,YA)
                        PLO(X,THD)
                        END
    500.        .0023769
    500.        .0002238
    900.        .0023769
    900.        .0002238
```

Fig. 3.29 MIMIC program for the pilot-ejection system.

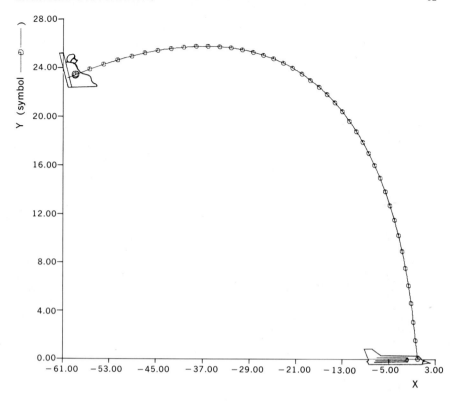

Fig. 3.30 Plot of the ejection path of the pilot-and-seat combination with respect to the aircraft.

trajectory of the combination with respect to the earth.   Figure 3.32 shows that the angle θ, initially at about 4.51°, tilts downward to about $-1.72°$.   The computation was actually terminated when X first reached -60 ft.

3.3.2 AIRCRAFT-ARRESTING GEAR SYSTEM†

A system is designed to halt a moving aircraft quickly during landing in order to avoid possible overrun at the end of a runway.   To halt such a moving aircraft, a system consisting of hydraulic shock absorbers, springs, pulleys, and cables is formed, as shown in Fig. 3.33.   It is necessary to determine the aircraft weights and speeds that could be accommodated by the system without exceeding the limits of the cables and the absorbers.

† Taken from ref. 8, which is based on an analog simulation performed at the Electronic Associates, Inc., Princeton Computating Center for the All-American Engineering Company, Wilmington, Delaware.

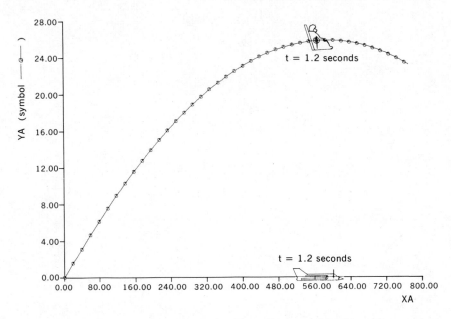

Fig. 3.31 Plot of the ejection path of the pilot-and-seat combination with respect to the earth.

The aircraft during landing is pulled by the forces $2f_{k1}$ produced by a pair of springs, each with a constant k_1. Thus, the equation of motion of the aircraft is

$$m_1 \ddot{x} = -2f_{k1} \sin \theta \qquad (3.38)$$

where θ is the angle shown in Fig. 3.33, and x and m_1 are the displacement and mass of the aircraft, respectively. Sin θ can be determined from the geometry in Fig. 3.33 as follows:

$$\sin \theta = \frac{x}{h + y_1} = \frac{x}{\sqrt{x^2 + h^2}} \qquad (3.39)$$

where

$$y_1 = \sqrt{x^2 + h^2} - h \qquad (3.40)$$

The moving carriage is pulled by force $2f_{k1}$ due to the spring with spring constant k_1 at one side and by force f_{k2} due to the spring with spring constant k_2 at the other side. Thus, the equation of motion of the moving carriage is

$$m_2 \ddot{y}_2 = 2f_{k1} - f_{k2} \qquad (3.41)$$

where y_2 and m_2 are the displacement and mass of the moving carriage.

The shock absorber (or so-called "water squeezer"), which converts the kinetic energy into heat, consists essentially of a piston and a cylinder. The piston is pulled by spring force f_{k2} on the one side and on the other side by damping force f_d. The damping force is due to the motion of the liquid forced to move from one chamber of the cylinder to the other as the cylinder is separated into two chambers by the moving piston. Thus, we have

$$m_3 \ddot{y}_3 = f_{k2} - f_d \qquad\qquad (3.42)$$

where m_3 and y_3 are the mass and the travel of the piston. The damping force f_d is proportional to the square of displacement y_3, or

$$f_d = f(y_3)(\dot{y}_3)^2 \qquad\qquad (3.43)$$

where function $f(y_3)$ represents the drag coefficient of the piston. This nonlinear coefficient is shown in Table 3.2.

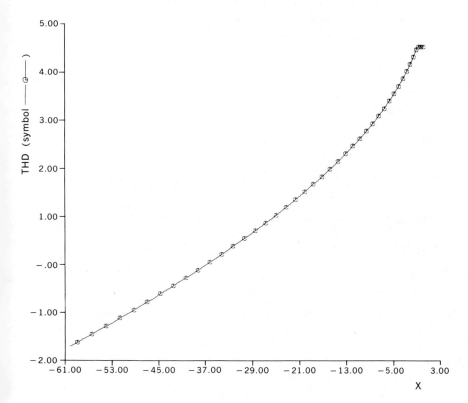

Fig. 3.32 Plot of angle of rotation (in degrees) of the pilot after the ejection.

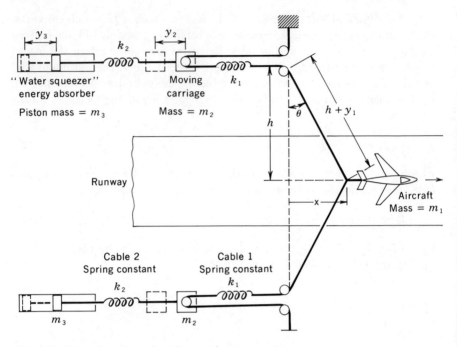

Fig. 3.33 Geometry of an aircraft-arresting-gear system.

The above spring force f_{k1} is proportional to the relative displacement $(y_1 - 2y_2)$, and it exists only if y_1 is equal to or larger than $2y_2$. Thus, we have

$$f_{k1} = \begin{cases} k_1(y_1 - 2y_2) & \text{for } y_1 \geq 2y_2 \\ 0 & \text{for } y_1 < 2y_2 \end{cases} \tag{3.44}$$

Similarly, the spring force f_{k2} is proportional to the relative displacement $(y_2 - y_3)$, and it exists only if y_1 is equal to or larger than y_3. We have

$$f_{k2} = \begin{cases} k_2(y_2 - y_3) & \text{for } y_2 \geq y_3 \\ 0 & \text{for } y_2 < y_3 \end{cases} \tag{3.45}$$

A MIMIC program for the arresting-gear system is shown in Fig. 3.34. Equivalent symbols and the data for computation are shown in Table 3.3. This program requires the specification of a DTMIN to overcome discontinuous functions. The computation is to be terminated when T reaches 10 sec, or if y_2 goes negative by 1 ft, or when x reaches 1,000 ft. Note that y_2 becoming negative indicates a physically unreal situation.

Table 3.2   Drag coefficient $f(y_3)$

y_3	f
0	8.33
30	4.0
60	1.6
120	5.2
150	5.2
180	6.6
210	8.3
240	10.7
270	16.0
282	21.0
294	28.0
306	41.0
312	50.0
324	90.0

The results of the computation are shown in the plots of Figs. 3.35 through 3.37.   Figure 3.35 shows the plot of $f(y_3)$, which indicates that argument y_3 has been as large as about 375 ft.   Figure 3.36 shows that the speed (1DX) of the aircraft is slowed down rapidly to about 20 mph in 6 sec, and the aircraft almost stops after a travel of about 870 ft.   The

Table 3.3   Equivalent symbols and computation data for arresting-gear system

Program symbol	Equation symbol	Value
X, 1DX, 2DX	$x,\ \dot{x},\ \ddot{x}$	
Y2, 1DY2, 2DY2	$y_2,\ \dot{y}_2,\ \ddot{y}_2$	
Y3, 1DY3, 2DY3	$y_3,\ \dot{y}_3,\ \ddot{y}_3$	
FY3, Y1	$f,\ y_1$	
FK1, FK2, FD	$f_{k1},\ f_{k2},\ f_d$	
M1	m_1	1,400 slugs
M2	m_2	45.28 slugs
M3	m_3	20 slugs
K1	k_1	4,550 lb/ft
K2	k_2	25,300 lb/ft
H	h	125 ft
	$x(0)$	0
1DXO	$\dot{x}(0)$	200 fps
	$y_2(0)$	0
	$\dot{y}_2(0)$	0
	$y_3(0)$	0
	$\dot{y}_3(0)$	0

```
*****AIRCRAFT ARRESTING GEAR SYSTEM
CONSTANT FUNCTION
         FY3     = CFN(14.)
PARAMETERS
                   PAR(1DX0)
CONTROL CONSTANTS
         DT      = 0.05
         DTMIN   = .0001
CONSTANTS
         M1      = 1400.
         M2      = 45.28
         M3      = 20.
         K1      = 4550.
         K2      = 25300.
         H       = 125.
SOLVE EQUATIONS
         2DY3    = (FK2-FD)/M3
         1DY3    = INT(2DY3,0.)
         Y3      = INT(1DY3,0.)
         FD1     = FUN(FY3,Y3)
         FD      = FD1*1DY3*1DY3
         2DY2    = (2.*FK1-FK2)/M2
         1DY2    = INT(2DY2,0.)
         Y2      = INT(1DY2,0.)
         2DX     = (-2.*FK1*SINTHE)/M1
         1DX     = INT(2DX,1DX0)
         X       = INT(1DX,0.)
         Y1      = SQR(X*X+H*H)-H
         SINTHE  = X/(H+Y1)
         Y12Y2   = Y1-2.*Y2
         Y2Y3    = Y2-Y3
         Y2GEY3  = FSW(Y2Y3,FALSE,TRUE,TRUE)
         Y2LTY3  = NOT(Y2GEY3)
Y2GEY3   FK2     = Y2Y3*K2
Y2LTY3   FK2     = 0.
         Y1GEY2  = FSW(Y12Y2,FALSE,TRUE,TRUE)
         Y1LTY2  = NOT(Y1GEY2)
Y1GEY2   FK1     = K1*Y12Y2
Y1LTY2   FK1     = 0.
FINISH STATEMENTS
                   FIN(T,10.)
                   FIN(-Y2,1.)
                   FIN(X,1000.)
HEADERS
                   HDR(TIME,ACCY3,VELY3,Y3,FY3,FD)
                   HDR( ,ACCY2,VELY2,Y2,Y2Y3,FK2)
                   HDR( ,ACCX,VELX,X,Y12Y2,FK1)
                   HDR( , Y1, SIN)
                   HDR
OUTPUT
                   OUT(T,2DY3,1DY3,Y3,FY3,FD)
                   OUT( ,2DY2,1DY2,Y2,Y2Y3,FK2)
                   OUT( ,2DX, 1DX, X,Y12Y2,FK1)
                   OUT( , Y1,SINTHE)
                   PLO(T,X,Y2,Y2Y3,1DX)
                   PLO(T,Y1,Y12Y2,Y3)
                   PLO(Y3,FD1)

                   END
0.          8.33
30.         4.0
60.         1.6
120.        5.2
150.        5.2
180.        6.6
210.        8.3
240.        10.7
270.        16.0
282.        21.0
294.        28.0
306.        41.0
312.        50.0
324.        90.0
290.
200.
```

Fig. 3.34   MIMIC program for the aircraft-arresting-gear system.

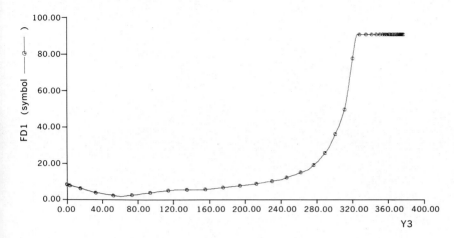

Fig. 3.35   Plot of function $f(y_3)$.

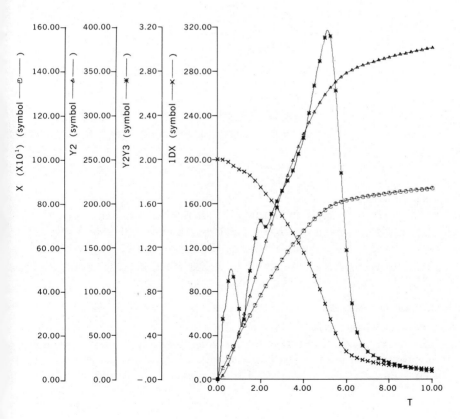

Fig. 3.36   Plot of x, y_2, $y_2 - y_3$, and $\dot{x}$ versus t.

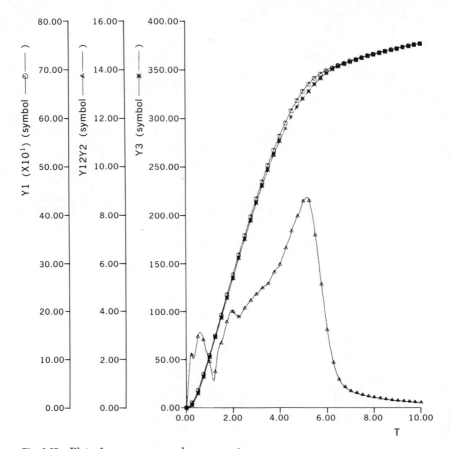

Fig. 3.37 Plot of y_1, $y_1 - y_2$, and y_3 versus t.

moving carriage travels about 400 ft.   There are some oscillations in the
relative displacement between y_2 and y_3.   Figure 3.37 shows displacement y_1, relative displacement between y_1 and y_2, and displacement y_3.
There are some oscillations again in the relative displacement, and y_1 follows y_3 closely but travels twice as much as y_3.

3.3.3 DOPPLER FREQUENCY FROM A SATELLITE

A radio receiver for tracking a satellite has a very narrow bandwidth in
order to extract the minute satellite beacon signal from its associated noise
background.   Since the satellite is moving, the received signal frequency
is constantly changing because of the doppler effect.   In order to maintain the signal in the receiver bandwidth, it is necessary to shift the local
oscillator frequency by an amount equal to the doppler frequency shift.

The doppler shift and its rate determine the characteristics of the local oscillator and must be known in order to design the receiver properly. Equations are now derived for computing the doppler frequency shift and the doppler rate.

We consider here the case where the satellite is in a circular orbit and passes directly over the tracking station. Figure 3.38 shows the geometry between the tracking station and the satellite. The earth's gravity g is

$$g = \frac{g_0 R^2}{R + H} \tag{3.46}$$

where g_0 = gravitational pull at earth's surface,
  R = earth radius,
  H = height of orbit.

This gravitational force g is equal to the centrifugal force of the orbiting satellite,

$$\frac{V_t^2}{R + H} = g \tag{3.47}$$

or

$$V_t = \sqrt{g(R + H)} \tag{3.48}$$

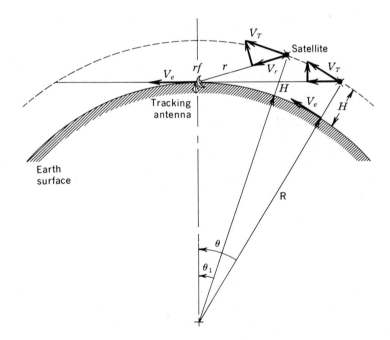

Fig. 3.38 Geometry of tracking a satellite.

where V_t is the tangential velocity of the satellite. The initial contact angle θ_i, as shown in Fig. 3.38, is the angle at the earth's center formed by the earth's radius which passes through the tracking station and the earth's radius which passes the intersection of the horizon and the orbit. By geometry, this angle can be computed by

$$\theta_i = \arctan \frac{\sqrt{H^2 + 2RH}}{R} \tag{3.49}$$

And the angle θ, which indicates the whereabouts of the satellite, is obtained by

$$\theta = \theta_i - \omega t \tag{3.50}$$

where t is time and ω the earth's rotation rate, which can be computed by

$$\omega = \dot{\theta} = \frac{V_t}{R + H} - V_e \cos \alpha \tag{3.51}$$

Angle α is the orbit inclination with respect to the equator, and V_e the earth's rotation rate. From the geometry in Fig. 3.38, we have slant range r,

$$r = \sqrt{4R(R + H) \sin^2 \left(\frac{\theta}{2}\right) + H^2} \tag{3.52}$$

which is obtained by applying the law of cosine. If the above equation is differentiated, we obtain the rate of change of the slant range r,

$$V_r = \dot{r} = -V_t R \sin \frac{\theta}{r} \tag{3.53}$$

If the above V_r is differentiated, we obtain the rate of change of velocity V_r along slant range A_r, or

$$A_r = \frac{dV_r}{dt} = \ddot{r} = -\frac{V_t^2 R \cos \theta}{(R + H)r} + \frac{V_t^2 R^2 \sin^2 \theta}{r^3} \tag{3.54}$$

Finally, doppler frequency shift f_d and doppler rate f_r are computed as below:

$$f_d = f_t \frac{V_r}{c} \tag{3.55}$$

and

$$f_r = f_t \frac{A_r}{c} \tag{3.56}$$

where f_t is the transmitter frequency and c the velocity of light.

A MIMIC program to compute the doppler shift and the doppler rate and other quantities is shown in Fig. 3.39. Equivalent symbols and the data for computation are shown in Table 3.4. Note that this pro-

```
***.**COMPUTATION OF DOPPLER FREQUENCY FROM A SATELLITE
                      CON(R,C,GO,VE)
                      PAR(H,FT)
*
        DT       = 10.
        ALPHA    = 0.49
*
*PRECOMPUTED CONSTANTS
        TEQO     = FSW(T,FALSE,TRUE,FALSE)
TEQO    C        = GO*R*R/((R+H)*(R+H))
TEQO    THI      = ATN(SQR(H*H+2.*R*H),R)
TEQO    VT       = SQR(G*(R+H))
TEQO    W        = VT/(R+H)-VE*COS(ALPHA)
*
*EQUATIONS
        TH       = THI-W*T
        SR       = SQR(4.*R*(R+H)*SIN(.5*TH)*SIN(.5*TH)+H*H)
        VR       = -VT*R*SIN(TH)/SR
        AR       = (VT*VT*R/SR)*(R*SIN(TH)*SIN(TH)/(SR*SR)-COS(TH)/(R+H))
*
        FD       = VR*FT/C
        FR       = AR*FT/C
*
                  FIN(-THI,TH)
                  FIN(T,500.)
                  HDR(T,FD,FR,SR,VR,AR)
                  OUT(T,FD,FR,SR,VR,AR)
                  PLO(T,FD,FR)
                  PLO(T,SR,VR,AR)
                  END
3963.34    186000.        .0060983      .0000727
150.       +1.70000E+09
```

Fig. 3.39 MIMIC program for the computation of the doppler frequency from a satellite.

Table 3.4   Equivalent symbols and computation data for doppler frequency calculation

Program symbol	Equation symbol	Value
R	R	3,963.34 miles
H	H	150 miles
FT	f_t	1,700 Mc
C	c	186,000 miles/sec
GO	g_0	0.0060983 miles/sec^2
VE	V_e	7.27×10^{-5} rad/sec
ALPHA	α	0.49 rad
G	g	
VT	V_t	
SR	r	
VR	V_r	
AR	A_r	
TH	θ	
W	$\omega = \dot{\theta}$	
THI	θ_i	
FD	f_d	
FR	f_r	

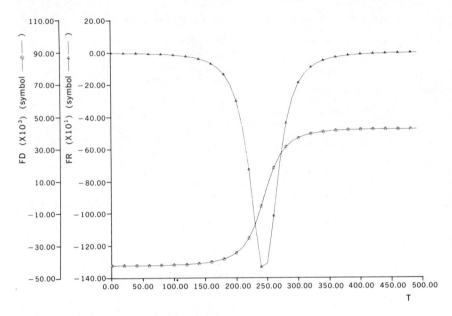

Fig. 3.40 Plot of doppler shift and doppler rate.

gram uses no INT statement, as this example is merely one of computation, not one of solving a differential equation. The results are shown by the plot in Fig. 3.40, which shows that the doppler frequency changes from about -42.5 kc to about $+42.5$ kc, and the largest doppler rate is about 1.335 kc, which occurs when the slant range is the shortest.

3.3.4 ATTACK COURSES OF AN AIRBORNE FIRE–CONTROL SYSTEM

An airborne fire-control system is one which positions automatically a weapon such as a gun or a missile mounted on an airborne platform (i.e., a fighter or interceptor). The projectiles fired from the weapon will be able to hit a target such as a bomber. In a fixed fire-control system, the weapon is mounted rigidly with respect to the airborne platform. The flight path which an interceptor is pursuing in making a firing run is called an attack course. It is assumed here that the fighter's speed is constant, and that the projectile's direction is aligned with the velocity direction of the fighter. It is further assumed that the attack course occurs in a plane; such a plane is called a tactical plane. The tactical plane is determined by the fighter's and target's directions and constitutes the basis of the two-dimensional model in this example.

In the tactical plane, the line connecting the target and the fighter is called the *line of sight* or *sightline*, as this is the line along which the fighter's radar sees the target. The distance along the line of sight between the target and the fighter is called the *range*, which is measured by the airborne radar. The radar also measures the *sightline rate* $\dot{\theta}$ (or the angular rate of change of the sightline) by means of rate gyros mounted on the gimbals of the antenna of the radar.

Two kinds of attack courses are to be introduced here: pure pursuit and lead pursuit. A pure-pursuit course is one in which the sightline is always coincident with the fighter's velocity direction; it is like the course of a dog pursuing his master. Such a course in a tactical plane is shown in Fig. 3.41. Note that at every instant the fighter's velocity direction is along the line of sight. The pure-pursuit course may be readily followed in clear weather by merely using a fixed reticle on the windshield of the fighter. However, it would not be flown in firing an unguided projectile, because such a projectile fired along the sightline will not strike the target. For example, in Fig. 3.41, a projectile fired at point A crosses the target's flight path at point B. While the projectile is in flight, the target is moving toward point C, and the projectile is passing astern of the target.

The two-dimensional model of the pure-pursuit course is shown in Fig. 3.42, which shows the two velocity vectors, the line of sight, the sight, the range R, and the "angle-off" the target θ. The sightline rate is actually the rate of change of the angle-off. The target's velocity V_t

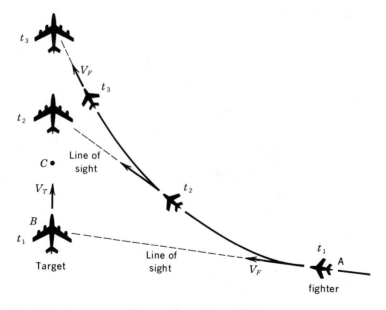

Fig. 3.41   A pure-pursuit course in earth coordinates.

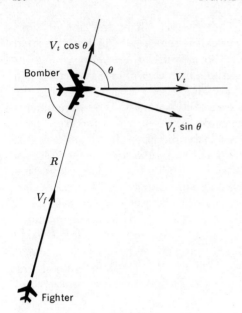

Fig. 3.42 Two-dimensional model of the pure-pursuit course.

may be decomposed into two components, one parallel to and another perpendicular to the sightline. The two speed relations along these two directions are

$$\frac{dR}{dt} = V_t \cos \theta - V_f \tag{3.57}$$

$$R \frac{d\theta}{dt} = - V_t \sin \theta \tag{3.58}$$

where dR/dt = range rate
$d\theta/dt$ = sightline rate
V_t = target speed
V_f = fighter speed
R = range
θ = angle-off

When Eq. (3.57) is divided by Eq. (3.58), we have

$$\int_{R_0}^{R} \frac{dR}{R} = \int_{\theta_0}^{\theta} \frac{V_t \cos \theta - V_f}{- V_t \sin \theta} \, d\theta \tag{3.59}$$

where R_0 and θ_0 represent a known point on the pure-pursuit course. Upon integration on both sides, we have, after simplification,

$$\frac{R}{R_0} = \frac{\sin \theta_0}{\sin \theta} \left(\frac{\tan \theta/2}{\tan \theta_0/2} \right)^m \tag{3.60}$$

where $m = V_f/V_t$.

A MIMIC program for computing the pure-pursuit attack course by using Eqs. (3.57) and (3.58) is shown in Fig. 3.43.   Initial range of 15,000 ft and initial angle-off of 90° are chosen.   Equivalent symbols and computation data are shown in Table 3.5.

The attack course in Fig. 3.41 is plotted in earth coordinates.   A more useful presentation is to plot the course in target coordinates; this is a plot in relative coordinates with the target stationary.   The two coordinates in the target coordinates are range R and angle-off θ.   In the

```
*****PURE PURSUIT COURSES OF A FIGHTER AIRPLANE
*
                          CON(DPR)
                          PAR(RO,THO)
*DPR IS IN DEGREES PER RADIAN
*
              DT        = 1.0
              VF        = 600.
              VT        = 480.
*
*TH IS IN DEGREE AND 1DTH IS IN RADIANS PER SECOND
              1DR       = VT*COS(TH/DPR)-VF
              R         = INT(1DR,RO)
              1DTH      = -VT*SIN(TH/DPR)/R
              TH        = INT(1DTH*DPR,THO)
*
              XR        = R*COS(TH/DPR)
              YR        = R*SIN(TH/DPR)
              X         = XR-VT*T
              Y         = YR
*
                          FIN(500.,R)
                          HDR(T,XR,YR,X,Y)
                          HDR( ,   ,  ,R,TH)
                          HDR( ,   ,  ,1DR,1DTH)
                          HDR
                          OUT(T,XR,YR,X,Y)
                          OUT( ,   ,  ,R,TH)
                          OUT( ,   ,  1DR,1DTH)
                          OUT
*
                          PLO(X,Y)
                          PLO(XR,YR)
                          PLO(T,R,TH)
                          END
57.2957795
15000.0        30.0
15000.0        60.0
15000.0        90.0
15000.0       120.0
```

Fig. 3.43 MIMIC program for the pure-pursuit course of a fighter airplane.

Table 3.5 Equivalent symbols and data for attack course computation

Program symbol	Equation symbol	Value
R, 1DR	$R, \dot{R}$	
TH, 1DTH	$\theta, \dot{\theta}$	
VT	V_t	480 fps
VF	V_f	600 fps
RO	$R(0) = R_0$	15,000 ft
THO	$\theta(0) = \theta_0$	90°
VO	V_0	2,500 ft
L	L	
RF	R_f	

program of Fig. 3.43, X and Y are the two earth coordinates, while XR and YR are the two target coordinates; both are in rectangular form. The results of the computation are shown in Figs. 3.44 through 3.46.   As shown in Fig. 3.45, the pure-pursuit course is a curved course with the

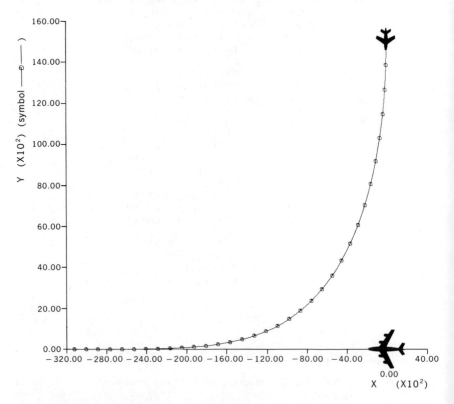

Fig. 3.44 Plot of a pure-pursuit course in earth coordinates.

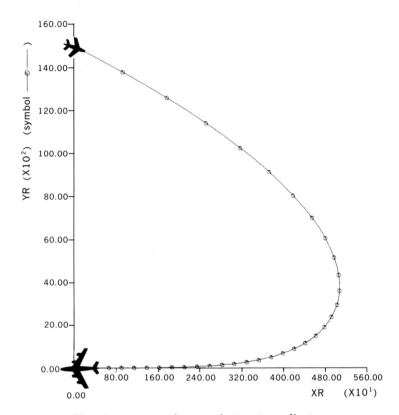

Fig. 3.45   Plot of a pure-pursuit course in target coordinates.

fighter's direction always aiming at the target.   For pursuit courses, the fighter is generally required to fly faster than the target so that it can close in behind the target's tail.   Note that the sightline rate is equal to the rate of the fighter's heading, and that the angle-off changes rapidly and then approaches to zero.

A lead-pursuit course is one in which the fighter flies with its velocity vector leading the sightline by a lead angle L.   Because of the lead angle, the projectiles fired along this course will strike the target.   Figure 3.47 shows a lead-pursuit course in earth coordinates in the tactical plane. Note that the fighter flies in a direction ahead of the line of sight by the lead angle L.   The distance AB along the fighter's velocity direction is the distance that the projectile should travel for a hit.

The two-dimensional model of a lead-pursuit course is shown in Fig. 3.48.   The model is a triangle.   As in the case of the pure-pursuit course, the target's velocity can be decomposed into two components, one perpendicular and one parallel to the sightline.   The two speed relations

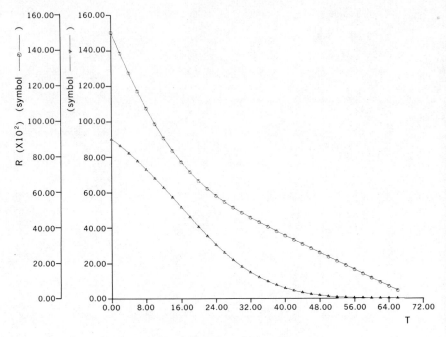

Fig. 3.46   Plot of a range and angle-off of a pure-pursuit course.

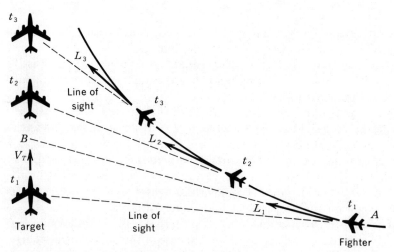

Fig. 3.47   A lead-pursuit course in earth coordinates.

along these two directions are

$$\frac{dR}{dt} = V_t \cos \theta - V_f \cos L \tag{3.61}$$

$$R \frac{d\theta}{dt} = -V_t \sin \theta + V_f \sin L \tag{3.62}$$

The side of the triangle along which the fighter travels consists of the sum of distances $V_f t_f$ and $V_0 t_f$. The former is the distance which the fighter travels with respect to the earth during the required time of flight of the projectile, while the latter is the distance which the projectile travels with respect to the fighter during the same time of flight. V_0, the relative projectile velocity, assumed to be constant here, may be regarded as the average velocity during the projectile's time of flight t_f, which is determined from projectile ballistics. The above distance $V_0 t_f$ is called the *future range* R_f. The above required geometry for a hit gives the following two relations:

$$R + t_f \frac{dR}{dt} = R_f \cos L \tag{3.63}$$

$$-t_f R \frac{d\theta}{dt} = R_f \sin L \tag{3.64}$$

Note that the pure-pursuit course is a special case of a lead-pursuit course where both L and t_f are equal to 0.

Analytical solution for the above four equations can be readily obtained if the following assumption is made:

$$\cos L \approx 1 \tag{3.65}$$

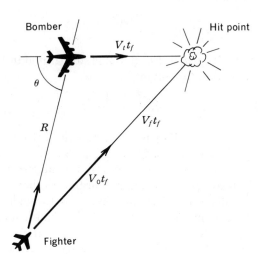

Fig. 3.48 Two-dimensional model of a lead-pursuit course.

This assumption is reasonable because the lead angle is quite small, particularly during the firing range. With this assumption, Eq. (3.61) is replaced by the following:

$$\frac{dR}{dt} = V_t \cos\theta - V_f \tag{3.66}$$

By substituting $\sin L$ from Eq. (3.64) into Eq. (3.62), we have, after simplification,

$$\frac{R\, d\theta/dt}{k} = -V_t \sin\theta \tag{3.67}$$

where $k = V_0/(V_0 + V_f)$. When Eq. (3.66) is divided by Eq. (3.67), we have

$$k \int_{R_0}^{R} \frac{dR}{R} = -\int_{R_0}^{R}\left(\cot\theta + \frac{V_f}{V_t}\csc\theta\right) d\theta \tag{3.68}$$

where R_0 and θ_0 represent a known point on the lead-pursuit course. Upon integration on both sides, we have, after simplification,

$$\left(\frac{R}{R_0}\right)^k = \frac{\sin\theta_0}{\sin\theta}\left(\frac{\tan\theta/2}{\tan\theta_0/2}\right)^m \tag{3.69}$$

where $m = V_f/V_t$.

A MIMIC program for computing the lead-pursuit course is shown in Fig. 3.49 by using Eqs. (3.61) through (3.64) without using the assumption (3.65). Initial range of 15,000 ft and initial angle-off of 90° are again chosen. Equivalent symbols and computation data are also shown in Table 3.5. In Fig. 3.49, Eq. (3.63) has been rewritten for solving R_f as shown below,

$$R_f = \frac{R V_0}{V_0 \cos L - dR/dt} \tag{3.70}$$

and $R\, d\theta/dt$ in Eq. (3.62) is substituted in Eq. (3.64), giving the following equation for solving L:

$$\sin L = (\sin\theta)\frac{V_t}{V_0 + V_f} \tag{3.71}$$

An IMP statement is used in the MIMIC program of Fig. 3.49 to solve the above algebraic equation (3.71).

In Fig. 3.49, X and Y are the two earth coordinates, and XR and YR are the two target coordinates, both in the rectangular form. The results are shown in Figs. 3.50 through 3.52. Figure 3.51 shows the course in target coordinates. Figure 3.52 shows R, θ, L, and R_f as functions of time. Note that lead angle L is no more than 9° and is only about 1° when in the firing range of 2,000 ft.

```
*****LEAD PURSUIT COURSES OF A FIGHTER AIRPLANE
*
                        CON(DPR)
                        PAR(RO,THO,LL)
*DPR IS IN DEGREES PER RADIAN
*
            DT      = 1.0
            VT      = 480.
            VF      = 600.
            VO      = 2500.
*
*TH IS IN DEGREE AND 1DTH IS IN RADIANS PER SECOND
            1DR     = +VT*COS(TH/DPR)-VF*COS(LL)
            R       = INT(1DR,RO)
            1DTH    = (-VT*SIN(TH/DPR)+VF*SIN(LL))/R
            TH      = INT(1DTH*DPR,THO)
*
*L IS IN DEGREE,LL IS L IN RADIANS
            LL      = IMP(LL,LL+SIN(LL)-SIN(TH/DPR)*VT/(VO+VF))
            L       = LL*DPR
            RF      = R*VO/(VO*COS(LL)-1DR)
*
            XR      = R*COS(TH/DPR)
            YR      = R*SIN(TH/DPR)
            X       = XR-VT*T
            Y       = YR
*
                        FIN(500.,R)
                        HDR(T,XR,YR,X,Y)
                        HDR( ,   ,  ,R,TH)
                        HDR( ,   ,  ,1DR,1DTH)
                        HDR( ,   ,  , L,   RF)
                        OUT(T,XR,YR,X,Y)
                        OUT( ,   ,  ,R,TH)
                        OUT( ,   ,  1DR,1DTH)
                        OUT( ,   ,  , L,   RF)
                        OUT
*
                        PLO(X,Y)
                        PLO(XR,YR)
                        PLO(T,R,TH,L,RF)
                        END
57.2957795
15000.0          30.0              0.
15000.0          60.0              0.
15000.0          90.0              0.
15000.0          120.0             0.
```

Fig. 3.49   MIMIC program for the lead-pursuit course of a fighter airplane.

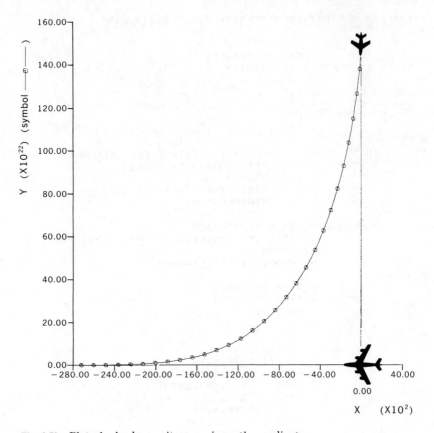

Fig. 3.50 Plot of a lead-pursuit course in earth coordinates.

The lead-pursuit course is also a curved course. The fighter does not fly directly toward the target but with a lead angle in order to score a hit. Because projectiles may be fired continuously along the course, it may be referred to as a continuous release course. It also requires that the fighter fly faster than the target for the final closing in behind the target.

3.4 SIMULATION OF NONLINEAR FEEDBACK CONTROL SYSTEMS

3.4.1 SIMULATION OF RELAY SERVOS

A relay servo is a feedback control system in which the corrective power from the motor is applied discontinuously. Because the corrective power is operated at full power, the relay servo responds rapidly. The simplicity and economy of a relay servo are attractive, provided that the requirements in static accuracy, stability, and transient performance can be met.

The characteristic of the relay is very important in determining the stability and accuracy of the servo. The four most common types of relay characteristics are shown in Fig. 3.53. In these characteristics, there are no more than three corrective levels: a positive maximum, zero, and a negative maximum.

Four relay servos are simulated. Each is a linear second-order servo incorporated additionally with one of the above four types of relays. Furthermore, the linear servo alone is also simulated for comparison. These five cases are listed in Table 3.6. The block diagram of the relay servos is shown in Fig. 3.54, from which the following relations are obtained:

$$E = Y - X \tag{3.72}$$

$$\frac{X}{G} = \frac{A}{S(BS + 1)} \tag{3.73}$$

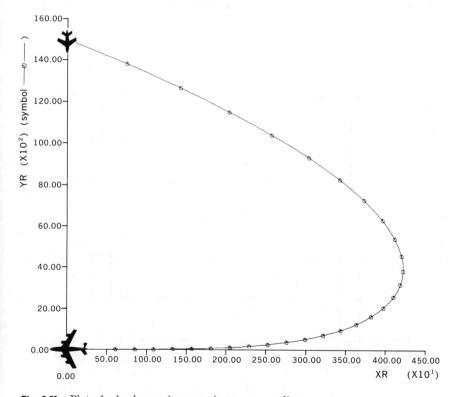

Fig. 3.51 Plot of a lead-pursuit course in target coordinates.

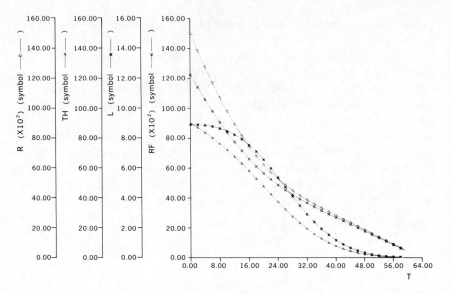

Fig. 3.52 Plot of range, angle-off, lead angle, and future range of a lead-pursuit course.

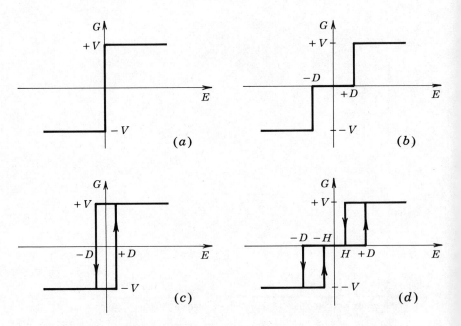

Fig. 3.53 Characteristics of four relays. (*a*) Simple relay; (*b*) relay with dead space; (*c*) relay with hysteresis; (*d*) relay with dead space and hysteresis.

Table 3.6   Values of constants and parameters for five simulated relay servos

	Constants					Parameters	
Servo	*A*	*B*	*V*	*D*	*H*	1DX0	X0
Linear	2	0.5	—	—	—	0	1.5
With a simple relay	2	0.5	1	—	—	0	1.5
With a dead-space relay	2	0.5	1	0.2	—	0	1.5
With a hysteresis relay	2	0.5	1	0.2	—	0	1.5
With a dead-space and hysteresis relay	2	0.5	1	0.2	0.1	0	1.5

where Y and X are, respectively, the input and output of the servo, and E (error signal) and G are, respectively, the input and output of the relay. A is the gain of the loop without the relay, and B is the time constant of the motor.   The above transfer function X/G can be written into the following expression:

$$S^2X = -\frac{SX}{B} + \frac{GA}{B} \qquad (3.74)$$

For computing the response of each of these cases, input Y is taken to be zero, but output X is initially displaced; thus, X is equal to $-E$. The transient response of the output of these servos and the phase trajectories are to be plotted.   The chosen values of the constants and parameters for these five cases are listed in Table 3.6, where constants A and B are defined in Eq. (3.73) and constants V, D, and H are defined in Fig. 3.53.   Simulation is terminated when time t reaches 5 sec.

3.4.1.1   A linear servo   The linear second-order servo is represented by Eqs. (3.72) and (3.74) in addition to the relation $G = E$.   The use of this redundant relation enables one to use the same variable names for all the five cases.

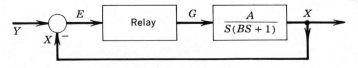

Fig. 3.54   Block diagram of a relay servo.

```
*****LINEAR SERVO SIMULATION
*
                    CON(A,B)
                    PAR(1DX0,X0)
*
        DT        = 0.01
*
        2DX       = -1DX/B+G*A/B
        1DX       = INT(2DX,1DX0)
        X         = INT(1DX,X0)
        F         = Y-X
        Y         = 0.0
*
        G         = E
*
                    FIN(T,5.0)
                    HDR(TIME,X,XDOT)
                    HDR
                    OUT(T,X,1DX)
                    PLO(T,X)
                    PLO(X,1DX)
                    END
2.0               0.5
0.0               1.5
```

Fig. 3.55 MIMIC program for a linear servo simulation.

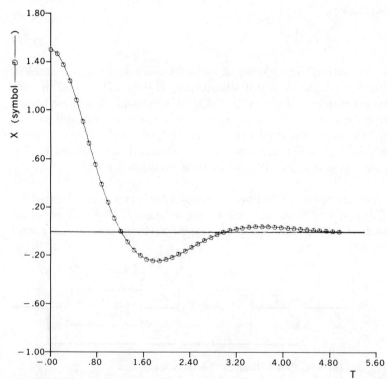

Fig. 3.56 Time response of a linear servo.

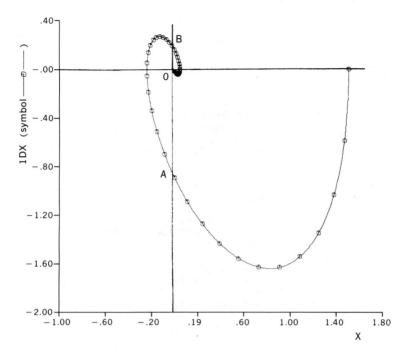

Fig. 3.57 Phase-plane plot of a linear servo.

The MIMIC program for the linear servo is shown in Fig. 3.55.   The transient error response is shown in Fig. 3.56, where it exhibits the commonly desired, slightly underdamped response.   The phase trajectory is shown in Fig. 3.57.   It is a continuous curve, which begins at X equal to 1.5 and $\dot{X}$ equal to 0.   Section AB of the trajectory shows the overshoot portion, and section $B0$ the undershoot portion.   The trajectory approaches the origin exponentially in time.

3.4.1.2 A simple relay servo   The simple relay servo is represented by Eqs. (3.72) and (3.74) and the bang-bang characteristic shown in Fig. 3.53a.   This characteristic, which exhibits three power levels ($+V$, 0, and $-V$), can be described as below:

$$G = +V \qquad \text{when } E > 0 \tag{3.75}$$
$$G = -0 \qquad \text{when } E = 0 \tag{3.76}$$
$$G = -V \qquad \text{when } E < 0 \tag{3.77}$$

Condition $E > 0$ can be expressed by using logical control variable E1 determined by the FSW statement

$$E1 = FSW(E, FALSE, FALSE, TRUE) \tag{3.78}$$

```
*****SIMULATION OF A SIMPLE RELAY SERVO
*
                        CON(A,B,V)
                        PAR(1DX0,X0)
*
        DT         = 0.01
*
        2DX        = -1DX/B+G*A/B
        1DX        = INT(2DX,1DX0)
        X          = INT(1DX,X0)
        F          = Y-X
        Y          = 0.0
*
  F1    G          = V
  F3    G          = 0.
  E2    G          = -V
*
        E1         = FSW(E,FALSE,FALSE,TRUE)
        E2         = FSW(E,TRUE,FALSE,FALSE)
        E3         = NOT(IOR(F1,E2))
*
                        FIN(T,5.0)
                        HDR(TIME,X,XDOT)
                        HDR
                        OUT(T,X,1DX)
                        PLO(T,X)
                        PLO(X,1DX)
                        END
2.0             0.5              1.0
0.0             1.5
```

Fig. 3.58 MIMIC program for the simulation of a simple
relay servo.

which states that E1 is true whenever $E > 0$; otherwise E1 is false.   Similarly, condition $E < 0$ can be expressed by using logical control variable
E2 determined by the following statement:

$$E2 = FSW(E,TRUE,FALSE,FALSE) \tag{3.79}$$

Condition $E = 0$ is equivalent to the condition when both E1 and E2 are
false; this can be expressed by the logical control variable E3, which is
determined by the nesting statement

$$E3 = NOT(IOR(E1,E2)) \tag{3.80}$$

where NOT and IOR denote logical NOT and logical OR operations,
respectively.   The above six statements (3.75) through (3.80) are shown
in the MIMIC program in Fig. 3.58.

The transient error response is shown in Fig. 3.59, and the phase
trajectory in Fig. 3.60.   Since the corrective power reverses instantane-
ously as the error signal goes through zero, the output X oscillates about

the horizontal axis, as shown in Fig. 3.59. The oscillation is ultimately damped to the origin of Fig. 3.60 because of the damping by the motor. The vertical axis in Fig. 3.60 is the line where the switching of the relay occurs; this line divides the phase plane into positive- and negative-torque regions.

3.4.1.3 A relay servo with a dead space in the relay The relay in this servo has the dead-space characteristic shown in Fig. 3.53b, where there are also three power levels $+V$, 0, and $-V$. This characteristic can be described as below:

$$G = +V \qquad \text{when } E > +D \tag{3.81}$$
$$G = 0 \qquad \text{when } -D \leq E \leq +D \tag{3.82}$$
$$G = -V \qquad \text{when } E < -D \tag{3.83}$$

As in the case of the simple relay servo, these conditions can be expressed by logical control variables E1, E2, and E3, determined by the following

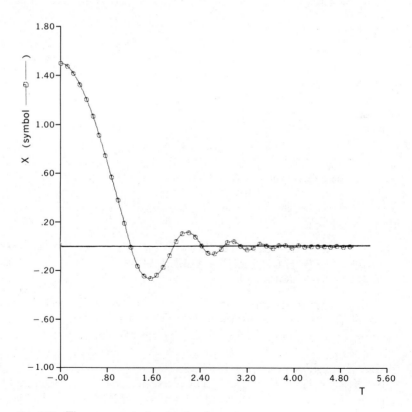

Fig. 3.59 Time response of a simple relay servo.

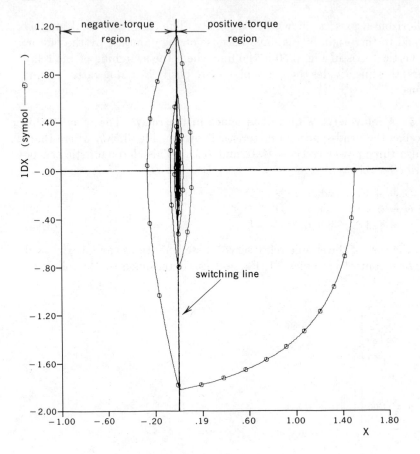

Fig. 3.60 Phase-plane plot of a simple relay servo.

three statements:

$$E1 = FSW(E-D,FALSE,FALSE,TRUE) \qquad (3.84)$$
$$E2 = FSW(E+D,TRUE,FALSE,FALSE) \qquad (3.85)$$
$$E3 = NOT(IOR(E1,E2)) \qquad (3.86)$$

The MIMIC program for this servo is shown in Fig. 3.61, which contains the above six statements (3.81) through (3.86). The transient error response is shown in Fig. 3.62. Output X approaches the amount of dead space D (that is, 0.2); this limits the static accuracy. The phase trajectory is shown in Fig. 3.63, where the relay switches at two vertical lines: $X = -D$ and $X = +D$. The phase plane is thus divided into three regions: the positive-, zero-, and negative-torque regions. In the zero-torque region, the corrective power is not activated, and the load coasts across the dead space with little change in speed.   The zero-torque region helps stabilization, because the servo can come to rest and stay within the dead space instead of going into a limit cycle; however, there is a larger static error due to the dead space.   Instead of using the above six statements to describe the dead-space characteristic of the relay, one can use the following two statements:

$$F = DSP(E, -D, +D) \tag{3.87}$$
$$G = FSW(F, -V, 0., +V) \tag{3.88}$$

The DSP statement gives the dead space specified by $+D$ and $-D$, and the FSW statement gives the three levels of $+V$, 0, and $-V$.

3.4.1.4 A relay servo with a hysteresis in the relay   The relay in this servo has the hysteresis characteristic shown in Fig. 3.53c.   This characteristic can be described as follows.   If G is initially $+V$, then G remains

```
*****SERVO SIMULATION WITH DEAD SPACE IN THE RELAY
*
                        CON(A,B,V,D)
                        PAR(1DX0,X0)
*
            DT      = 0.01
*
            2DX     = -1DX/B+G*A/B
            1DX     = INT(2DX,1DX0)
            X       = INT(1DX,X0)
            F       = Y-X
            Y       = 0.0
*
   E1       G       = V
   E3       G       = 0.0
   E2       G       = -V
*
            E1      = FSW(E-D,FALSE,FALSE,TRUE)
            F2      = FSW(E+D,TRUE,FALSE,FALSE)
            F3      = NOT(IOR(E1,F2))
*
                        FIN(T,5.0)
                        HDR(TIME,X,XDOT)
                        HDR
                        OUT(T,X,1DX)
                        PLO(T,X)
                        PLO(X,1DX)
                        END
   2.0              0.5             1.0             0.2
   0.0              1.5
```

Fig. 3.61 MIMIC program for a servo simulation with dead space in the relay.

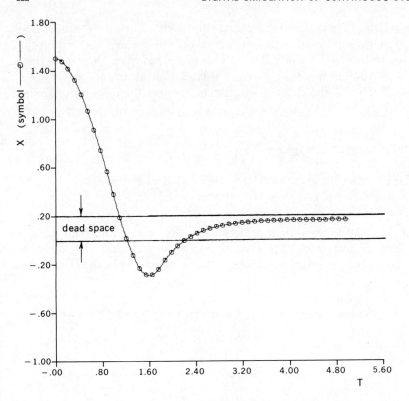

Fig. 3.62 Time response of a relay servo with dead space in the relay.

at $+V$ if $E > -D$; otherwise, G becomes $-V$. If G is initially $-V$, then G remains at $-V$ if $E < +D$; otherwise, G becomes $+V$.

If G is equal to $+V$ or $-V$ when H is true or false, respectively, then we have the following LSW statement:

$$G = \text{LSW}(H, +V, -V) \tag{3.89}$$

Let E1 be true when $E > +D$ and E2 be true when $E < -D$; then we have

$$E1 = \text{FSW}(E - D, \text{FALSE}, \text{FALSE}, \text{TRUE}) \tag{3.90}$$
$$E2 = \text{FSW}(E + D, \text{TRUE}, \text{FALSE}, \text{FALSE}) \tag{3.91}$$

The initial status of G is to be stored in a flip-flop, which can be described by an FLF statement. The FLF statement has three arguments, say E1, E2, and R, where E1 and E2 denote inputs to the flip-flop and R denotes the status at time equal to 0 (to be arbitrarily chosen true here).

Let H be the status of the flip-flop.   The FLF statement

$$H = FLF(E1, E2, TRUE) \tag{3.92}$$

prescribes that H becomes true when E1 is true, becomes false when E2 is true, and remains unchanged when either E1 or E2 is false.

If G is initially at $+V$, H is true and remains true until E2 is true (this means until $E < -D$).   If G is initially at $-V$, H is false and remains false until E1 is true (this means until $E > +D$).   Both E1 and E2 are false when $-D \leq E \leq +D$, and that both E1 and E2 are true is impossible.   Thus, the above four statements (3.89) through (3.92) prescribe the hysteresis characteristic in Fig. 3.53c and are shown in the MIMIC program in Fig. 3.64.

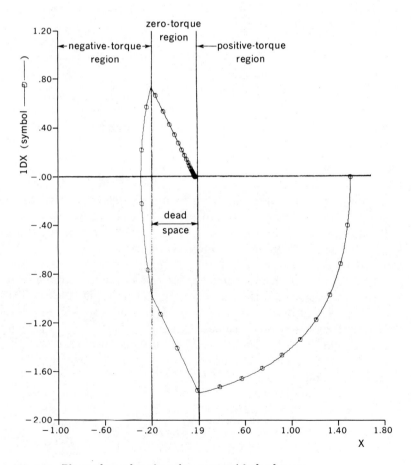

Fig. 3.63   Phase-plane plot of a relay servo with dead space.

```
*****SERVO SIMULATION WITH HYSTERESIS IN THE RELAY
*
                        CON(A,B,V,D)
                        PAR(1DX0,X0)
*
            DT          = 0.01
*
            2DX         = -1DX/B+G*A/B
            1DX         = INT(2DX,1DX0)
            X           = INT(1DX,X0)
            E           = Y-X
            Y           = 0.0
*
            E1          = FSW(E-D,FALSE,FALSE,TRUE)
            F2          = FSW(E+D,TRUE,FALSE,FALSE)
            H           = FLF(E1,E2,TRUE)
            G           = LSW(H,V,-V)
*
                        FIN(T,5.0)
                        HDR(TIME,X,XDOT)
                        HDR
                        OUT(T,X,1DX)
                        PLO(T,X)
                        PLO(X,1DX)
                        END
2.0             0.5             1.0             0.2
0.0             1.5
```

Fig. 3.64 MIMIC program for a servo simulation with hysteresis in
the relay.

The transient error response is shown in Fig. 3.65 and the phase
trajectory in Fig. 3.66. Since the hysteresis delays the switching operation, the corrective power is not reversed until the output X has passed
the desired zero point. As can be seen on the phase plane, the effect is
destabilizing. There exists a limit cycle, as shown in Fig. 3.66.

3.4.1.5 A servo with both a dead space and a hysteresis in the relay The
relay in this servo has the characteristic shown in Fig. 3.53d. This characteristic can be described as follows. If G is initially $+V$, then G remains
at $+V$ if $E > +H$ but becomes 0 when $E \leq +H$. If G is initially $-V$,
then G remains at $-V$ if $E < -H$ but becomes 0 when $E \geq -H$. If G
is initially 0, then G remains 0 if $-D \leq E \leq +D$, becomes $+V$ if
$E > +D$, and becomes $-V$ if $E < -D$.

Let S1 be true when $E > D$, S2 be true when $E > -D$, R1 be true
when $E \leq H$, and R2 be true when $E \geq -H$. Then we have

$$S1 = FSW(E-D,FALSE,FALSE,TRUE) \tag{3.93}$$
$$S2 = FSW(E+D,TRUE,FALSE,FALSE) \tag{3.94}$$
$$R1 = FSW(E-H,TRUE,TRUE,FALSE) \tag{3.95}$$
$$R2 = FSW(E+H,FALSE,TRUE,TRUE) \tag{3.96}$$

Let L1 represent the status of a flip-flop in such a manner that L1 is true or false when S1 is true or when R1 is true, respectively; otherwise L1 remains unchanged.   Let L2 represent the status of another flip-flop in such a way that L2 is true or false when S2 is true or when R2 is true, respectively; otherwise L2 remains unchanged.   Note that the case that both S1 and R1 are true is impossible; so is the case that both S2 and R2 are true.   We then have

$$L1 = FLS(S1,R1,TRUE) \tag{3.97}$$
$$L2 = FLF(S2,R2,TRUE) \tag{3.98}$$

When L1 is true, G is equal to $+V$.   When L2 is true, G is equal to $-V$.   When both L1 and L2 are false, G is equal to 0.   These three when-clauses can be translated into the following three logical statements:

$$E1 = LSW(L1,TRUE,FALSE) \tag{3.99}$$
$$E2 = LSW(L2,TRUE,FALSE) \tag{3.100}$$
$$E3 = NOT(IOR(E1,E2)) \tag{3.101}$$

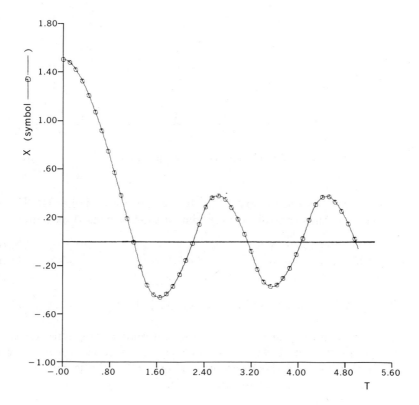

Fig. 3.65   Time response of a relay servo with hysteresis in the relay.

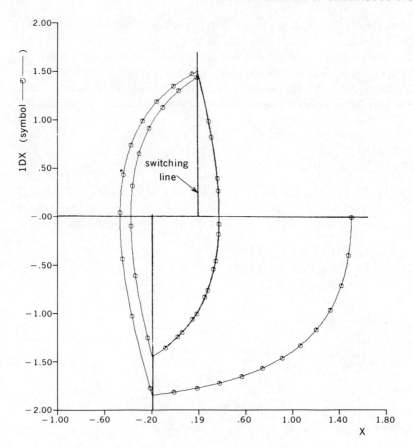

Fig. 3.66   Phase-plane plot of a relay servo with hysteresis.

These logical statements give three logical control variables E1, E2, and E3, which in turn control the execution of the following three statements:

E1	G	= V	(3.102)
E3	G	= 0.	(3.103)
E2	G	= −V	(3.104)

The above 12 statements (3.93) through (3.104) are shown in the MIMIC program of Fig. 3.67.

   If G is initially at $+V$, L1 is true and remains true until R1 is true (this means until $E \leq H$).   If G is initially at $-V$, L2 is true and remains true until R2 is true (this means until $E \geq -H$).   If G is initially 0, both L1 and L2 are false and remain false until S1 is true (this means until $E > D$), when G becomes $+V$, or until S2 is true (this means until

$E < -D$), when G becomes $-V$. Thus, these statements prescribe the hysteresis–dead-space characteristic of the relay.

The transient error response is shown in Fig. 3.68 and the phase trajectory in Fig. 3.69. Notice the two vertical lines at which the switching of the relay occurs; these lines are offset along the horizontal axis. Since hysteresis of dead space contributes destabilization and static error, the existence of both gives a larger static error and a limit cycle with a larger amplitude than either alone.

Instead of using the above 12 statements to describe the dead-space and hysteresis characteristic of the relay, one can make use of the sym-

```
*****SERVO  SIMULATION  WITH  DEAD  SPACE  AND  HYSTERESIS
*
                    CON(A,B,V,D,H)
                    PAR(1DX0,X0)
*
          DT       = 0.01
*
          2DX      = -1DX/B+G*A/B
          1DX      = INT(2DX,1DX0)
          X        = INT(1DX,X0)
          E        = Y-X
          Y        = 0.0
*
          S1       = FSW(E-D,FALSE,FALSE,TRUE)
          S2       = FSW(E+D,TRUE,FALSE,FALSE)
          R1       = FSW(E-H,TRUE,FALSE,FALSE)
          R2       = FSW(E+H,FALSE,FALSE,TRUE)
          L1       = FLF(S1,R1,TRUE)
          L2       = FLF(S2,R2,TRUE)
*
   E1     G        = V
   E3     G        = 0.0
   E2     G        = -V
*
          E1       = LSW(L1,TRUE,FALSE)
          E2       = LSW(L2,TRUE,FALSE)
          E3       = NOT(IOR(E1,E2))
*
                    FIN(T,5.0)
                    HDR(TIME,X,XDOT)
                    HDR
                    OUT(T,X,1DX)
                    PLO(T,X)
                    PLO(X,1DX)
                    END
2.0            0.5            1.0          0.2          0.1
0.0            1.5
```

Fig. 3.67 MIMIC program for a servo simulation with dead space and hysteresis.

metry of the characteristic and use the following five statements:

$$S = FSW(ABS(E) - D, FALSE, FALSE, TRUE) \quad\quad (3.105)$$
$$R = FSW(ABS(E) - H, TRUE, FALSE, FALSE) \quad\quad (3.106)$$
$$L = FLF(S, R, TRUE) \quad\quad (3.107)$$
$$F = LSW(L, V, 0.) \quad\quad (3.108)$$
$$G = FSW(E, -F, 0., +F) \quad\quad (3.109)$$

The first two statements (3.105) and (3.106) generate the logical values of TRUE or FALSE as the inputs to the FLF statement in the way described above, except that the polarity of the input E is ignored. The LSW statement then translates the logical value from the FLF statement into the level of V or 0. These four statements (3.105) through (3.108) describe only the positive portion of the characteristic. Statement (3.109) determines the polarity of the input E and then selects the proper polarity for the output of the relay.

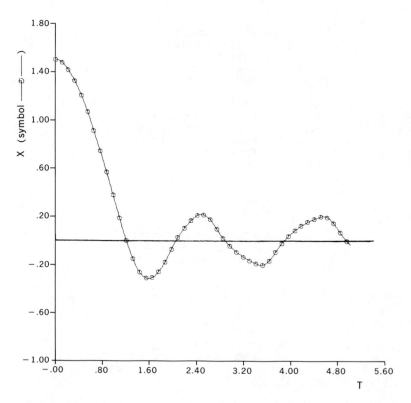

Fig. 3.68 Time response of a relay servo with dead space and hysteresis in the relay.

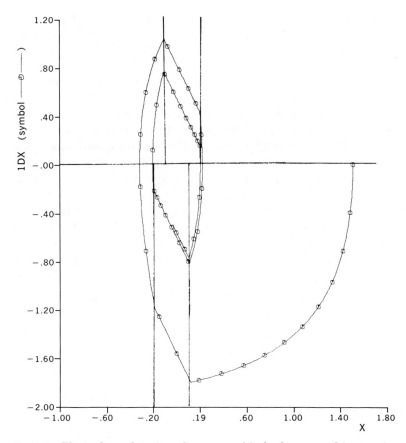

Fig. 3.69 Phase-plane plot of a relay servo with dead space and hysteresis in the relay.

3.4.2 AEROBEE ROCKET ATTITUDE CONTROL SYSTEM

The Aerobee is a small rocket which is used as a research vehicle to carry varied scientific payloads into space.   The rocket is rather small, 30 ft in length and 15 in. in diameter, and carries about 270 lb of payload to a peak altitude of about 120 miles.   The rocket, after its engine burns for about 50 sec, follows a ballistic trajectory, rises to its peak altitude, and then returns to the earth.   A large portion of the flight after burnout (typically 5 min) is well above the atmosphere; thus, scientific observations free from atmospheric distortion can be performed.   Missions of the rocket range from atmospheric studies to observations of the spectral distribution of the energy emitting from stars.   Data can be recorded on film, which is recovered by parachuting the payload back to the earth, or they can be telemetered back if payload recovery is not possible. Many of the experiments which are flown as the payload of the rocket can be reflown aboard satellites after relatively inexpensive flight tests abroad an Aerobee.

When the rocket is well above the atmosphere where the disturbance is low, the rocket and its instruments, by means of an attitude control system, are controlled to point to various objects such as the sun, planets, stars, or earthbound objects such as the horizon, and they can be held there with relatively little force. This control system makes use of two free gyros having two degrees of freedom each as the reference elements and three orthogonally oriented rate gyros to measure the rates. The system controls the attitude only in the coast phase of the flight. Simulation of such a system can give an opportunity to study the effects of parameter variations, control innovations, and varied operating conditions. For simplicity, only a single-axis simulation is described here.

A block diagram of the control system is shown in Fig. 3.70. The free gyro produces an error voltage V_e:

$$V_e = G_2 \sin (\theta_r - \theta) \tag{3.110}$$

where G_2 = sensitivity of gyro
$\qquad \theta_r$ = reference angle
$\qquad \theta$ = angle of orientation of rocket

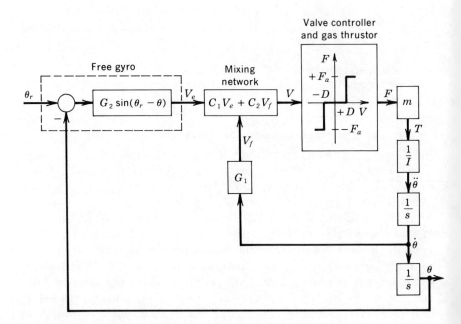

Fig. 3.70   Block diagram for the Aerobee rocket control system.

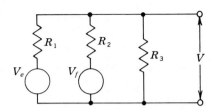

Fig. 3.71 Schematic of the mixing network.

This error voltage V_e is added with a feedback voltage V_f from a rate gyro by a mixing network, shown in Fig. 3.71.   The voltage output from the network V is

$$V = C_1 V_e + C_2 V_f \qquad (3.111)$$

where

$$C_1 = \frac{1}{1 + (1 + R_3/R_2)(R_1/R_3)}$$

$$C_2 = \frac{1}{1 + (1 + R_3/R_1)(R_2/R_3)}$$

where R_1, R_2, and R_3 are the resistances shown in Fig. 3.71.   The voltage V_f from the rate gyro is

$$V_f = -G_1 \dot{\theta} \qquad (3.112)$$

where G_1 is the sensitivity of the rate gyro.

The control system employs gas thrustors to control the angular orientation.   These thrustors, which use the residual helium gas in the rocket fuel tanks after combustion has ended, are controlled by a valve controller.   The combined characteristic of the controller and the thrustors is also shown in Fig. 3.70; there are three levels of forces: $+F_a$, 0, $-F_a$, in addition to a dead space of $2D$.   The dynamics of the rocket can be simply taken as

$$\ddot{\theta} = \frac{Fm}{I} \qquad (3.113)$$

where F = force produced by thrustors
  m = moment arm
  I = moment of inertia of rocket about longitudinal axis

A MIMIC program for simulating this nonlinear feedback control system is shown in Fig. 3.72.   Equivalent symbols and simulation data are shown in Table 3.7.   The dead space D represents the trip voltage of the controller; the value of 0.025 volt in Table 3.7 corresponds to an angle of orientation of about $\frac{1}{8}°$.   The valve controller and the gas thrustors

```
*****AEROBEE ROCKET ATTITUDE CONTROL SYSTEM
                    CON(PI)
                    PAR(X0)
*
*****CONSTANTS
        XR      = 0.
        I       = 900.
        M       = 12.5
        FA      = 4.
        G1      = 0.13
        G2      = 11.9
        D       = 0.025
        R1      = 33000.
        R2      = 33000.
        R3      = 25000.
*
******FREE GYRO
***  X IS IN DEGREES
        VE      = G2*SIN((XR-X)*PI/180.)
*
*****RATE GYRO
        VF      = -G1*1DX
*
*****NETWORK
        V       = C1*VE+C2*VF
        C1      = 1./(1.+(1.+R3/R2)*(R1/R3))
        C2      = 1./(1.+(1.+R3/R1)*(R2/R3))
*
*****VALVE CONTROLLER AND GAS MOTOR
        H       = DSP(V,-D,+D)
        F       = FSW(H,-FA,0.,+FA)
*
*****ROCKET DYNAMICS
        2DX     = (F*M/I)*(180./PI)
        1DX     = INT(2DX,0.)
        X       = INT(1DX,X0)
*
                    FIN(T,30.)
                    HDR(T,X,1DX)
                    HDR
                    OUT(T,X,1DX)
                    PLO(T,X,1DX)
                    PLO(X,1DX)
                    END
3.14159265
15.0
90.0
```

Fig. 3.72 MIMIC program for the Aerobee rocket attitude
control system.

are described by the following DSP and FSW statements:

$$H = DSP(V,-D,+D) \tag{3.114}$$
$$F = FSW(H,+FA,0.,-FA) \tag{3.115}$$

The DSP statement gives the dead space, while the FSW statement gives

Table 3.7 Equivalent symbols and simulation data for attitude control system

Program symbol	Equation symbol	Value
X, 1DX, 2DX	θ, $\dot{\theta}$, $\ddot{\theta}$	
VF, VE, V, T, F	V_f, V_e, V, T, F	
X0	$\theta(0)$	15°
1DX0	$\dot{\theta}(0)$	0
XR	θ_r	0
I	I	900 slug-ft²
M	m	12.5 ft
FA	F_a	4 lb
G1	G_1	0.13 volt/(deg)(sec)
G2	G_2	11.9 volts
D	D	0.025 volt
R1	R_1	33,000 ohms
R2	R_2	33,000 ohms
R3	R_3	25,000 ohms

one of the three possible levels according to whether the values of V are positive, 0, or negative. Note that X, 1DX, and 2DX in Fig. 3.72 are expressed in terms of degrees, not radians.

The computed results are shown in the plots of Figs. 3.73 and 3.74. Figure 3.73 shows the time response of the angle of orientation and the

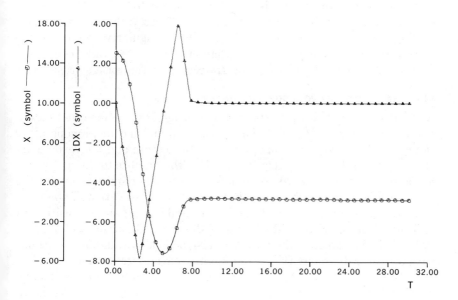

Fig. 3.73 Time response of the angle of orientation and the body rate.

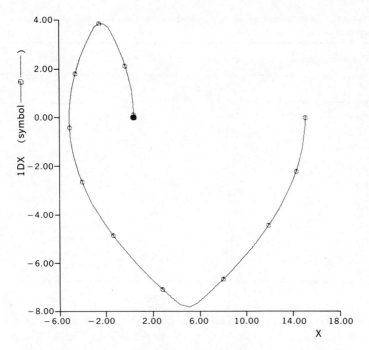

Fig. 3.74 Phase-plane plot of the rocket orientation.

body rate, when the rocket is initially displaced by 15°. The angle of
orientation is essentially recovered in about 7 sec with one undershoot,
leaving an inaccuracy of about 0.25°. The triangular waveform of the
body rate is due to the bang-bang characteristic of the valve controller.
Figure 3.74 shows the phase-plane trajectory of the rocket orientation.

3.4.3 A SATELLITE ROLL-AXIS CONTROL SYSTEM

A three-axis-oriented solar experiment package is to be mounted onto a
manned orbiting spacecraft. This package would include, among other
things, a 14-in. telescope, together with still-picture and television cameras. A control system is required to point the satellite to the sun, which
has a diameter of about 20 arc-minutes. It is also required to point the
satellite to a position off the sun but within the observation of the sun's
corona; consequently, the control system should be capable of positioning
a displacement of 1° from the center of the sun. On account of the lim-
itations of the cameras, the position must be held within 60 arc-seconds
with a jitter rate of less than 1 arc-minute per minute of time.

In the discussion here, only the control of the roll axis is considered.
The block diagram of the control system is shown in Fig. 3.75. As shown

there, the roll axis is controlled through a position servo loop. A high-grade rate-integrating gyro is chosen for measuring attitude position, and a dc direct-drive torque motor for control actuation. A maximum roll excursion of 7.5 arc-minutes in 15 time-minutes is required. This could be met by using the gyro with a drift of no more than 7.5/15, or 0.5 arc-second per second of time, and by choosing a proper loop gain such that the transient position errors are kept below 1 arc-minute. Also, a maximum roll rate of 1 arc-minute per minute of time is required throughout the 15-min observation period. This could be met by properly selecting the torque motor and the loop gain.

As shown in the block diagram, the error X_e from the gyro is

$$X_e = X_c - X \tag{3.116}$$

where X is the orientation angle of the roll axis and X_c the command angle, and the transfer function of the gyro is approximated by

$$\dot{Y} = \frac{K_1 X_e - Y}{\tau_1} \tag{3.117}$$

where Y is the output voltage of the rate-integrating gyro. The output

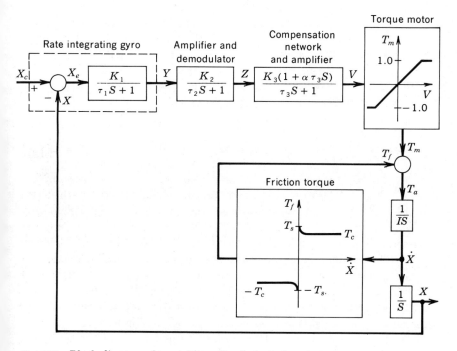

Fig. 3.75 Block diagram of a satellite roll-axis control system.

of the gyro is ac-amplified and demodulated. The transfer function of
the demodulation is

$$\dot{Z} = \frac{K_2 Y - Z}{\tau_2} \tag{3.118}$$

where Z is the output of the demodulator. The output of the modulator
is then compensated by a lead-lag network and then amplified to drive
the torque motor. The transfer function of the combination of the compensation network and the amplifier is

$$\dot{V} = \frac{-V + K_3 Z + \alpha \tau_3 Z}{\tau_3} \tag{3.119}$$

where V is the output from the amplifier. The torque T_m from the torque
motor has a saturation characteristic as shown in the block diagram in
Fig. 3.75.

The dynamics of the satellite about the roll axis is approximated by

$$T_a = I\ddot{X} \tag{3.120}$$

where I is the moment of inertia of the satellite about the roll axis and
T_a the torque available to overcome the inertia torque. The characteristic of the friction torque T_f is also shown in Fig. 3.75, where T_s is the
static friction torque and T_c the coulomb friction torque. Both T_s and
T_c are assumed constant. The effect of the speed and the motor torque
T_m on the friction torque T_f can be described in the following manner:

1. When $\dot{X} = 0$, $T_f = T_s$ if $|T_m| > T_s$; otherwise, $T_f = 0$.
2. When $\dot{X} \neq 0$, $T_f = T_c$ if $|T_m| > T_c$; otherwise, $T_f = 0$.

And the available torque T_a is

$$T_a = T_m - T_f \tag{3.121}$$

A MIMIC program simulating the control system in Fig. 3.75 is
shown in Fig. 3.76. Equivalent symbols and simulation data are shown
in Table 3.8. Constant DPR is the conversion factor of 57.2958° rad by
which another conversion factor, CONV, of arc-seconds per radian is
obtained. The saturation characteristic is described by a LIM statement. The friction characteristic is described by 24 statements, the last
16 statements of which are to generate eight logical control variables L1
through L8 by means of which the proper value of T_f is selected.

The results for the case when the input is a step function of 1,800
arc-seconds are shown in Figs. 3.77 through 3.80. Figure 3.77 shows the
output of the compensation network and amplifier V and the output of
torque motor T_m. Torque T_m is limited by the saturation characteristic

```
****A SATELLITE ROLL AXIS CONTROL SYSTEM
                CON(CONV1)
                PAR(XC)
        I      = 200.0
        DTMIN  = 0.0001
        ALPHA  = 10.
        T1     = 0.006
        T2     = 0.01
        T3     = 0.0555
        K1     = 15.0
        K2     = 1000.
        K3     = 0.1
        TC     = 0.1
        TS     = 0.2
*****CONV2 IS IN ARC-SEC PER RADIAN
        CONV2  = CONV1*3600.
*****RATE INTEGRATING GDRD
        XE     = (XC/CONV2)-X
        1DY    = (K1*XE-Y)/T1
        Y      = INT(1DY,0.)
*****AMPLIFIER-DEMODULATOR
        1DZ    = (K2*Y-Z)/T2
        Z      = INT(1DZ,0.)
*****COMPENSATION NETWORK-AMPLIFIER
        1DV    = (K3*Z+K3*ALPHA*T3*1DZ-V)/T3
        V      = INT(1DV,0.)
*****TORQUE MOTOR
        TM     = LIM(V,-1.,+1.)
*****FRICTION TORQUE
L1      TF     = -TM
L2      TF     = TM
L3      TF     = -TS
L4      TF     = TS
L5      TF     = -TC
L6      TF     = TC
L7      TF     = -TM
L8      TF     = TM
        L1     = AND(1DXEQZ,TMLETS,TMNE)
        L2     = AND(1DXEQZ,TMLETS,TMPZ)
        L3     = AND(1DXEQZ,TMGTTS,TMNE)
        L4     = AND(1DXEQZ,TMGTTS,TMPZ)
        L5     = AND(1DXNEZ,TMGTTC,TMNE)
        L6     = AND(1DXNEZ,TMGTTC,TMPZ)
        L7     = AND(1DXNEZ,TMLETC,TMNE)
        L8     = AND(1DXNEZ,TMLETC,TMPZ)
        1DXEQZ = FSW(1DX,FALSE,TRUE,FALSE)
        1DXNEZ = NOT(1DXEQZ)
        TMGTTS = FSW(ABS(TM)-TS,FALSE,FALSE,TRUE)
        TMLETS = NOT(TMGTTS)
        TMGTTC = FSW(ABS(TM)-TC,FALSE,FALSE,TRUE)
        TMLETC = NOT(TMGTTC)
        TMPZ   = FSW(TM,FALSE,TRUE,TRUE)
        TMNE   = NOT(TMPZ)
*****AVAILABLE TORQUE
        TA     = TM-TF
*****SATELLITE DYNAMICS
        2DX    = TA/I
        1DX    = INT(2DX,0.)
        X      = INT(1DX,0.)
*****UNITS CONVERSION
*****X  IS IN RADIANS. 1DX  IS IN RADIANS PER SEC
*****XX IS IN ARC-SEC, 1DXX IS IN ARC-SEC PER SEC
        XX     = CONV2*X
        1DXX   = CONV2*1DX
*
                FIN(T,6.0)
                HDR(T,XE,XX,V,TM,TA)
                HDR(,Y,1DY,Z,1DZ,X)
                OUT(T,XE,XX,V,TM,TA)
                OUT(,Y,1DY,Z,1DZ,X)
                OUT
                PLO(T,V,TM)
                PLO(T,TA)
                PLO(T,XX,1DXX)
                PLO(XX,1DXX)
                END
57.2957795
1800.0
```

Fig. 3.76 MIMIC program for a satellite roll-axis control system.

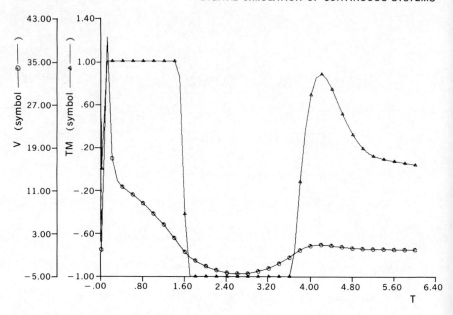

Fig. 3.77   Plot of the amplifier output V and torque-motor output T_m.

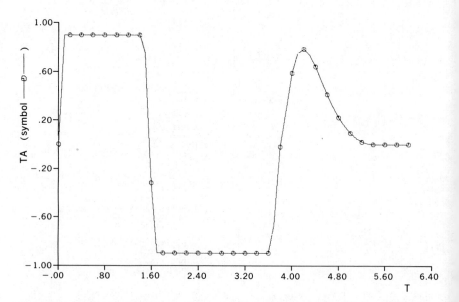

Fig. 3.78   Plot of the available torque T_a.

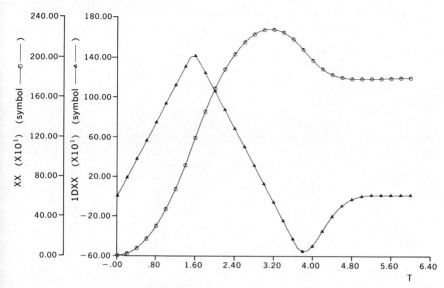

Fig. 3.79 Plot of the orientation angle of the roll axis and the angular rate.

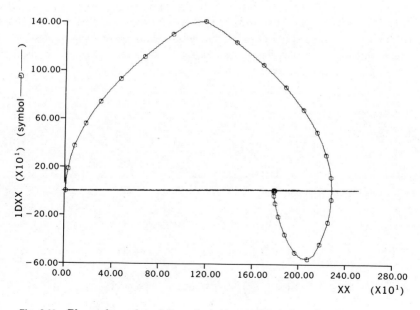

Fig. 3.80 Phase-plane plot of the orientation angle of the roll axis.

Table 3.8 Equivalent symbols and simulation data for roll axis control system

Program symbol	Equation symbol	Value
I	I	200 slug-ft^2
ALPHA	α	10
T1	τ_1	0.006 sec
T2	τ_2	0.01 sec
T3	τ_3	0.0555 sec
K1	K_1	15 volts/rad
K2	K_2	1,000 volts/volt
K3	K_3	0.1 volt/volt
TC	T_c	0.1 ft-lb
TS	T_s	0.2 ft-lb
X, 1DX, 2DX	$X, \dot{X}, \ddot{X}$	
Y, 1DY	$Y, \dot{Y}$	
Z, 1DZ	$Z, \dot{Z}$	
TM, TA, TF	T_m, T_a, T_f	
XC	X_c	1,800 arc-seconds
XE	X_e	

† Initial values of all integrators are zero.

of the torque motor. Figure 3.78 shows the available torque T_a, where the effect of the friction torque is not pronounced. Figure 3.79 shows output X and its derivative $\dot{X}$. The speed is almost zero after 4 sec of response time, and the angular error is less than 1 arc-second. A phase-plane plot of the response is shown in Fig. 3.80, where the angle of orientation settles to the command value of 1,800 arc-seconds.

PROBLEMS

3.1. Given the equations

$$x = A(\phi - \sin \phi) \qquad y = A(1 - \cos \phi)$$

generate a cycloid by MIMIC programming.

3.2. Given the equations

$$x = C \cos \phi - A \cos \left(\frac{C\phi}{A}\right) \qquad y = C \sin \phi - A \sin \left(\frac{C\phi}{A}\right)$$

generate an epicycloid by MIMIC programming.

3.3. Given the equations

$$x = B \cos \phi + A \cos \left(\frac{B\phi}{A}\right) \qquad y = B \sin \phi - A \sin \left(\frac{B\phi}{A}\right)$$

generate a hypocycloid by MIMIC programming.

3.4. Given the equations

$$r = A(1 + \cos \theta) \qquad x = r \cos \theta \qquad y = r \sin \theta$$

generate a cardioid by MIMIC programming.

3.5. Given the MIMIC program in Fig. 3.81, show the family of curves generated by the program.

3.6. Given the MIMIC program in Fig. 3.82, show the curve it generates when

(a) N = 1   (b) N = 2   (c) N = 3   (d) N = 4   (e) N = 5

3.7. By MIMIC programming, find the magnitude and angle spectra of the transfer function

$$\frac{X}{Y} = \frac{1}{1 + j\tau\omega}$$

(a) When $\tau = 0.1$ (b) When $\tau = 1$
(c) When $\tau = 10$

```
                    DT        = .02
                    DTMIN     = 0.01
                    Y1        = SIN(6.28*T)
                    C1        = LIN(TRUE,T,0..10.)
                    C2        = LIN(TRUE,T,10.01,20.)
                    C3        = LIN(TRUE,T,20.01,30.)
                    C4        = LIN(TRUE,T,30.01,40.)
                    C5        = LIN(TRUE,T,40.01,50.)
                    C6        = LIN(TRUE,T,50.01,60.)
                    C7        = LIN(TRUE,T,60.01,70.)
                    C8        = LIN(TRUE,T,70.01,80.)
          C1        Y         = Y1
          C2        Y         = Y1-0.1
          C3        Y         = Y1-0.2
          C4        Y         = Y1-0.3
          C5        Y         = Y1-0.4
          C6        Y         = Y1-0.5
          C7        Y         = Y1-0.6
          C8        Y         = Y1-0.7
                    X1        = T
          C1        X         = X1
          C2        X         = X1-10.
          C3        X         = X1-20.
          C4        X         = X1-30.
          C5        X         = X1-40.
          C6        X         = X1-50.
          C7        X         = X1-60.
          C8        X         = X1-70.
                    FIN(T,80.)
                    HDR(T,X,Y)
                    PLO(X,Y)
                    END
```

Fig. 3.81 MIMIC program for generating a family of curves.

```
                        PAR(N)
        PI        =  3.1416
        ONE       =  FSW(T-PI.TRUE.TRUE.FALSE)
        TWO       =  FSW(T-2.*PI.TRUE.TRUE.FALSE)
        THREE     =  FSW(T-4.*PI.TRUE.TRUE.FALSE)
        FOUR      =  FSW(T-6.*PI.TRUE.TRUE.FALSE)
        FIVE      =  FSW(T-8.*PI.TRUE.TRUE.FALSE)
        SECOND    =  AND(TWO.NOT(ONE))
        THIRD     =  AND(THREE.NOT(TWO))
        FOURTH    =  AND(FOUR.NOT(THREE))
        FIFTH     =  AND(FIVE.NOT(FOUR))
        SIXTH     =  NOT(FIVE)
ONE         A     =  2.
SECOND      A     =  4.
THIRD       A     =  8.
FOURTH      A     =  16.
FIFTH       A     =  32.
SIXTH       A     =  64.
        RHO       =  A*SIN(N*T)
        X         =  RHO*COS(T)
        Y         =  RHO*SIN(T)
                     FIN(T,10.*PI)
                     PLO(X,Y)
                     END
```

Fig. 3.82   MIMIC program for generating a family of curves.

3.8. Given the transfer function

$$\frac{X}{Y} = \frac{1}{(ju)^2 + 2\zeta ju + 1}$$

where $u = \omega/\omega_n$, find the magnitude and angle spectra of this function by MIMIC programming

(a) When $\zeta = 0.1$, $\omega_n = 1$ (b) When $\zeta = 0.4$, $\omega_n = 1$
(c) When $\zeta = 0.7$, $\omega_n = 1$ (d) When $\zeta = 1.0$, $\omega_n = 1$

3.9. Compute the solution of the differential equation in Prob. 1.1 by MIMIC programming.

3.10. Compute the solution of the differential equation in Prob. 1.2 by MIMIC programming.

3.11. Compute the solution of the differential equation in Prob. 1.3 by MIMIC programming.

3.12. A small spacecraft has a folded appendage assembly which can fit inside the limited shroud space during launch.   Figure 3.83 shows the spacecraft and the appendages.   The appendages are two diametrically opposed, relatively heavy weights attached to the end of a very light boom.   After launch, the appendages are released and the centrifugal force pulls them out away from the spacecraft until they are locked into place.   During this short period, the appendages experience forces and accelerations while at the same time the complete assembly despins before being injected into orbit.

Assume that the weights M slide frictionlessly on the booms and are initially located at $R(0)$ and that the spacecraft has constant moment of inertia I and initial spin rate $\theta(0)$. The equations of motion of the weights can be described by

$$\ddot{R} = R(\theta)^2 \qquad \ddot{\theta} = -\frac{2MR\dot{R}\theta}{I + MR^2}$$

where θ and $\dot{\theta}$ are the angular speed and acceleration of the weights, respectively, and R, $\dot{R}$, and $\ddot{R}$ are the radial distance, speed, and acceleration of the weights, respectively. Given the values of constants and initial conditions

$$M = 0.25 \text{ slug} \qquad I = 10.5 \text{ slug-ft}^2$$
$$R(0) = 1 \text{ ft} \qquad \dot{R}(0) = 0 \text{ fps}$$
$$\theta(0) = 0 \text{ rad} \qquad \theta(0) = 4.85 \text{ rad/sec}$$

compute the solution of the equations of motion by MIMIC programming until the time reaches 2 sec.

3.13. The equation of motion for a mass and nonlinear spring system is

$$M\ddot{x} + F(x) = 0$$

where M is the mass and F the nonlinear spring force. The nonlinear spring force F, in pounds, is approximated by the following relation:

$$F(x) = 1,900[(x + 1)^2 - 1]$$

Given the values of constant and initial conditions

$$M = 0.12 \text{ slug}$$
$$\dot{x}(0) = 0$$
$$x(0) = -0.3, -0.6, -0.9 \text{ in.}$$

compute, by MIMIC programming, the transient response of the system until time reaches 0.5 sec.

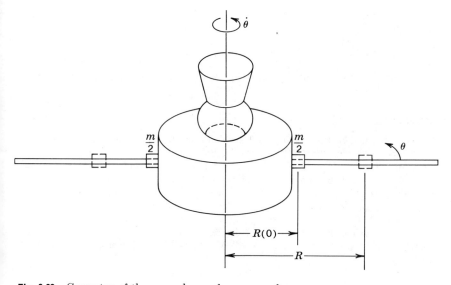

Fig. 3.83   Geometry of the appendages of a spacecraft.

3.14. The complex relation

$$E(\theta) = I_1 \exp\left[j2\pi\left(\frac{d_1}{\lambda}\right)\sin\theta\right] + I_2 \exp\left[j2\pi\left(\frac{d_2}{\lambda}\right)\sin\theta\right]$$
$$+ I_3 \exp\left[j2\pi\left(\frac{d_3}{\lambda}\right)\sin\theta\right] + I_4 \exp\left[j2\pi\left(\frac{d_4}{\lambda}\right)\sin\theta\right]$$

gives the radiation pattern of a four-element antenna array with unequal element spacings. This array has the current intensities which follow a binomial distribution. Given the values of constants

$$I_1 = 1 \qquad I_2 = 2 \qquad I_3 = 2 \qquad I_4 = 1$$
$$\frac{d_1}{\lambda} = 0 \qquad \frac{d_2}{\lambda} = 1 \qquad \frac{d_3}{\lambda} = 2 \qquad \frac{d_4}{\lambda} = 3$$

compute, by MIMIC programming, the magnitude of $E(\theta)$ in decibels for the range of θ equal to 0 to 180°.

3.15. The motion of the earth orbiting about the sun in the orbit plane may be described by the two equations of motion

$$\frac{d^2x}{dt^2} = -\mu^2\frac{x}{r^3} \qquad \frac{d^2y}{dt^2} = -\mu^2\frac{y}{r^3}$$

where $r = \sqrt{x^2 + y^2}$
$\mu^2 = n^2a^3$
$n = 2\pi/P$

In the above, a is the semimajor axis of the ellipse, P is the period of the orbit, and e is the eccentric anomaly. Given the values of constants and initial conditions

$a = 1$ astronomical unit
$n = 1°$/mean solar day
$e = 0.02$
$x(0) = a(1 - e)$
$\dot{x}(0) = 0$
$y(0) = 0$
$$\dot{y}(0) = \frac{a\sqrt{1 - e^2}}{1 - e}\frac{\pi n}{180}$$

compute the complete orbit by MIMIC programming.

REFERENCES

1. Chu, Y., and S. Haas: Iso-parameter Contours for Airborne Fixed Fire Control Systems, *Proc. Natl. Electron. Conf.*, 1957, pp. 155–166.
2. Pipes, L. A.: "Applied Mathematics for Engineers and Physicists," 2d ed., McGraw-Hill Book Company, New York, 1958.
3. Schwartz, M.: "Information Transmission, Modulation, and Noise," McGraw-Hill Book Company, New York, 1959.
4. Rogers, A. E., and T. W. Connolly: "Analog Computation in Engineering Design," McGraw-Hill Book Company, New York, 1960.
5. Fifer, S.: "Analogue Computation," McGraw-Hill Book Company, New York, 1960.
6. Danby, J. M. A.: "Fundamentals of Celestial Mechanics," The Macmillan Company, New York, 1962.

7. Levine, L.: "Methods for Solving Engineering Problems Using Analog Computers," McGraw-Hill Book Company, New York, 1964.
8. Harnett, R. T., F. J. Sansom, and L. M. Warshawsky: Midas Programming Guide, *Tech. Rept.* SEQ-TDR-64-1, Directorate of Systems Dynamic Analysis, Wright-Patterson Air Force Base, Ohio, January, 1964.
9. Hausner, A.: "Simple Analog Computer Oscilloscope Display," pp. 38–45, Simulation Councils, Inc., December, 1964.
10. James, M. L., G. M. Smith, and J. C. Wolford: "Analog Computer Simulation of Engineering Systems," International Textbook Company, Scranton, Pa., 1966.
11. Chu, Y.: Application of Mimic Language at GSFC, *Rept.* X-700-67-96, Goddard Space Flight Center, NASA, February, 1967.
12. April, G. C., R. W. Pike, and C. L. Smith: Calculation of Temperature Profile in Ablator Char Using Mimic, *Simulation*, April, 1967, pp. 219–225.
13. Digital Simulation of Continuous Systems, *Proc. IBM Sci. Computing Symp.*, IBM Corporation, 1967.
14. Sansom, F. J., and H. E. Petersen: Mimic Programming Manual, *Tech. Rept.* SEG-TR-67-31, Wright-Patterson Air Force Base, Ohio, July, 1967.
15. Chu, Y.: Digital Analog Simulation Techniques, *Proc. Fifth Congr. Intern. Assoc. Analogue Computation, Lausanne, Switzerland*, 1967.
16. Nobel, B.: "Applications of Undergraduate Mathematics in Engineering," The Macmillan Company, New York, 1967.

4
Mathematical Applications

In this chapter, mathematical applications of MIMIC programming are presented. MIMIC programming is applied to the Fourier series, the Fourier integral, autocorrelation, crosscorrelation, ordinary differential equations, and partial differential equations. The equations in most of the examples in this chapter are well known, and their analytical solutions are available. They are chosen in order to show how closely the MIMIC language resembles the mathematical equations and to offer some comparisons between the computed and analytical results.

4.1 FOURIER SERIES

4.1.1 PERIODIC FUNCTIONS

A time function $F(t)$ is said to be periodic of period P if the following relation holds for all t:

$$F(t) = F(t + P) \tag{4.1}$$

A number of periodic functions are shown in Fig. 4.1. If a periodic function holds for the additional relation

$$F(t) = F(-t) \tag{4.2}$$

then the function is said to be an *even function*. Figure 4.1a, c, and f are examples of even functions. If a periodic function holds, instead, for the additional relation

$$F(t) = -F(-t) \tag{4.3}$$

then the function is said to be an *odd function*. Figure 4.1b, d, and e are examples of odd functions. Some odd functions can be shifted to become even functions (or vice versa); an example is the odd function in Fig. 4.1b, which becomes an even function like that shown in Fig. 4.1a when the origin is shifted for a quarter period along the horizontal direction. If a periodic function is neither even nor odd, it can be resolved into an even part and an odd part; the periodic function is the superposition of these two parts. For example, the function in Fig. 4.1g is the superposition of the even function in Fig. 4.1a and the odd function in Fig. 4.1d.

4.1.2 EXPANSION OF A PERIODIC FUNCTION

A periodic time function $F(t)$ with a period P can be expanded into an infinite series of the following form, called the *Fourier series:*

$$F(t) = A_0 + \sum_{n=1}^{\infty} (A_n \cos n\omega_0 t + B_n \sin n\omega_0 t) \tag{4.4}$$

where

$$A_0 = \frac{1}{P} \int_0^P F(t) \, dt \tag{4.5}$$

$$A_n = \frac{2}{P} \int_0^P F(t) \cos n\omega_0 t \, dt \tag{4.6}$$

$$B_n = \frac{1}{P} \int_0^P F(t) \sin n\omega_0 t \, dt \tag{4.7}$$

and

$$P = \frac{2\pi}{\omega_0} \tag{4.8}$$

The above expansion requires that $F(t)$ have a finite number of discontinuities and meet the following condition:

$$\int_0^P |F(t)| \, dt < \infty \tag{4.9}$$

In the above equations, ω_0 is called the *fundamental frequency* and $n\omega_0$ the *nth harmonic*. The A's and B's are called Fourier coefficients. If a peri-

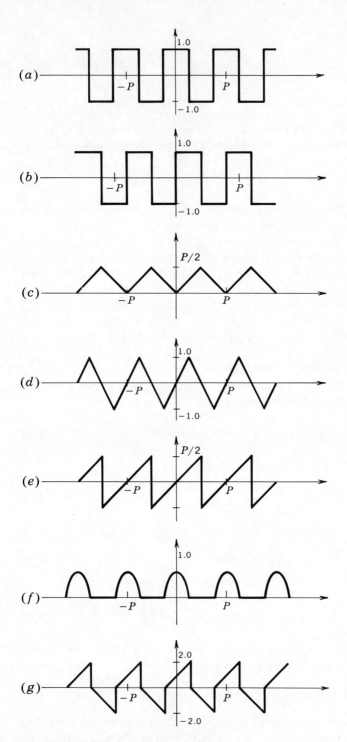

Fig. 4.1 Periodic functions.

148

odic function is even, coefficients B_n are all zero. If it is odd, coefficients A (that is, A_0 and A_n) are all zero. It is apparent from Eq. (4.4) that a periodic time function may contain both positive and negative frequencies which are harmonically related to the fundamental.

The series in Eq. (4.4) may be written into the following equivalent form:

$$F(t) = C_0 + \sum_{n=1}^{\infty} C_n \cos(n\omega_0 t + \phi_n) \tag{4.10}$$

where

$$C_n = \sqrt{A_n{}^2 + B_n{}^2} \tag{4.11}$$

$$\phi_n = \arctan\left(\frac{-B_n}{A_n}\right) \tag{4.12}$$

Coefficients C_n and ϕ_n are called, respectively, the magnitude (or amplitude) and the phase of the nth harmonic of the periodic function. The plots of magnitude C_n and phase ϕ_n versus n (or $n\omega_0$) are called the spectra of the given periodic function. Since these spectra are lines, they are line spectra.

4.1.3 AN EXAMPLE

Expansion of a periodic function into a Fourier series is the determination of the coefficients in either Eq. (4.4) or Eq. (4.10). The coefficients for the periodic functions in Fig. 4.1 that are determined from Eq. (4.5) are shown in Table 4.1. As an example, coefficients of the periodic function in Fig. 4.1f are now determined. As shown in Fig. 4.1f, $F(t)$ for the interval 0 to P is

$$F(t) = \begin{cases} \cos\left(\dfrac{2\pi t}{P}\right) & \text{for } 0 \le t \le \dfrac{P}{4} \text{ and } \dfrac{3P}{4} \le t \le P \\[2ex] 0 & \text{for } \dfrac{P}{4} \le t \le \dfrac{3P}{4} \end{cases} \tag{4.13}$$

By using Eqs. (4.5) through (4.8) and making use of the symmetry of $F(t)$, we have

$$A_0 = \frac{2}{P} \int_0^{P/4} \cos\left(\frac{2\pi t}{P}\right) dt$$

$$A_n = \frac{4}{P} \int_0^{P/4} \cos\left(\frac{2\pi t}{P}\right) \cos\left(\frac{2\pi n t}{P}\right) dt \tag{4.14}$$

$$B_n = \frac{4}{P} \int_0^{P/4} \cos\left(\frac{2\pi t}{P}\right) \sin\left(\frac{2\pi n t}{P}\right) dt$$

Table 4.1 Fourier expansion of periodic functions in Fig. 4.1

Fig.	A_0	A_n	B_n
(a)	$A_0 = 0$	$A_n = \begin{cases} 0 & \text{for even } n \\ (-1)^{(n-1)/2}\left(\dfrac{4}{n\pi}\right) & \text{for odd } n \end{cases}$	$B_n = 0$
(b)	$A_0 = 0$	$A_n = 0$	$B_n = \begin{cases} \dfrac{4}{n\pi} & \text{for odd } n \\ 0 & \text{for even } n \end{cases}$
(c)	$A_0 = \dfrac{\pi}{2}$	$A_n = \begin{cases} -\dfrac{4}{n^2\pi} & \text{for odd } n \\ 0 & \text{for even } n \end{cases}$	$B_n = 0$
(d)	$A_0 = 0$	$A_n = 0$	$B_n = \begin{cases} (-1)^{(n-1)/2}\left(\dfrac{8}{n^2\pi^2}\right) & \text{for odd } n \\ 0 & \text{for even } n \end{cases}$
(e)	$A_0 = 0$	$A_n = 0$	$B_n = (-1)^{n+1}\left(\dfrac{2}{n}\right)$
(f)	$A_0 = \dfrac{1}{\pi}$	$A_1 = 0.5$ $A_n = 0 \quad$ for odd n of 3, 5, 7, . . . $A_n = \dfrac{1}{(n-1)\pi}\sin\dfrac{(n-1)\pi}{2} + \dfrac{1}{(n+1)\pi}\sin\dfrac{(n+1)\pi}{2} \quad$ for even n	$B_n = 0$
(g)	$A_0 = 0$	$A_n = \begin{cases} (-1)^{(n-1)/2}\left(\dfrac{4}{n\pi}\right) & \text{for odd } n \\ 0 & \text{for even } n \end{cases}$	$B_n = \begin{cases} (-1)^{(n-1)/2}\left(\dfrac{8}{n^2\pi^2}\right) & \text{for odd } n \\ 0 & \text{for even } n \end{cases}$

After simplification, we have

$$A_0 = \frac{1}{\pi}$$

$$A_n = \frac{1}{(n-1)\pi} \sin \frac{(n-1)\pi}{2} + \frac{1}{(n+1)\pi} \sin \frac{(n+1)\pi}{2} \qquad (4.15)$$

$$B_n = 0$$

B_n's are zero, as function $F(t)$ is an even function. With these coefficients, the given periodic function can now be expressed as below:

$$F(t) = \frac{1}{\pi} + \frac{1}{2} \cos \omega_0 t + \frac{2}{3\pi} \cos 2\omega_0 t - \frac{2}{15\pi} \cos 4\omega_0 t$$

$$+ \frac{2}{25\pi} \cos 6\omega_0 t \cdots \qquad (4.16)$$

The numerical values of A_n for n equal to 0 to 9 are shown in the second column of Table 4.2. By means of Eqs. (4.11) and (4.12), the magnitude and phase are

$$C_0 = A_0 + \frac{1}{\pi}$$

$$C_n = |A_n| \qquad (4.17)$$

$$\phi_n = 0$$

4.1.4 COMPUTATION OF FOURIER COEFFICIENTS

The values of Fourier coefficients of a periodic function $F(t)$, as determined by Eqs. (4.5) through (4.8) or by Eqs. (4.11) and (4.12), can be obtained by MIMIC programming. A MIMIC program for the periodic

Table 4.2 Comparison of the values of Fourier coefficients

| Coeff. | Analytical results | MIMIC results | |
		Using cosine function	Using table look-up
A_0	$1/\pi = 0.318310$	0.318310	0.3175011
A_1	0.5	0.500000	0.498729
A_2	$2/(3\pi) = 0.212207$	0.212207	0.211663
A_3	0	-0.0000000087	-0.0000006
A_4	$-2/(15\pi) = -0.0424413$	-0.0424413	-0.0423339
A_5	0	0.000000017	0.0000005
A_6	$2/(35\pi) = 0.0181891$	0.0181891	0.0181473
A_7	0	-0.0000000001	-0.0000007
A_8	$-2/(63\pi) = -0.0101051$	-0.0101051	-0.0100821
A_9	0	0.0000000002	-0.0000004

```
*****FOURIER SERIES EXPANSION OF A PERIODIC FUNCTION
*
                        CON(2PI)
                        PAR(N)
*
            P        = 1.
            DT       = P/40.
            X        = 2PI*T/P
            F        = COS(X)
*
            NEONE    = FSW(N-1.,TRUE,TRUE,FALSE)
   NEONE    AO       = INT(F,0.)*2./P
            A        = INT(F*COS(N*X),0.)*4./P
                        FIN(T,P/4.)
   NEONE             HDR(T,AO)
                     HDR(T,A)
                     HDR
   NEONE             OUT(T,AO)
                     OUT(T,A)
                     OUT
                     END
6.28318531
1.
2.
3.
4.
5.
6.
7.
8.
9.
```

Fig. 4.2   MIMIC program for the Fourier expansion of a periodic function.

function in Fig. 4.1f is shown in Fig. 4.2, where N is a parameter for N from 1 to 9.   The case where N is equal to 0 is computed during the run when N is 1; this is achieved by logical control variable NEONE (N not Equal to ONE) placed at the appropriate statements.   Note that the value of P is inserted in the program by using an arithmetic statement, while constant 2π is denoted by a CON statement.   This choice is due to the rule that a fixed-point decimal number not over four digits (if there is a sign and a decimal point) can be inserted by an arithmetic statement, while a similar number up to 10 digits (if there is a sign and a decimal point) can be inserted by a CON statement.   The result is shown in the third column of Table 4.2.   Compare these values with those in the second column; they are almost identical.

The analytical approach to the evaluation of Fourier coefficients is rather limited because periodic functions which arise from practical applications are arbitrary and not amenable to analytical treatment.   However, digital analog simulation can be employed to compute readily the values of Fourier coefficients of these arbitrary periodic functions.

As an illustration, assume that the periodic function of the above example is arbitrary. Take one period of this function and convert it into a table as shown in Table 4.3, where the argument is expressed in degrees. The use of one half-period of the function is sufficient because of the symmetry existing in the function. The MIMIC program using this table is shown in Fig. 4.3. This program is almost identical to that

```
*****FOURIER EXPANSION OF AN ARBITRARY PERIODIC FUNCTION
*
                        CON(2PI,DEGPR)
            HALCOS =    CFN(10.)
                        PAR(N)
            P      =    1.
            DT     =    P/40.
            X      =    2PI*T*DEGPR/P
            F      =    FUN(HALCOS,X)
  *
            NEONE  =    FSW(N-1.,TRUE,TRUE,FALSE)
  NEONE     AO     =    INT(F,0.)*2./P
            A      =    INT(F*COS(N*X),0.)*4./P
                        FIN(T,P/4.)
  NEONE                 HDR(T,AO)
                        HDR(T,A)
                        HDR
  NEONE                 OUT(T,AO)
                        OUT(T,A)
                        OUT
                        END
  6.28318531   57.295779513
  0.0          1.0
  10.          0.98481
  20.          0.93969
  30.          0.86603
  40.          0.76604
  50.          0.64279
  60.          0.50000
  70.          0.34202
  80.          0.17365
  90.          0.0
  1.
  2.
  3.
  4.
  5.
  6.
  7.
  8.
  9.
```

Fig. 4.3 MIMIC program for the Fourier expansion of an arbitrary periodic function.

```
*****APPROXIMATION OF A FUNCTION BY FOURIER SERIES
*
                        CON(2PI)
                        CON(A0,A1,A2,A3,A4)
                        CON(A5,A6)
*
            DT      = 0.01
            P       = 1.
            X       = 2PI*T/P
*
            F1      = A0+A1*COS(1.*X)
            F2      = F1+A2*COS(2.*X)
            F3      = F2+A3*COS(3.*X)
            F4      = F3+A4*COS(4.*X)
            F5      = F4+A5*COS(5.*X)
            F6      = F5+A6*COS(6.*X)
*
            L1      = FSW(X-0.25*2PI,TRUE,FALSE,FALSE)
            L2      = FSW(X-0.75*2PI,FALSE,FALSE,TRUE)
            L3      = IOR(L1,L2)
            L4      = AND(NOT(L1),NOT(L2))
*
   L3       ERROR1 = F1-COS(X)
   L3       ERROR2 = F2-COS(X)
   L3       ERROR4 = F4-COS(X)
   L3       ERROR6 = F6-COS(X)
*
   L4       ERROR1 = F1
   L4       ERROR2 = F2
   L4       ERROR4 = F4
   L4       ERROR6 = F6
*
                        FIN(T,P)
                        HDR(T,F1,F2,F4,F6)
                        HDR(,ERROR1,ERROR2,ERROR4,ERROR6)
                        HDR
                        OUT(T,F1,F2,F4,F6)
                        OUT(,ERROR1,ERROR2,ERROR4,ERROR6)
                        OUT
                        PLO(T,F1,F2)
                        PLO(T,F4,F6)
                        PLO(T,ERROR1,ERROR2,ERROR4)
                        PLO(T,ERROR6)
                        END
6.28318531
0.318310        0.5             0.212207        0.0             -0.0424413
0.0             0.0181891
```

Fig. 4.4 MIMIC program for the approximation of a function by a Fourier series.

in Fig. 4.2, except that a pair of CFN and FUN statements now replaces
the statement which analytically defines function F.   Constant DEGPR,
57.2958° rad, is inserted by the CON statement.   The result, which is
shown in the fourth column of Table 4.2, is accurate to at least three
digits; this accuracy is limited by the accuracy of the values in Table 4.3.

Table 4.3   Cosine function

X, deg	COS(X)
0	1.00000
10	0.98481
20	0.93969
30	0.86603
40	0.76604
50	0.64279
60	0.50000
70	0.34202
80	0.17365
90	0.00000

Figure 4.4 shows a program to compute function F itself by using a limited number of terms in Eq. (4.16).   The values of constants A are those in the second column of Table 4.2.   Functions $F(t)$ with two and three terms are shown in Fig. 4.5; and the errors of $F(t)$ with two, three, and four terms, in Fig. 4.6.   The largest errors occur at the discontinuities

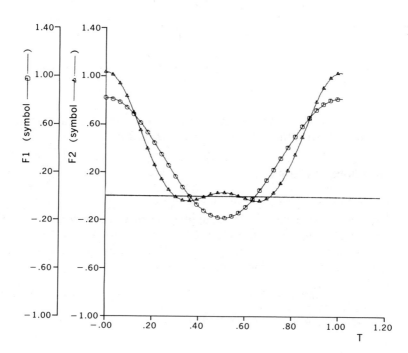

Fig. 4.5   Plot of function $F(t)$ with two and three terms of Fourier series expansion.

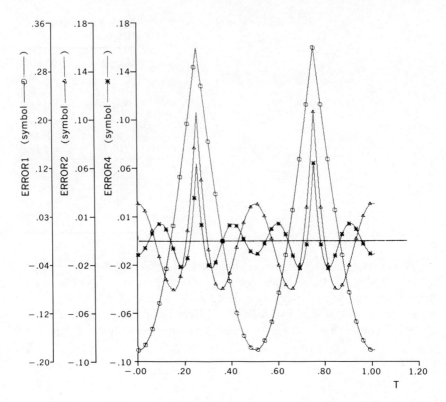

Fig. 4.6 Plot of errors of $F(t)$ with two, three, and four terms of Fourier series expansion.

of $F(t)$. Note that this example gives a reasonably accurate representation of $F(t)$ with only three terms (function F2).

4.2 FOURIER INTEGRAL

4.2.1 EXPANSION OF A NONPERIODIC FUNCTION

Expansion of Fourier series is applicable to periodic functions, and the resulting spectra are discrete. Certain nonperiodic functions may be expanded by the Fourier integral, and the resulting spectra are continuous.

If function $F(t)$ meets the condition

$$\int_{-\infty}^{\infty} |F(t)|\, dt < \infty \tag{4.18}$$

then the Fourier integral of function $F(t)$ is

$$G(j\omega) = \int_{-\infty}^{\infty} F(t)e^{-j\omega t}\, dt \tag{4.19}$$

which is also called the Fourier transform of function $F(t)$. And the Fourier inverse transform of $G(j\omega)$ is

$$F(t) = \frac{1}{2\pi} \int_{-\infty}^{\infty} G(j\omega)e^{j\omega t}\, dt \tag{4.20}$$

Expressions (4.19) and (4.20) constitute a pair of mutually inverse integral relations referred to as a Fourier pair.

Fourier integral (4.19) can also be written as

$$G(j\omega) = A(\omega) + jB(\omega) \tag{4.21}$$

where functions $A(\omega)$ and $B(\omega)$ are

$$A(\omega) = \int_{-\infty}^{\infty} F(t)\cos \omega t\, dt \tag{4.22}$$

$$B(\omega) = -\int_{-\infty}^{\infty} F(t)\sin \omega t\, dt \tag{4.23}$$

and amplitude M and phase ϕ of $G(j\omega)$ are

$$M = |G(j\omega)| = \sqrt{A(\omega)^2 + B(\omega)^2} \tag{4.24}$$

$$\phi = \arctan\left(\frac{B(\omega)}{A(\omega)}\right) \tag{4.25}$$

The plots of amplitude M and phase ϕ versus frequency ω are the spectra of function $F(t)$; they are continuous.

4.2.2 AN EXAMPLE

Continuous spectra of an exponential pulse, a rectangular pulse, a triangular pulse, and a cosine are shown in Fig. 4.7. As an example, the Fourier integral of the exponential pulse is now evaluated. Consider the following exponential pulse:

$$F(t) = e^{-t} \qquad \text{for } t \geq 0 \tag{4.26}$$

By using expressions (4.22) and (4.23), we have

$$A(\omega) = \int_0^{\infty} e^{-t}\cos \omega t\, dt = \frac{1}{1 + \omega^2} \tag{4.27}$$

$$B(\omega) = -\int_0^{\infty} e^{-t}\sin \omega t\, dt = \frac{-\omega}{1 + \omega^2} \tag{4.28}$$

The values of A and B for frequencies between 0 and 40 are shown in the second and third columns of Table 4.4.

4.2.3 COMPUTATION OF THE FOURIER INTEGRAL

The Fourier integral of the above exponential pulse can be computed from Eqs. (4.22) through (4.25) by MIMIC programming. Such a MIMIC program is shown in Fig. 4.8, where frequency ω is programmed as a

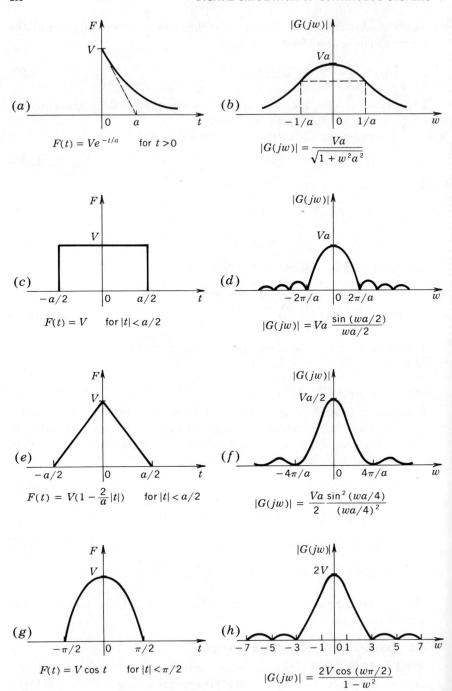

(a)

$F(t) = Ve^{-t/a}$ 　　for $t > 0$

(b)

$|G(jw)| = \dfrac{Va}{\sqrt{1 + w^2 a^2}}$

(c)

$F(t) = V$ 　　for $|t| < a/2$

(d)

$|G(jw)| = Va\,\dfrac{\sin\,(wa/2)}{wa/2}$

(e)

$F(t) = V(1 - \dfrac{2}{a}|t|)$ 　　for $|t| < a/2$

(f)

$|G(jw)| = \dfrac{Va}{2}\dfrac{\sin^2\,(wa/4)}{(wa/4)^2}$

(g)

$F(t) = V\cos t$ 　　for $|t| < \pi/2$

(h)

$|G(jw)| = \dfrac{2V\cos\,(w\pi/2)}{1 - w^2}$

Fig. 4.7 Fourier transforms of several functions.

Table 4.4 Comparison of the values of a Fourier transform

| Frequency, ω | Analytic results | | MIMIC results | | | |
	A	B	A	B	M	Phase, deg
0	1.00000	0	1.00000	0	1.00000	0
0.25	0.941176	−0.235294	0.941177	−0.235294	0.970143	−14.0362
0.5	0.800000	−0.400000	0.800000	−0.400000	0.894427	−26.5650
1	0.500000	−0.500000	0.500000	−0.500000	0.707107	−45.0000
1.5	0.307692	−0.461528	0.307692	−0.461538	0.554700	−56.3100
2	0.200000	−0.400000	0.200000	−0.400000	0.447214	−63.4350
2.5	0.137931	−0.344828	0.137931	−0.344827	0.371390	−68.1985
3	0.100000	−0.300000	0.100000	−0.299999	0.316227	−71.5650
4	0.0588235	−0.235294	0.0588225	−0.235295	0.242536	−75.9640
6	0.0270270	−0.162162	0.0270276	−0.162162	0.164399	−80.5375
8	0.0153846	−0.0123077	0.0153835	−0.213077	0.124035	−82.8755
10	0.00990099	−0.0990099	0.00990073	−0.0990097	0.0995035	−84.2895
20	0.00249377	−0.0498753	0.00249369	−0.0498760	0.0499383	−87.1377
40	0.00062461	−0.0249844	0.000625294	−0.0249834	0.0249912	−88.5663

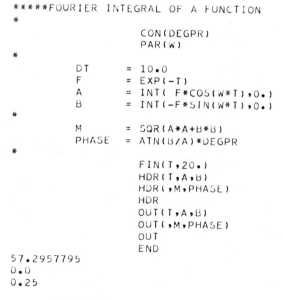

```
*****FOURIER  INTEGRAL  OF  A  FUNCTION
*
                        CON(DEGPR)
                        PAR(W)
*
             DT      =  10.0
             F       =  EXP(-T)
             A       =  INT( F*COS(W*T),0.)
             B       =  INT(-F*SIN(W*T),0.)
*
             M       =  SQR(A*A+B*B)
             PHASE   =  ATN(B/A)*DEGPR
*
                        FIN(T,20.)
                        HDR(T,A,B)
                        HDR( ,M,PHASE)
                        HDR
                        OUT(T,A,B)
                        OUT( ,M,PHASE)
                        OUT
                        END
57.2957795
0.0
0.25
```

Fig. 4.8 MIMIC program for computing the Fourier integral of a function.

parameter. The integration is terminated at T equal to 20, as e^{-20} is about 0.25×10^{-8}. The values of A, B, M, and ϕ are shown in the fourth through seventh columns of Table 4.4. In comparing the analytical and computed results in Table 4.4, the differences are indeed very small, as a sufficiently large T has been chosen.

4.3 CORRELATION FUNCTIONS

4.3.1 AUTOCORRELATION FUNCTION

The autocorrelation function of a random process $F(t)$ is defined as

$$R(\tau) = \lim_{P \to \infty} \frac{1}{2P} \int_{-P}^{P} F(t)F(t + \tau) \, dt \tag{4.29}$$

where argument τ is the time displacement. $R(\tau)$ is a real and even function. It has its maximum value at the origin, and approaches zero as the argument approaches infinity if $F(t)$ contains no average value and no periodical elements. It is continuous if it is continuous at τ equal to zero.

If $F(t)$ is a periodic function, it can be shown that the mean value of $F(t)F(t + \tau)$ taken over an infinite time interval as a limit can be replaced by that over one period. As an example, let $F(t)$ be the following periodic function:

$$F(t) = A \sin \omega t \tag{4.30}$$

Then, by using Eq. (4.29) and taking the mean value over one period, the autocorrelation function is

$$R(\tau) = \frac{\omega A^2}{2\pi} \int_0^{2\pi/\omega} \sin \omega t \sin \omega(t + \tau) \, dt$$

or

$$R(\tau) = \frac{A^2}{2} \cos \omega \tau \tag{4.31}$$

which is also periodic. In general, $R(\tau)$ is periodic if $F(t)$ is a periodic time function.

4.3.2 POWER SPECTRAL DENSITY

The Fourier transform of an autocorrelation function of a random process is

$$G(\omega) = \int_{-\infty}^{\infty} R(\tau)e^{-j\omega t} \, dt \tag{4.32}$$

and the inverse transform of $G(\omega)$ is

$$R(\tau) = \frac{1}{2\pi} \int_{-\infty}^{\infty} G(\omega)e^{j\omega t} \, d\tau \tag{4.33}$$

Equations (4.32) and (4.33) form a Fourier transform pair. $G(\omega)$ is called the *power spectral density*. The integral of $G(\omega)$ with respect to the angular frequency ω over the entire range of angular frequencies represents the mean-square value of function $F(t)$ and is related to $R(0)$, or

$$R(0) = \frac{1}{2\pi} \int_{-\infty}^{\infty} G(j\omega)\, d\omega \tag{4.34}$$

Thus, if $F(t)$ is a voltage or current for a unit-ohm load, the above integral gives the mean power taken by the load. Since $R(\tau)$ is a real and even function, its transform $G(\omega)$ is also a real and even function. Sometimes, it is preferred to express Eqs. (4.32) and (4.33) as the following cosine transforms:

$$R(\tau) = \frac{1}{2\pi} \int_{-\infty}^{\infty} G(\omega) \cos \omega\tau\, d\omega \tag{4.35}$$

$$G(\omega) = \int_{-\infty}^{\infty} R(\tau) \cos \omega\tau\, d\tau \tag{4.36}$$

In short, the autocorrelation function of a random process is related to its power spectral density by the above Fourier cosine transform pair.

4.3.3 COMPUTATION OF THE AUTOCORRELATION FUNCTION

Since the data represented by $F(t)$ are collected in a finite time interval, the integration of $F(t)$ over an infinite time duration as required by Eq. (4.29) or (4.35) is not practical. Instead of $F(t)$, a truncated $F(t)$, denoted by $FT(t)$, is used. $FT(t)$ is obtained by choosing a sufficiently long time duration of $2P$ from the observed data of $F(t)$, as the accuracy of the autocorrelation function depends on the duration. We then have

$$FT(t) = \begin{cases} F(t) & \text{for } 0 < t < 2P \\ 0 & \text{elsewhere} \end{cases} \tag{4.37}$$

Let RT be the approximated autocorrelation function. We have

$$RT(\tau) = \frac{1}{2P} \int_0^{2P} FT(t)FT(t + \tau)\, dt \tag{4.38}$$

To compute $RT(\tau)$ by MIMIC programming, $FT(t)$ is first converted into a table. Assume that there are 100 points and call the table DATA. The following CFN and FUN statements will produce functions $FT(t)$ and $FT(t + \tau)$:

```
         PAR(TAU)
DATA =   CFN(100.)
FT   =   FUN(DATA, T)
FTAU =   FUN(DATA, T+TAU)
```

```
*****COMPUTATION OF AN AUTOCORRELATION FUNCTION
*
                        CON(2PI)
                        PAR(TAU)
*
           DT       =  0.01
           E        =  10.0
           P        =  1.0
*
           F        =  E*SIN(2PI*T/P)
           FTAU     =  E*SIN(2PI*(T+TAU)/P)
           R        =  INT(F*FTAU,0.)/P
*
                        FIN(T,P)
                        HDR(T,F,FTAU,R)
                        HDR
                        OUT(T,F,FTAU,R)
                        FLO(T,F,FTAU,R)
                        END
6.28319
0.0
0.1
0.2
0.3
0.4
0.5
0.6
0.7
0.8
0.9
1.0
```

Fig. 4.9 MIMIC program for computing an autocorrelation function.

Table 4.5   The computed values of an autocorrelation function RT

τ	RT
0.0	0.500000
0.1	0.404508
0.2	0.154508
0.3	−0.154509
0.4	−0.404509
0.5	−0.500000
0.6	−0.404507
0.7	−0.154507
0.8	0.154510
0.9	0.404509
1.0	0.500000

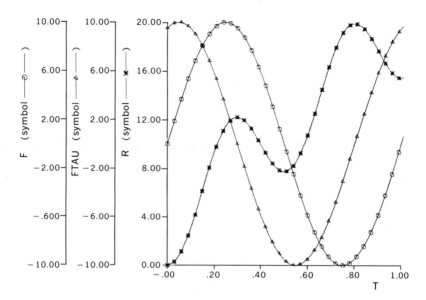

Fig. 4.10 Plot from the MIMIC program in Fig. 4.9 ($\tau = 0.2$).

And the autocorrelation function is

$$RT = INT(FT*FTAU, 0.)/2.*P$$
$$FIN(T, 2.*P)$$

An example of computing the autocorrelation function of the periodic function $F(t)$ of Eq. (4.30) is shown in the MIMIC program of Fig. 4.9. The value of the period is chosen to be 1. The time displacement τ is chosen as a parameter. The computed values of R are shown in Table 4.5; they agree well with the values from Eq. (4.31).

A plot of $F(t)$, $F(t + \tau)$, and R with τ equal to 0.2 is shown in Fig. 4.10. The correct value of R is located where t is equal to 1.

4.3.4 CROSSCORRELATION FUNCTION

The crosscorrelation function of two random processes $F1(t)$ and $F2(t)$ is defined as

$$R12(\tau) = \lim_{p \to \infty} \frac{1}{2P} \int_{-P}^{P} F1(t)F2(t + \tau) \, dt \qquad (4.39)$$

where argument τ is the time displacement. It may also be defined as

$$R21(\tau) = \lim_{p \to \infty} \frac{1}{2P} \int_{-P}^{P} F2(t)F1(t + \tau) \, dt \qquad (4.40)$$

Function $R12$ is related to function $R21$ as below:

$$R12(\tau) = R21(-\tau) \tag{4.41}$$

Unlike the autocorrelation function, the crosscorrelation function $R12$ or $R21$ is not necessarily even, and its value is not necessarily maximum at τ equal to zero. It is continuous if the autocorrelation function of $F1(t)$ or $F2(t)$ is continuous at τ equal to zero.

If $F1(t)$ and $F2(t)$ are both periodic and have the same fundamental frequency, the mean value of $F1(t)F2(t + \tau)$ taken over the infinite time interval as a limit can be replaced by that taken over one period.

```
*****COMPUTATION OF A CROSSCORRELATION FUNCTION
*
                      CON(2PI)
                      PAR(TAU)
          DT        = 0.01
          E         = 1.0
          P         = 1.0
*
  B1      W         = 1.0
  B2      W         = -1.0
          A1        = FSW(T,     0.,1.,1.)
          B1        = FSW(T-.5,A1,0.,,0.)
          A2        = FSW(T-.5,0.,1.,,1.)
          B2        = FSW(T-1.,A2,0.,,0.)
*
          F         = F*SIN(2PI*T/P)
          FTAU      = E*SIN(2PI*(T+TAU)/P)
          R21       = INT(W*FTAU,0.)/P
*
                      FIN(T,P)
                      HDR(T,F,FTAU,W,R21)
                      OUT(T,F,FTAU,W,R21)
                      PLO(T,F,FTAU,W,R21)
                      END
6.28319
0.0
0.1
0.2
0.3
0.4
0.5
0.6
0.7
0.8
0.9
1.0
```

Fig. 4.11 MIMIC program for computing a crosscorrelation function.

Table 4.6   The computed values of a crosscorrelation function $R21$

τ	$R21$
0.0	0.636619
0.1	0.515053
0.2	0.196739
0.3	−0.196721
0.4	−0.515019
0.5	−0.636619
0.6	−0.515052
0.7	−0.196737
0.8	0.196723
0.9	0.515020
1.0	0.636619

The Fourier transform of a crosscorrelation function is

$$G12(\omega) = \int_{-\infty}^{\infty} R12(\tau)e^{-j\omega\tau}\, d\tau \qquad (4.42)$$

where $G12$ is called the *cross-power spectral density*. The inverse transform of $G12$ is

$$R12(\tau) = \frac{1}{2\pi} \int_{-\infty}^{\infty} G12(\omega)e^{j\omega\tau}\, d\omega \qquad (4.43)$$

Equations (4.42) and (4.43) form a Fourier transform pair.

As an example, let us find the crosscorrelation function of the periodic sinusoidal function $F(t)$ of Eq. (4.30) and a periodic square-wave function with the same period and amplitude. A MIMIC program for computing this crosscorrelation function $R21$ is shown in Fig. 4.11. Since the given functions are periodic, the average is computed for one period. The computed result is shown in Table 4.6.

4.4   ORDINARY DIFFERENTIAL EQUATIONS

Many mathematical models studied by engineers and physicists are represented by differential equations. A differential equation is an equation which contains derivatives of a dependent variable with respect to one or more independent variables. An ordinary differential equation contains only derivatives with respect to a single independent variable. A partial differential equation contains partial derivatives with respect to one or more independent variables.

Ordinary differential equations may be linear or nonlinear. An ordinary linear differential equation contains terms of the first degree in the dependent variable and its derivatives. A nonlinear ordinary differential equation may have terms of second or higher degree in the dependent variable and its derivatives; these terms can be products and powers of the dependent variable and its derivatives as well as transcendental functions of the dependent variable.

The coefficients of the terms of a linear ordinary differential equation may all be constants or functions of the independent variable. Ordinary linear differential equations with constant coefficients are not to be further discussed in this chapter, as their solutions can be readily obtained analytically or, as will be amply illustrated, by MIMIC programming.

4.4.1 LINEAR ORDINARY DIFFERENTIAL EQUATIONS

Engineering and physical systems give rise to mathematical models that may be represented by ordinary linear differential equations. The most general form of this type of equation is

$$a_n(t)\frac{d^n y}{dt^n} + \cdots + a_1(t)\frac{dy}{dt} + a_0(t) = f(t) \tag{4.44}$$

This is a linear ordinary differential equation because the equation, except the forcing function $f(t)$, is a sum of terms each of which is a linear function of the dependent variable or its derivative, and the coefficients of each term are functions only of the independent variable. Some of the most common differential equations of this type are now introduced.

```
*****SOLVING MATHIEU'S EQUATION
*
              PAR(A)
*
      Q        = 0.5*A
      W        = 2.0
      2DY      = -(A-2.*Q*COS(W*T))*Y
      1DY      = INT(2DY,0.)
      Y        = INT(1DY,1.)
*
              FIN(T,100.)
              HDR(T,Y,1DY)
              OUT(T,Y,1DY)
              PLO(T,Y)
              END
0.5
1.0
3.5
4.0
```

Fig. 4.12 MIMIC program for solving Mathieu's equation.

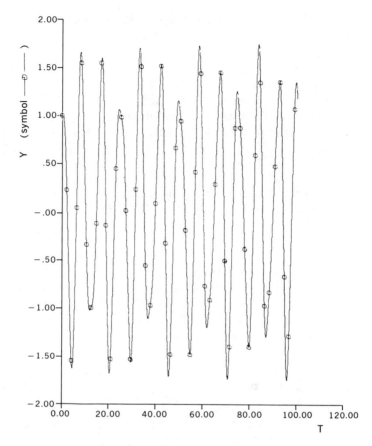

Fig. 4.13 Time response of a solution of Mathieu's equation ($a = 0.5$ and $q = a/2$).

4.4.1.1 Mathieu's equation The following second-order differential equation with a time-varying coefficient,

$$\frac{d^2y}{dt^2} + (a - 2q \cos \omega t)y = 0 \tag{4.45}$$

is known as Mathieu's equation where a, q, and ω are constants. It describes a number of physical and engineering systems. As an example, consider first a simple, frictionless pendulum with a weightless rod of length L. If A, the angle between the rod and the vertical, is small, the angular motion of the pendulum is described by the following linearized equation:

$$\ddot{A} = \frac{g}{L} A = 0 \tag{4.46}$$

where g is the gravitational constant.   If the support to which one end of the rod is tied moves vertically in a sinusoidal motion, we have

$$y = Y \cos \omega t$$

where y = vertical motion of support
   Y = amplitude of vertical motion
   ω = angular rate of vertical motion
This vertical motion causes a vertical acceleration of

$$\frac{d^2y}{dt^2} = -\omega^2 Y \cos \omega t$$

which accelerates the entire pendulum and modulates the gravitational force on the pendulum.   Equation (4.46) thus becomes

$$\frac{d^2A}{dt^2} + \left(\frac{g}{L} - \frac{\omega^2 Y}{L} \cos \omega t \right) A = 0 \tag{4.47}$$

which is Mathieu's equation.

A MIMIC program solving Eq. (4.45) is shown in Fig. 4.12, where a is taken as the parameter, q is equal to $0.5a$, and ω is equal to 2.   The chosen values of a are 0.5, 1.0, 3.5, and 4.0.   The computer results are shown in Figs. 4.13 through 4.18.   The solution with a equal to 0.5 is

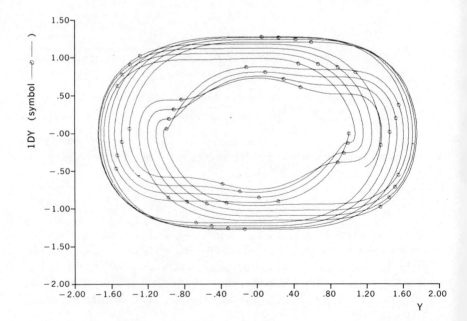

Fig. 4.14   Phase-plane plot of a solution of Mathieu's equation ($a = 0.5$ and $q = a/2$).

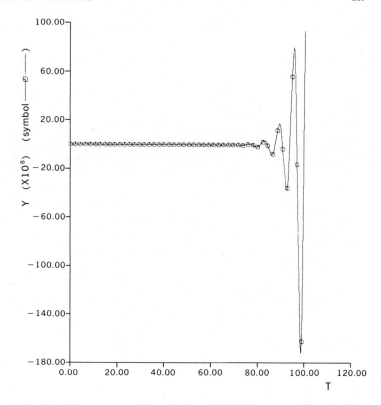

Fig. 4.15 Time response of a solution of Mathieu's equation ($a = 1.0$ and $q = a/2$).

shown in Fig. 4.13, and the phase-plane trajectory in Fig. 4.14; the solution is stable and nonperiodic. The solution with a equal to 1 is shown in Fig. 4.15, and the phase-plane trajectory in Fig. 4.16; the solution is unstable. The solution with a equal to 3.5 is shown in Fig. 4.17, and the phase-plane trajectory in Fig. 4.18; the solution is stable and periodic. The solution with a equal to 4, similar to that in Fig. 4.15, is unstable. These results agree with those from the analytical study, which shows that, in a chart of a versus q, there are stable and unstable regions.

4.4.1.2 Legendre's equation The differential equation

$$(1 - x^2) \frac{d^2y}{dx^2} - 2x \frac{dy}{dx} + n(n + 1)y = 0 \qquad (4.48)$$

is known as Legendre's differential equation of degree n. It arises, for example, in the process of obtaining solutions of Laplace's equation in spherical coordinates.   We shall consider only the important special case where n is a positive integer or zero.

The general solution of this equation is

$$y = a_0 \left[1 - \frac{n(n+1)}{2!} x^2 + \frac{n(n-2)(n+1)(n+3)}{4!} x^4 \cdots \right]$$
$$+ a_1 \left[x - \frac{(n-1)(n+2)}{3!} x^3 \right.$$
$$\left. + \frac{(n-1)(n-3)(n+2)(n+4)}{5!} x^5 \cdots \right] \quad (4.49)$$

where a_0 and a_1 are arbitrary constants.   If n is an even integer, the first series in Eq. (4.49) reduces to a polynomial; if n is an odd integer, the second series reduces to a polynomial.   Now if the value of a_0 or a_1, whichever the case may be, is so chosen that the polynomial becomes 1 when x

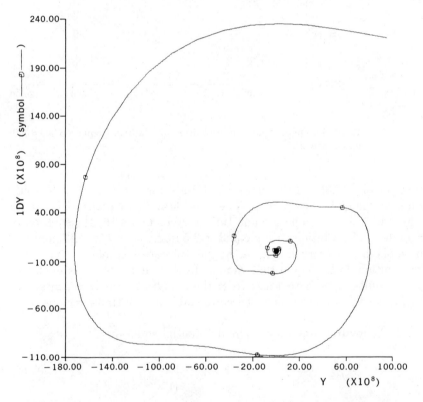

Fig. 4.16 Phase-plane plot of a solution of Mathieu's equation ($a = 1.0$ and $q = a/2$).

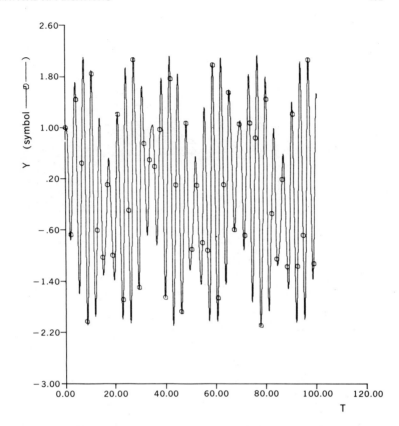

Fig. 4.17 Time response of a solution of Mathieu's equation ($a = 3.5$ and $q = a/2$).

is 1, we then obtain the following set of polynomials $P_i(x)$:

$$P_0(x) = 1$$
$$P_1(x) = x$$
$$P_2(x) = \frac{3x^2 - 1}{2}$$
$$P_3(x) = \frac{5x^3 - 3x}{2}$$
$$P_4(x) = \frac{35x^4 - 30x^2 + 3}{8} \qquad (4.50)$$
$$P_5(x) = \frac{63x^5 - 70x^3 + 15x}{8}$$
$$P_6(x) = \frac{231x^6 - 315x^4 + 105x^2 - 5}{16}$$

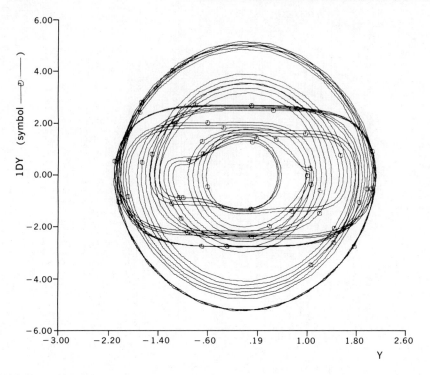

Fig. 4.18 Phase-plane plot of a solution of Mathieu's equation ($a = 3.5$ and $q = a/2$).

The initial conditions that make P_i equal to 1 when x is 1 can be computed and are shown in Table 4.7. The general polynomial $P_n(x)$ is given by the series

$$P_n(x) = \sum_{i=0}^{N} (-1)^i \frac{(2n - i)!}{2^n i!(n - i)!(n - 2i)!} x^{n-2i} \tag{4.51}$$

where $N = n/2$ for n even and $N = (n - 1)/2$ for n odd. These polynomials are called *Legendre polynomials*. Each satisfies a Legendre differential equation for which n has the value indicated by the subscript.

A MIMIC program for solving Legendre's equation (4.48) is shown in Fig. 4.19. Since the factor $(1 - x^2)$ becomes 0 when x reaches 1, derivative 2DY may become infinite (though the computer does not permit "infinity" to occur). Therefore, the computation is terminated at X slightly less than 1. DT is chosen as the small time interval before X reaches 1. Figure 4.20 shows the computed results where polynomials P_i for i equal to 0 to 6 are plotted.

The division by $(1 - x^2)$ produces a value of infinity when x is equal to 1. Hausner [21] has shown that this division can be avoided if parametric representations are employed for all the variables in the equation. Let us define

$$y' = \frac{dy}{dx} \quad \text{and} \quad \frac{dy'}{dx} = \frac{d^2y}{dx^2}$$

Then we have, from Eq. (4.48),

$$\frac{dy'}{dx} = \frac{2xy' - n(n+1)y}{1 - x^2}$$

Let t be the parameter. The above equation can be converted into the following three differential equations which have t as the independent variable:

$$\frac{dy'}{dt} = 2xy' - n(n+1)y$$
$$\frac{dy}{dt} = y'(1 - x^2) \tag{4.52}$$
$$\frac{dx}{dt} = 1 - x^2$$

No special precaution is now required when x approaches 1.

```
******LEGENDRE'S DIFFERENTIAL EQUATION
*
               PAR(N,YO,1DYO)
*
        X       =  T
        DT      =  .02
        2DY     =  (2.*X*1DY-N*(N+1.)*Y)/(1.-X*X)
        1DY     =  INT(2DY,1DYO)
        Y       =  INT(1DY,YO)
*
               FIN(X,1.-DT)
               HDR(X,Y)
               HDR
               OUT(X,Y)
               PLO(X,Y)
               END
   0.        1.            0
   1.        0.            1.
   2.       -.5            0
   3.        0            -1.5
   4.        .375          0
   5.        0             1.875
   6.       -.3125         0
```

Fig. 4.19 MIMIC program for solving Legendre's equation.

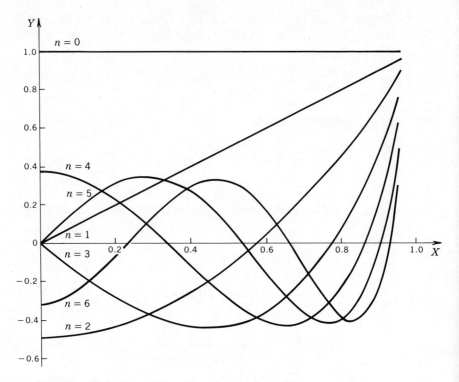

Fig. 4.20 Plot of solutions of Legendre equation $(n = 0, 1, \ldots, 6)$.

```
*****LEGENDRE'S DIFFERENTIAL EQUATION--PARAMETRIC FORM
*
                 PAR(N,Y0,YP0)
*
        DT      = .02
        YP      = INT(2.*X*YP-N*(N+1.)*Y,YP0)
        Y       = INT(YP*(1.-X*X),Y0)
        X       = INT((1.-X*X),0.)
                 FIN(X,.99)
                 HDR(T,X,Y)
                 OUT(T,X,Y)
                 PLO(X,Y)
                 END
0.          1.              0
1.          0.              1.
2.          -.5             0
3.          0               -1.5
4.          .375            0
5.          0               1.875
6.          -.3125          0
```

Fig. 4.21 MIMIC program for solving Legendre's equation in parametric form.

Table 4.7   Initial conditions for Legendre's equation

n	$y(0)$	$\dot{y}(0)$
0	1	0
1	0	1
2	$\frac{1}{2}$	0
3	0	$-\frac{3}{2}$
4	$\frac{3}{8}$	0
5	0	$1\frac{5}{8}$
6	$-\frac{5}{16}$	0

A MIMIC program for solving the Legendre equation in this parametric form is shown in Fig. 4.21. Note that symbols x, y, dx/dt, dy/dt, y', and dy'/dt of Eq. (4.52) are represented in the program by X, Y, 1DX, 1DY, YP, and 1DYP, respectively. Initial conditions $y(0)$ and $\dot{y}(0)$ are those in Table 4.7; they are represented by Y0 and YP0, respectively. Initial condition $x(0)$ is zero.

4.4.1.3   Bessel's equation   The equation

$$t^2 \frac{d^2y}{dt^2} + t \frac{dy}{dt} + (t^2 - n^2)y = 0 \qquad (4.53)$$

is a classical differential equation with variable coefficients. The general solution of the equation is

$$y = C_1 J_n(x) + C_2 Y_n(x) \qquad (4.54)$$

where C_1 and C_2 are arbitrary constants. $J_n(x)$ and $Y_n(x)$ are the nth-order Bessel functions of the first and second kind, respectively. Tables of $J_n(x)$ and $Y_n(x)$ are available. When n is 0 or a positive integer, $J_n(x)$ can be computed from the following infinite series:

$$J_n(x) = \sum_{i=0}^{\infty} \frac{(-1)^i}{i!(n+i)!} \left(\frac{x}{2}\right)^{n+2i} \qquad (4.55)$$

For x equal to 0, we then have the following initial values of J_n:

$$\begin{aligned} J_0(0) &= 1 \\ J_n(0) &= 0 \qquad \text{for } n = 1, 2, 3, \ldots \end{aligned} \qquad (4.56)$$

Bessel functions of the first kind have been applied to spectrum analysis of a frequency-modulated (FM) wave F. Let F be represented as

$$F = E \cos (\omega_c t + m_f \sin \omega_m t) \qquad (4.57)$$

which becomes, after expansion,

$$F = E \cos \omega_c \cos (m_f \sin \omega_m t) - \sin \omega_c t \sin (m_f \sin \omega_m t)$$

By means of the following relations between Bessel functions and trigonometric functions,

$$\cos (m_f \sin \omega_m t) = J_0(m_f) + 2J_2(m_f) \cos 2\omega_m t + 2J_4(m_f)$$
$$\cos 4\omega_m t + \cdots$$
$$\sin (m_f \sin \omega_m t) = 2J_1(m_f) \sin \omega_m t + 2J_3(m_f)$$
$$\sin 3\omega_m t + \cdots$$
$$(4.58)$$

We have, after substituting Eqs. (4.58) into (4.57),

$$
\begin{aligned}
F = E\{ & J_0(m_f) \cos \omega_c t \\
& - J_1(m_f)[\cos (\omega_c + \omega_m)t - \cos (\omega_c - \omega_m)t] \\
& + J_2(m_f)[\cos (\omega_c + 2\omega_m)t + \cos (\omega_c - 2\omega_m)t] \\
& - J_m(m_f)[\cos (\omega_c + 3\omega_m)t - \cos (\omega_c - 3\omega_m)t] \\
& + \cdots \}
\end{aligned}
\qquad (4.59)
$$

Equation (4.59) shows that Bessel functions of the first kind are related to the magnitudes of each frequency component of an FM spectrum.

4.4.1.4 Derivatives of Bessel functions If relation (4.55) is manipulated algebraically and differentiated, we obtain the following two relations:

$$x\dot{J}_n(x) = nJ_n(x) - xJ_{n+1}(x) \qquad (4.60)$$
$$x\dot{J}_n(x) = xJ_{n-1}(x) - nJ_n(x) \qquad (4.61)$$

When Eqs. (4.60) and (4.61) are combined, we have

$$\dot{J}_n(x) = \tfrac{1}{2}[J_{n-1}(x) - J_{n+1}(x)] \qquad (4.62)$$

Equations (4.60) through (4.62) are alternative expressions for the derivative of a Bessel function of the first kind with respect to the argument. By combining Eqs. (4.60) and (4.61), we have

$$2nJ_n(x) = x[J_{n-1}(x) + J_{n+1}(x)] \qquad (4.63)$$

which is a recurrence relation. By using Eqs. (4.60) and (4.62) together with initial values of (4.56), we obtain the following initial values of $\dot{J}_n$:

$$\dot{J}_0(0) = 0$$
$$\dot{J}_1(0) = 0.5 \qquad (4.64)$$
$$\dot{J}_n(0) = 0 \qquad \text{for } n = 2, 3, 4, \ldots$$

4.4.1.5 Generation of Bessel functions Bessel functions of the first kind can be generated by solving the Bessel equation (4.53) with initial conditions (4.56) and (4.64). The initial conditions for the zeroth and first orders are

$$J_0(0) = 1 \quad \text{and} \quad \dot{J}_0(0) = 0$$
$$J_1(0) = 0 \quad \text{and} \quad \dot{J}_1(0) = 0.5 \tag{4.65}$$

For the higher orders, the initial conditions are all zero. Thus, by solving Eq. (4.53), zeroth- and first-order Bessel functions of the first kind can be obtained, but one has to find a way to start the computation for higher orders. A MIMIC program for obtaining these two Bessel functions is shown in Fig. 4.22.

However, Bessel functions of the first kind can be obtained by solving the following system of differential equations:

$$\dot{J}_0(t) = -J_1(t)$$

$$\dot{J}_1(t) = J_0(t) - \frac{1}{t} J_1(t)$$

$$\dot{J}_2(t) = J_1(t) - \frac{2}{t} J_2(t)$$

$$\dot{J}_3(t) = J_2(t) - \frac{3}{t} J_3(t) \tag{4.66}$$

$$\dot{J}_4(t) = J_3(t) - \frac{4}{t} J_4(t)$$

$$\cdot \quad \cdot \quad \cdot \quad \cdot \quad \cdot \quad \cdot \quad \cdot \quad \cdot \quad \cdot \quad \cdot \quad \cdot$$

which are obtained from Eq. (4.61) by substituting n equal to 0, 1, 2, etc.

A MIMIC program which computes Eqs. (4.66) for n equal to 0 through 4 is shown in Fig. 4.23 with the initial values (4.56). The problem of dividing zero by zero in Eqs. (4.66) at t equal to 0 can be handled

```
*****SOLUTION OF BESSEL DIFFERENTIAL EQUATION
*
                              PAR(N,Y0,1DY0)
                   DT       = 0.02
*
                   2DY      = -(T*1DY+(T*T-N*N)*Y)/(T*T)
                   1DY      = INT(2DY,1DY0)
                   Y        = INT(1DY,Y0)
*
                              FIN(T,20.)
                              HDR(TIME,Y)
                              HDR
                              OUT(T,Y)
                              PLO(T,Y)
                              END
          0.              1.0              0.0
          1.0             0.0              0.5
```

Fig. 4.22 MIMIC program for solving the Bessel equation.

```
******GENERATION  OF  BESSEL'S  FUNCTION  OF  THE  FIRST  KIND
*
            J0      =  INT(-J1,1.0)
            J1      =  INT(J0-K0,0.)
            J2      =  INT(J1-K1,0.)
            J3      =  INT(J2-K2,0.)
            J4      =  INT(J3-K3,0.)
*
            K0      =  J1/T
            K1      =  2.*J2/T
            K2      =  3.*J3/T
            K3      =  4.*J4/T
*
                    FIN(T,16.)
                    HDR(TIME,J0,J1,J2,J3,J4)
                    HDR
                    OUT(T,J0,J1,J2,J3,J4)
                    PLO(T,J0,J1,J2,J3,J4,)
                    END
```

Fig. 4.23 MIMIC program for generating Bessel functions of the first kind
of the orders 0 through 4.

by logical control variable and FSW statements. Since the IBM 7094
computer is built to yield a result of zero when division of a number by
zero occurs, this hardware feature is made use of to give a slightly simpler
program of Fig. 4.23.   A plot of the computed result from this program
is shown in Fig. 4.24.

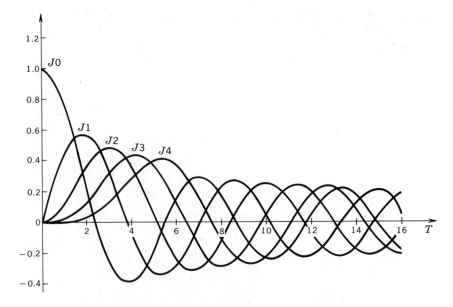

Fig. 4.24 Plot of Bessel functions of the first kind ($n = 0, 1, 2, 3, 4$).

4.4.2 NONLINEAR ORDINARY DIFFERENTIAL EQUATIONS

Nonlinear differential equations arise in more exact scientific and engineering analyses. More often than not, attempts are made to justify linear approximations (though plausible in many occasions) because of severe difficulty in obtaining solutions of nonlinear differential equations. In fact, there exists no general theoretical background for solution of nonlinear differential equations. The use of digital analog simulation offers an effective means of obtaining numerical solutions, usually in a plot of the dependent variable vs. the independent variable.

Instead of seeking a solution in terms of the independent variable, another approach applicable to a single second-order nonlinear differential equation is the so-called *phase-plane* analysis. It is a graphic method whereby a trajectory or a path is plotted on a rectangular coordinate with the abscissa and ordinate representing, respectively, the dependent variable and its first derivative. Phase-plane analysis is applicable in general to systems that are not driven by an external force. Thus, the phase plane is used to study the transient behavior of a system subject to initial conditions but otherwise unexcited.

Many simple examples of nonlinear equations of practical interest describe oscillations; these equations are usually second-order equations. Several examples now follow to show transient responses and phase-plane trajectories.

4.4.2.1 A simple pendulum The differential equation which describes the large motion of a simple, frictionless pendulum with a weightless rod of length L is

$$\ddot{A} + \frac{g}{L} \sin A = 0 \tag{4.67}$$

where A is the angle between the rod and the vertical and g is the gravitational constant. For a given pendulum, its angular motion depends on the initial conditions A_0 and $\dot{A}_0$. If initial angular rate $\dot{A}_0$ is nonzero and/or initial angle A_0 is large, the pendulum swings back and forth nonsinusoidally. With a sufficiently large initial angular rate $\dot{A}_0$, the pendulum can be caused to rotate continuously. A transitional case of neither oscillation nor rotation is shown in Fig. 4.25. A MIMIC program for solving nonlinear equation (4.67) is shown in Fig. 4.26, where A is expressed in degrees and $\dot{A}$ in radians per second. Constant DPG is the conversion factor of $57.2957795°/\text{rad}$.

The relation between the potential and kinetic energies of the system gives a better understanding of the motion of the pendulum. The potential energy of the pendulum at any angle is

$$\text{Potential energy} = mgL(1 - \cos A) \qquad (4.68)$$

where m is the mass of the pendulum bob, and the kinetic energy at any angle is

$$\text{Kinetic energy} = \tfrac{1}{2}mL^2\dot{A}^2 \qquad (4.69)$$

If angle A and angular rate $\dot{A}$ in Eqs. (4.68) and (4.69) are replaced, respectively, by initial angle A_0 and angular rate $\dot{A}_0$, we then have the expressions for the initial potential and kinetic energies. The sum of the potential and kinetic energies of the pendulum at any instant is equal to the sum of the initial potential and kinetic energies, or

$$mgL(1 - \cos A_0) + \tfrac{1}{2}mL^2\dot{A}_0^2 = mgL(1 - \cos A) + \tfrac{1}{2}mL^2\dot{A}^2 \qquad (4.70)$$

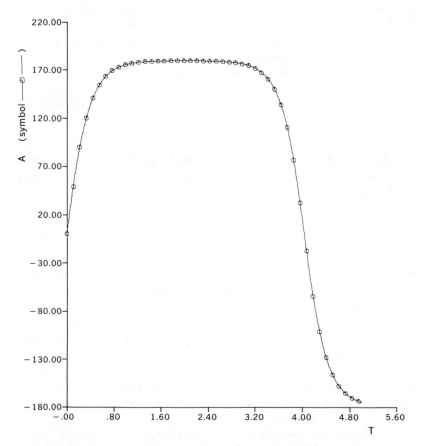

Fig. 4.25 Plot of the motion of a single pendulum (a transition case).

```
*****MOTION OF A SIMPLE PENDULUM
*
                        CON(DPR)
                        PAR(A0,1DA0)
*
            DT      =  0.01
            G       =  32.16
            L       =  2.01
*
*****A AND A0 ARE IN DEGREES*****
*****1DA, 2DA, AND 1DA0 ARE IN RADIANS PER SECOND
*
            2DA     = -(G/L)*SIN(A/DPR)
            1DA     = INT(2DA,1DA0)
            A       = INT(1DA*DPR,A0)
*
                        FIN(T,1.)
                        HDR(T,A,1DA,2DA)
                        PLO(T,A)
                        PLO(A,1DA)
                        END
57.29578
90.0            0.0
120.0           0.0
150.0           0.0
180.            0.0
90.0            5.656856
0.0             8.
0.0             10.
0.0             15.0
0.0             20.0
0.0             25.0
```

Fig. 4.26 MIMIC program for computing the motion of a simple pendulum.

which, after simplification, becomes

$$\dot{A}^2 = \frac{2g}{L}\cos A + C$$

$$C = \dot{A}_0{}^2 - \frac{2g}{L}\cos A_0$$

(4.71)

where C is a constant determined by initial conditions. For each set of initial conditions, Eqs. (4.71) give a trajectory on the phase plane. Since $\cos(+A)$ is equal to $\cos(-A)$ and $(+\dot{A})^2$ is equal to $(-\dot{A})^2$, the trajectory is symmetrical with respect to both the ordinate and the abscissa.

The condition which can cause the pendulum to rotate is derived as follows. The maximum potential energy of the pendulum, which occurs when the pendulum swings to its highest position, is

Maximum potential energy $= 2mgL$

If the sum of the initial potential and kinetic energies is larger than the above maximum potential energy, then the pendulum rotates continuously. Thus, the condition that the pendulum rotates continuously is

$$mgL(1 - \cos A_0) + \tfrac{1}{2}mL^2 \dot{A}_0^2 > 2mgL$$

or, after simplification,

$$\dot{A}_0^2 > \frac{2g}{L}(1 + \cos A_0) \tag{4.72}$$

or

$$\dot{A}_0^2 > \frac{4g}{L}\cos^2\left(\frac{A_0}{2}\right) \tag{4.73}$$

If the sum is less than the above maximum potential energy, then the pendulum oscillates continuously. The condition for continuous oscillations is

$$\dot{A}_0^2 < \frac{4g}{L}\cos^2\left(\frac{A_0}{2}\right) \tag{4.74}$$

and the transition condition is

$$\dot{A}_0^2 = \frac{4g}{L}\cos^2\left(\frac{A_0}{2}\right) \tag{4.75}$$

At this transition condition, there is neither oscillation nor rotation, and the pendulum swings to the highest position and stays there. The trajectory of Eq. (4.75) on the phase plane is the boundary between the region of continuous oscillation and the region of continuous rotation.

As an example, let g be 32.16 ft/sec² and L be 2.01 ft. The transition condition becomes

$$\dot{A}_0 = 8\cos\left(\frac{A_0}{2}\right) \tag{4.76}$$

The following are the pairs of values for the transition boundary on the phase plane:

$$
\begin{aligned}
A &= +180°, +120°, \quad +90°, \quad +60°, +0°, \quad -60°, \\
&\qquad\qquad\qquad\qquad -90°, -120°, -180° \\
\dot{A} &= \quad 0, \quad \pm4, \pm4\sqrt{2}, \pm4\sqrt{3}, \pm8, \pm4\sqrt{3}, \\
&\qquad\qquad\qquad\qquad \pm4\sqrt{2}, \quad \pm4, \quad 0
\end{aligned}
\tag{4.77}
$$

And Eqs. (4.71) for the phase-plane trajectories become

$$\dot{A}^2 = 32\cos A + C \tag{4.78}$$
$$C = \dot{A}_0^2 - 32\cos A_0$$

A MIMIC program for computing the trajectories on the phase plane by using Eqs. (4.78) is shown in Fig. 4.27, and the trajectories are shown in Fig. 4.28. In Fig. 4.28, the closed paths describe the motion of the pendulum at continuous oscillation about the lowest position. The open paths describe the motion of the pendulum at continuous rotation with the angular rate never changing the sign. The two paths which seemingly cross the axis actually do not cross the axis but stop there, as the pendulum comes to rest at a point of equilibrium which is the highest position of the pendulum motion. This kind of equilibrium is unstable and corresponds to the singular points in the phase plane of Fig. 4.28 at $\dot{A}$ equal to 0 and A equal to $\pm\pi$, $\pm3\pi$, etc. The previous plot of the pendulum motion in Fig. 4.25 is such a transition case. This plot is obtained by using MIMIC to compute the solution of Eq. (4.67) initially with A equal to 0° and $\dot{A}$ equal to $+8$ rad/sec. As shown in Fig. 4.25, most of the time taken by the pendulum occurs when A is near $\pm180°$. Another kind of equilibrium which corresponds to the singular points in the phase plane of Fig. 4.28 at $\dot{A}$ equal to 0 and A equal to 0, $\pm2\pi$, etc., is stable but trivial, as the pendulum bob is stationary at the lowest point.

```
*****PHASE PLANE TRAJECTORIES OF THE MOTION OF A SIMPLE PENDULUM
*
                        CON(DPR)
                        PAR(A0,ADOTO,TER)
*
            DT          = 1.0
            G           = 32.16
            L           = 2.01
            A           = T
*
*****A,A0,T ARE IN DEGREES
*****ADOT AND ADOTO ARE IN RADIANS PER SECOND
*
            ADOT        = SQR(2.*G*COS(A/DPR)/L + C)
            C           = ADOTO*ADOTO - 2.*G*COS(A0/DPR)/L
*
                        FIN(T,TER)
                        HDR(T,ADOT)
                        OUT(T,ADOT)
                        PLO(T,ADOT)
                        END
57.29578
30.0            0.0             30.
60.0            0.0             60.
90.0            0.0             90.
120.            0.0             120.
180.            0.0             180.0
0.0             10.             360.
0.0             13.             360.
0.0             16.             360.
```

Fig. 4.27 MIMIC program for computing the phase-plane trajectories of a simple pendulum.

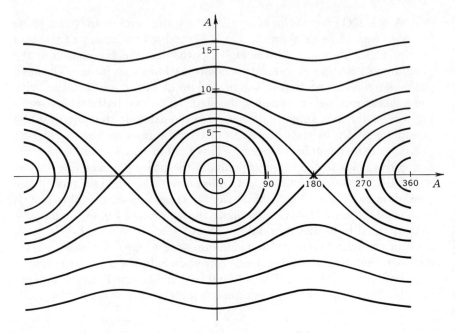

Fig. 4.28   Phase-plane plot of the motion of a simple pendulum.

4.4.2.2   Duffing's equation   The current i and the flux linkage ϕ of an iron-cored inductor may be approximated by

$$i = a_1\phi + a_3\phi^3 + a_5\phi^5 + \cdots \tag{4.79}$$

where there are only odd-power terms because of the symmetry of the magnetization curve about the origin.   The magnitudes of coefficients a_i for i equal to 5 or larger are becoming increasingly smaller than a_1 and a_3. Therefore, the behavior of an iron-cored inductor can be reasonably well described by the first two terms.

Consider a circuit which consists of a capacitor, an iron-cored inductor, and a sinusoidal voltage source.   The voltage equation is

$$\frac{d\phi}{dt} + \frac{1}{C} \int i\, dt = E \sin \omega t \tag{4.80}$$

where C = capacitance
$\quad\quad\;\; E$ = amplitude
$\quad\quad\;\; \omega$ = frequency of voltage source

When Eq. (4.80) is differentiated with respect to time and then i is substituted by Eq. (4.79), we have

$$\ddot{\phi} + \frac{a_1}{C}\phi + \frac{a_3}{C}\phi^3 = E\omega \cos \omega t \tag{4.81}$$

This equation is known as *Duffing's equation*. Without the ϕ^3 term, this equation is a linear second-order differential equation with constant coefficients.

Consider a spring-mass system with a nonlinear spring and a sinusoidal excitation. If the restoring force F_r of the spring is

$$F_r = Kx + Qx^3$$

then the system is described by

$$M\ddot{x} + Kx + Qx^3 = F \sin \omega t \tag{4.82}$$

where M = mass
K, Q = spring constants
F = amplitude
ω = frequency of excitation

This is again the Duffing equation. If Q is positive, the restoring force corresponds to a so-called hard spring; if Q is negative, the restoring force corresponds to a soft spring. The restoring force of a soft spring is shown in Fig. 4.29, where K is equal to 10 lb/in. and Q equal to -0.4 lb/in.^{3} for

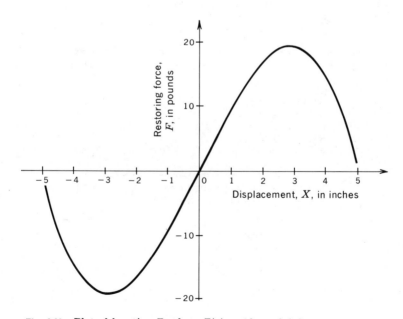

Fig. 4.29 Plot of function F, where $F(x) = 10x - 0.4x^3$.

$|x|$ equal to or less than 5 in.   With a soft spring, the restoring force can reach the point that it can decrease with the increase of the amplitude of oscillation and may cause the spring to collapse.

A MIMIC program which computes solutions of Duffing's equation (4.82) is shown in Fig. 4.30, where the restoring force is that in Fig. 4.29. In addition, the following values have been chosen:

$$Mg = 16.1 \text{ lb}$$
$$F = 5 \text{ lb}$$
$$\omega = 10 \text{ rad/sec}$$

The computed results are shown in the plots of Figs. 4.31 and 4.32.   Figure 4.31 shows that the time response is nonsinusoidal but is becoming aperiodic.   This response is corroborated by the trajectory in the phase plane of Fig. 4.32.

Periodic solutions of the Duffing equation have a fundamental period which is equal to the period of the external exciting force (that is, $2\pi/\omega$). Experiments show that permanent oscillations with a frequency of 1/2, 1/3, . . . $1/n$ of that of the exciting force can occur in a nonlinear system. This phenomenon is called *subharmonic resonance.*

```
*****SOLVING DUFFING'S EQUATION
*
                PAR(F,W)
*
*****G IN INCHES PER SECOND SQUARE, WT IN LBS
*****K IN LBS PER INCH, Q IN LB PER CUBIC INCH
*
        DT      = 0.01
        WT      = 16.1
        G       = 390.0
        K       = 10.0
        Q       = -0.4
        M       = WT/G
*
        2DX     = (F*SIN(W*T)-K*X-Q*X*X*X)/M
        1DX     = INT(2DX,0.)
        X       = INT(1DX,0.)
*
                FIN(T,4.0)
                HDR(T,X)
                OUT(T,X)
                PLO(T,X)
                PLO(X,1DX)
                END
5.0             10.
```

Fig. 4.30   MIMIC program for solving Duffing's equation.

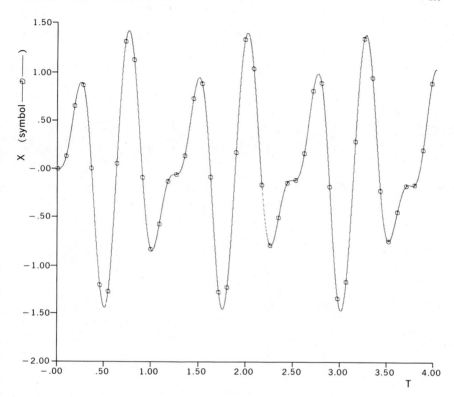

Fig. 4.31   Time response of a solution of Duffing's equation ($F = 5$ and $\omega = 10$).

4.4.2.3   Van der Pol's equation   Van der Pol showed that the behavior of an electronic oscillator could be described by a nonlinear differential equation of the form

$$\ddot{x} - A(1 - x^2)\dot{x} + Bx = 0 \qquad\qquad (4.83)$$

where $\dot{x}$ and $\ddot{x}$ are the first and second derivatives of x in time t, and A and B are positive constants.   A system characterized by this equation exhibits a limit cycle (oscillation of fixed amplitude and period) on the phase plane.   The limit cycle is due to the coefficient $A(1 - x^2)$, which can become positive, zero, or negative when the absolute value of x becomes less than, equal to, or larger than 1.   At a proper value of x, the oscillation becomes stable.

As an example, the values of constant B and parameter A, as well as the initial values of x_0 and $\dot{x}_0$, are shown in Table 4.8.   A MIMIC program for computing the solutions of van der Pol's equation by using the data in Table 4.8 is shown in Fig. 4.33.   The results for the two cases are

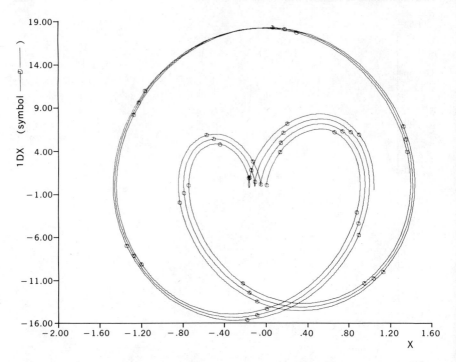

Fig. 4.32 Phase-plane plot of a solution of Duffing's equation ($F = 5$ and $\omega = 10$).

```
*****SOLVING VAN DER POL'S EQUATION
*
                    CON(B)
                    PAR(A,X0,1DX0)
*
        2DX     = A*1DX-A*1DX*X*X-B*X
        1DX     = INT(2DX,1DX0)
        X       = INT(1DX,X0)
*
                    FIN(T,30.)
*
                    HDR(TIME,X,XDOT)
                    HDR
                    OUT(T,X,1DX)
*
                    PLO(T,X)
                    PLO(X,1DX)
*
                    END
1.0
0.2         1.0             0.0
1.5         3.0             0.0
```

Fig. 4.33 MIMIC program for solving van der Pol's
equation.

Table 4.8 Data for computing van der Pol's equation

Case	(a)	(b)
B	1.0	1.0
A	0.2	1.5
x_0	1.0	3.0
$\dot{x}_0$	0	0

shown in Figs. 4.34 through 4.37.   The time responses are shown in Figs. 4.34 and 4.35, and the phase-plane plots in Figs. 4.36 and 4.37.   The phase-plane plots show that the system has a stable limit cycle since the paths converge to a single closed path in the plane, and the time-response plots show that the oscillations reach a fixed amplitude and period.   For

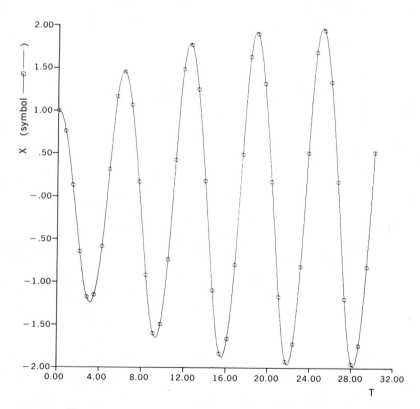

Fig. 4.34   Time response of a solution of van der Pol's equation ($A = 0.2$ and $B = 1$).

the solution where the value of A is smaller, the limit cycle is nearly circular (Fig. 4.36) and the oscillation is nearly sinusoidal (Fig. 4.34).   For the solution with a larger value of A, the limit cycle is no longer circular (Fig. 4.37), and the oscillation is not quite sinusoidal (Fig. 4.35).

The value of DT in Fig. 4.33 is 0.1 sec, as it has not been explicitly specified in the program.   It is possible to use logical control variables to give different values of DT during different time periods.   For example, one may require more points during the initial period of a transient response, fewer points as the response approaches a steady state, and a few points as the response arrives at a steady state.   As an example, in the MIMIC program of Fig. 4.33, DT may remain 0.1 sec when t is less than 1 sec. DT is chosen to be 1 sec when t is equal to or larger than 1 sec but less than 10 sec.   And DT is chosen to be 10 sec when t is equal to or larger than 10 sec.   The program in Fig. 4.33 is rewritten and shown

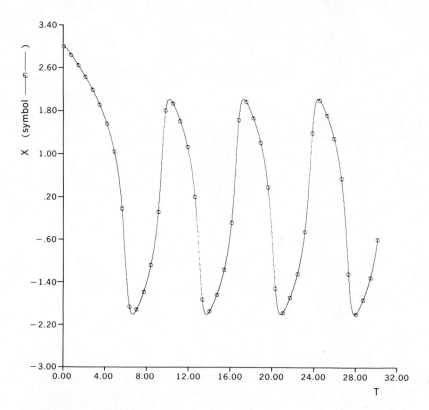

Fig. 4.35   Time response of a solution of van der Pol's equation ($A = 1.5$ and $B = 1$).

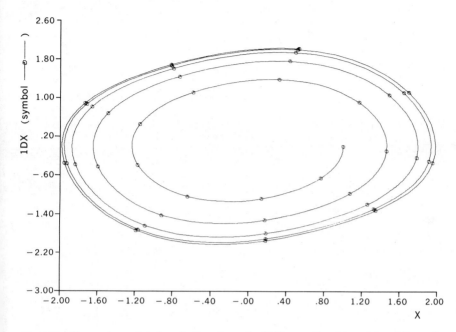

Fig. 4.36 Phase-plane plot of a solution of van der Pol's equation ($A = 0.2$ and $B = 1$).

in Fig. 4.38, where logical control variables D1, D2, and D3 control three values of DT. These logical control variables are determined by logical relations among variables C1, C2, and C3, which represent the time at less than 1 sec, at less than 10 sec, and at larger than or equal to 10 sec, respectively. These relations and representations are specified by FSW, AND, and NOT statements. The table output of this program is shown in Fig. 4.39, where there are only 29 (yet adequate) entries (or points) instead of possibly a table with pages of entries.

4.5 PARTIAL DIFFERENTIAL EQUATIONS

Partial differential equations are those differential equations with more than one independent variable. They contain partial derivatives of dependent variables with respect to one or more independent variables. Analyses in heat flow, wave propagation, transmission along a line, vibrations, hydrodynamics, elasticity, and the like involve partial differential equations. In this section some commonly known linear partial differential equations are introduced, and then the method of finite difference is applied to transform a partial differential equation into a system of ordinary differential equations.

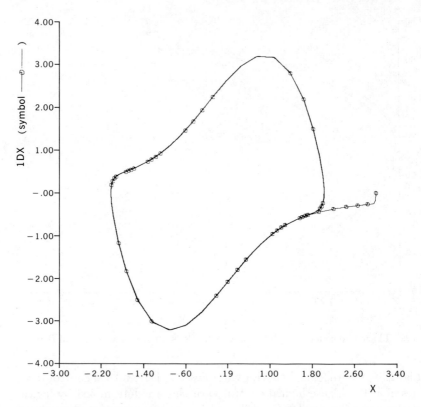

Fig. 4.37 Phase-plane plot of a solution of van der Pol's equation ($A = 1.5$ and $B = 1$).

4.5.1 SECOND-ORDER PARTIAL DIFFERENTIAL EQUATIONS

Our discussion on partial differential equations is limited to a second-order equation of the type

$$A(x,y) \frac{\partial^2 u}{\partial x^2} + B(x,y) \frac{\partial^2 u}{\partial x\, \partial y} + C(x,y) \frac{\partial^2 u}{\partial y^2}$$
$$+ f\left(x,y,u, \frac{\partial u}{\partial x}, \frac{\partial u}{\partial y}\right) = 0 \quad (4.84)$$

where u is the dependent variable and x and y are the two independent variables. This equation is linear in the second-order terms, but term $f(x,y,u,\partial u/\partial x,\partial u/\partial y)$ may be linear or nonlinear.

Equation (4.84) is called *elliptic* if $B^2 - 4AC < 0$. Laplace's equation

$$\frac{\partial^2 u}{\partial x^2} + \frac{\partial^2 u}{\partial y^2} = 0 \quad\quad\quad (4.85)$$

and Poisson's equation

$$\frac{\partial^2 u}{\partial x^2} + \frac{\partial^2 u}{\partial y^2} = f(x,y) \tag{4.86}$$

are important examples of elliptic equations. The solution of elliptic partial differential equations by the finite-difference method results generally in a system of simultaneous, linear, algebraic equations which cannot be solved advantageously by presently available digital analog simulation software. For this reason, elliptic equations are not further discussed.

Equation (4.84) is called *parabolic* if $B^2 - 4AC = 0$. The one-dimensional heat-flow equation

$$\alpha \frac{\partial^2 u}{\partial x^2} = \frac{\partial u}{\partial t} \tag{4.87}$$

is an important example of parabolic equations. Equation (4.84) is called

```
*****SOLVING VAN DER POL'S EQUATION WITH MULTIPLE VALUES OF DT
*
                    CON(B)
                    PAR(A,X0,1DX0)
*
D1        DT      = .1
D2        DT      = 1.
D3        DT      = 10.
*
          D1      = C1
          D2      = AND(C2,NOT(C1))
          D3      = AND(C3,NOT(C1),NOT(C2))
*
          C1      = FSW(T-1., TRUE,FALSE,FALSE)
          C2      = FSW(T-10.,TRUE,FALSE,FALSE)
          C3      = NOT(C2)
*
          2DX     = A*1DX-A*1DX*X*X-B*X
          1DX     = INT(2DX,1DX0)
          X       = INT(1DX,X0)
*
          FIN(T,100.)
*
          HDR(TIME,X,XDOT)
          HDR
          OUT(T,X,1DX)
*
          END
1.0
0.2            1.0            0.0
1.5            3.0            0.0
```

Fig. 4.38 MIMIC program for solving van der Pol's equation with multiple values of DT.

A	XO	1DXO
2.00000E-01	1.00000E 00	0.

TIME	X	XDOT
0.	1.00000E 00	0.
1.00000E-01	9.95004E-01	-9.98384E-02
2.00000E-01	9.80063E-01	-1.98748E-01
3.00000E-01	9.55313E-01	-2.95912E-01
4.00000E-01	9.20963E-01	-3.90628E-01
5.00000E-01	8.77289E-01	-4.82289E-01
6.00000E-01	8.24624E-01	-5.70361E-01
7.00000E-01	7.63353E-01	-6.54355E-01
8.00000E-01	6.93905E-01	-7.33794E-01
9.00000E-01	6.16762E-01	-8.08185E-01
1.00000E 00	5.32454E-01	-8.76987E-01
2.00000E 00	-5.36682E-01	-1.08709E 00
3.00000E 00	-1.22912E 00	-1.48837E-01
4.00000E 00	-7.94283E-01	9.51898E-01
5.00000E 00	4.56126E-01	1.36776E 00
6.00000E 00	1.42421E 00	3.47235E-01
7.00000E 00	1.07102E 00	-9.70920E-01
8.00000E 00	-2.99046E-01	-1.60171E 00
9.00000E 00	-1.55026E 00	-5.94221E-01
1.00000E 01	-1.33287E 00	9.28230E-01
2.00000E 01	7.25612E-01	-1.69192E 00
3.00000E 01	3.22739E-01	2.03610E 00
4.00000E 01	-1.37422E 00	-1.60221E 00
5.00000E 01	1.95387E 00	4.46530E-01
6.00000E 01	-1.89276E 00	5.08337E-01
7.00000E 01	1.34421E 00	-1.33927E 00
8.00000E 01	-4.49562E-01	1.87068E 00
9.00000E 01	-6.51746E-01	-2.01458E 00
1.00000E 02	1.60941E 00	1.30475E 00

Fig. 4.39 Table output of van der Pol's equation with multiple values of DT.

hyperbolic if $B^2 - 4AC > 0$. The one-dimensional wave equation

$$v^2 \frac{\partial^2 u}{\partial x^2} = \frac{\partial^2 u}{\partial t^2} \qquad (4.88)$$

is an important example of hyperbolic equations.

4.5.1.1 Electric current transmission Consider the one-dimensional flow of an electric current in a transmission line with a series resistance per unit length R, a shunt conductance per unit length G, an inductance per unit length L, and a shunt capacitance per unit length C. The current i and the voltage e at any point of the line can be specified by one spatial coordinate x and time variable t. The change in voltage along a linear segment of length Δx is

$$\Delta e = -iR\,\Delta x - L\,\Delta x\,\frac{\partial i}{\partial t}$$

and the change in current is

$$\Delta i = -Ge\,\Delta x - C\,\Delta x\,\frac{\partial e}{\partial t}$$

When Δx approaches zero as a limit, these two relations become a pair of partial differential equations

$$\frac{\partial e}{\partial x} + Ri + L\,\frac{\partial i}{\partial t} = 0$$

$$\frac{\partial i}{\partial x} + Ge + C\,\frac{\partial e}{\partial t} = 0$$

If the first of the above two equations is differentiated with respect to x and the second with respect to t and if the two resulting equations are solved for e, we have the following second-order partial differential equation:

$$\frac{\partial^2 e}{\partial x^2} = LC\,\frac{\partial^2 e}{\partial t^2} + (RC + LG)\,\frac{\partial e}{\partial t} + RGe \qquad (4.89)$$

If the first equation is differentiated with respect to t and the second with respect to x and if the resulting equations are solved for i, we have

$$\frac{\partial^2 i}{\partial x^2} = LC\,\frac{\partial^2 i}{\partial t^2} + (RC + LG)\,\frac{\partial i}{\partial t} + RGi \qquad (4.90)$$

These two equations, which are exactly the same in form, are sometimes known as the *telephone equations*, as they are used in analyzing telephone transmission.

In certain telegraph applications, the conductance per unit length G and inductance per unit length L are small and negligible, or

$$G = L = 0$$

Equations (4.89) and (4.90) then become

$$\frac{\partial^2 i}{\partial x^2} = RC\,\frac{\partial i}{\partial t} \qquad \frac{\partial^2 e}{\partial x^2} = RC\,\frac{\partial e}{\partial t}$$

These are known as the *telegraph equations*.

For high frequencies, the values of the terms with second derivatives in Eqs. (4.89) and (4.90) are large. If the resistance per unit length R and the conductance per unit length G are thus neglected in Eqs. (4.89) and (4.90), we have the equations for the case of a dissipationless transmission line:

$$\frac{\partial^2 i}{\partial x^2} = LC \frac{\partial^2 i}{\partial t^2} \qquad \frac{\partial^2 e}{\partial x^2} = LC \frac{\partial^2 e}{\partial t^2} \tag{4.91}$$

4.5.1.2 Wave propagation   The three-dimensional *wave equation* has the following form:

$$\nabla^2 u = \frac{\partial^2 u}{\partial x^2} + \frac{\partial^2 u}{\partial y^2} + \frac{\partial^2 u}{\partial z^2} = \frac{1}{v^2} \frac{\partial^2 u}{\partial t^2} \tag{4.92}$$

where ∇^2 = laplacian operator
$\qquad v$ = constant having a dimension of velocity
$\qquad t$ = time
$\qquad x, y, z$ = rectangular coordinates
$u(x,y,z,t)$ = physical quantity under consideration
The wave equation may describe displacement of a tightly stretched string, deflection of a stretched membrane, propagation of currents and voltages along an electric transmission line, or propagation of electromagnetic waves in free space.   In all these physical phenomena, energy is propagated with a finite velocity to distant points, and the wave disturbance travels through the medium that supports it without giving the medium any permanent displacement.

For the one- and two-dimensional cases in the rectangular coordinates, *wave equation* (4.92) becomes

$$v^2 \frac{\partial^2 u}{\partial x^2} = \frac{\partial^2 u}{\partial t^2} \tag{4.93}$$

$$\frac{\partial^2 u}{\partial x^2} + \frac{\partial^2 u}{\partial y^2} + \frac{1}{v^2} \frac{\partial^2 u}{\partial t^2} \tag{4.94}$$

For example, Eq. (4.93) describes displacement of a tightly stretched oscillating string.   In comparing Eqs. (4.91) and (4.93), we notice $v = 1/\sqrt{LC}$.   Thus, a dissipationless transmission line propagates waves of current and potential with a velocity equal to $1/\sqrt{LC}$.   If Eq. (4.93) describes transverse motion of a string under tension, then v is equal to T/ρ, where T is tension and ρ is density of the string.

The two-dimensional wave equation in polar coordinates is

$$\frac{\partial^2 u}{\partial r^2} + \frac{1}{r} \frac{\partial u}{\partial r} + \frac{1}{r^2} \frac{\partial^2 u}{\partial \theta^2} = \frac{1}{v^2} \frac{\partial^2 u}{\partial t^2} \tag{4.95}$$

where r and θ are the two polar coordinates.   This equation can describe, for example, the vibration of a circular membrane.   If the motion is a function only of r and t and independent of the angle θ, the one-dimensional wave equation in polar coordinates is

$$\frac{\partial^2 u}{\partial r^2} + \frac{1}{r}\frac{\partial u}{\partial r} = \frac{1}{v^2}\frac{\partial^2 u}{\partial t^2} \tag{4.96}$$

4.5.1.3 Diffusion or heat conduction   The three-dimensional equation

$$\nabla^2 u = \frac{\partial^2 u}{\partial x^2} + \frac{\partial^2 u}{\partial y^2} + \frac{\partial^2 u}{\partial z^2} = \frac{1}{\alpha}\frac{\partial u}{\partial t} \tag{4.97}$$

is called the *equation of heat conduction*, or *equation of diffusion*, where u is the physical quantity under consideration, ∇^2 is the laplacian operator, and α is the diffusivity.   This equation may describe flow of heat in a uniform medium or diffusion of concentration in a material.   It may also describe, for example, in the one-dimensional case, propagation of voltage and current along a transmission line with negligible leakage and inductive effects, ac distribution in a homogeneous conducting medium (the so-called skin effect), distribution of current density in a metal, or propagation of excess hydrostatic pressure in a soil.

For one- and two-dimensional cases in rectangular coordinates, Eq. (4.97) becomes

$$\frac{\partial^2 u}{\partial x^2} = \frac{1}{\alpha}\frac{\partial u}{\partial t} \tag{4.98}$$

$$\frac{\partial^2 u}{\partial x^2} + \frac{\partial^2 u}{\partial y^2} = \frac{1}{\alpha}\frac{\partial u}{\partial t} \tag{4.99}$$

The physical quantities which constitute the diffusivity depend on the application.   For example, if Eq. (4.95) describes temperature distribution of the heat flow in a medium, diffusivity α is equal to $k/(c\rho)$, where k is the thermal conductivity, c the specific heat of the medium, and ρ the density of the medium.   In case Eq. (4.96) describes distribution of the current density in a metal, diffusivity is the product of permeability μ and conductivity σ.   In case of propagation of the voltage along a transmission line, diffusivity is the product of resistance per unit length R and capacitance per unit length C.

The one- and two-dimensional cases of the heat conduction and diffusion equation in polar coordinates can be similarly obtained from Eqs. (4.95) and (4.96).   A complete specification for the solution of a partial differential equation should include initial conditions and boundary conditions, and the solution must satisfy both conditions.

4.5.2 CONVERSION TO DIFFERENTIAL DIFFERENCE EQUATIONS

In the MIMIC processor, there is a counter which represents the independent variable denoted by T.   However, in a partial differential equation, there are more than one independent variables.   The more generally acceptable approach is to apply finite difference to the space variables of the partial differential equation and thus to convert a partial differential equation into a system of differential difference equations. This conversion leads to an approximate mathematical representation of the original partial differential equation.

When the finite difference is applied to a single space variable x, the maximum value of x (say L) is divided into a discrete set of values of x: $x_0 = 0$, $x_1 = \Delta x$, $x_2 = 2\Delta x$, . . . , $x_n = n\,\Delta x = L$. We shall consider here only fixed increments of x. Partial derivatives with respect to x are then replaced by the suitably chosen finite differences at the chosen set of values of x.

The partial derivative of function $u(x,t)$ with respect to x can be expressed as

$$\frac{\partial u}{\partial x} = \lim_{\Delta x \to 0} \frac{u(x + \Delta x, t) - u(x - \Delta x, t)}{2\Delta x} \tag{4.100}$$

If Δx is not allowed to approach the limit of zero but is replaced by a finite value, the partial derivative $\partial u/\partial x$ at $x = x_i$ can be approximately represented by

$$\left(\frac{\partial u}{\partial x}\right)_{x_i} \approx \frac{u(x_i + \Delta x, t) - u(x_i - \Delta x, t)}{2\Delta x}$$

or

$$\left(\frac{\partial u}{\partial x}\right)_{x_i} \approx \frac{1}{2\Delta x}(u_{i+1} - u_{i-1}) \tag{4.101}$$

The partial derivative $\partial^2 u/\partial x^2$ at $x = x_i$ can be approximately represented by

$$\left(\frac{\partial^2 u}{\partial x^2}\right)_{x_i} \approx \frac{1}{\Delta x}\left[\left(\frac{\partial u}{\partial x}\right)_{x_i + \Delta x/2} - \left(\frac{\partial u}{\partial x}\right)_{x_i - \Delta x/2}\right]$$

or

$$\left(\frac{\partial^2 u}{\partial x^2}\right)_{x_i} \approx \frac{1}{(\Delta x)^2}\{[u(x_i + \Delta x, t) - u(x_i,t)]$$
$$- [u(x_i,t) - u(x_i - \Delta x, t)]\}$$

or

$$\left(\frac{\partial^2 u}{\partial x^2}\right)_{x_i} \approx \frac{1}{\Delta x^2}(u_{i+1} - 2u_i + u_{i-1}) \tag{4.102}$$

These finite-difference approximations are called *first-order central differences*. Two other difference approximations are the forward difference and the backward difference, which approximate derivatives at a point by including points on one side only. Formulas for the central, forward, and backward differences for the first- and second-order approximations

Table 4.9 Central-, forward-, and backward-difference formulas for the first and second partial derivatives

Type		Formula	First-error term
First-order approximations:			
Central difference	(a)	$\left(\dfrac{\partial u}{\partial x}\right)_i = \dfrac{u_{i+1} - u_{i-1}}{2(\Delta x)}$	$-\dfrac{(\Delta x)^2}{6}\left(\dfrac{\partial^3 u}{\partial x^3}\right)_i$
	(b)	$\left(\dfrac{\partial^2 u}{\partial x^2}\right)_i = \dfrac{u_{i+1} - 2u_i + u_{i-1}}{(\Delta x)^2}$	$-\dfrac{(\Delta x)^2}{12}\left(\dfrac{\partial^4 u}{\partial x^4}\right)_i$
Forward difference	(a)	$\left(\dfrac{\partial u}{\partial x}\right)_i = \dfrac{u_{i+1} - u_i}{\Delta x}$	$-\dfrac{\Delta x}{2}\left(\dfrac{\partial^2 u}{\partial x^2}\right)_i$
	(b)	$\left(\dfrac{\partial^2 u}{\partial x^2}\right)_i = \dfrac{u_{i+2} - 2u_{i+1} + u_i}{(\Delta x)^2}$	$-(\Delta x)\left(\dfrac{\partial^3 u}{\partial x^3}\right)_i$
Backward difference	(a)	$\left(\dfrac{\partial u}{\partial x}\right)_i = \dfrac{u_i - u_{i-1}}{\Delta x}$	$\dfrac{\Delta x}{2}\left(\dfrac{\partial^2 u}{\partial x^2}\right)_i$
	(b)	$\left(\dfrac{\partial^2 u}{\partial x^2}\right)_i = \dfrac{u_i - 2u_{i-1} + u_{i-2}}{2(\Delta x)}$	$\Delta x\left(\dfrac{\partial^3 u}{\partial x^3}\right)_i$
Second-order approximations:			
Central difference	(a)	$\left(\dfrac{\partial u}{\partial x}\right)_i = \dfrac{-u_{i+2} + 8u_{i+1} - 8u_{i-1} + u_{i-2}}{12(\Delta x)}$	$\dfrac{(\Delta x)^4}{30}\left(\dfrac{\partial^5 u}{2x^5}\right)_i$
	(b)	$\left(\dfrac{\partial^2 u}{\partial x^2}\right)_i = \dfrac{-u_{i+2} + 16u_{i+1} - 30u_i + 16u_{i-1} - u_{i-2}}{12(\Delta x)^2}$	$\dfrac{(\Delta x)^4}{90}\left(\dfrac{x^6 u}{\partial x^6}\right)_i$
Forward difference	(a)	$\left(\dfrac{\partial u}{\partial x}\right)_i = \dfrac{-u_{i+2} + 4u_{i+1} - 3u_i}{2(\Delta x)}$	$\dfrac{(\Delta x)^2}{3}\left(\dfrac{\partial^3 u}{\partial x^3}\right)_i$
	(b)	$\left(\dfrac{\partial^2 u}{\partial x^2}\right)_i = \dfrac{-u_{i+3} + 4u_{i+2} - 5u_{i+1} + 2u_i}{(\Delta x)^2}$	$\dfrac{11(\Delta x)^2}{12}\left(\dfrac{\partial^4 u}{\partial x^4}\right)_i$
Backward difference	(a)	$\left(\dfrac{\partial u}{\partial x}\right)_i = \dfrac{-3u_i + 4u_{i-1} - u_{i-2}}{2(\Delta x)}$	$-\dfrac{(\Delta x)^2}{3}\left(\dfrac{\partial^3 u}{\partial x^3}\right)_i$
	(b)	$\left(\dfrac{\partial^2 u}{\partial x^2}\right)_i = \dfrac{2u_i - 5u_{i-1} + 4u_{i-2} - u_{i-3}}{(\Delta x)^2}$	$-\dfrac{11(\Delta x)^2}{12}\left(\dfrac{\partial^4 u}{\partial x^4}\right)_i$

are shown in Table 4.9. Formulas for the backward differences are symmetrical with the forward-difference formulas.

When the partial derivative $\partial^2 u/\partial x^2$ in Eq. (4.93) is replaced by the approximation in Eq. (4.102), we have

$$\frac{d^2 u_i}{dt^2} = \frac{v^2}{(\Delta x)^2}(u_{i+1} - 2u_i + u_{i-1}) \qquad \text{for } i = 0, 1, \ldots, n \qquad (4.103)$$

This is a set of $(n + 1)$ ordinary differential equations (sometimes called differential difference equations). These equations are to be solved for variables u_i, where i is equal to 0 through n, and the solution has to satisfy the initial and boundary conditions. Similarly, when partial derivative $\partial^2 u/\partial x^2$ in Eq. (4.98) is replaced by the approximation in Eq. (4.102), we again have a set of $(n + 1)$ ordinary differential equations as below:

$$\frac{du_i}{dt} = \frac{\alpha}{(\Delta x)^2}(u_{i+1} - 2u_i + u_{i-1}) \qquad \text{for } i = 0, 1, \ldots, n \qquad (4.104)$$

When the finite difference is applied to two space variables x and y, we have the following first-order approximation:

$$\frac{\partial^2 u}{\partial x^2} + \frac{\partial^2 u}{\partial y^2} \approx \frac{u(x + \Delta x, y) - 2u(x,y) + u(x - \Delta x, y)}{(\Delta x)^2}$$
$$+ \frac{u(x, y + \Delta y) - 2u(x,y) + u(x, y - \Delta y)}{(\Delta y)^2} \quad (4.105)$$

The four neighboring points $(x \pm \Delta x)$ and $(y \pm \Delta y)$ in the above equation are a part of the rectangular grid. If we choose

$$\Delta x = \Delta y = h$$

we then have a square grid, and Eq. (4.105) becomes

$$\frac{\partial^2 u}{\partial x^2} + \frac{\partial^2 u}{\partial y^2} \approx \frac{1}{h^2} [u(x + h, y) + u(x - h, y)$$
$$+ u(x, y + h) + u(x, y - h) - 4u(x,y)] \quad (4.106)$$

There are other types of grids, such as triangular and hexagonal, which are useful for certain problems where boundary conditions are not easily satisfied with the square grid. When the approximation in Eq. (4.106) is applied to the wave equation (4.94), we have

$$\frac{d^2 u_i}{dt^2} = \frac{v^2}{h^2} [u(x_j + h, y_k) + u(x_j - h, y_k) + u(x_j, y_k + h)$$
$$+ u(x_j, y_k - h) - 4u(x_j,y_k)] \quad (4.107)$$

There may be as many equations like (4.107) as the number of the chosen grid points, and these ordinary differential equations are to be solved simultaneously with a proper set of initial boundary conditions. An equation similar to (4.107) can be obtained for the heat-conduction equation (4.99).

The finite-difference approximations can also be applied to the partial differential equation in polar coordinates. For a one-dimensional case with the first-order approximation, Eq. (4.96) becomes

$$\frac{d^2 u_i}{dt^2} = \frac{v^2}{(\Delta r)^2} \left[\left(1 + \frac{\Delta r}{2r_i}\right) u_{i+1} - 2u_i + \left(1 - \frac{\Delta r}{2r_i}\right) u_{i-1} \right] \quad (4.108)$$

For a two-dimensional case with the first-order approximation, Eq. (4.95) becomes

$$\frac{d^2 u}{dt^2} = \frac{v^2}{(\Delta r)^2} \left[\left(1 + \frac{\Delta r}{2r_j}\right) u(r_j + \Delta r, \theta_k) - 2u(r_j,\theta_k) \right.$$
$$\left. + \left(1 - \frac{\Delta r}{2r_j}\right) u(r_j - \Delta r, \theta_k) \right] + \frac{v^2}{r_j^2(\Delta \theta)^2} [u(r_j, \theta_k + \Delta \theta)$$
$$- 2u(r_j,\theta_k) + u(r_j, \theta_k - \Delta \theta)] \quad (4.109)$$

Again, there may be as many differential equations like Eq. (4.109) as the number of the grid points.

Although the independent variable t is regarded as continuous in the digital analog simulation, numerical integration in t is actually performed with Δt automatically chosen by the MIMIC processor (if not specified by the programmer). Courant and his coworkers have shown that it is impossible to choose Δt and Δx arbitrarily if a stable solution of Eq. (4.111) is to be obtained. By considering the error which is the difference between the analytical solution from the differential equation (4.98) and that from its corresponding difference equation, it was shown that this error is bounded if

$$\Delta t \leq \frac{(\Delta x)^2}{2\alpha} \tag{4.110}$$

Otherwise, the error grows exponentially with t. It follows that unlimited decrease in the value of Δx will not lead to an improved accuracy unless accompanied by a suitable decrease in Δt.

4.5.3 AN EXAMPLE

Consider the one-dimensional heat flow of a medium with thermal conductivity k, specific heat c, and density ρ. This medium is held between two infinite slabs at a distance L apart. The slabs are held at a temperature of zero, while the medium initially has a uniform temperature of T_m °F. It is required to find the temperature distribution of the medium. Let T be the temperature. The partial differential equation for the temperature distribution is

$$\frac{\partial T}{\partial t} = \frac{k}{c\rho} \frac{\partial^2 T}{\partial x^2} \tag{4.111}$$

The boundary conditions of the medium are

$$T(0,t) = T(L,t) = 0 \tag{4.112}$$

and the initial condition of the medium is

$$T(x,0) = T_m \tag{4.113}$$

The analytical solution of this equation is

$$T(x,t) = \frac{4T_m}{\pi} \sum_{n=1}^{\infty} \frac{1}{n} \sin \frac{n\pi x}{L} \exp\left[-\left(\frac{k}{c\rho}\right)\left(\frac{n^2\pi^2 t}{L^2}\right) \right]$$
$$\text{for } n = 1, 3, 5, \ldots \tag{4.114}$$

This solution actually represents an infinite number of sinusoidal temperature distributions across the medium from $x = 0$ to $x = L$. At $t = 0$ the sine waves all add up to give the initial flat temperature distribution. For $t > 0$, the sine waves decay exponentially at different rates; those sine waves with a larger value of n decay faster. The following values are chosen:

$$T_m = 100°F$$
$$L = 1 \text{ ft}$$
$$k = 2.4 \text{ Btu/(min)(ft)(°F)}$$
$$c = 0.2 \text{ Btu/(lb)(°F)}$$
$$\rho = 150 \text{ lb/ft}^3$$
$$n = 20$$

(4.115)

For n equal to 20, the medium is divided into 20 segments.

```
*****SOLUTION OF ONE-DIMENSIONAL HEAT FLOW EQUATION
*
          L        = 1.
          K        = 2.4
          C        = 0.2
          P        = 150.
          DELTAX   = L/20.
          Z        = K/(C*P*DELTAX*DELTAX)
          IC       = 100.
*
          T0       = 0.
          T1       = INT(Z*(T2 -2.*T1 +T0 ),IC)
          T2       = INT(Z*(T3 -2.*T2 +T1 ),IC)
          T3       = INT(Z*(T4 -2.*T3 +T2 ),IC)
          T4       = INT(Z*(T5 -2.*T4 +T3 ),IC)
          T5       = INT(Z*(T6 -2.*T5 +T4 ),IC)
*
          T6       = INT(Z*(T7 -2.*T6 +T5 ),IC)
          T7       = INT(Z*(T8 -2.*T7 +T6 ),IC)
          T8       = INT(Z*(T9 -2.*T8 +T7 ),IC)
          T9       = INT(Z*(T10-2.*T9 +T8 ),IC)
          T10      = INT(Z*(T11-2.*T10+T9 ),IC)
*
          T11      = INT(Z*(T12-2.*T11+T10),IC)
          T12      = INT(Z*(T13-2.*T12+T11),IC)
          T13      = INT(Z*(T14-2.*T13+T12),IC)
          T14      = INT(Z*(T15-2.*T14+T13),IC)
          T15      = INT(Z*(T16-2.*T15+T14),IC)
*
          T16      = INT(Z*(T17-2.*T16+T15),IC)
          T17      = INT(Z*(T18-2.*T17+T16),IC)
          T18      = INT(Z*(T19-2.*T18+T17),IC)
          T19      = INT(Z*(T20-2.*T19+T18),IC)
          T20      = 0.
*
          FIN(T,5.0)
*
          HDR(T,T2,T4,T6,T8,T10)
          HDR
          OUT(T,T2,T4,T6,T8,T10)
          PLO(T,T2,T4,T6,T8,T10)
          END
```

Fig. 4.40 MIMIC program for solving a one-dimensional heat-flow equation.

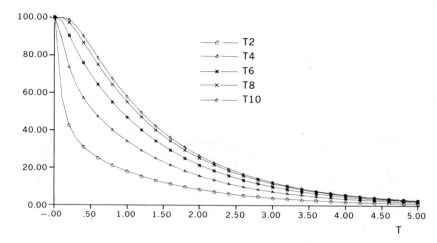

Fig. 4.41 Time response of temperature distribution of a one-dimensional heat-flow problem.

By using the first-order central-difference approximations, we have the following set of ordinary differential equations:

$$\frac{dT_i}{dt} = Z(T_{i+1} - 2T_i + T_{i-1}) \qquad \text{for } i = 1, 2, \ldots, 19 \qquad (4.116)$$

where $Z = \alpha/(\Delta x)^2$
$\alpha = k/(c\rho) = 0.08$
$\Delta x = L/20 = 0.05$
The boundary conditions are

$$T_0 = T_{20} = 0 \qquad \text{for all values of } t \qquad (4.117)$$

and the initial conditions are

$$T_1 = T_2 = \cdots = T_{19} = 100 \qquad \text{at } t = 0 \qquad (4.118)$$

Because the boundary conditions are given at $x = 0$ and $x = L$, there are only 19 differential equations. From relation (4.110), the choice of Δt must satisfy the following inequality:

$$\Delta t \leq \frac{1}{64}$$

Otherwise the solution becomes unstable.

A MIMIC program for computing the solution of Eqs. (4.116) with the boundary and initial conditions (4.117) and (4.118) is shown in Fig. 4.40. This program consists essentially of 19 INT statements. Computation is terminated when T reaches 5. The computed results are shown in two plots. Figure 4.41 shows a family of curves with temperature vs.

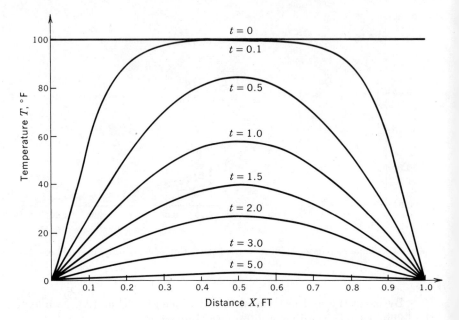

Fig. 4.42 Spatial response of temperature distribution of a one-dimensional heat-flow problem.

time with x_i as the parameter, while Fig. 4.42 shows a family of curves with temperature T versus distance x with t as the parameter.

The analytical solution (4.114) assumes that the thermal conductivity k, specific heat c, and density ρ are constants. If any one or more of these quantities are not constants, the analytical solution is no longer valid. However, it may still be possible to obtain a solution from Eq. (4.116), provided that variations of these quantities are known. For example, assume that the specific heat varies across the medium of $c = f(x)$. This can be accommodated by using different values of c to compute Z at various values of x_i.

4.5.4 HIGHER-ORDER FINITE DIFFERENCES

Replacements of partial derivatives by finite differences are approximations. The errors inherent in this method can be examined by using Taylor series expansion. The Taylor series expansion for the function $u(x,t)$ at a point x_i in terms of the function and its derivatives at a neighboring point is

$$u(x_{i+1},\, t) = u(x_i,t) + (x_{i+1} - x_i)\left(\frac{\partial u}{\partial x}\right)_{x_i}$$
$$+ \frac{x_{i+1} - x_i}{2!}\left(\frac{\partial^2 u}{\partial x^2}\right)_{x_i} + \frac{x_{i+1} - x_i}{3!}\left(\frac{\partial^3 u}{\partial x^3}\right)_{x_i} + \cdots$$

or

$$u_{i+1} = u_i = \Delta x \left(\frac{\partial u}{\partial x}\right)_{x_i} + \frac{(\Delta x)^2}{2!}\left(\frac{\partial^2 u}{\partial x^2}\right)_{x_i}$$
$$+ \frac{(\Delta x)^3}{3!}\left(\frac{\partial^3 u}{\partial x^3}\right)_{x_i} + \cdots \quad (4.119)$$

Similarly, if x_i is a point at a distance x on the other side of x_i, we have

$$u_{i-1} = u_i - \Delta x \left(\frac{\partial u}{\partial x}\right)_{x_i} + \frac{(\Delta x)^2}{2!}\left(\frac{\partial^2 u}{\partial x^2}\right)_{x_i}$$
$$- \frac{(\Delta x)^3}{3!}\left(\frac{\partial^3 u}{\partial x^3}\right)_{x_i} + \cdots \quad (4.120)$$

When Eqs. (4.119) and (4.120) are combined, we have

$$\left(\frac{\partial u}{\partial x}\right)_{x_i} = \frac{u_{i+1} - u_{i-1}}{2(\Delta x)} - \frac{(\Delta x)^2}{6}\left(\frac{\partial^3 u}{\partial x^3}\right)_{x_i} + \cdots \quad (4.121)$$

The second term on the right side of the above equation is the first-error term of the first-order approximation of the central-difference formula. From Eq. (4.119), we obtain

$$\left(\frac{\partial u}{\partial x}\right)_i = \frac{u_{i+1} - u_i}{\Delta x} - \frac{(\Delta x)}{2}\left(\frac{\partial^2 u}{\partial x^2}\right)_{x_i} - \cdots \quad (4.122)$$

The second term is, similarly, the first-error term of the first-order approximation of the forward-difference formula. From Eq. (4.120), we obtain

$$\left(\frac{\partial u}{\partial x}\right)_i = \frac{u_i - u_{i-1}}{\Delta x} + \frac{(\Delta x)}{2}\left(\frac{\partial^2 u}{\partial x^2}\right)_{x_i} - \cdots \quad (4.123)$$

The second term is, similarly, the first-error term of the first-order approximation of the backward-difference formula. All these first-error terms are shown in the last column in Table 4.9. The errors represented by these error terms are proportional both to $(\Delta x)^2$ and to the second or third derivative of the function at the point in question.

The finite-difference approximation error for the second partial derivative can also be obtained from Eqs. (4.119) and (4.120). For example, if Eq. (4.119) is combined with Eq. (4.120), we obtain

$$\left(\frac{\partial^2 u}{\partial x^2}\right)_{x_i} = \frac{u_{i+1} - 2u_i + u_{i-1}}{(\Delta x)^2} - \frac{(\Delta x)^2}{12}\left(\frac{\partial^4 u}{\partial x^4}\right)_{x_i} - \cdots \quad (4.124)$$

The first-error term is also shown in Table 4.9.

Central, forward, and backward approximations of second and higher orders may also be obtained from Taylor series expansions; these approximations give more accurate finite-difference approximations. Second-order approximations for the first and second partial derivatives are shown in Table 4.9. In general, the approximation error is proportional to $(\Delta x)^n$ for an nth-order approximation.

4.6 DOUBLE INTEGRATION OF A FUNCTION

As mentioned, there exists only one independent variable in the MIMIC processor. Double integration of a function implies that there exist two independent variables. Use of numerical integration to one independent variable can be similarly applied.

As an example, consider the volume V of a sphere with a unity radius which can be expressed as

$$V = \int_{-1}^{1} \int_{0}^{\sqrt{1-x^2}} 2\pi y \, dy \, dx \tag{4.125}$$

where x and y are the distances along X and Y coordinates whose origin is located at the center of the sphere. This integration can be analytically evaluated, and the exact volume of the sphere is $4\pi/3$.

If we cut the sphere along the x axis into slices of equal thickness (i.e., slices perpendicular to the x axis), Eq. (4.125) can be written into

$$V = 4\pi \int_{0}^{1} Y_i \, dx \tag{4.126}$$

where

$$Y_i = \int_{0}^{y_i} y \, dy \tag{4.127}$$

and

$$y_i = \sqrt{1 - x_i^2} \tag{4.128}$$

Integral (4.127) gives Y_i, which is the volume of the ith slice of the sphere, and integral (4.126) sums the volumes of all the slices to give the volume of the sphere. The latter integral is to be numerically computed. Let the radius along the x axis be divided into six equal increments of h; then h is equal to $1/6$. Various numerical methods of integration are available. Three methods are selected, and their formulas are shown in Table 4.10.

In evaluating integral (4.127), the integration limits y_i must be

Table 4.10   Numerical-integration formulas and results

Method	*Integration formula*	*Result*
Exact	$V = 4\pi/3$	4.18879
Euler	$V = (y_0 + y_1 + y_2 + y_3 + y_4 + y_5)(4\pi h)$	4.68309
Simpson	$V = (y_0 + 4y_1 + 2y_2 + 4y_3 + 2y_4 + 4y_5 + y_6)(4\pi h/3)$	4.18857
Weddle	$V = (y_0 + 5y_1 + y_2 + 6y_3 + y_4 + 5y_5 + y_6)(12\pi h/10)$	4.18857

```
*****DOUBLE INTEGRATION OF A FUNCTION
*
                        CON(PI)
          DT      = .01
*
          YO      = INT(DYO,0.)
          Y1      = INT(DY1,0.)
          Y2      = INT(DY2,0.)
          Y3      = INT(DY3,0.)
          Y4      = INT(DY4,0.)
          Y5      = INT(DY5,0.)
          Y6      = 0.
***FUNCTION SWITCHES DYI AND S
          DYO     = FSW(T-TO,T,T,0.)
          DY1     = FSW(T-T1,T,T,0.)
          DY2     = FSW(T-T2,T,T,0.)
          DY3     = FSW(T-T3,T,T,0.)
          DY4     = FSW(T-T4,T,T,0.)
          DY5     = FSW(T-T5,T,T,0.)
          S       = FSW(T-(1.-DT),FALSE,TRUE,TRUE)
***TIME TO TERMINATE THE INTEGRATORS
          TO      = 1.
          T1      = SQR(35.)/6.
          T2      = SQR(32.)/6.
          T3      = SQR(27.)/6.
          T4      = SQR(20.)/6.
          T5      = SQR(11.)/6.
*
***EXACT VALUE
  S       VEXACT = PI*4./3.
***USE EULER'S RULE FOR N = 6
  S       X       = (YO+Y1+Y2+Y3+Y4+Y5+Y6)*4.*PI/6.
***USE SIMPSON'S RULE FOR N = 6
  S       V1      = 4.*(Y1+Y3+Y5)
  S       V2      = 2.*(Y2+Y4)
  S       V       = (YO+V1+V2+Y6)*4.*PI/18.
***USE WEDDLE'S RULE FOR N = 6
  S       W1      = 5.*(Y1+Y5)
  S       W2      = YO+Y2+Y4+Y6
  S       W       = (W2+W1+6.*Y3)*4.*PI/20.
***TERMINATION
                    FIN(T,1.)
***OUTPUT
                    HDR(T,VEXACT,X,V,W)
                    HDR
  S                 OUT(T,VEXACT,X,V,W)
                    END
3.14159265
```

Fig. 4.43 MIMIC program for double integration of a function.

known. These limits are computed by Eq. (4.128), as shown below:

$$
\begin{aligned}
x_0 &= 0h = 0 & y_0 &= \sqrt{1 - x_0{}^2} = 1 \\
x_1 &= 1h = \frac{1}{6} & y_1 &= \sqrt{\frac{35}{6}} \\
x_2 &= 2h = \frac{2}{6} & y_2 &= \sqrt{\frac{32}{6}} \\
x_3 &= 3h = \frac{3}{6} & y_3 &= \sqrt{\frac{27}{6}} \\
x_4 &= 4h = \frac{4}{6} & y_4 &= \sqrt{\frac{20}{6}} \\
x_5 &= 5h = \frac{5}{6} & y_5 &= \sqrt{\frac{11}{6}}
\end{aligned}
\tag{4.129}
$$

A MIMIC program for evaluating integrals (4.126) and (4.127) is shown in Fig. 4.43, where T represents variable y. Integral (4.126) is computed numerically by all three integration formulas in Table 4.10. There are six INT statements for the six slices of the sphere. Since the size of each slice is different, each INT statement has to be terminated at a different time. Each INT statement is terminated by setting its integrand DY_i equal to zero. DY_i is set to zero by the FSW statements when time T_i (that is, y_i) reaches the termination value in (4.129). The logical control variable S causes numerical integration only when independent variable T reaches the terminating value of unity. The result of the program is also shown in Table 4.10. In comparing the results from the three integration formulas with the exact value, it is obvious that Simpson and Weddle integration formulas give a result accurate to four digits. Better accuracy can be readily obtained by cutting the sphere into more slices.

PROBLEMS

4.1. Compute by MIMIC programming the coefficients of Fourier series by relations (4.5) through (4.8) for the following periodic functions:
- (a) Rectangular function in Fig. 4.1a
- (b) Rectangular function in Fig. 4.1b
- (c) Triangular function in Fig. 4.1c
- (d) Triangular function in Fig. 4.1d
- (e) Sawtooth function in Fig. 4.1e
- (f) Half-cosine function in Fig. 4.1f

4.2. Compute by MIMIC programming the coefficients of Fourier series from the analytical relations in Table 4.1 for the following functions:
- (a) Rectangular function in Fig. 4.1a
- (b) Rectangular function in Fig. 4.1b
- (c) Triangular function in Fig. 4.1c

(d) Triangular function in Fig. 4.1d
(e) Sawtooth function in Fig. 4.1e
(f) Half-cosine function in Fig. 4.1f

4.3. Compare the results in Prob. 4.1 with those in Prob. 4.2.

4.4. Compute by MIMIC programming amplitude spectra $|G(j\omega)|$ with frequency ω as a parameter by relations (4.22) through (4.24) for the following cases:

(a) Rectangular pulse in Fig. 4.7c
(b) Triangular pulse in Fig. 4.7e
(c) Half-cosine pulse in Fig. 4.7g

4.5. Compute by MIMIC programming amplitude spectra $|G(j\omega)|$ with frequency ω as a parameter by using the analytical relation

(a) In Fig. 4.7d　　(b) In Fig. 4.7f　　(c) In Fig. 4.7h

4.6. Compare the results in Prob. 4.4 with those in Prob. 4.5.

4.7. Compute by MIMIC programming autocorrelation functions of the following periodic functions by relation (4.29):

(a) Rectangular function in Fig. 4.1a
(b) Rectangular function in Fig. 4.1b
(c) Triangular function in Fig. 4.1c
(d) Triangular function in Fig. 4.1d
(e) Sawtooth function in Fig. 4.1e
(f) Half-cosine function in Fig. 4.1f

4.8. Compute by MIMIC programming crosscorrelation functions of the following pairs of periodic functions by relation (4.39), assuming that each pair has the same period of unity.

(a) Rectangular function in Fig. 4.1a and triangular function in Fig. 4.1c
(b) Rectangular function in Fig. 4.1b and triangular function in Fig. 4.1d
(c) Rectangular function in Fig. 4.1b and sawtooth function in Fig. 4.1e
(d) Rectangular function in Fig. 4.1a and half-cosine function in Fig. 4.1f

4.9. Given the differential equation

$$y\frac{dy}{dx} - y^2 + 2x = 0$$

compute the solution by MIMIC programming until x is equal to 5 for $y(0) = 1$.

4.10. Given the differential equation

$$\frac{d^3y}{dx^3} + xy = 0$$

and the initial conditions

$$y(0) = 0 \qquad \frac{dy(0)}{dx} = 1 \qquad \frac{d^2y(0)}{dx^2} = 0$$

compute the solution by MIMIC programming until x is equal to 1.

4.11. Given the differential equation

$$\frac{d^3y}{dt^3} + y\frac{d^2y}{dt^2} = 0$$

and the initial conditions

$$y(0) = 0 \qquad \frac{dy(0)}{dt} = 0 \qquad \frac{d^2y(0)}{dt^2} = 1$$

compute the solution by MIMIC programming until t is equal to 2.

4.12. The following is Rayleigh's equation,

$$\frac{dx^2}{dt^2} - e\left[1 - \frac{1}{3}\left(\frac{dx}{dt}\right)^2\right]\frac{dx}{dt} + x = 0$$

where e is a parameter.   Choose several values of e from the range

$$0.1 \le e \le 10$$

and compute the solutions by MIMIC programming; plot phase-plane trajectories for the following cases of initial conditions:
   (a) $x(0) = 2$, $\dot{x}(0) = 0$
   (b) $x(0) = 0$, $\dot{x}(0) = 2$
   (c) $x(0) = 2$, $\dot{x}(0) = 2$

4.13. Compute by MIMIC programming the volume of an elliptic cylinder of unit length, where the ellipse is described by the equation

$$\frac{x^2}{4} + \frac{y^2}{9} = 1$$

for the following cases:
   (a) By Euler's rule
   (b) By Simpson's rule
   (c) By Weddle's rule

4.14. Prepare a table to describe the ellipse in Prob. 4.13.   Use a CFN statement to enter the table into the MIMIC program and compute the volume of elliptic cylinder of unit length for the following three cases:
   (a) By Euler's rule
   (b) By Simpson's rule
   (c) By Weddle's rule
   Note: The use of the table is to illustrate the point that the volume of an arbitrary shape of the cylinder can be computed.

4.15. Compare the results in Prob. 4.13 with those in Prob. 4.14.

4.16. A thin, uniform rod has a uniform cross-sectional area and length L.   The equation which describes the heat flow in the rod [see Eq. (4.87)] is

$$\alpha\frac{\partial^2 T}{\partial x^2} = \frac{\partial T}{\partial t}$$

where $T(x,t)$ is the temperature of the rod and α the diffusivity of the rod.   The rod is kept at a constant but different temperature at each end and is well insulated at the lateral sides.   Given the values of constants and initial conditions

$$L = \text{rod length} = 10 \text{ ft}$$
$$\alpha = \text{diffusivity} = 0.05 \text{ ft}^2/\text{min}$$
$$T(0,t) = 100°F$$
$$T(10,t) = 200°F$$
$$T(x,0) = 150°F$$

compute by MIMIC programming the temperature distribution of the rod with time.

4.17. An elastic string stretched under uniform tension is fixed at both ends.   The equation which describes the string lateral displacement $y(x,t)$ is [see Eq. (4.88)]

$$v^2\frac{\partial^2 y}{\partial x^2} = \frac{\partial^2 y}{\partial t^2}$$

and

$$v^2 = \frac{TGL}{W}$$

where T = tension = 5 lb
G = gravitational constant = 32.2 fps
L = string length = 10 ft
W = string weight = 0.8 lb
Given the initial conditions

$$y(0,t) = 0 \qquad y(10,t) = 0 \qquad y(x,0) = 0$$

$$\frac{\partial y}{\partial t}(x,0) = 2$$

compute by MIMIC programming the displacement of the string with time.

REFERENCES

1. Van der Pol, B.: On Relaxation Oscillations, *Phil. Mag.*, vol. 17, no. 2, p. 986, 1926.
2. Carslaw, H. S.: "Introduction to the Theory of Fourier's Series and Integrals," 3d ed., Dover Publications, Inc., New York, 1930.
3. McLachlan, N. W.: "Bessel Functions for Engineers," Oxford University Press, London, 1934.
4. McLachlan, N. W.: "Theory and Application of Mathieu Functions," Oxford University Press, London, 1947.
5. Gray, H. J., R. Merwin, and J. G. Brainerd: Solutions of the Mathieu Equation, *AIEE Trans.*, vol. 67, 1948.
6. Howe, R. M., and V. S. Haneman: The Solution of Partial Differential Equations by Difference Methods Using the Electronic Differential Analyzer, *Proc. IRE*, October, 1953, pp. 1497–1508.
7. Webster, A. G.: "Partial Differential Equations of Mathematical Physics," Dover Publications, Inc., New York, 1955.
8. Kopal, A.: "Numerical Analysis," John Wiley & Sons, Inc., New York, 1955.
9. Crandall, S. H.: "Engineering Analysis," McGraw-Hill Book Company, New York, 1956.
10. Fisher, M. E.: Higher Order Differences in the Analogue Solution of Partial Differential Equations, *J. ACM*, vol. 3, no. 10, pp. 325–347, 1956.
11. Margenau, H., and G. M. Murphy: "The Mathematics of Physics and Chemistry," D. Van Nostrand Company, Inc., Princeton, N.J.; vol. 1, 1956; vol. 2, 1964.
12. Booth, A. D.: "Numerical Methods," 2d ed., Butterworth Scientific Publications, London, 1957.
13. Pipes, L. A.: "Applied Mathematics for Engineers and Physicists," 2d ed., McGraw-Hill Book Company, New York, 1958.
14. Karplus, W. J., and W. W. Soroka: "Analog Methods," 2d ed., McGraw-Hill Book Company, New York, 1959.
15. Irving, J., and M. Mullineux: "Mathematics in Physics and Engineering," Academic Press, Inc., New York, 1959.
16. Lee, Y. W.: "Statistical Theory of Communication," John Wiley & Sons, Inc., New York, 1960.
17. Jackson, A. S.: "Analog Computation," McGraw-Hill Book Company, New York, 1960.

18. Forsythe, G. E., and W. R. Wasow: "Finite-difference Methods for Partial Differential Equations," John Wiley & Sons, Inc., New York, 1960.
19. Collatz, L.: "The Numerical Treatment of Differential Equations," Springer-Verlag OHG, Berlin, 1960.
20. Salvadori, M. G., and M. L. Baron: "Numerical Methods in Engineering," 2d ed., Prentice-Hall, Inc., Englewood Cliffs, N.J., 1961.
21. Hausner, A.: Parametric Techniques for Eliminating Division and Treating Singularities in Computer Solutions of Ordinary Differential Equations, *IRE Trans. Electron. Computers*, February, 1962, p. 42.
22. Dettman, J. W.: "Mathematical Methods in Physics and Engineering," McGraw-Hill Book Company, New York, 1962.
23. Huskey, H. D., and G. A. Korn: "Computer Handbook," McGraw-Hill Book Company, New York, 1961.
24. Fox, L.: "Numerical Solution of Ordinary and Partial Differential Equations," Pergamon Press, New York, 1962.
25. Hausner, A.: Multiple Integrals on a Non-repetitive Analog Computer, *Proc. Spring Joint Computer Conf.*, 1963, pp. 205–212.
26. Froberg, C. E.: "Introduction to Numerical Analysis," Addison-Wesley Publishing Company, Inc., Reading, Mass., 1965.
27. Smith, G. D.: "Numerical Solution of Partial Differential Equations," Oxford University Press, Fair Lawn, N.J., 1965.
28. Bingulac, S. P., and E. A. Humo: Analog Computer Generation of Bessel Functions of Arbitrary Order, *IEEE Trans. Electron. Computers*, December, 1965, pp. 886–889.
29. Lathi, B. P.: "Signals, Systems and Communication," John Wiley & Sons, Inc., New York, 1965.
30. Richtmyer, R. R.: "Difference Methods for Initial-value Problems," 2d ed., John Wiley & Sons, Inc., New York, 1967.
31. Hausner, A.: Accurate Analog Computer Generation of Bessel Functions for Large Ranges, *Simulation*, November, 1967, pp. 249–254.

5
Simulation by FORTRAN Programming

A *program* is a written procedure prepared for a digital computer to calculate the solution of a problem. The *FORTRAN* (FORmula TRANslation) *language* is a set of statements which is formulated primarily for mathematically oriented applications. A program written in FORTRAN language is called a *FORTRAN program*. A FORTRAN program is called a *source program* because it must be first translated into a machine-language program by a FORTRAN compiler (or FORTRAN processor). This machine-language program is called an *object program* because only execution of the object program by the computer produces the numerical result.

There are many versions of the FORTRAN language. The word FORTRAN is used here to mean version 13 of FORTRAN IV [18]. The approach here is first to introduce the language rather briefly and then to explain the syntax of the language in more detail by means of a series of examples in solving a nonlinear differential equation. Also by means of these examples, programming techniques and numerical methods are in-

troduced. Other examples of FORTRAN programming will be shown in
the later chapters.

5.1 FORTRAN LANGUAGE ELEMENTS

A FORTRAN program is a sequence of FORTRAN statements. FOR-
TRAN statements are composed of these elements: constants, variables,
subscripts, operators, and expressions. This section describes these elements as well as the card format.

5.1.1 CARD FORMAT

Table 5.1 shows the card format of FORTRAN statements. Columns 1
to 5 are for a statement number, which is an unsigned integer ranging
from 1 to 32767. Blanks and leading zeros are ignored in these columns.
Any executable statement may be labeled with a statement number, but
statement numbers for specification statements (Sec. 5.2.5) should be
avoided. Each statement must have one or more cards. Column 6
should be blank or a zero; if it is not, it is a *continuation card*. Columns
7 to 72 contain the statement proper. Blanks in these columns are
ignored except in an alphameric field. Columns 73 to 80 are not processed by the FORTRAN processor and may be used for identification.
One special format is for cards with character C in column 1; these are
called comment cards. They are not processed, and columns 2 to 72 may
be used for comments.

   The order of execution of the statements in a source program follows the sequence of the statements (i.e., the order in a deck of cards)
unless specified by control statements. Some statements have to be
placed in a particular order, which will be mentioned when these statements are introduced.

5.1.2 CHARACTER SET

FORTRAN employs a limited set of characters, as shown in Table 5.2.
It consists of 10 digit symbols, 26 capital letters, and 12 special char-

Table 5.1   Card format for FORTRAN statements

Column	Description
1–5	Statement number.
6	Any character except a blank or a zero in this column means a continuation card. Maximum number of continuation cards for one statement is 19.
7–72	Statement proper. Blanks are ignored by FORTRAN processor.
73–80	Not processed by Fortran processor but may be used for identification.

Table 5.2   Character set

Character	Symbols
Decimal digits	0, 1, 2, . . . , 9
Alphabetics	A, B, C, . . . , Z
Special characters	+ − * / . ,) (= ' S blank

acters including the blank. They are called alphameric characters. Because of the limited set of characters, special combinations of characters are used to represent operators, such as .LT., and to represent subscripts, such as B(1).

5.1.3 FORTRAN NUMBERS

By FORTRAN numbers, we mean the following seven types of numbers:

1. Integer (i.e., decimal integer)
2. Real (i.e., real and single precision)
3. Double-precision (i.e., real and double-precision)
4. Complex (i.e., a pair of real numbers)
5. Logical (i.e., boolean numbers)
6. Octal (i.e., octal numbers)
7. Alphameric (i.e., a string of characters)

Octal and alphameric numbers are not allowed in FORTRAN arithmetic statements. Therefore, no TYPE statement is needed to declare octal or alphameric numbers.

5.1.4 CONSTANTS

FORTRAN numbers can be expressed as constants. Formats and examples for the seven types of constants are shown in Table 5.3. An integer constant is written with no decimal point, while a real constant must include a decimal point. Since the fixed-point format of a binary number in the IBM 7090/94 computer has 35 number bits, an integer constant can be as large as $2^{35} - 1$. However, when an integer constant is used as a subscript or as an index of a DO statement (see Table 5.8), the value of the integer constant is computed mod 2^{15} (because the memory address of the computer is 15 bits). An integer constant has up to 11 decimal digits, while a real constant has up to nine digits (because a real number represented in the floating-point format in the computer has 27 number bits). The magnitude of a real constant must be between approximate limits of 10^{38} and 10^{-38} or must be zero.

Table 5.3   Formats of constants†

Constant	Format	Example
Integer	It consists of 1 to 11 decimal digits written without a decimal point.	5, 19, 251
Real	It consists of (1) one to nine significant decimal digits written with a decimal point but not followed by a decimal exponent or (2) a sequence of decimal digits written with a decimal point followed by a decimal exponent which is letter E followed by a signed or unsigned integer constant.	105. 0. -9.235 $2.1E-5$ $-5.5E+8$
Double-precision	It consists of (1) ten or more significant decimal digits written with a decimal point but not followed by a decimal exponent or (2) a sequence of decimal digits written with a decimal point followed by a decimal exponent which is letter D followed by a signed or unsigned integer constant.	1.23456789 $12.3D+4$ $-0.345D-2$
Complex	It consists of an ordered pair of signed or unsigned real constants separated by a comma and enclosed in parentheses.	$(2.5, -16.2)$ $(-9.5, 0.0)$ $(5.E5, -2.)$
Logical	It has two forms, .TRUE. and .FALSE.	.TRUE. .FALSE.
Octal	It consists of a letter O followed by 1 to 12 signed or unsigned octal digits.	0123456 0777777777777
Alphameric	It consists of two letters nH followed by n alphameric characters. Blanks are significant in alphameric constants.	6H00000S 8H6Y.bcHUb

† Octal constants and alphamerical constants are not allowed in FORTRAN arithmetic statements.

A double-precision constant has 16 decimal digits (as it is represented in the double-precision floating-point format in the computer). The magnitude of a double-precision constant must lie between the approximate limits of 10^{-29} and 10^{38} or must be zero.   Numbers between 10^{-29} and 10^{-38} may be used, but only eight decimal digits are significant.

A complex constant consists of a pair of real constants; the first real constant represents the real part, while the second real constant represents the imaginary part.

A logical constant has two values, which are represented by .TRUE. and .FALSE.   An octal constant is written as letter O followed by 1 to 12 signed or unsigned octal digits.   An alphameric constant is written as nH followed by n alphameric characters.   Blanks are characters in alphameric constants.

5.1.5 VARIABLES

Since octal and alphameric numbers are not allowed in FORTRAN arithmetic statements, there are only five types of variables: integer, real, double-precision, complex, and logical.   The rule to form a variable name is that the name consists of one to six alphameric characters, the first of which must be alphabetic.   The format of a variable name and examples are shown in Table 5.4.   As previously mentioned, the type of a variable must be declared by a TYPE statement (Sec. 5.2.5) but with one important exception.   If the first character of a variable name is letter I, J, K, L, M, or N, it is an integer variable name; if it is not, it is a real variable name.   Since this can be conveniently applied, the need of TYPE statements to declare integer and real variables is greatly reduced.   The above rule of forming a variable name is referred to as the rule to form a symbolic name and is also applied to constant name, function name, subroutine name, entry name of a subroutine, list name in a NAMELIST statement (see Table 5.9), and block name in a labeled COMMON statement (see Table 5.14).

Table 5.4   Formats of variables

Name	*Format*	*Example*
Variable	It consists of one to six alphameric characters, the first of which must be alphabetic.	JLEFT Z00012 MIMC0
Subscript	It takes only one of the following forms: v or c $v + c$ or $v - c$ $c*v$ or $c*v + c'$ or $c*v - c'$ v is an unsigned, nonsubscripted integer variable. c and c' are unsigned integer constants.	JOHN K999 JEEP-25 6*I 4*K-8 8$+$I (invalid) 8$+$4*K (invalid)
Subscripted variable	It consists of a variable name followed by parentheses enclosing one to seven subscripts that are separated by commas.	A(I) K(3) B(4*K-8,6*I,J)

5.1.6 SUBSCRIPTS

An array of one to seven dimensions may be represented by a variable having one to seven subscripts.   Such a variable is called a subscripted variable.   Formats and examples of subscripts and subscripted variables are also shown in Table 5.4.   As shown there, the subscript can be a constant, a variable, or an expression; in the case of an expression, it must be one of the five types shown in Table 5.4.   The value of a subscript expression must be positive and nonzero.

The dimension of a subscripted variable must be declared by a DIMENSION, a COMMON, or a TYPE (except EXTERNAL statement) statement, which must precede the first appearance of the subscripted variable in any executable, NAMELIST, or DATA statement (see Table 5.14).

5.1.7 OPERATORS

An operator denotes an operation such as addition, comparison of two numbers, or a logical operation.   When an operator is associated with one FORTRAN number, it is called a unary operator; when associated with two, it is called a binary operator.

There are three types of operators: arithmetic, logical, and relational.   There are five arithmetic operators, three logical operators, and six relational operators; their symbols and operations are shown in Table 5.5.   Notice that logical and relational operators must have a period immediately before and immediately after the letters.   All these operators are binary, except that (1) operator .NOT. is unary and (2) operators + and − can be either unary or binary.

Table 5.5   FORTRAN operators

Type	Symbol	Operation
Arithmetic	+	Addition
	−	Subtraction
	*	Multiplication
	/	Division
	**	Exponentiation
Logical	.NOT.	Logical NOT
	.AND.	Logical AND
	.OR.	Logical OR
Relational	.GT.	Greater than
	.GE.	Greater than or equal to
	.LT.	Less than
	.LE.	Less than or equal to
	.EQ.	Equal to
	.NE.	Not equal to

Table 5.6   Precedence of operations

Operation	Precedence
Function	1 (highest)
**	2
*, /	3
+, −	4
.LT., .LE., .EQ., .NE., .GT., .GE.	5
.NOT.	6
.AND.	7
.OR.	8 (lowest)

5.1.8 EXPRESSIONS

An expression is a meaningful combination of operators and numbers. When it is evaluated, there should exist a value, numerical or logical. If an expression consists of more than one type of FORTRAN number, it is called a mixed-mode expression. With a few exceptions, mixed-mode expressions are not permitted.

There are two types of expressions, arithmetic and logical. An arithmetic expression contains arithmetic operators, while a logical expression contains logical and/or relational operators. Examples of arithmetical and logical expressions can be found in the arithmetic IF and logical IF statements (see Table 5.8). When an arithmetic expression is evaluated, it gives a numerical value. When a logical expression is evaluated, it gives a logical value.

Parentheses are used in an expression to specify the order in which operations are to be evaluated. Where parentheses are omitted, the order of the operations in an expression follows the precedence shown in Table 5.6.

5.1.9 FORTRAN ARITHMETIC

There are several special arithmetic rules in FORTRAN language which are referred to as FORTRAN arithmetic.

(a) *Truncation after integer division*   When two integers are divided, the quotient is usually not an integer. If the quotient is not an integer, the fractional part of the quotient is truncated and the quotient becomes an integer. For example, 7/3 is 2; 5/3*4 is 4; 4*5/3 is 6.

(b) *Use of parentheses*   Two arithmetic operators should not appear next to each other. For example, in the expressions X*−A and K/−I, where a minus symbol follows an arithmetic operator, a pair of parentheses must be used to indicate that the minus symbol indicates change of sign of variable I, not a subtraction. These expressions should be written as $X*(-A)$ and $K/(-I)$.

When an expression is being compiled, it is scanned from the left to the right; this implies a left-to-right precedence. If such a precedence is not desired, parentheses are required. For example, $A*B/C*D$ does not mean $(A*B)/(C*D)$. If the latter is desired, one should write $A*B/(C*D)$ or $(A*B)/(C*D)$.

A third case in which a pair of parentheses is required is the expression $A**B**C$. This expression is not permitted. It must be written as either $A**(B**C)$ or $(A**B)**C$, whichever is intended.

(c) *Mixed-mode arithmetic expressions*   A mixed-mode arithmetic expression is one in which integers are mixed with real numbers. For example, $I+1.5$, $X*3$, and $A**3$ are mixed-mode arithmetic expressions. Mixed-mode arithmetic expressions are not permitted. An important exception is in exponentiation: mixed-mode expressions such as $A**J$ and $X**2$ are permitted, but mixed-mode expressions such as $2**X$ and $K**B$ are not valid. (However, a real number or a real expression can have a real exponent.)

(d) *Mixed-mode arithmetic statements*   The mode on the left side of an arithmetic statement should be the same as that on the right side. If they are not the same, it is a mixed-mode arithmetic statement. A mixed-mode statement converts a real expression into an integer and vice versa. For example, the following are two mixed-mode statements:

$$I = X*Y + Z$$
$$W = J*K + 4$$

When the expression $X*Y+Z$ in the first statement is computed, the fractional part is discarded and the integral value is assigned to I. In the second statement, the result after evaluating the expression $J*K+4$ is converted into a real number and is then assigned to W. This conversion property of an arithmetic statement can sometimes be useful.

5.2 FORTRAN STATEMENTS

FORTRAN statements may be divided into five groups: arithmetic, control, input-output, subroutine, and specification. These statements are introduced in this section, and will be explained in detail when they are being illustrated in FORTRAN programs in the later sections.

5.2.1 ARITHMETIC STATEMENTS

The arithmetic statement prescribes a numerical or logical calculation. The format is shown in Table 5.7. Examples of arithmetic statements are

$$I = I + 1$$
$$BCD(2,I) = FDIV * 3.1$$
$$PAUL = .TRUE.$$
$$A = B.GT.C.AND.D.LE.E$$

where I, FDIV, PAUL, A, B, C, D, and E are called *variables;* 1, 2, 3.1, and .TRUE. are called *constants;* and BCD(2,I) is called a *subscripted variable,* 2 and I being the two *subscripts.* Symbols + and * are called *arithmetical operators;* .GT. and .LE. are called *relational operators;* and .AND. is called a *logical operator.*

An arithmetic statement often closely resembles a conventional arithmetic formula. However, the equal symbol in the format in Table 5.7 does not mean equality, but rather replacement (i.e., the value, after evaluation, of the right side of the equal symbol replaces the value on the left side).

5.2.2 CONTROL STATEMENTS

The control statements control or terminate the execution sequence of a FORTRAN program. Table 5.8 shows the formats and examples of 11 control statements. As shown in Table 5.8, the GO TO statement causes the sequence to be transferred to a specified statement number n. The computed GO TO statement causes the control to be transferred to the statement number n_1, n_2, . . . , or n_m, depending on whether the value of i at the time of execution is 1, 2, . . . , m, respectively. The assigned GO TO statement causes the control of the computation sequence to be transferred to statement number i, which must be n_1, n_2, . . . , or n_m. The actual value of statement number i must have been previously assigned by an ASSIGN statement.

There are two conditional control statements. The arithmetic IF statement (see Table 5.8) causes control of the sequence to be transferred to the statement number n_1, n_2, or n_3, depending on whether the numerical value of an arithmetic expression a is less than, equal to, or greater than zero, respectively. The logical IF statement (see Table 5.8) causes statement s to be executed if logical expression t has a logical value of TRUE. If t has a logical value of FALSE, statement s is skipped. In either case,

Table 5.7   Arithmetic statement

Statement	Format	Note
Arithmetic	$a = b$	a is a subscripted or nonsubscripted variable, and b is an expression.

Table 5.8 Control statements†

Statement	Format	Example	Note
GO TO	GO TO n	GO TO 101	n is a statement number in this table.
Computed GO TO	GO TO $(n_1, n_2, \ldots , n_m)$, i	GO TO(10,20,5,15),JOHN	$n_1, n_2, \ldots , n_m$ are statement numbers in this table. i is a nonsubscripted integer variable in this table.
Assigned GO TO	GO TO i, $(n_1, n_2, \ldots , n_m)$	GO TO IBM, (25,30,15)	i must have a value assigned by a previously executed ASSIGN statement.
ASSIGN	ASSIGN n TO i	ASSIGN 9 to KING	i must be the nonsubscripted integer variable that appears later in an assigned GO TO statement.
Arithmetic IF	IF$(a)n_1, n_2, n_3$	IF (D(J,K)−X) 10,20,30 IF (A*B+C/D) 10,5,8	a is an arithmetic expression (not complex).

Logical IF	IF (t) s	IF (A.AND.B) $x=y**5$
		IF (10.LT.MA) GO TO 8
		IF (X.OR.Y.GT.Z) GO TO(1,5),I
		IF (PM) CALL MARY
			t is a logical expression. s is any executable statement except a DO statement or another logical IF statement.

DO	DO n $i = m_1, m_2, m_3$	DO 100 I = 1,10 DO 20 I=J,K,5	m_1, m_2, m_3 are each either an unsigned integer constant or a nonsubscripted integer variable. If m_3 is not stated, it is taken to be 1.
CONTINUE	CONTINUE	CONTINUE	
PAUSE	PAUSE PAUSE C	PAUSE PAUSE 345	C is an unsigned octal integer constant of one to five digits.
END	END	END	
STOP	STOP or STOP C	STOP STOP 123	

† END statement is a nonexecutable statement.

control is transferred to the next statement in the sequence except in the particular case where statement s is a GO TO statement and t is TRUE.

The DO statement permits formation of a computation loop. The extent of the loop is called the range. The range covers those statements which begin from the statement immediately following the DO statement through the statement with number n. For each index i, the statements in the range are executed and then the index is incremented. The initial value of index i is m_1, the increment is m_3, and the final value of index i is m_2. When i exceeds m_2, the DO statement is terminated. The values of m_1, m_2, and m_3 must be greater than zero when the DO statement is executed. Nesting of DO statements is permitted to form multiple loops. However, an inner loop must be enclosed by the outer loop, and no loop crossing is permitted.

The CONTINUE statement is a dummy statement. It is commonly used as the last statement in the range of a DO statement to provide a statement number for reference. An IF statement cannot be the last statement of a DO loop; in this case, a CONTINUE statement is used instead. The PAUSE statement causes the computer to halt with an octal integer constant C in the address field of the storage register of the memory of the computer. If C is not there, it is taken to be zero. When the START key is depressed after a pause, the program resumes its execution. The END statement terminates compilation of a FORTRAN program and must physically be the last statement of the program. The STOP statement terminates the execution of the program and returns the control to the operating system.

5.2.3 INPUT–OUTPUT STATEMENTS

The input and output statements cause a specified list of values to be transferred between the magnetic-core memory and an input or output device. There are five types of input and output statements; Table 5.9 shows their formats and examples.

An INPUT or OUTPUT statement contains a list which is an ordered string of list items separated by commas. A list item may be a variable, a subscripted variable, or an implicit DO expression. An example of the list is

$$X(4), Y, (W(J,K), Z(J), J = 1,5)$$

where list item $(W(J,K), Z(J), J = 1,5)$ is a DO expression to be evaluated according to the following indexing:

```
  DO 1 J = 1, 5
  Z(J)
1 W(J,K)
```

Table 5.9 Input-output statements†

Statement	Format		Example	Note
INPUT	READ n,list	(cards on-line)	READ 5(X(J),J=1,10)	n is a FORMAT statement number. x is a NAMELIST name, and i is an unsigned integer constant or an unsubscripted integer variable. i refers to an input (or output) device. List means an ordered list of variables to be inputted; it can be empty.
	READ (i,n)list	(BCD data)	READ (5,20) X,Y,(Z(I),I=1,5)	
	READ (i)list	(binary data)	READ (K,5) J,W(I)	
	READ (i,x)	(BCD data)	READ (3), (Y(I),I=1,20)	
			READ (N), (Y(I),I=1,20)	
			READ (5,FMT)	
OUTPUT	WRITE (i,n)list	(BCD data)	WRITE (6,20)X,Y,(Z(I),I=1,5)	For n, x, i, see the above note.
	WRITE (i,x)	(BCD data)	WRITE (N,10)J,A(K)	
	WRITE (i)list	(binary record)	WRITE (2) (A(K),K=1,10)	
	PUNCH n,list	(cards on-line)	WRITE (M) A,B,C	
	PRINT n,list	(print on-line)	WRITE (6,NAME)	
			PUNCH 5,(X(I),I=1,15)	
			PRINT 3,(Y(J),J=1,10)	
MAGNETIC TAPE	END FILE i		END FILE 5	
	REWIND i		END FILE K	
	BACKSPACE		REWIND 3	
			REWIND K	
			BACKSPACE 4	
FORMAT	FORMAT$(S_1,S_2,\ldots,S_n/S_1',S_2',\ldots,S_n'/\ldots)$		FORMAT(3F12.8,2I4,1PE20.8)	S_i or S_i' is a field. Each field prescribes a format specification. For i, see the above note.
			FORMAT(I5/(E12.6,F10.4))	
			FORMAT(12A6)	
NAMELIST	NAMELIST/X/A,$\ldots$,B/Y/C,$\ldots$,D/Z/E,$\ldots$		DIMENSION A(10), I(5.5),L(10)	X, Y, Z, $\ldots$ are NAMELIST names. A, B, C, D, $\ldots$ are variable or array names.
			NAMELIST/N1/A,B,I,J,L/N2/A,C,J,K	

† FORMAT and NAMELIST are nonexecutable statements.

The READ statement, as shown in Table 5.9, has four forms. The first form causes cards to be read on-line from the card reader. The second and third forms cause BCD and binary information to be read respectively off-line from symbolic input device i (except the card reader). The fourth form causes BCD information relating to variables and arrays associated with the NAMELIST name x to be read off-line from symbolic input device i (except the card reader).

The WRITE statement, as shown in Table 5.9, has three forms. The first and third WRITE statements cause BCD and binary information to be written respectively off-line on symbolic output device i. The second WRITE statement causes all variable and array names (as well as their values) that belong to NAMELIST name x to be written off-line on symbolic output device i. The PUNCH statement causes alphameric cards to be punched on-line. The PRINT statement causes data to be output on the on-line printer. When a WRITE statement refers to a NAMELIST name, the values and names of all variables and arrays belonging to the NAMELIST name are written, each according to its type.

The END FILE statement causes an end-of-file mark to be written on symbolic magnetic tape i. The REWIND statement causes symbolic tape unit i to be rewound. The BACKSPACE statement causes symbolic tape i to be backspaced one physical record if i refers to an input/output device in the BCD mode, or it causes tape i to be backspaced one logical record if i refers to an input/output device in the binary mode.

In addition to a list, the BCD input-output statements require a FORMAT statement to describe the types of fields and their specifications for each item in the list. Each field (S or S') in the FORMAT statement describes the type and specification. There are nine types of fields: D, E, F, T, O, A, H, L, and X. Table 5.10 shows formats and examples for these fields; their explanation is deferred until later.

The NAMELIST statement specifies namelists each of which is an input (or output) list of variable names and array names, and the data cards associated with the statement specify the values of the namelists. Therefore, the use of a NAMELIST statement omits the use of a FORMAT statement and an input (or output) list in an INPUT (or OUTPUT) statement in reading (writing) data. Table 5.9 shows the format of the NAMELIST statement; an example of its use is

    DIMENSION X(10), I(3,3), K(20)
    NAMELIST /N1/X,Y,I,J,K/N2/X,Z,J,M
    READ(5,N1)

The above example shows that arrays X, I, and K and variables Y and J belong to the namelist with name N1, and the array X and variables Z,

Table 5.10   Field specifications for FORMAT statement

Field	Specification	Example	Note
Numeric	$Dw.d$, $mDw.d$ $Ew.d$, $mEw.d$ $Fw.d$, $mFw.d$ Iw mIw Ow mOw	D25.16 3E20.8 F10.6 1018 06	w and m are unsigned integer constants. w represents field width of data. d represents number of digit positions to the right of decimal point. m represents m successive fields in the same format, and is interpreted the same below.
Complex number	Two numeric fields	2E10.2 E8.3,F8.4	
Alphameric	Aw, mAw, nH	A6 4Hbxy = 4A6	w, n, and m are unsigned integer constants. w represents number of characters to be read. n represents number of characters to be introduced into a FORMAT statement.
Logical	Lw, mLw	L2 L4 4L4	w is defined above. For input, if the leftmost nonblank character is T(F), the value is .TRUE.(.FALSE.). A blank field is regarded as .FALSE.. For output, T or F is printed with $(w-1)$ leading blanks.
Blank	nx	10X	n, as defined above, should not be larger than 132. On input, n characters are skipped. On output, n blanks are introduced.

J, and M belong to the namelist with name N2. Namelist names are enclosed in slashes. Only name N1 is referred to in the above READ statement (5 refers to an input device). The above statements may have, as an example, the following data cards:

column 2
↓

First data card: $N1 I(2,2) = 6, J = 8.4, Y = 6
Second data card: X(3) = 9.0,5.5, K = 2,3,4,5,16*9.0$

The character in the first column of these data cards is ignored. The first card is searched for a $, which should be followed immediately by a namelist name and again followed immediately by one or more blanks. If the search fails, additional cards are examined consecutively until a match occurs. When a match is found between the namelist name on a data card and the namelist name referred to in a READ statement, the data items on the cards (which can be integer constant, real constant, double-precision constant, complex constant, or logical constant) are converted and stored. For the above example, the match is found on the first card. Integer constant 6 is stored in $I(2,2)$, real constant 8.4 is converted to an integer and then stored in J, and integer constant 6 is converted to real and then stored in Y. Since no more data items remain on the first card, the next card is read. Real constant 9.0 is stored in $X(3)$, and real constant 5.5 is stored in $X(4)$. Since K is an array name not followed by a subscript, the entire array is filled with the succeeding constants. Therefore, integer constants 2, 3, 4, and 5 are stored in $K(1)$ through $K(4)$, respectively, and real constant 9.0 is first converted to an integer and then stored in $K(5)$ through $K(20)$. The last character $ terminates the READ operation.

A namelist name is defined only once by its appearance in a NAMELIST statement, which must precede any appearance of the name in the program. Thereafter, the namelist name may appear only in READ or WRITE statements in the program. A namelist name must not become any other name in the program, and a dummy argument in a FUNCTION, SUBROUTINE, or ENTRY statement cannot become a variable in a NAMELIST statement. If a NAMELIST statement contains a dimensioned variable, the statement which defines the dimension of the variable must precede the NAMELIST statement.

5.2.4 SUBROUTINE STATEMENTS

A subroutine is a sequence of statements which perform a desired function. Once such a sequence is written, it can be referenced or called many times without the need of rewriting the sequence. Another usage of subroutines is that a program may be organized to consist of a main program and a number of subroutines, which can be separately programmed. Thus, one job can be divided into several smaller jobs, and these jobs may be distributed to several programmers for faster completion. There are four types of subroutines in FORTRAN: (1) arithmetic statement functions, (2) built-in functions, (3) FUNCTION subprograms, and (4) SUBROUTINE subprograms. The subroutine statements enable the programmer to write these subroutines. Table 5.11 lists the seven subroutine statements and shows their formats and examples.

Subroutines may be divided into functions and SUBROUTINE subprograms. Functions are returned with only a single value, and are referenced by an arithmetic expression containing their names. SUBROUTINE subprograms are returned with one or more values and are referenced by a CALL statement. Furthermore, a subroutine can be either open or closed. An open subroutine, though written once, is

Table 5.11 Subroutine statements†

Statement	Format	Example	Note
ARITHMETIC STATEMENT FUNCTION	$c = d$	TERM(Z) = A + B/Z THIRD(C,D) = TERM(C)*D MAX(A,I) = A**I−X LFUN(A,B,C) = A*B.LE.B*C	c is a function name followed by arguments in parentheses. Arguments must be distinct, nonsubscripted variables separated by commas. d is an expression having no subscripted variables.
FUNCTION	FUNCTION name $(a_1,a_2, \ldots ,a_n)$ REAL FUNCTION name $(a_1,a_2, \ldots ,a_n)$ INTEGER FUNCTION name $(a_1,a_2, \ldots ,a_n)$ DOUBLE PRECISION FUNCTION name $(a_1, \ldots ,a_n)$ COMPLEX FUNCTION name $(a_1,a_2, \ldots ,a_n)$ LOGICAL FUNCTION name $(a_1,a_2, \ldots ,a_n)$	FUNCTION ARCTAN(RAD) REAL FUNCTION TYPE(X,Y,Z) INTEGER FUNCTION PAR(IN,OUT) DOUBLE PRECISION FUNCTION X(R,S) COMPLEX FUNCTION C(T) LOGICAL FUNCTION L(W,Q)	name is the symbolic name of a single-valued function. $a_1, \ldots ,a_n$ $(n \geq 1)$ are nonsubscripted variable names of a dummy name of a SUBROUTINE or a FUNCTION subprogram.
SUBROUTINE	SUBROUTINE subr SUBROUTINE subr $(a_1,a_2, \ldots ,a_n)$ SUBROUTINE subr $(a_1, \ldots ,a_n,*, \ldots ,*)$	SUBROUTINE NUMBER SUBROUTINE BEST (A,I,B,C) SUBROUTINE WORK (X,Y,Z,*,*)	subr is the symbolic name of a SUBROUTINE subprogram. $a_1, \ldots ,a_n$ are nonsubscripted variable names or dummy names of a SUBROUTINE or a FUNCTION subprogram. * denotes a nonstandard return.
CALL	CALL subr $(b_1, \ldots ,b_n)$ CALL subr $(b_1, \ldots ,b_n,\$n_1, \ldots ,\$n_m)$	CALL NUMBER CALL BEST (X,2,Y,5.5) CALL WORK (A,B,C,\$20,\$40) EXTERNAL R CALL SUBR (R,S,T)	subr is the symbolic name of a SUBROUTINE subprogram. $b_1, \ldots ,b_n$ are arguments which can be constants, subscripted or nonsubscripted variables, a string of alphabetic characters, expressions, or names of SUBROUTINE or FUNCTION subprograms. n's are statement numbers.

228

ENTRY	ENTRY ename $(b_1, \ldots, b_n)$ ENTRY ename $(b_1, \ldots, b_n, *, \ldots, *)$	ENTRY FIRST (X,Y,Z) ENTRY NEXT (I,J,*,*)	ename is the symbolic name of an entry point. $b_1, \ldots, b_n$ are arguments as described above.
RETURN	RETURN RETURN i	RETURN 3 RETURN K	i is an integer constant or variable which denotes the ith nonstandard return in the argument list of a SUBROUTINE or ENTRY statement, reading left to right.
BLOCK DATA	BLOCK DATA	BLOCK DATA DIMENSION B(4) DATA (B(I),I = 1,4)/1,2,2*3./	First statement for a BLOCK DATA subprogram.

† FUNCTION, SUBROUTINE, ENTRY, and BLOCK DATA statements are nonexecutable statements.

inserted into the object program each time it is referred to in the source program, while a closed subroutine is inserted only once in the object program. The above built-in-function type of subroutine is an open subroutine, while the other three types are closed subroutines.

(a) *Arithmetic statement function* This function is defined by an ARITHMETIC STATEMENT FUNCTION statement shown in Table 5.11. The name of the function is selected according to the previously mentioned rule for a symbolic name. The complete function name consists of this name followed immediately by an enclosed string of one or more arguments separated by commas, as illustrated in Table 5.11. These arguments are dummy variables. The function definition is an expression which does not involve subscripted variables (though it may involve a precedingly defined function). Those variables in the expression which are not arguments are the parameters of the function. All ARITHMETIC STATEMENT FUNCTION definitions must precede the first executable statement of the source program.

(b) *Built-in functions* The built-in functions are predefined, open subroutines that have been incorporated in the FORTRAN processor. A partial list of these functions is shown in Table 5.12. In this table, X's and K's represent real and integer arguments, respectively. Function names beginning with letters A, F, S, and D give a result of type real, while those beginning with letters I and M give a result of type integer. Some functions such as AMAXO accept integer arguments but give real results, while some other functions such as IFIX accept real arguments but give integer results. The logical functions accept either real or integer arguments but give real results.

(c) *FUNCTION subprogram* A FUNCTION subprogram requires a FUNCTION statement as the first statement and a RETURN statement as the last. As shown in Table 5.11, there are six FUNCTION statements; their choice depends on the type required. The name of the function must appear at least once as a variable on the left side of an arithmetic statement or in an input statement, and it cannot be used in a NAMELIST statement.

The arguments in the function name are dummy variables. The actual arguments may be (1) any type of constants, (2) any type of subscripted or nonsubscripted variables, (3) an arithmetic or a logical expression, and (4) the name of a FUNCTION or SUBROUTINE subprogram; they must correspond in number, order, and type with the dummy arguments. When a dummy argument is an array name, a statement with dimension information must appear in the FUNCTION subprogram. The FUNCTION subprogram may contain any FORTRAN statements

Table 5.12   FORTRAN built-in functions

Name	Function†
ABS(X)	Absolute value of real variable X.
IABS(K)	Absolute value of integer K.
AINT(X)	Largest integer $/X/$ with sign of X (that is, truncation).
INT(X)	Ditto, except that the result is an integer.
AMOD(X_1,X_2)	$X_1 - \text{AINT}(X_1/X_2)$ (that is, remainder).
MOD(K_1,K_2)	$K_1 - \text{INT}(K_1/K_2)$ (that is, remainder).
AMAXO($K_1, \ldots, K_n$)	Largest value of integer arguments. Result is real.
AMAX/($X1, \ldots, X_n$)	Largest value of real arguments. Result is real.
MAXO($K_1, \ldots, K_n$)	Largest value of integer arguments. Result is integer.
MAX/($X_1, \ldots, X_n$)	Largest value of real arguments. Result is integer.
AMZNO($K_1, \ldots, K_n$)	Smallest value of integer arguments. Result is real.
AMIN/($X_1, \ldots, X_n$)	Smallest value of real arguments. Result is real.
MZNO($K_1, \ldots, K_n$)	Smallest value of integer arguments. Result is integer.
MZNI($X_1, \ldots, X_n$)	Smallest value of real arguments. Result is integer.
FLOAT(K)	Conversion of an integer argument into a real argument.
IFIX(X)	Conversion of a real argument into an integer.
SZGN(X_1,X_2)	Value of X_1 with sign of X_2. Result is real.
ISIGN(K_1,K_2)	Value of K_1 with sign of K_2. Result is integer.
DIM(X_1,X_2)	$X_1 - \text{AMIN}/(X_1,X_2)$ (that is, positive difference).
IDIM(K_1,K_2)	$K_1 - \text{MZNO}(K_1,K_2)$ (that is, positive difference).
AND(X_1,X_2)	Logical intersection of two 36-bit arguments. Result is real.
AND(K_1,K_2)	Ditto.
OR(X_1,X_2)	Logical union of two 36-bit arguments. Result is real.
OR(K_1,K_2)	Ditto.
COMPL(X)	Logical is complement of a 36-bit argument. Result is real.
COMPL(K)	Ditto.
BOOL(X)	Logical 36-bit argument from signed 36-bit argument.
BOOL(K)	Ditto.

† X's are real and K's are integers.   Function names beginning with A, F, S, and D give a real result, and those beginning with I and M give an integer result.   Results of the four logical functions are all real.

except SUBROUTINE or another FUNCTION statement. A FUNC-
TION subprogram is referenced by using its name as an operand in an
arithmetic expression.

The FORTRAN processor is incorporated with many built-in
FUNCTION subprograms which are known as mathematical subroutines.
A partial list of these mathematical FUNCTION subprograms is shown in
Table 5.13. These are, among others, exponential, logarithmic, and
trigonometric functions. The arguments as well as the results of all
these functions in this table are real.

(*d*) *SUBROUTINE subprogram* A SUBROUTINE subprogram
requires a SUBROUTINE statement as the first statement and a
RETURN statement as the last executable statement. As shown in
Table 5.11, there are three forms of SUBROUTINE statement: the first
one without arguments, the second with arguments, and the third with
nonstandard returns.

A CALL statement is used to refer to a SUBROUTINE statement.
It transfers control to the subprogram and presents it with the actual
arguments. Table 5.11 shows three forms of CALL statements: the
first one without arguments, the second with arguments, and the third
with nonstandard returns. The arguments of a CALL statement can be
constants, subscripted or nonsubscripted variables, arithmetic or logical
expressions, strings of alphameric characters, or names of FUNCTION

Table 5.13 Mathematical FUNCTION subprograms

Name	Function
EXP(X)	Exponential of X
ALOG(X)	Natural logarithm of X
ALOG10(X)	Common logarithm of X
SIN(X)	Sine of X
COS(X)	Cosine of X
TAN(X)	Tangent of X
COTAN(X)	Cotangent of X
ATAN(X)	Arctangent of X
ATAN2(X1,X2)	Arctangent of (X1/X2)
ARSIN(X)	Arcsine of X
ARCOS(X)	Arccosine of X
SINH(X)	Hyperbolic sine of X
COSH(X)	Hyperbolic cosine of X
TANH(X)	Hyperbolic tangent of X
SQRT(X)	Square root of X
ERF(X)	Error function of X
GAMMA(X)	Gamma function of X
ALGAMA(X)	Logarithm of gamma function of X

or SUBROUTINE subprograms. When the names are FUNCTION and
SUBROUTINE subprograms, they must be declared by an EXTERNAL
statement in order to distinguish these subprogram names from ordinary
variable names; an example is shown in Table 5.11.

A SUBROUTINE subprogram may use one or more of its arguments as the outputs. Such arguments must appear on the left side of
an arithmetic statement or in an input list within the subprogram. The
arguments of the subroutine are dummy variables which are replaced by
the actual arguments in the CALL statement. The actual arguments
must correspond in number, order, and type with the dummy arguments.
When a dummy argument is an array name, a statement specifying its
dimension must appear in the SUBROUTINE subprogram, and the corresponding actual argument in the CALL statement must be a dimensioned array name. A SUBROUTINE subprogram may contain any
FORTRAN statements except FUNCTION statements, another SUB-
ROUTINE statement, or BLOCK DATA statements.

When the subprogram has a normal return, the first SUBROUTINE
statement and the first CALL statement in Table 5.11 are used when no
arguments are required (a COMMON statement is usually used in this
case); and the second SUBROUTINE statement and the second CALL
statement are used where there are arguments. In these cases, the first
RETURN statement is used to indicate the normal exit of the subprogram, and the next executable statement in the calling program is the
one following the CALL statement in the calling program.

When the subprogram requires nonstandard returns, the third SUB-
ROUTINE statement and the third CALL statement are used. The
nonstandard returns are denoted by as many characters * as the arguments of nonstandard returns in the SUBROUTINE statement, and by a
string of such characters $n_1, \ldots, n_m (where m denotes the number of
nonstandard returns) as the calling arguments in the CALL statement.
The second RETURN statement is used where i denotes the ith nonstandard return. The return to the calling program from the ith nonstandard return is to continue from the statement with number n_i in the
calling program.

The normal entry to a SUBROUTINE (or FUNCTION) subprogram is the first executable statement following the SUBROUTINE (or
FUNCTION) statement. However, it is also possible to enter a subprogram by a CALL statement (or by a function reference) to an ENTRY
statement in the subprogram. In this case, entry of a subprogram is the
first executable statement following the ENTRY statement in the subprogram. The formats and examples of ENTRY statements are shown
in Table 5.11. There can be more than one ENTRY statement in a subprogram, as well as more than one nonstandard return. ENTRY state-

ments are nonexecutable.   Each CALL statement (or function reference) must agree in order, type, and number with the referenced SUBROUTINE (or FUNCTION) or ENTRY statement.   No subprogram may refer to itself directly or through any of its ENTRY statements, nor may it refer to any other subprogram whose RETURN statement has not been satisfied.

The FORTRAN processor is incorporated with some built-in SUB-ROUTINE subprograms.   There are subroutines EXIT, DUMP, and PDUMP.   In addition, there are five subroutines for machine indicator tests: SLITE, SLITET, SSWTCH, OVERFL, and DVCHK.

(e) *BLOCK DATA subprogram*   The last statement in Table 5.11 enables one to write a BLOCK DATA subprogram which makes it possible to enter data into a labeled COMMON block during compilation. This subprogram may contain only the DATA, COMMON, DIMEN-SION, and TYPE statements associated with the data being defined. The BLOCK DATA statement is the first statement of a BLOCK DATA subprogram, and the END statement is the last statement.   An example of a BLOCK DATA subprogram is shown below:

```
BLOCK DATA
DIMENSION X(4), Z(3)
COMMON /ED/X,Y,Z
DATA (X(I),I=1,4)/4*1.5/,Y/3.14159/
END
```

Notice that all items of a COMMON block must be listed in the COM-MON statement even though they do not all appear in the DATA state-ment.   Data may be entered into more than one COMMON block in one BLOCK DATA subprogram.

5.2.5 SPECIFICATION STATEMENTS

The specification statements provide information about storage allocation and about the constants and variables used in the program, and allow com-ments or messages to be inserted in a FORTRAN program to improve readability of the FORTRAN program.   There are six specification statements: DIMENSION, COMMON, EQUIVALENCE, DATA, TYPE, and COMMENT.   General forms and examples of these state-ments are shown in Table 5.14.

A COMMENT statement consists of a string of characters of the set shown in Table 5.2.   This string is ignored by the FORTRAN proc-essor and serves merely to furnish commentary information to the reader. A comment may appear anywhere in a program as long as it is ahead of the END statement.   As shown in Table 5.14, character C must appear in column 1.

Table 5.14 Specification statements†

Statement	Format	Note
DIMENSION	DIMENSION $V_1(i_1), V_2(i_2), \ldots$ e.g., DIMENSION P(95), R(2500), S(2500) DIMENSION BCD(10,900), FF(9100)	Each V_n is an array variable. Each i_n is composed of from one to seven unsigned integer constants and/or integer variables, separated by commas.
COMMON	COMMON $a,b,c, \ldots ./r/d,e,f, \ldots ./s/g,h, \ldots$ e.g., COMMON P,R,S,FF COMMON D,E(10)/X,F(3),G/Y/H COMMON /Z/A,Q(5)//R,T	$a, b, \ldots /r/, /s/, \ldots$ are variables that may be dimensioned. $/r/, /s/, \ldots$ are variables that are block names.
EQUIVALENCE	EQUIVALENCE $(a,b,c, \ldots), (d,e,f, \ldots)$ e.g., DIMENSION BCD(10,900), FF(9100), B(10), IM(8) EQUIVALENCE (BCD,FF(101)), (AA,IAA) EQUIVALENCE (FCTN,B(2)), (IRA,IM(1))	$a, b, c, d, e, f, \ldots$ are variables that may be subscripted; these subscripts must be integer constants. The number of subscripts appended to a variable either must be equal to the number of dimensions of the variable or must be equal to 1.
DATA	DATA list$/d_1, d_2, \ldots, d_m/$ list$/d_1, d_2, k*d_3, \ldots, d_m/ \ldots$ e.g., DATA DS, TRUE/6H000008,077777777777/ DATA (X(I),Y(I),I=1,20,2)/2.0,3.0,18*10.0/	Word list means the names of the variables being defined. d is the data literal (i.e., constant), and k is an integer constant. k followed by an * and then followed by a d indicates that the data literal is repeated k times.
TYPE	INTEGER $a(i_1), b(i_2), c(i_3), \ldots$ REAL $a(i_1), b(i_2), c(i_3), \ldots$ DOUBLE PRECISION $a(i_1), b(i_2), c(i_3), \ldots$ COMPLEX $a(i_1), b(i_2), c(i_3), \ldots$ LOGICAL $a(i_1), b(i_2), c(i_3), \ldots$ EXTERNAL x, y, c e.g., INTEGER B(100), D(5,10), MAR REAL IOUT,FF,HORCI DOUBLE PRECISION Q,J,DSIN EXTERNAL MIMCO, SMO4 COMPLEX C(2,10) LOGICAL LA,LB,LC,LD DATA LA,LB,LC,LD/F,.TRUE.,.FALSE.,T/	$a, b, c, \ldots$ are variable or function names appearing within the program. $x, y, z, \ldots$ are function names appearing within the program. Each i_n is composed of from one to seven integer constants and/or integer variables. Subscripts may be appended only to variable names appearing within the program, not to function names.
COMMENT	Character C is column 1; e.g., C****VAN DER POL'S EQUATION	Comment or message is in columns 2 to 72.

† All these statements are nonexecutable statements.

235

A DIMENSION statement declares the name of a group of variables; such a group is called an array. All the members of the array carry the same name but identify themselves by subscripts, such as $X(10)$ and $Z(5)$. An array may have as many as seven subscripts to represent seven dimensions. Each subscript of an array name in a DIMENSION statement can be an integer constant or an integer variable which gives the maximum size of each dimension of the array. The DIMENSION statement must generally precede the first appearances of the variables to which are referred in any executable, NAMELIST, or DATA statement in the program. A single DIMENSION statement may specify the dimensions of more than one array. Dimensions may also be declared in a COMMON or a TYPE statement. If a variable is dimensioned in a DIMENSION statement, it must not be dimensioned elsewhere.

A COMMON statement defines a common storage area to be shared by a program and its subprograms. It must generally precede any executable, NAMELIST, and DATA statements in a program. The locations in the COMMON area are assigned to the variables according to the sequence in which these variables appear in the COMMON statement, beginning with the first COMMON statement of the program.

There are two kinds of COMMON statements: blank COMMON and labeled COMMON. As shown in Table 5.14, a labeled COMMON is indicated by a block name embedded in slashes and placed before the variable names of the statement. A blank COMMON is indicated either by omitting the block name if it appears at the beginning of the COMMON statement or by preceding the blank COMMON variable names by two consecutive slashes. All COMMON blocks must have the same length in all the programs that are executed together. A DATA statement is used to enter data into a labeled COMMON statement, but not into a blank COMMON statement.

An EQUIVALENCE statement controls the allocation of data storage by causing two or more variables to share the same core-storage location. An EQUIVALENCE statement must generally precede any executable, NAMELIST, and DATA statements in the program. As shown in Table 5.14, each pair of parentheses in the statement encloses the names of two or more variables that are to be stored in the same location during execution of the object program; any number of equivalences may be given. Two variables in a COMMON area or in two different COMMON areas should not be made equivalent to each other, directly or indirectly.

A DATA statement is used to cause data to be compiled into an object program. The constants that can be specified in a DATA statement are shown in Table 5.3. There must be a one-to-one correspondence between the variable names and the constants in a DATA statement.

The DATA statement in a BLOCK DATA subprogram causes the subprogram to compile data into the COMMON area of the program.

A TYPE statement specifies the type of one or more variables and/or functions. As shown in Table 5.14, there are six TYPE statements to specify integer, real, double-precision, complex, logical, and external variables and functions. Variables that appear in an EXTERNAL statement are subprogram names. If subprogram names are the arguments of other subprograms or if they are the names of built-in functions which are used as the names of a FUNCTION or SUBROUTINE subprogram, they must appear in an EXTERNAL statement.

There is a very important exception. If a variable name has I, J, K, L, M, or N as the first character, it is automatically regarded as an integer variable name. If the variable name with I, J, K, L, M, or N as the first character is not an integer variable name, then it must be properly declared by a TYPE statement. (This rule also applies to function names.) Thus, TYPE statements for such names are not required. Appearance of a name in a TYPE statement, except an EXTERNAL statement, must precede the first appearances of the variables to which they refer in any executable, NAMELIST, or DATA statements in the program. Any variable that is dimensioned by a TYPE statement may not be dimensioned elsewhere.

5.3 COMPUTING THE SOLUTION OF A DIFFERENTIAL EQUATION—VERSION 1

Having introduced FORTRAN statements and elements of the statements, we can now show a complete FORTRAN program. This program is to compute the solution of van der Pol's equation by using a minimum number of types of statements. It is to be referred to as version 1, as the same equation will again be used in introducing other programming techniques and numerical methods.

5.3.1 VAN DER POL'S EQUATION

The van der Pol equation, together with the values of parameters and initial conditions, is again shown:

$$\ddot{x} + A(x^2 - 1)\dot{x} + Bx = 0 \tag{5.1}$$

where

$$A = 0.1 \quad \text{and} \quad B = 1$$
$$x(0) = 1 \quad \text{and} \quad \dot{x}(0) = 0$$

With the above values of A and B, Eq. (5.1) can be rewritten as

$$\ddot{x} = -0.1(x^2 - 1)\dot{x} - x \tag{5.2}$$

Table 5.15   Equivalent symbols

Equation symbol	Program symbol
x	X0
$\dot{x}$	X1 or DX
$\ddot{x}$	X2DX
t	T
	KOUNT

In terms of FORTRAN language, Eq. (5.2) can be written as

$$\text{X2DX} = -.1*(\text{X0*X0}-1.0)*\text{X1}-\text{X0} \tag{5.3}$$
$$\text{DX} = \text{X1}$$

FORTRAN variables X2DX, DX, etc., and the respective equation symbols are shown in Table 5.15. Also shown in Table 5.15 is T, which represents the time t which is the independent variable, and KOUNT, which represents a counter which counts the number of iterations during numerical solution of the differential equation. Note that x is represented by either DX or X1; the reason for this representation will become apparent later.

5.3.2 NUMERICAL SOLUTION

The differential equation is to be solved by a numerical method in which the simplest Euler integration formula is employed. By this method, variables x and $\dot{x}$ are incremented in the following manner:

$$x = x + \dot{x}H$$
$$\dot{x} = \dot{x} + \ddot{x}H \tag{5.4}$$

where H represents the increment in time t and is called the step size of integration. In terms of FORTRAN language, with H equal to 0.001, we have

$$\text{X0} = \text{X0} + 0.001*\text{DX}$$
$$\text{X1} = \text{X1} + 0.001*\text{X2DX} \tag{5.5}$$

The numerical procedure to compute the solution is as follows. Since the values of X0 and X1 at T equal to 0 are known, the values of X2DX and DX at T equal to 0 are computed by Eq. (5.3). These values of X2DX and DX at T equal to 0 are then used in Eq. (5.5) to compute X0 and X1 at T equal to H, which are then used in Eq. (5.3) to compute X2DX and DX at T equal to H. The values of X2DX and DX at T equal to H are used in Eq. (5.5) to compute X0 and X1 at T equal to 2H, which are then used in Eq. (5.3) to compute X2DX and DX at T equal to 2H. This process of alternately computing the derivatives X2DX and DX by Eq. (5.3) and integrating the variables X0 and X1 by Eq. (5.5) continues until T reaches the chosen value for termination.

5.3.3 FLOWCHART

Figure 5.1 is a flowchart which shows the above computing process in addition to the necessary initialization, time incrementing, termination testing, print-output counting, and print outputting. The print count is represented by the variable KOUNT. Initially, the values of X1 and T are set to 0, and those of X0 and KOUNT are set to 1. The printer then skips the paper to the top of the next page. KOUNT is next decremented by 1 and then tested for 0. Since KOUNT is 0 at this first time, the initial values of T, X0, and X1 are printed. The derivatives X2DX and DX are computed, and the variables X0 and X1 are integrated. The time T is incremented by 0.001 and then tested for 3. If it is less than or equal to 3, the computing process returns to the step where KOUNT is decremented by 1; this forms a loop, as shown in Fig. 5.1. This loop continues until T is larger than 3. At that time, the final values of T, X0, and X1 are printed.

5.3.4 WRITE AND FORMAT STATEMENTS

The procedure shown in the flowchart of Fig. 5.1 is translated into the FORTRAN program in Fig. 5.2. In this program, there are the following WRITE and FORMAT statements:

```
     WRITE(6,80)
     WRITE(6,90), T,X0,X1
  80 FORMAT(1H1)
  90 FORMAT(1H ,1PE30.8,1P2E20.8)
```

As indicated in Table 5.9, the WRITE statement is of the form WRITE(i,n) list, where i indicates an output device, n is the statement number of an associated FORMAT statement, and list is a list of variables. (The list can be empty.) This statement prepares a BCD tape that can be used for off-line print output. For program control, the first character of each BCD record carries a special function. For this reason, this character is called a carriage control character which controls spacing of the print output. Some control characters and their functions are shown in Table 5.16. The control character is not printed. Program control of print output is obtained by beginning with a field specification (in the FORMAT statement) which consists of three characters: 1H immediately followed by the desired control character. The field specifications in the above two FORMAT statements, 1H1 and 1Hb (b means blank), are two examples.

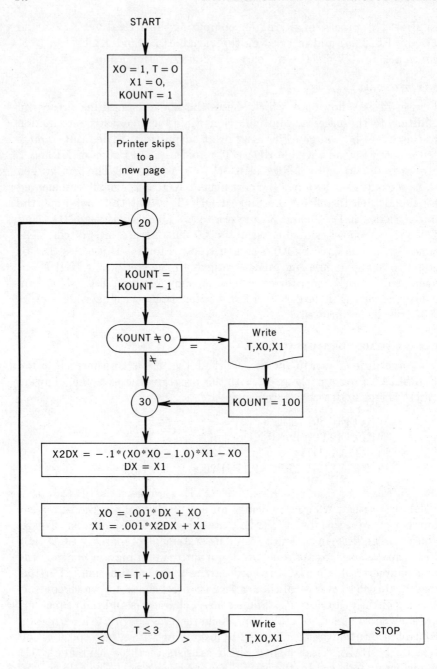

Fig. 5.1 Flowchart for computing the solution of van der Pol's equation, version 1.

```
$EXECUTE          JB JOB
$ID   CHU   *305/65/020*3M$
$ JB JOB
$IBFTC VER1
C******SOLVING VAN DER POL'S EQUATION    VERSION 1
C******DATA, LOGICAL IF, GO TO, ARITH. STATEMENTS.
C******WRITE AND FORMAT STATEMENTS
C******ONE RUN, ONE LOOP, EULER INTEGRATION.
       DATA X0,X1,T,KOUNT/1.0,2*0.0,1/
C******SKIP TO THE TOP OF NEW PAGE
       WRITE(6,80)
    80 FORMAT(1H1)
C******DECREMENT THE COUNTER
    20 KOUNT=KOUNT-1
C******TEST FOR COUNTER BEING ZERO
       IF(KOUNT.NE.0) GO TO 30
C******PRINT RESULT
       WRITE(6,90) T,X0,X1
    90 FORMAT(1H ,1PE30.8,1P2E20.8)
C******RESET PRIOR COUNTER
       KOUNT=100
C******COMPUTING DERIVATIVES
    30 X2DX=-.1*(X0*X0-1.0)*X1-X0
       DX=X1
C******INTEGRATION
    40 X0=.001*DX+X0
       X1=.001*X2DX+X1
C******INCREMENT TIME COUNTER
       T=T+.001
C******TEST FOR TERMINATION
       IF(T.LE.3.0) GO TO 20
C******PRINT THE RESULT OF THE LAST INTERATION
       WRITE(6,90) T,X0,X1
       STOP
       END
```

Fig. 5.2 FORTRAN program for computing the solution of van der Pol's equation, version 1.

Quantities 1PE30.8 and 1P2E20.8 are specifications for the numerical fields in the FORMAT statements. For numerical fields, there are five types, as were shown in Table 5.10: $Dw.d$, $Ew.d$, $Fw.d$, Iw, and Ow, which denote, respectively, double-precision number, floating-point number, fixed-point number, integer, and octal number. Examples of these types are:

D25.10	indicates	bbbbbbbbb$-$.1234567890Db02
E20.8	indicates	bbbbbb$-$.12345678E$+$05
F12.6	indicates	bbb$-$12.345600
I5	indicates	bbb25
08	indicates	bbb12345

Table 5.16   Printer control characters (standard mode)

Control character	Function
1	Skip immediately to the top of next page and space one line after printing.
0	Space one line before printing and one line after printing.
Blank	Space one line after printing.

In the above, w is an unsigned integer constant that represents the field width for the converted data; this field width may be purposely specified larger than that required in order to provide column spacing between numbers. For the above five examples, the widths are 25-, 20-, 12-, 5-, and 8-character positions. The spacings obtained by using a larger-than-necessary width are filled in with b's (blanks). The letter d is also an unsigned integer or zero to represent the number of positions that appear to the right of the decimal point. For the above examples, there are 10, 8, and 6 fractional digits for the D, E, and F fields, respectively. If a fixed-point number has more fractional digits than specified by d in an F field, the excess fractional digits on the less significant end are lost. If an integer has more digits than specified by w in an I field, the excess digits on the more significant end and the sign digit are lost. If a real number specified by a D, E, or F field requires more spaces than are allowed by the width w, the number is disregarded and the field is filled with asterisks.

A scale factor followed by letter P may precede the field specification to indicate the number of integral digits in the D, E, and F fields. Examples of the use of scale factors are:

E20.8	indicates	bbbbbb−.12345678Eb05
1PE20.8	indicates	bbbbb−1.23456780Eb04
−1PE20.8	indicates	bbbbbb−.01234567Eb06

The scale factor is assumed to be zero if no other value has been given. However, once a value has been given, it will hold for all D, E, and F field specifications following the scale factor within the same FORMAT statement. (This applies to both single-record format and multiple-record format.) The scale factor has no effect on I and O fields.

It is often desired to print (or read) n successive numbers of the same type of field. This can be specified by placing an unsigned integer immediately to the left of a D, E, F, I, L, O, or A specification. For example,

E16.4	indicates	bbbbbb−.1234Eb02
2E16.4	indicates	bbbbbb−.1234Eb02bbbbbbb.4321Eb04
1P2E16.4	indicates	bbbbb−1.2343Eb01bbbbbb4.3212Eb03

The above repetition of field specifications can be extended to a group of field specifications by using parentheses. This is better illustrated by the following examples:

FORMAT(2(F10.6,E12.4),I4)   indicates
FORMAT(F10.6,E12.4,F10.6,E12.4,I4)

Up to two levels of parentheses are allowed in addition to the pair of parentheses required by the FORMAT statement. The second level of parentheses facilitates the specification of complex numbers.

The field specifications so far described are limited to one line of print. It is possible to use a single FORMAT statement to specify more than one line of print by using the slash (/). The slash denotes that the printer turns to a new line. For example, (3F10.4/5E16.6) would specify a multiline block of print in which lines 1, 3, 5, . . . have field specification (3F10.4) and lines 2, 4, 6, . . . have specification (5E16.6) until the data are exhausted, and (3F10.4//5E16.6) would specify a block in which lines 1, 4, 7, . . . have specification (3F10.4), lines 2, 5, 8, . . . are blanks, and lines 3, 6, 9, . . . have specification (5E16.6) until the data are exhausted.

5.3.5 FORTRAN PROGRAM

The first four cards (or lines) of the FORTRAN program in Fig. 5.2 are control cards. The $EXECUTIVE card, which contains the name IBJOB, signals the beginning of a job segment. When this card is read by the supervisor of the IBSYS operating system, it passes control to the IBJOB processor. The $ID card gives the identification of the user, project number, and options such as a limit on execution time of the program. The next $IBJOB card initiates the IBJOB processor and specifies options such as compile and execute. The $IBFTC card carries the deck name VER1, which identifies the deck that follows. When this card is read, the FORTRAN IV compiler is brought into the core memory to process the deck. There can be options on list, symbol table, punch, instruction set, and index register on the $IBJOB card. If there are data cards (there are no data cards in this program), a $DATA control card must be placed immediately after the END card, and the data cards follow immediately thereafter.

The next four cards, together with other cards with character C in column 1, are COMMENT statements; these cards are listed but otherwise ignored by the FORTRAN processor. The COMMENT statements are inserted to provide remarks so as to improve the readability of the program.

The DATA statement initializes X0, X1, T (real variables), and KOUNT (an integer variable) to the values of 1, 0, 0, and 1, respectively. The pair of WRITE and FORMAT statements causes the off-line printer

to skip the paper to the top of the next page because the control character
is 1.   Variable KOUNT is now decremented by 1 and then tested for a
nonzero value.   If it is zero, the values of T, X0, and X1 are printed out.
Otherwise, KOUNT is set to 100.   This is followed by the computation
of derivatives X20X and DX, by the integration of variables X0 and X1,
and by incrementing T.   If T is 3 or less, then the computation returns
to the decrementing of KOUNT and thus forms a loop for iteration.   The
computation terminates when T exceeds 3.   The STOP statement terminates the execution and returns the control to IBSYS.   The END
statement terminates the compilation.

The result of the computation is shown in Fig. 5.3, where the values
in the first, second, and third columns are, respectively, the values of T,
X0, and X1.   Notice that the print interval is approximately 0.1 because
conversion of a binary fractional number to a decimal number is not exact.

Version 1 shows integer constants, integer variables, real constants,
and real variables.   It illustrates the COMMENT, DATA, WRITE,

0.	1.00000000E 00	0.
9.99999595E-02	9.95053482E-01	-9.98407400E-02
1.99999814E-01	9.80162358E-01	-1.98727730E-01
2.99999642E-01	9.55467165E-01	-2.95758000E-01
3.99999472E-01	9.21195602E-01	-3.90094939E-01
4.99999303E-01	8.77655745E-01	-4.80964178E-01
5.99998760E-01	8.25230467E-01	-5.67644972E-01
6.99998218E-01	7.64372510E-01	-6.49459869E-01
7.99997675E-01	6.95600599E-01	-7.25762445E-01
8.99997127E-01	6.19497156E-01	-7.95925874E-01
9.99996591E-01	5.36706668E-01	-8.59333408E-01
1.09999532E 00	4.47935176E-01	-9.15371990E-01
1.19999403E 00	3.53949884E-01	-9.63430095E-01
1.29999274E 00	2.55578825E-01	-1.00290076E 00
1.39999145E 00	1.53710428E-01	-1.03318986E 00
1.49999017E 00	4.92910635E-02	-1.05373240E 00
1.59998888E 00	-5.66784650E-02	-1.06401083E 00
1.69998759E 00	-1.63149045E-01	-1.06358120E 00
1.79998630E 00	-2.69031975E-01	-1.05210127E 00
1.89998502E 00	-3.73210520E-01	-1.02935933E 00
1.99998373E 00	-4.74554455E-01	-9.95301783E-01
2.09998244E 00	-5.71936882E-01	-9.50057209E-01
2.19998115E 00	-6.64253569E-01	-8.93950260E-01
2.29997987E 00	-7.50442761E-01	-8.27509296E-01
2.39997858E 00	-8.29505467E-01	-7.51460832E-01
2.49997729E 00	-9.00524437E-01	-6.66713101E-01
2.59997600E 00	-9.62681246E-01	-5.74329364E-01
2.69997472E 00	-1.01526985E 00	-4.75492281E-01
2.79997343E 00	-1.05770674E 00	-3.71463707E-01
2.89997214E 00	-1.08953728E 00	-2.63542175E-01
2.99997085E 00	-1.11043642E 00	-1.53023319E-01
3.00097084E 00	-1.11058944E 00	-1.51909316E-01

Fig. 5.3 Table output from the FORTRAN program in Fig. 5.2 (version 1).

FORMAT, logical IF, arithmetic, GO TO, STOP, and END statements. It shows the use of a flowchart to describe a computation procedure. It also shows how to compute the solution of a differential equation.

5.4 VERSION 2

The computed result in Fig. 5.3 for van der Pol's equation consists merely of three columns of numbers. It does not show which computation it is, what the values in these columns represent, or what the values of constants and parameters are. Furthermore, the program in Fig. 5.2 does not allow multiple runs with different parameters, and has no READ statements or data cards. Version 2 removes all these deficiencies.

5.4.1 PRINT OUTPUT DESIGN

In order to provide titles and headings as well as the values of constants and parameters, one needs to lay out the output that he wishes to have from the printer. An example is shown in Fig. 5.4. In this layout, the first, second, and fourth lines show the titles, and the sixth line shows the headings for the three columns of the numerical results. Figure 5.4 also shows the names and values of the constants and parameters as well as the spacings between the lines. Such a layout may be referred to as a print output design.

5.4.2 FIELD SPECIFICATIONS OF ALPHAMERIC DATA

There are two fields which specify alphameric data that are stored internally in BCD. These are the A field and the H field, as shown in Table 5.10. Specification Aw causes w characters to be read into or written from a variable or from an array, while nH specifies a string of n characters in a FORMAT statement. The data specified by field A are represented by a variable name or an array name and thus can be referenced. The data specified by field H carry no name and cannot be referenced.

(a) A field When an A field is referenced by an INPUT statement, specification nAw means that the next n successive fields of w characters are to be stored internally as BCD information in successive locations of the core memory. If w is larger than 6, only the six rightmost characters are significant; if w is less than 6, the characters are left-adjusted and the memory word filled out with blanks. For example, the following three statements and one data card,

```
      DIMENSION TITLE(12)
      READ(5,100) TITLE
  100 FORMAT(12A6)
  (1H1,9X, 34HSOLUTION OF VAN DER POL'S EQUATION)
```

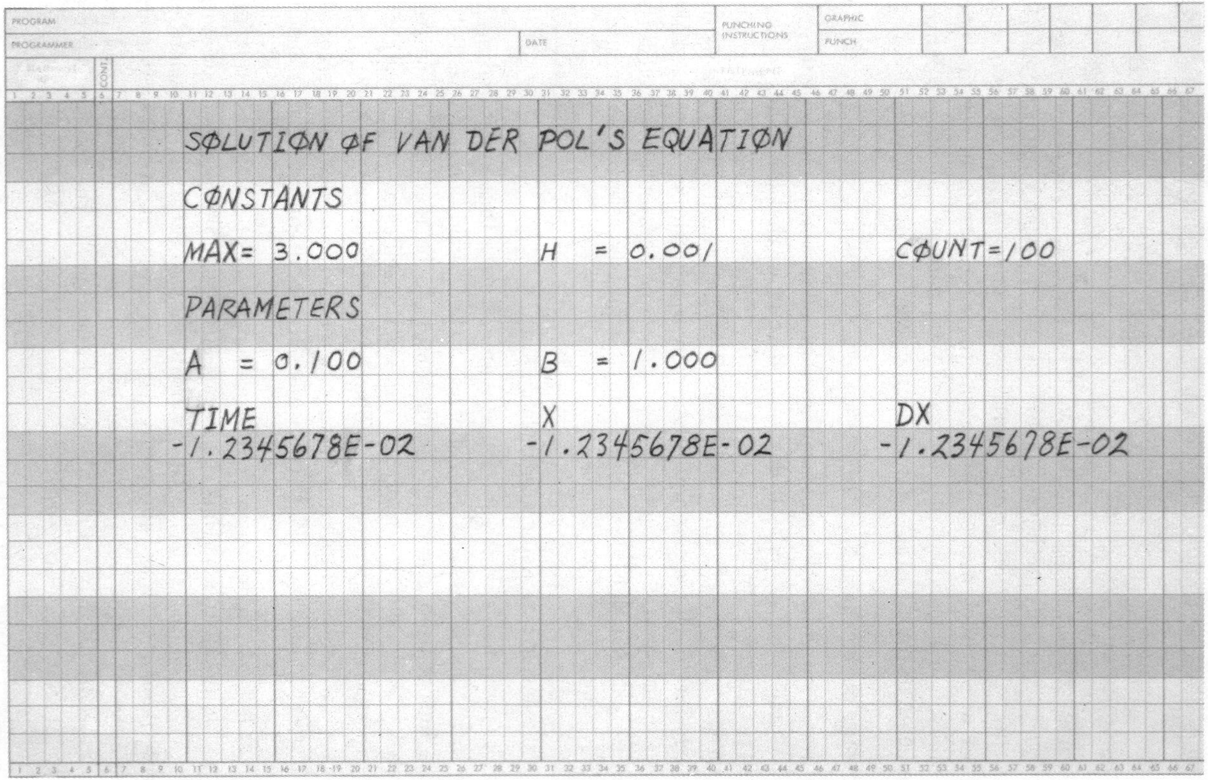
PROGRAM
PROGRAMMER
DATE
PUNCHING INSTRUCTIONS
GRAPHIC
PUNCH
CONT.
SØLUTIØN ØF VAN DER POL'S EQUATIØN
CØNSTANTS
MAX= 3.000
H = 0.001
CØUNT=100
PARAMETERS
A = 0.100
B = 1.000
TIME
X
DX
-1.2345678E-02
-1.2345678E-02
-1.2345678E-02

Fig. 5.4 Print output design for the FORTRAN program in Fig. 5.6 (version 2).

cause the data to be stored into the array TITLE consisting of twelve 6-character words in the following manner:

(1H1,9
X,34HS
OLUTIO
NbOFbV
ANbDER
bPOL'S
bEQUAT
ION)bb
bbbbbb
bbbbbb
bbbbbb
bbbbbb

where b means blank.   (1H1,9 can be referred to as TITLE(1), and word ION)bb as TITLE(8).

When an A field is referenced by an OUTPUT statement, specification nAw means that the next n successive fields of w characters are transferred from the memory to an output device.   If w exceeds 6, only six characters of output are transferred and then preceded by $(w - 6)$ blanks; if w is less than 6, the w leftmost characters of the word are transferred.

(b) *Blank field*   Before discussing the H field, the blank field is introduced.   Field nX specifies n blank characters in an input/output record where $0 \leq n \leq 132$.   For an INPUT statement, nX causes n characters in the input record to be skipped.   For an OUTPUT statement, nX causes n blanks to be introduced into the output record.

(c) *H field*   The nH field (or Hollerith field) specifies a string of n characters (including blanks) to be reproduced exactly.   These n characters are placed immediately after the letters nH.   For example, the following statements cause the first line in Fig. 5.4 to be printed:

WRITE(6,90)
90 FORMAT(1H1,9X, 34HSOLUTION OF VAN DER POL'S
                                        EQUATION)

There are three fields in the FORMAT statement.   The first field, 1H1, causes the printer to skip the paper to the top of the next page and to space one line after printing.   The second field, 9X, a blank field, specifies a skip of 9 character spaces.   Actually, there are 10 blank character spaces because the control character in field 1H1 is counted but not printed.   As another example, the following statements cause the second and third lines in Fig. 5.4 to be printed:

WRITE(6,91) MAX,H,COUNT
91 FORMAT(1H0,9X,9HCONSTANTS//10X,4HMAX
        = F6.3,10X,4HHbb = F6.3,10X,6HCOUNT = I3)

The first field in the FORMAT statement, 1H0, causes the printer to space one line before printing and one line after printing. The second field, 9X, skips 9 character spaces (again, a total of 10 blank character spaces). The third field prints the string CONSTANTS. The two slashes, as explained previously, cause the printer to space two lines. The next field, 10X, provides 10 blank character spaces for the third printed line in Fig. 5.4. Field 4HMAX = F6.3 causes the printing of the value of MAX in equation form; the value occupies six-character spaces with three fractional digits. The next field causes a skip of 10-character spaces. Field 4HHbb = F6.3 causes the printing of the value of H in equation form. The next field, 10X, again provides 10 blank character spaces, and field 6HCOUNT = I3 causes the printing of the value of COUNT in equation form, the value consisting of three integer digits. In short, the field specifications in the above FORMAT statement describe the form of the second and third lines in Fig. 5.4.

5.4.3 FLOWCHART

In order to print the output as in Fig. 5.4, the flowchart in Fig. 5.1 has been modified as shown in Fig. 5.5. In Fig. 5.5, there are blocks to write the problem title, to read and write the title and the constants, to read and write the title and parameters, to read initial conditions, and to write output headings. There are two loops: an inner loop similar to that in Fig. 5.1 for numerical solution of the differential equation, and an outer loop which permits multiple runs. The runs continue until all the data cards for the READ statements of the program are exhausted.

Figure 5.4 also indicates that the termination condition MAX, integration step size H, and the number of counts for print interval K are chosen as constants, and coefficients A and B in van der Pol's equation as parameters. The values of constants are not changed during multiple runs, while the values of parameters and initial conditions can be changed for each run.

5.4.4 READ STATEMENT AND DATA CARDS

A FORTRAN program for the flowchart in Fig. 5.5 is written and shown in Fig. 5.6. In this FORTRAN program there are the following READ and FORMAT statements, together with an associated data card:

READ(5,101) MAX,H,K
101 FORMAT(2F10.0,I3)
3.0   0.001   100
↑
└─column 1

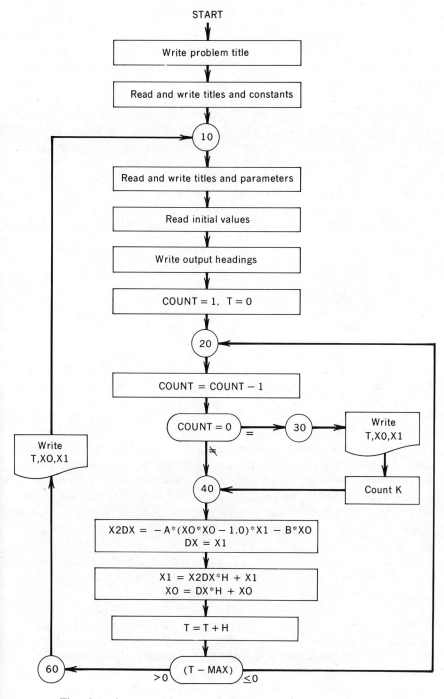

Fig. 5.5 Flowchart for computing the solution of van der Pol's equation, version 2.

The READ statement causes input device 5 (that is, the card reader) to read the values of variables MAX, H, and K; the formats of these values are specified in the FORMAT statement whose statement number is 101. The first field, 2F10.0, specifies two successive fields, each having a width of 10 characters but no fractional digits; these are the formats for the values of MAX and H.   The second field, I3, specifies a field for a three-digit integer for the value of K.   The third line above represents a data card; real number 3.0 in the first 10-character positions is the value of MAX, real number 0.001 in the second 10-character positions is the value of H, and integer 100 in the third 3-character positions is the value of K. Notice that there are disagreements in fractional digits between those specified in the FORMAT statement and those on the data cards.   In such cases, it is always the numbers on the data cards that prevail.

The other READ and FORMAT statements in the program of Fig. 5.6 are

```
 10  READ(5,102)  A,B
102  FORMAT(8F10.0)
     READ(5,102)X0,X1
0.1              1.0
1.0              0.0
↑
└──column 1
```

The above two READ statements share the same FORMAT statement. Again, the numbers on the data cards prevail for the disagreements in the fractional digits.

5.4.5 FORTRAN PROGRAM

The FORTRAN program is shown in Fig. 5.6.   The first two statements after the four control cards and four COMMENT statements declare variable MAX to be real and COUNT to be integer.   The next two statements cause the title to be printed.   The next four statements write the title "CONSTANTS" as well as read and write the values for constants MAX, H, and K in equation form.   Similarly, the next four statements write the title "PARAMETERS" as well as read and write the values of parameters A and B.   The next statement reads the initial values X0 and X1, and the next two statements write the headings for the tabular output. All these statements are to produce the designed output shown in Fig. 5.4.

The remaining part of version 2 is essentially the same as that of version 1.   However, in version 2, there are data cards which are located immediately after the control card $DATA.   The first data card contains the values of the constants.   The second and third data cards contain the values of parameters and initial conditions for the first run, the fourth and fifth for the second run, and the sixth and seventh for the third run.

```
$EXECUTE        IBJOB
$ID    CHU    *305/65/020*3M$
$IBJOB
$IBFTC VER2
C*****SOLVING VAN DER POL'S EQUATION     VERSION 2
C*****TYPE, ARITH., GO TO, ARITH. IF, LOGICAL IF STATEMENTS.
C*****READ, WRITE, AND FORMAT STATEMENTS. DATA CARDS.
C*****MORE THAN ONE RUN. TWO LOOPS. EULER INTEGRATION.
       REAL MAX
       INTEGER COUNT
C*****WRITE THE TITLE
       WRITE(6,90)
   90 FORMAT(1H1,9X,34HSOLUTION OF VAN DER POL'S EQUATION)
C*****READ AND WRITE CONSTANTS
       READ(5,101) MAX,H,K
  101 FORMAT(2F10.0,I3)
       WRITE(6,91) MAX,H,K
   91 FORMAT(1H0,9X,9HCONSTANTS//10X,4HMAX=F6.3,10X,4HH   =F6.3,10X,
      16HCOUNT=I3)
C*****READ AND WRITE PARAMETERS
   10 READ(5,103) A,B
  103 FORMAT(8F10.0)
       WRITE(6,92) A,B
   92 FORMAT(1H0,9X,10HPARAMETERS//10X,4HA   =F6.3,10X,4HB  =F6.3)
C*****READ INITIAL VALUES
       READ(5,103) X0,X1
C*****WRITE THE OUTPUT HEADINGS
       WRITE(6,94)
   94 FORMAT(1H0,9X,5HTIME ,15X,5HX    ,15X,5HDX   )
C*****SET PRINT COUNTER TO ONE
       COUNT=1
C*****SET TIMER TO ZERO
       T=0.0
C*****BEGIN OF COMPUTATION
   20 COUNT=COUNT-1
C*****TEST FOR COUNTER BEING ZERO
       IF(COUNT.EQ.0) GO TO 30
       GO TO 40
C*****PRINT RESULT
   30 WRITE(6,95) T,X0,X1
   95 FORMAT(1H ,8X,2(1PE14.7,6X), 1PE14.7)
C*****RESET PRINT COUNTER
       COUNT=K
C*****COMPUTING DERIVATIVES
   40 X2DX=-A*(X0*X0-1.0)*X1-B*X0
       DX=X1
C*****INTEGRATIONS
       X1=X2DX*H+X1
       X0=DX*H+X0
       T=T+H
C*****TEST FOR TERMINATION
       IF(T-MAX) 20,20,60
C*****PRINT THE RESULT OF THE LAST ITERATION
   60 WRITE(6,95) T,X0,X1
C*****SKIP TO NEXT PAGE FOR NEXT RUN
       WRITE(6,96)
   96 FORMAT(1H1)
       GO TO 10
       END
$DATA
3.0         0.001      100
0.1         1.0
1.0         0.0
0.5         1.0
3.0         0.0
1.0         1.0
3.0         3.0
```

Fig. 5.6 FORTRAN program for computing the solution of van der Pol's equation, version 2.

SOLUTION OF VAN DER POL'S EQUATION

CONSTANTS

| MAX= 3.000 | H = 0.001 | COUNT=100 |

PARAMETERS

| A = 0.100 | B = 1.000 |

TIME	X	DX
0.	1.0000000E 00	0.
9.9999959E-02	9.9505348E-01	-9.9840740E-02
1.9999981E-01	9.8016236E-01	-1.9872773E-01
2.9999964E-01	9.5546716E-01	-2.9575800E-01
3.9999947E-01	9.2119560E-01	-3.9009494E-01
4.9999930E-01	8.7765574E-01	-4.8096418E-01
5.9999876E-01	8.2523047E-01	-5.6764497E-01
6.9999822E-01	7.6437251E-01	-6.4945987E-01
7.9999768E-01	6.9560060E-01	-7.2576244E-01
8.9999713E-01	6.1949716E-01	-7.9592587E-01
9.9999659E-01	5.3670667E-01	-8.5933341E-01
1.0999953E 00	4.4793518E-01	-9.1537199E-01
1.1999940E 00	3.5394988E-01	-9.6343009E-01
1.2999927E 00	2.5557882E-01	-1.0029008E 00
1.3999915E 00	1.5371043E-01	-1.0331899E 00
1.4999902E 00	4.9291064E-02	-1.0537324E 00
1.5999889E 00	-5.6678465E-02	-1.0640108E 00
1.6999876E 00	-1.6314905E-01	-1.0635812E 00
1.7999863E 00	-2.6903197E-01	-1.0521013E 00
1.8999850E 00	-3.7321052E-01	-1.0293593E 00
1.9999837E 00	-4.7455446E-01	-9.9530178E-01
2.0999824E 00	-5.7193688E-01	-9.5005721E-01
2.1999812E 00	-6.6425357E-01	-8.9395026E-01
2.2999799E 00	-7.5044276E-01	-8.2750930E-01
2.3999786E 00	-8.2950547E-01	-7.5146083E-01
2.4999773E 00	-9.0052444E-01	-6.6671310E-01
2.5999760E 00	-9.6268125E-01	-5.7432936E-01
2.6999747E 00	-1.0152698E 00	-4.7549228E-01
2.7999734E 00	-1.0577067E 00	-3.7146371E-01
2.8999721E 00	-1.0895373E 00	-2.6354218E-01
2.9999709E 00	-1.1104364E 00	-1.5302332E-01
3.0009708E 00	-1.1105894E 00	-1.5190032E-01

Fig. 5.7 Table output for the FORTRAN program in Fig. 5.6 (version 2).

The output of version 2 is shown in Fig. 5.7. There is no difference in the numerical result between versions 1 and 2 except the annotations in version 2.

Version 2 shows a FORTRAN program with two loops. It shows READ and FORMAT statements, and data cards as well as A field and H field. It also illustrates the use of TYPE, arithmetic GO TO, arith-

metic IF, and logical IF statements.   It also presents an example of print
output design.

5.5 VERSION 3

Version 2 gives a tabulated output complete with the titles, headings, constants, and parameters.   However, it is written specifically for computing
the solution of a particular differential equation.   In version 3, the program is rewritten so that it may be used to compute the solution of other
differential equations with a minimum of changes.

To accomplish the above objective, computation of the derivatives
is programmed as a subroutine.   In this way, when the solution of a given
differential equation is to be computed, only this subroutine (and the
necessary data) needs to be changed.   For a similar reason in using different integration subroutines later, the numerical integration is also programmed as a subroutine.   Furthermore, subscripted variables and variable formats are needed so that the title as well as the names and formats
of constants, parameters, and initial conditions can be read in as data
without the least change in the main program.

5.5.1 SUBSCRIPTED VARIABLES

For programming simplicity, variables which belong to one class may be
grouped to form an array and assigned with an array name; each variable
of the array is referenced by a subscripted variable name.   For example,
parameters A and B in version 2 can be grouped to form an array called
PAR.   If A and B are assigned to be the first and second members of the
array, they are referenced by subscripted variable names PAR(1) and
PAR(2).

A DIMENSION statement declares one or more arrays and the
name, number of subscripts, and maximum size of each of these arrays.
The format of the DIMENSION statement is shown in Table 5.14, and
the format of the subscript in Table 5.12.   In version 3, we have the following DIMENSION statement:

DIMENSION X(50),P(50),CON(50),KON(50),PAR(50)

The DIMENSION statement reserves memory locations for these arrays
to store real constants, integer constants, parameters, dependent variables, and derivatives of dependent variables.   A size of 50 elements has
been chosen for each of these arrays.   Computing the solution of van der
Pol's equation is again chosen as an example for version 3.   The assign-
ments of constants, parameters, etc., to the members of these arrays are
shown in Table 5.17.

Table 5.17   Names of subscripted variables in version 3

Version 2	Version 3	Remark
MAX H	CON(1) CON(2)	Array for real constants
K	KON(1)	Array for integer constants
A B	PAR(1) PAR(2)	Array for parameters
X0 X1	X(1) X(2)	Array for dependent variables
DX X2DX	P(1) P(2)	Array for derivatives of $X(i)$

5.5.2 READ AND WRITE STATEMENTS FOR SUBSCRIPTED VARIABLES

In version 3, there are the following READ and WRITE statements for subscripted variables:

```
      READ  (5,103) (CON(I),I = 1,L)
      READ  (5,101) (KON(2),I = 1,L)
      WRITE (6,CONST) (CON(I),I = 1,L), (KON(I),I = 1,K)
   10 READ  (5,103) (PAR(I),I = 1,M)
      WRITE (6,WPAR) (PAR(I),I = 1,M)
      READ  (5,103) (X(I),I = 1,N)
   30 WRITE (6,OUT) T, (X(I),I = 1,N)
```

These statements employ a DO expression which has been introduced previously and shown in Table 5.8.   Each of these DO expressions functions like a DO loop and assigns the values of the subscripted variable according to the field specifications in a FORMAT statement or according to the "format data."   The above first, second, fourth, and sixth statements are specified by FORMAT statements with statement number 101 or 103, while the above third, fifth, and seventh statements are specified by format data, as will be shown.

5.5.3 VARIABLE FORMATS

It is possible in FORTRAN to provide the field specifications of FORMAT statements on data cards; this gives the convenience of supplying the formats as data.   In version 3, there are the following statements and data cards by means of which formats are read as data:

```
      DIMENSION TITLE(24),INDEX(24),CONST(24)
      DIMENSION WPAR(24),HDR(24),OUT(24)
      READ (5,100) TITLE,INDEX,CONST,WPAR,HDR,OUT
  100 FORMAT (12A6)
(1H1,9X,34HSOLUTION OF VAN DER POL'S EQUATION)
(1H0,9X,4HK   = I6,10X,4HL   = I6//10X,4HM   = I6,10X,4HN
  = I6)
(1H0,9X,4HMAX = F6.3,10X,4HH   = F6.3,10X,6HCOUNT = I3)
(1H0,9X,4HA   = F6.3,10X,4HB   = F6.3)
(1H0,9X,5HTIME ,15X,5HX   ,15X,5HDX   )
(1H ,9X,2(1PE14.7,6X),1PE14.7)
```

The above DIMENSION statement declares array variables TITLE, INDEX, CONST, WPAR, HDR, and OUT where the formats for the title, index limits, constants, parameters, output headings, and print output are to be stored. Thus, these array variables are format variables. The above READ statement reads in these format data on the data cards. For a dimension size of 24 words, there are two data cards per array (thus, one blank card is required after each of the above data cards). The data are stored in a format of six-character words, as described earlier. Notice that the above format data are identical to the field specifications in the respective FORMAT statements in version 2.

In version 3, the following WRITE statements use format variables:

```
      WRITE (6,TITE)
      WRITE (6,INDEX) K,L,M,N
      WRITE (6,CONST) (CON(I),I = 1,L), (KON(J),J = 1,K0)
      WRITE (6,WPAR) (PAR(I),I = 1,M)
      WRITE (6,HDR)
   30 WRITE (6,OUT) T, (X(I),I = 1,N)
```

By means of these format variables, no FORMAT statements are necessary, and the exact format specifications are not required until the computation of a particular solution.

5.5.4 TWO SUBROUTINES

The subroutine to compute the derivatives of van der Pol's equation is programmed as below:

```
$IBFTC SUB2
      SUBROUTINE DERV(X,P,PAR,T)
      DIMENSION X(50),P(50),PAR(50)
      P(1) = X(2)
      P(2) = -PAR(1)*(X(1)*X(1)-1.0)*X(2)-PAR(2)*X(1)
      RETURN
      END
```

The above $IBFTC card is a control card which causes the FORTRAN processor to compile the deck with the name SUB2. The second card is a SUBROUTINE statement (which is shown in Table 5.11) with name DERV and arguments X, P, PAR, and T. X's are inputs and P's are outputs. The above DIMENSION statement is required in the subroutine because variables X, P, and PAR are arrays. The van der Pol equation is written in two statements in terms of the subscripted variables in Table 5.17. These statements are followed by a RETURN statement, and the subroutine is completed by an END statement.

The numerical integration is also programmed as a subroutine. This subroutine employing the Euler integration formula is shown below:

```
$IBFTC SUB1
        SUBROUTINE INTEGR(X,P,CON,N)
        DIMENSION X(50),P(50),CON(50)
        DO 10 I = 1, N
    10 X(I) = X(I)+P(I)*CON(2)
        RETURN
        END
```

The name of this subroutine is INTEGR with arguments X, P, CON, and N. Arguments X, P, and CON are arrays which are declared in a DIMENSION statement. P's are inputs and X's are outputs. CON(2) is the integration step size. Index limit N specifies the number of "integrators."

The above subroutines are called by the following two CALL statements:

```
    40 CALL DERV(X,P,PAR,T)
        CALL INTEGR(X,P,CON,N)
```

The CALL statements have been previously introduced and also shown in Table 5.11. These CALL statements have standard returns, and the arguments must agree in number, order, type, and array size with the dummy arguments in the SUBROUTINE statements of the above two subroutines.

5.5.5 FORTRAN PROGRAM

The FORTRAN program is shown in Fig. 5.8. The DIMENSION, READ, WRITE, and FORMAT statements in this program are described above. The computation part of the program is almost identical to that of version 2, except that the subroutines and CALL statements replace the statements for numerical integration and derivative computation.

In Fig. 5.8, the main program is followed immediately by the two sub-routines and then by the $DATA control card. The data cards immediately follow this control card. There are 21 data cards, including 6 blank ones. The first 12 cards are punched with format data (the second, fourth, etc., are blank cards). The thirteenth data card is to provide the values of index limits, the fourteenth for the values of real constants, and the fifteenth for the value of an integer constant. The sixteenth and seventeenth are the values of parameters and initial conditions for the first run, the eighteenth and nineteenth for the second run, and the twentieth and twenty-first for the third run.

The printed output of the computation is shown in Fig. 5.9. The numerical results from versions 2 and 3 are identical, and the annotations between the two versions are the same except that there are index limits in version 3.

Version 3 shows a FORTRAN program with subscripted variables, subroutines, format variables, and format data cards. It shows DIMENSION and DO statements, READ and WRITE statements for subscripted variables, and SUBROUTINE and CALL statements. This version can be used to compute the solution of some other ordinary differential equation or equations, simply by providing a subroutine to compute the derivatives and preparing format and numerical data cards.

5.6 VERSION 4

The data which are shared by the main program and the subroutines can be better handled by using COMMON statements. This version 4 is to incorporate a COMMON statement in version 3 and, in addition, to replace the integration subroutine in version 3 by one with error control so that the integration step size varies automatically.

5.6.1 COMMON STATEMENT

In version 3, the data communication between the main program and a subroutine is by means of arguments. The use of arguments for communication becomes more difficult when one subroutine may call another subroutine. An alternative approach is to create a common region in the memory so that the main program and its subroutines can share the stored data, with no arguments to be specified in the subroutine statement. This common region is specified by a COMMON statement.

As previously shown in Table 5.14, a COMMON statement defines a common storage area to be shared by a program and its subprograms. It must generally precede any executable, NAMELIST, or DATA statements. The locations in the common area are assigned to the variables according to the sequence in which these variables appear in the COM-

```
$EXECUTE          IBJOB
$ID    CHU   *305/65/020*3M$
$IBJOB
$IBFTC VER3
C*****SOLVING VAN DER POL'S EQUATION    VERSION 3
C*****READ AND WRITE STATEMENT FOR SUBSCRIPTED VARIABLES
C*****DIMENSION AND DO STATEMENTS. FORMAT VARIABLES.
C*****TWO SUBROUTINES. EULER INTEGRATION.
      DIMENSION X(50),P(50),CON(50),KON(50),PAR(50)
      DIMENSION TITLE(24),INDEX(24),CONST(24)
      DIMENSION WPAR(24),HDR(24),OUT(24)
      READ(5,100) TITLE,INDEX,CONST,WEAR,HDR,OUT
  100 FORMAT (12A6)
C*****WRITE THE TITLE
      WRITE (6,TITLE)
C*****READ AND WRITE INDEX LIMITS
      READ(5,101) K,L,M,N
  101 FORMAT(8I10)
      WRITE(6,90)
   90 FORMAT(1H0,9X,12HINDEX LIMITS)
      WRITE(6,INDEX) K,L,M,N
C*****READ AND WRITE CONSTANTS
      READ(5,103) (CON(I),I=1,L)
      READ(5,101) (KON(I),I=1,K)
      WRITE (6,91)
   91 FORMAT(1H0,9X,9HCONSTANTS)
      WRITE(6,CONST) (CON(I),I=1,L),(KON(I),I=1,K)
C*****READ AND WRITE PARAMETERS
   10 READ(5,103) (PAR(I),I=1,M)
  103 FORMAT(8F10.0)
      WRITE (6,92)
   92 FORMAT(1H0,9X,10HPARAMETERS)
      WRITE (6,WPAR)     (PAR(I),I=1,M)
C*****READ INITIAL VALUES
      READ(5,103) (X(I),I=1,N)
C*****WRITE THE OUTPUT HEADINGS
      WRITE (6,HDR)
C*****SET PRINT COUNTER TO ONE
      KOUNT=1
C*****SET TIMER TO ZERO
      T=0.0
C*****BEGIN OF COMPUTATION
   20 KOUNT=KOUNT-1
C*****TEST FOR COUNTER BEING ZERO
      IF(KOUNT.EQ.0) GO TO 30
      GO TO 40
C*****PRINT RESULT
   30 WRITE(6,OUT) T,(X(I),I=1,N)
C*****RESET PRINT COUNTER
      KOUNT=KON(1)
   40 CALL DERV(X,P,PAR,T)
      CALL INTEGR(X,P,CON,N)
      T=T+CON(2)
      IF (T-CON(1)) 20,20,60
C*****PRINT THE RESULT OF THE LAST ITERATION
   60 WRITE(6,OUT) T,(X(I),I=1,N)
      WRITE (6,96)
   96 FORMAT(1H1)
      GO TO 10
      END
```

Fig. 5.8 FORTRAN program for computing the solution of van der Pol's equation, version 3.

```
$IBFTC SUB1
(*****INTEGRATIONS
      SUBROUTINE INTEGR(X,P,CON,N)
      DIMENSION X(50),P(50),CON(50)
      DO 10 I=1,N
   10 X(I)=X(I)+CON(2)*P(I)
      RETURN
      END
$IBFTC SUB2
      SUBROUTINE DERV(X,P,PAR,T)
      DIMENSION X(50),P(50),PAR(50)
C*****COMPUTING DERIVATIVE
      P(1)=X(2)
      P(2)=-PAR(1)*(X(1)*X(1)-1.0)*X(2)-PAR(2)*X(1)
      RETURN
      END
$DATA
(1H1,9X,34HSOLUTION OF VAN DER POL'S EQUATION)

(1H0,9X,4HK   =I6,10X,4HL   =I6//10X,4HM   =I6,10X,4HN   =I6)

(1H0,9X,4HMAX=F6.3,10X,4HH   =F6.3,10X,6HCOUNT=I3)

(1H0,9X,4HA   =F6.3,10X,4HB   =F6.3)

(1H0,9X,5HTIME ,15X,5HX   ,15X,5HDX   )

(1H ,8X,2(1PE14.7,6X),1PE14.7)
```

```
           1         2         2         2
3.0        0.001
           100
0.1        1.0
1.0        0.0
0.5        1.0
3.0        0.0
1.0        1.0
3.0        3.0
```

Fig. 5.8 (Continued)

MON statement. If the variables in a COMMON statement contain dimension information, they must not be dimensioned elsewhere.

In version 4, the COMMON statement

COMMON X(50),P(50),CON(50),PAR(50),N,T

creates a common region for variables X, P, CON, PAR, N, and T and declares the dimensions and sizes of these variables. These variables will store dependent variables, derivatives, constants, parameters, number of "integrators," and time (independent variable). The data stored in this common region are to be shared by the main program and the two subroutines. This statement should be present in the main program as well as in the two subroutines.

SCLUTICN OF VAN DER PCL'S EQUATICN

INDEX LIMITS

K =   1   L =   2

M =   2   N =   2

CCNSTANTS

MAX= 3.000   H = C.001   CCUNT=1CO

PARAMETERS

A = 0.1CO   B = 1.000

TIME	X	UX
C.	1.COCCCOOE OC	0.
9.9959959E-02	9.9505348E-01	-9.984074CE-02
1.9959981E-01	9.8016236E-01	-1.9872773E-01
2.9959964E-01	9.5546716E-01	-2.95758CCE-01
3.9959947E-01	9.2119560E-01	-3.9009494E-01
4.9959930E-01	8.7765574E-01	-4.8096418E-01
5.9959876E-01	8.2523047E-01	-5.6764497E-01
6.9999822E-01	7.6437251E-01	-6.4945987E-01
7.9959768E-01	6.9560060E-01	-7.2576244E-01
8.9959713E-01	6.1949716E-01	-7.9592587E-01
9.9959659E-01	5.3670667E-01	-8.5933341E-01
1.0959953E OC	4.4793518E-01	-9.1537199E-01
1.1959940E OO	3.5394988E-01	-9.6343CC9E-01
1.2959927E OO	2.5557882E-01	-1.0029008E OO
1.3959915E OO	1.5371043E-01	-1.0331899E OO
1.4959902E OO	4.9291064E-02	-1.C537324E OO
1.5959889E OO	-5.6678465E-02	-1.0640108E OO
1.6959876E OO	-1.6314905E-01	-1.0635812E OO
1.7959863E CO	-2.6903197E-01	-1.C521013E OO
1.8959850E OO	-3.7321052E-01	-1.0293593E OO
1.9959837E CC	-4.7455446E-01	-9.953C178E-01
2.0959824E OC	-5.7193688E-01	-9.5005721E-01
2.1959812E OO	-6.6425357E-01	-8.9395C26E-01
2.2959799E OO	-7.5044276E-01	-8.275C93CE-01
2.3959786E CC	-8.2950547E-01	-7.5146083E-01
2.4959773E CC	-9.C052444E-01	-6.667131CE-01
2.5959760E OO	-9.6268125E-01	-5.7432936E-01
2.6959747E OO	-1.0152698E OO	-4.7549228E-01
2.7959734E CO	-1.C577067E OO	-3.7146371E-01
2.8959721E CC	-1.C895373E OO	-2.6354218E-01
2.9959709E OO	-1.1104364E OC	-1.5302332E-01
3.C0C9708E CO	-1.1105894E OO	-1.519C932E-01

Fig. 5.9 Table output for the FORTRAN program in Fig. 5.7 (version 3).

5.6.2 VARYING–STEP EULER INTEGRATION

Varying-step integration means that the integration step size H is automatically changed according to an error evaluation. The simple Euler integration formula is still to be used for integration. The varying-step integration algorithm to be described here employs the parameters of DT (print interval of the output), DTMIN (minimum permissible H), and DTMAX (maximum permissible H), instead of H and COUNT as described in the previous versions. DTMIN can be chosen to be zero, but DTMAX should not be larger than DT.

The flowchart in Fig. 5.10 shows the varying-step version of Euler integration and is programmed as a subroutine. For each call of the subroutine, one or more integration steps take place until the next print time T_f is reached; at that time the next output is printed. The next print time T_f is obtained by adding the value of DT to the current time T. The value of H is initially set to DT. For each integration step, H is first chosen to be the minimum of the H from the last integration step, the print interval DT, and the time difference $(T_f - T)$. Euler integration for the current step is next calculated, T is incremented by H, and the derivatives of the dependent variables are calculated for the incremented T.

The measurement that makes the change of H automatically is the evaluation of a relative error RELERR. The RELERR is to be found as follows. The truncation error E of the Euler formula which can be obtained from the Taylor's series is

$$E = \frac{\ddot{x}(\tau)h^2}{2}$$

where τ is a value of independent variable t in the range of interest. The second derivative $\ddot{x}$ can be approximated as below:

$$\ddot{x} = \frac{\dot{x}(t + h) - \dot{x}(t)}{h}$$

By combining the above two relations, we have

$$E = \frac{[\dot{x}(t + h) - \dot{x}(t)]h}{2}$$

This error E may be converted into a relative error, which is obtained by taking the absolute value of this error E divided by x. Thus, the relative error E_r for one dependent variable is

$$E_r = \left| \frac{\dot{x}(t + h) - \dot{x}(t)}{x} \frac{h}{2} \right|$$

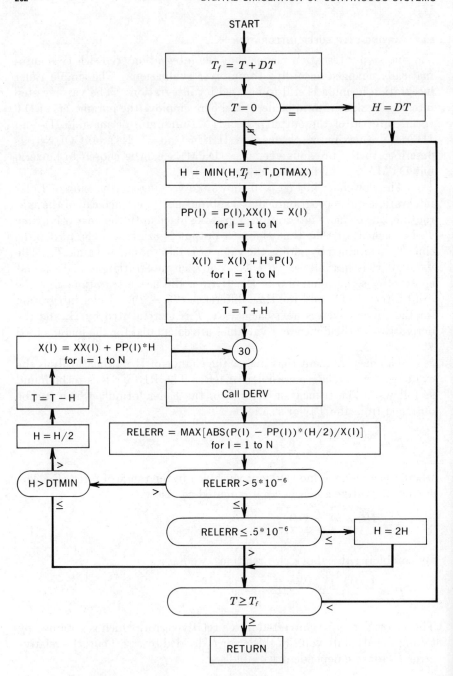

Fig. 5.10   Flowchart for a varying-step Euler integration.

and the RELERR is the maximum of E_r's for all the dependent variables. In terms of the variables for the subsequent FORTRAN program, we have

$$\text{RELERR} = \text{maximum of} \left[\frac{P(I) - PP(I)}{X(I)} \frac{H}{2} \right] \quad \text{for } I = 1 \text{ to } N$$

where $P(I)$, $PP(I)$, and $X(I)$ represent, respectively, $\dot{x}(t + h)$, $\dot{x}(t)$, and x. H represents the step size h, and N represents the number of dependent variables. The RELERR is the maximum of the relative errors that occur during the current integration step, not the maximum of the error of the solution. This is an important difference.

If RELERR is equal to or less than $0.5\text{E}-6$, then the step size H for the next integration step is doubled. If RELERR is larger than $5.0\text{E}-6$ and if H at this time is larger than DTMIN, then the step size is halved and the current integration step is performed again by using the new step size. If the RELERR is larger than $0.5\text{E}-6$ or it is equal to $5.0\text{E}-6$ or less, then the step size is retained for the next integration step. The integration continues step by step until the next print time is reached.

5.6.3 FORTRAN PROGRAM

The varying-step integration subroutine INTEGR is shown in the FORTRAN program of Fig. 5.11. The flowchart for the FORTRAN program is shown in Fig. 5.12. In the flowchart, the derivative computation, the time incrementing, and print counting all disappear, because these functions as well as integration are carried out in the subroutine INTEGR. This program, called version 4, is again written for the computation of the solution of van der Pol's equation.

The calling of subroutine DERV by subroutine INTEGR is required. These subroutines require no arguments because the COMMON statement defines a common storage area for data communication. The COMMON statement must appear exactly the same in the main program as in both subroutines.

In Fig. 5.11, the read-in of format data and numerical data and the print of the titles, constants, and parameters are almost identical to version 3.

The result of version 4 is shown in Fig. 5.13. This result is almost identical to that in Fig. 5.9 except for the appearance of DT, DTMAX, and DTMIN in Fig. 5.13 instead of H and COUNT as in Fig. 5.9.

5.6.4 VERSION 4PDE

Like version 3, version 4 can be used to compute the solution of some other differential equations by rewriting subroutine DERV and preparing the associated data cards. In order to illustrate this usage, the partial differential equation for one-dimensional heat flow described in an earlier

```
$EXECUTE        IBJOB
$ID   CHU   *305/65/020*3M$
$IBJOB
$IBFTC VER4
C*****SOLVING VAN DER POL'S EQUATION    VERSION 4
C*****TWO SUBROUTINES. COMMON STATEMENT. FORMAT VARIABLES
C*****VARYING-STEP EULER INTEGRATION
      COMMON X(50),P(50),CON(50),PAR(50),N,T
      DIMENSION TITLE(24),INDEX(24),CONST(24)
      DIMENSION WPAR(24),HDR(24),OUT(24)
      READ(5,100) TITLE,INDEX,CONST,WPAR,HDR,OUT
  100 FORMAT (12A6)
C*****WRITE THE TITLE
      WRITE (6,TITLE)
C*****READ AND WRITE INDEX LIMITS
      READ(5,101) K,L,M,N
  101 FORMAT(8I10)
      WRITE(6,90)
   90 FORMAT(1H0,9X,12HINDEX LIMITS)
      WRITE(6,INDEX) K,L,M,N
C*****READ AND WRITE CONSTANTS
      READ(5,103) (CON(I),I=1,L)
      WRITE (6,91)
   91 FORMAT(1H0,9X,9HCONSTANTS)
      WRITE(6,CONST) (CON(I),I=1,L)
C*****READ AND WRITE PARAMETERS
   10 READ(5,103) (PAR(I),I=1,M)
  103 FORMAT(8F10.0)
      WRITE (6,92)
   92 FORMAT(1H0,9X,10HPARAMETERS)
      WRITE (6,WPAR)    (PAR(I),I=1,M)
C*****READ INITIAL VALUES
      READ(5,103) (X(I),I=1,N)
C*****WRITE THE OUTPUT HEADINGS
      WRITE (6,HDR)
C*****BEGIN OF COMPUTATION
C*****SET TIMER TO ZERO
      T=0.0
C*****COMPUTING DERIVATIVE
      CALL DERV
C*****PRINT RESULT
   30 WRITE(6,OUT) T,(X(I),I=1,N)
C*****INTEGRATION
      CALL INTEGR
      IF (T-CON(1)) 30,30,60
C*****PRINT THE RESULT OF THE LAST ITERATION
   60 WRITE(6,OUT) T,(X(I),I=1,N)
C*****SKIP TO THE TOP OF NEXT PAGE
      WRITE (6,96)
   96 FORMAT(1H1)
      GO TO 10
      END
$IBFTC SUB1
      SUBROUTINE INTEGR
      COMMON X(50),P(50),CON(50),PAR(50),N,T
C*****VARYING-STEP EULER INTEGRATION
      DIMENSION XX(50),PP(50)
C*****INITIALIZATION
      DT  =CON(2)
      DTMAX=CON(3)
      DTMIN=CON(4)
```

Fig. 5.11 FORTRAN program for computing the solution of van der Pol's equation, version 4.

```
      TFINAL=T+DT
      IF (T.EQ.0.) H=DT
   10 H  = AMIN1(H,TFINAL-T,DTMAX)
C*****INTEGRATE ONE STEP
      DO 20 I=1, N
      PP(I)=P(I)
      XX(I)=X(I)
   20 X(I) =X(I)+H*P(I)
      T    =T+H
C*****COMPUTE DERIVATIVE
   30 CALL DERV
C*****COMPUTE APPROXIMATE MAXIMUM RELATIVE ERROR
      RELERR=0.
      DO 40 I=1, N
      ERROR = (P(I)-PP(I))*H/2.
   40 RELERR=AMAX1(RELERR,ABS(ERROR/X(I)))
C*****TEST FOR HALVING H
      IF ((RELERR.GT.+5.0E-6).AND.(H.GT.DTMIN)) GO TO 50
C*****TEST FOR DOUBLING H
      IF (RELERR.LE.0.5E-6)  H=2.*H
C*****TEST FOR TIME TO RETURN
      IF (T.GE.TFINAL) RETURN
C*****CONTINUE TO INTEGRATE
      GO TO 10
C*****HALVE THE H
   50 H  = H/2.
C*****SET    NEW T
      T  = T-H
      DO 60 I=1, N
   60 X(I)=XX(I) + PP(I)*H
C*****REPEAT ERROR TESTING
      GO TO 30
      END
$IBFTC SUB2
      SUBROUTINE DERV
      COMMON X(50),P(50),CON(50),PAR(50),N,T
      P(1)=X(2)
      P(2)=-PAR(1)*(X(1)*X(1)-1.0)*X(2)-PAR(2)*X(1)
      RETURN
      END
$DATA
(1H1,9X,34HSOLUTION OF VAN DER POL'S EQUATION)

(1H0,9X,4HK  =I6,10X,4HL  =I6//10X,4HM  =I6,10X,4HN  =I6)

(1H0,9X,4HMAX=F6.3,10X,4HDT =F6.3,10X,6HDTMAX=F6.3//30X,6HDTMIN=F6.3)

(1H0,9X,4HA  =F6.3,10X,4HB  =F6.3)

(1H0,9X,5HTIME ,15X,5HX  ,15X,5HDX  )

(1H ,8X,2(1PE14.7,6X),1PE14.7)
```

	0	4	2	2
3.0	0.1	0.001	0.0	
0.1	1.0			
1.0	0.0			
0.5	1.0			
3.0	0.0			
1.0	1.0			
3.0	3.0			

Fig. 5.11 (Continued)

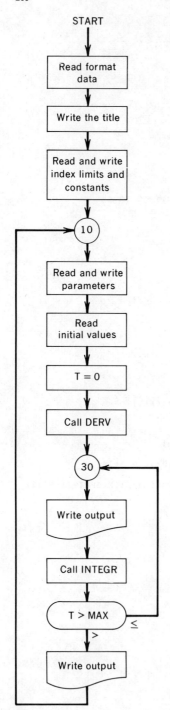

Fig. 5.12 Flowchart for version 4.

```
SOLUTICN OF VAN DER POL'S EQUATION

INDEX LIMITS

K   =      0            L   =      4

M   =      2            N   =      2

CONSTANTS

MAX= 3.000             DT = 0.100            DTMAX= 0.001

                       DTMIN= 0.

PARAMETERS

A   = 0.100            B   = 1.000

TIME                   X                     DX
0.                     1.0000000E 00         0.
1.0000000E-01          9.9505348E-01         -9.9840778E-02
2.0000000E-01          9.8016174E-01         -1.9872782E-01
3.0000000E-01          9.5546649E-01         -2.9575813E-01
3.9999999E-01          9.2119429E-01         -3.9009494E-01
4.9999990E-01          8.7765435E-01         -4.8096421E-01
5.9999998E-01          8.2522833E-01         -5.6764505E-01
6.9999998E-01          7.6437003E-01         -6.4946018E-01
7.9999997E-01          6.9559744E-01         -7.2576261E-01
8.9999996E-01          6.1949355E-01         -7.9592608E-01
9.9999995E-01          5.3670234E-01         -8.5933326E-01
1.0999999E 00          4.4792974E-01         -9.1537219E-01
1.1999999E 00          3.5394301E-01         -9.6342999E-01
1.2999999E 00          2.5557072E-01         -1.0029005E 00
1.3999999E 00          1.5370095E-01         -1.0331888E 00
1.4999999E 00          4.9280406E-02         -1.0537305F 00
1.5999999E 00          -5.6689965E-02        -1.0639898E 00
1.6999999E 00          -1.6315973E-01        -1.0635587E 00
1.7999999E 00          -2.6904160E-01        -1.0520769E 00
1.8999999E 00          -3.7321717E-01        -1.0293319E 00
1.9999999E 00          -4.7455949E-01        -9.9527297E-01
2.0999999E 00          -5.7193856E-01        -9.5002688E-01
2.1999999E 00          -6.6425321E-01        -8.9391879E-01
2.2999999E 00          -7.5044010E-01        -8.2747673E-01
2.3999999E 00          -8.2950052E-01        -7.5142759E-01
2.4999999E 00          -9.0051652E-01        -6.6667908F-01
2.5999998E 00          -9.6267065E-01        -5.7429513E-01
2.6999998E 00          -1.0152560E 00        -4.7545784E-01
2.7999998E 00          -1.0576901E 00        -3.7142959E-01
2.8999998E 00          -1.0895170E 00        -2.6350858E-01
2.9999998E 00          -1.1104131E 00        -1.5299063E-01
3.0999998E 00          -1.1201801E 00        -4.1133020E-02
```

Fig. 5.13   Table output for the FORTRAN program in Fig. 5.11 (version 4).

```
$EXECUTE        IBJOB
$ID    CHU   *305/65/020*3M$
$IBJOB
$IBFTC V4PDE
C*****SOLVING ONE-DIMENSIONAL HEAT FLOW. VERSION 4PDE
C*****TWO SUBROUTINES. COMMON STATEMENTS. FORMAT VARIABLE
C*****VARYING-STEP EULER INTEGRATION
      COMMON X(50),P(50),CON(50),PAR(50),N,T
      DIMENSION TITLE(24),INDEX(24),CONST(24)
      DIMENSION WPAR(24),HDR(24),OUT(24)
      READ(5,100) TITLE,INDEX,CONST,WPAR,HDR,OUT
  100 FORMAT (12A6)
C*****WRITE THE TITLE
      WRITE (6,TITLE)
C*****READ AND WRITE INDEX LIMITS
      READ(5,101) K,L,M,N
  101 FORMAT(8I10)
      WRITE(6,90)
   90 FORMAT(1H0,4X,12HINDEX LIMITS)
      WRITE(6,INDEX) K,L,M,N
C*****READ AND WRITE CONSTANTS
      READ(5,103) (CON(I),I=1,L)
      WRITE (6,91)
   91 FORMAT(1H0,4X,9HCONSTANTS)
      WRITE(6,CONST) (CON(I),I=1,L)
C*****READ AND WRITE PARAMETERS
   10 READ(5,103) (PAR(I),I=1,M)
  103 FORMAT(8F10.0)
      WRITE (6,92)
   92 FORMAT(1H0,4X,10HPARAMETERS)
      WRITE (6,WPAR)    (PAR(I),I=1,M)
C*****READ INITIAL VALUES
      READ(5,103) (X(I),I=1,N)
C*****WRITE THE OUTPUT HEADINGS
      WRITE (6,HDR)
C*****SET TIMER TO ZERO
      T=0.0
C*****BEGIN OF COMPUTATION
C*****COMPUTE DERIVATIVE
      CALL DERV
C*****PRINT RESULT
   30 WRITE(6,OUT) T,(X(I),I=2,10,2)
C*****INTEGRATION
      CALL INTEGR
C*****TEST TERMINATION
      IF (T-CON(1)) 30,30,60
C*****PRINT THE RESULT OF THE LAST ITERATION
   60 WRITE(6,OUT) T,(X(I),I=2,10,2)
C*****SKIP TO THE TOP OF NEXT PAGE
      WRITE (6,96)
   96 FORMAT(1H1)
      GO TO 10
      END
$IBFTC SUB1
      SUBROUTINE INTEGR
      COMMON X(50),P(50),CON(50),PAR(50),N,T
C*****VARYING-STEP EULER INTEGRATION
      DIMENSION XX(50),PP(50)
C*****INITIALIZATION
```

Fig. 5.14 FORTRAN program for computing the solution of a one-dimensional heat-flow equation, version 4PDE.

```
            DT    =CON(2)
            DTMAX=CON(3)
            DTMIN=CON(4)
            TFINAL=T+DT
            IF (T.EQ.0.) H=DT
      10 H    = AMIN1(H,TFINAL-T,DTMAX)
C*****INTEGRATE ONE STEP
            DO 20 I=1, N
            PP(I)=P(I)
            XX(I)=X(I)
      20 X(I)  =X(I)+H*P(I)
            T     =T+H
C*****COMPUTE DERIVATIVE
      30 CALL DERV
C*****COMPUTE APPROXIMATE MAXIMUM RELATIVE ERROR
            RELERR=0.
            DO 40 I=1, N
            ERROR = (P(I)-PP(I))*H/2.
      40 RELERR=AMAX1(RELERR,ABS(ERROR/X(I)))
C*****TEST FOR HALVING H
            IF ((RELERR.GT.+5.0E-6).AND.(H.GT.DTMIN)) GO TO 50
C*****TEST FOR DOUBLING H
            IF (RELERR.LE.0.5E-6)  H=2.*H
C*****TEST FOR TIME TO RETURN
            IF (T.GE.TFINAL) RETURN
C*****CONTINUE TO INTEGRATE
            GO TO 10
C*****HALVE THE H
      50 H    = H/2.
C*****SET    NEW T
            T    = T-H
            DO 60 I=1, N
      60 X(I)=XX(I) + PP(I)*H
C*****REPEAT ERROR TESTING
            GO TO 30
            END
$IBFTC SUB2
            SUBROUTINE DERV
            COMMON X(50),P(50),CON(50),PAR(50),N,T
            IF(T.GT.0.) GO TO 10
            DX=PAR(1)/20.
            Z=PAR(2)/(PAR(3)*PAR(4)*DX*DX)
            X0=0.
            X20=0.
      10 P(1)=Z*(X(2)-2.0*X(1)+X0)
            P(2)=Z*(X(3)-2.0*X(2)+X(1))
            P(3)=Z*(X(4)-2.0*X(3)+X(2))
            P(4)=Z*(X(5)-2.0*X(4)+X(3))
            P(5)=Z*(X(6)-2.0*X(5)+X(4))
            P(6)=Z*(X(7)-2.0*X(6)+X(5))
            P(7)=Z*(X(8)-2.0*X(7)+X(6))
            P(8)=Z*(X(9)-2.0*X(8)+X(7))
            P(9)=Z*(X(10)-2.0*X(9)+X(8))
            P(10)=Z*(X(11)-2.0*X(10)+X(9))
            P(11)=Z*(X(12)-2.0*X(11)+X(10))
            P(12)=Z*(X(13)-2.0*X(12)+X(11))
            P(13)=Z*(X(14)-2.0*X(13)+X(12))
            P(14)=Z*(X(15)-2.0*X(14)+X(13))
```

Fig. 5.14   (Continued)

```
      P(15)=Z*(X(16)-2.0*X(15)+X(14))
      P(16)=Z*(X(17)-2.0*X(16)+X(15))
      P(17)=Z*(X(18)-2.0*X(17)+X(16))
      P(18)=Z*(X(19)-2.0*X(18)+X(17))
      P(19)=Z*(X20-2.0*X(19)+X(18))
      RETURN
      END
$DATA
(1H1,4X,46HSOLUTION OF ONE-DIMENSIONAL HEAT FLOW EQUATION)

(1H0,4X,4HK   =I3,8X,4HL   =I3,8X,4HM   =I3,8X,4HN   =I3)

(1H0,4X,4HMAX=F6.3,5X,4HDT =F6.3,5X,6HDTMAX=F6.3,5X,6HDTMIN=F6.3)

(1H0,4X,7HLENGTH=F3.1,5X,8HCOND'TY=F4.2,3X,8HSP.HEAT=F3.1,4X,8HDENSIT
5.1)
(1H0,4X,4HTIME,11X,2HT2,13X,2HT4,13X,2HT6,13X,2HT8,13X,3HT10)

(1H ,3X,5(1PE14.7,1X),1PE14.7)
```

	1	4	4	19			
3.0	0.1	0.001	0.0				
1.0	2.4	0.2	150.0				
100.	100.	100.	100.	100.	100.	100.	1
100.	100.	100.	100.	100.	100.	100.	1
100.	100.	100.					

Fig. 5.14   (Continued)

chapter is chosen as the example. The FORTRAN program for this differential equation, to be called version 4PDE, is shown in Fig. 5.14. In subroutine DERV of Fig. 5.14, computation of a coefficient Z is required only once; this is handled by an IF statement. This subroutine essentially consists in computing 19 derivatives.

In the DIMENSION statement in the main program, a new array variable XINIT is added with a size of 48 (four cards) for the 19 initial values. The data cards are similar to those in version 4.

The computed result of this program is shown in Fig. 5.15. The output format is similar to that from version 4. Temperatures T0 and T20 are known and thus not printed out. Temperatures T2, T4, T6, T8, and T10 are printed out but not temperatures T12, T14, T16, and T18, because temperature distribution is known to be symmetrical with respect to the line where T10 is located.

5.7 OTHER VERSIONS

The numerical-integration method so far employed is the simple Euler formula. There are many other integration formulas available [1-5]. Here, the use of Runge-Kutta formulas as well as predictor-corrector formulas is illustrated; these FORTRAN programs are called versions 5 and 6, respectively. In addition, the use of double-precision computation for

SOLUTION OF ONE-DIMENSIONAL HEAT FLOW EQUATION

INDEX LIMITS

K = 1   L = 4   M = 4   N = 19

CONSTANTS

MAX= 3.000   DT = 0.100   DTMAX= 0.001   DTMIN= 0.

PARAMETERS

LENGTH=1.0   COND'TY=2.40   SP.HEAT=0.2   DENSITY=150.0

TIME	T2	T4	T6	T8	T10
0.	1.0000000E 02	1.0000000E 02	1.0000000E 02	1.0000000E 02	1.0000000E 02
1.0000000E-01	5.7170191E 01	8.8245168E 01	9.7903883E 01	9.9745473E 01	9.9563118E 01
2.0000000E-01	4.2459337E 01	7.3589094E 01	9.0432855E 01	9.7168863E 01	9.8771641E 01
3.0000000E-01	3.5233582E 01	6.2883339E 01	8.2651106E 01	9.2385194E 01	9.5265708E 01
3.9999999E-01	3.0724226E 01	5.6917166E 01	7.5776677E 01	8.6671019E 01	9.0170354E 01
4.9999999E-01	2.7504320E 01	5.1567539E 01	6.9707152E 01	8.0742567E 01	8.4415615E 01
5.9999998E-01	2.4979701E 01	4.7143586E 01	6.4257698E 01	7.4941044E 01	7.8557498E 01
6.9999998E-01	2.2868215E 01	4.3314077E 01	5.9304023E 01	6.9418768E 01	7.2871840E 01
7.9999997E-01	2.1026621E 01	3.9903739E 01	5.4767524E 01	6.4235429E 01	6.7481828E 01
8.9999996E-01	1.9379090E 01	3.6815500E 01	5.0595642E 01	5.9405420E 01	6.2433107E 01
9.9999995E-01	1.7883488E 01	3.3993912E 01	4.6750323E 01	5.4921892E 01	5.7733672E 01

Fig. 5.15 Table output for the FORTRAN program in Fig. 5.14 (version 4PDE).

the purpose of reducing the round-off error will also be exemplified; this FORTRAN program will be called version 7.

5.7.1 SELECTION OF INTEGRATION FORMULAS

An integration formula is one by means of which numerical integration is calculated. Its selection is one of the most crucial elements in digital analog simulation. The failure of most of the earlier digital analog simulations may be attributed in part to the failure to use a proper integration formula.

In choosing an integration formula, there are many factors that should be considered: accuracy, speed of computation, solution stability, discontinuity, self-starting, and error estimation. Considerations of some of these factors are discussed below.

The accuracy of a simulation is affected by three kinds of errors incurred at each step of integration. The first kind is called round-off error, which is due to insufficient digits of a computer word to represent the number in numerical integration. The second kind is called truncation error, which is due to inadequacy of an integration formula for computing the increment of an integration step accurately. Often, truncation error is the dominant error per step. The third kind is called propagated error, which is due to the round-off and truncation errors propagated from earlier steps of integration. A numerical-integration procedure is said to be unstable if the propagated error is unbounded. In other words, these errors can cause solution instability and the result becomes meaningless. Long-duration real-time simulation requires special attention to the stability problem.

The numerical solution of a differential equation requires many integration steps; thus, the computation time is directly proportional to the number of steps. For each integration step, the computation time is directly proportional to the time required for computing the integration formula. Therefore, the speed of a simulation depends on the step size and the particular integration formula. For a given accuracy, there may exist a combined choice of step size and integration formula that is an optimum in time.

Discontinuities occasionally arise in a simulation. The discontinuity may, for example, occur in the input or in a nonlinear element. If such a discontinuity occurs within an integration step, a large error may result. In case this error occurs where a varying-step integration algorithm is used, the step size may "oscillate across the discontinuity"; this oscillation may result in an undesirable computation loop. One way to avoid this large error and oscillation is to terminate the integration step at the location of discontinuity and then to start integration again from this location.

By self-starting, we mean that computation of the solution can be started with no values other than the initial conditions of the differential equation. Some integration formulas are self-starting, while others are not and require other methods to compute the necessary starting values. Since the error occurring at each step of integration may vary, it is desirable to change the step size in order to keep the error within a chosen value. Accurate error estimate of an integration formula is necessary if a varying-step algorithm of the formula is to be implemented. Error estimates of some integration formulas are relatively simple, while others are not.

5.7.2   RUNGE–KUTTA FORMULAS AND VERSION 5

The Runge-Kutta methods of numerical integration calculate the approximation of the dependent variable x_{n+1} at the independent variable t equal to t_{n+1} from the values of x_n, t_n, and step size h only. This method requires multiple evaluations of function f, where f is the derivative:

$$\frac{dx}{dt} = f(t,x)$$

Table 5.18 shows the Runge-Kutta formulas of second through fifth order.

Table 5.18   Runge-Kutta formulas

Second order:
$$k_1 = hf(t_n,x_n)$$
$$k_2 = hf(t_n + h,\, x_n + k_1)$$
$$x_{n+1} = x_n + (k_1 + k_2)/2$$
Third order:
$$k_1 = hf(t_n,x_n)$$
$$k_2 = hf(t_n + h/2,\, x_n + k_1/2)$$
$$k_3 = hf(t_n + h,\, x_n + 2k_2 - k_1)$$
$$x_{n+1} = x_n + (k_1 + 4k_2 + k_3)/6$$
Fourth order:
$$k_1 = hf(t_n,x_n)$$
$$k_2 = hf(t_n + h/2,\, x_n + k_1/2)$$
$$k_3 = hf(t_n + h/2,\, x_n + k_2/2)$$
$$k_4 = hf(t_n + h,\, x_n + k_3)$$
$$x_{n+1} = x_n + (k_1 + 2k_2 + 2k_3 + k_4)/6$$
Fifth order:
$$k_1 = hf(t_n,x_n)$$
$$k_2 = hf(t_n + h/3,\, x_n + k_1/3)$$
$$k_3 = hf[t_n + 2h/5,\, x_n + (6k_2 + 4k_1)/25]$$
$$k_4 = hf[t_n + h,\, x_n + (15k_3 - 12k_2 + k_1)/4]$$
$$k_5 = hf[t_n + 2h/3,\, x_n + (8k_4 - 50k_3 + 90k_2 + 6k_1)/81]$$
$$k_6 = hf[t_n + 4h/5,\, x_n + (8k_4 + 10k_3 + 36k_2 + 6k_1)/75]$$
$$x_{n+1} = x_n + (23k_1 + 125k_3 - 81k_5 + 125k_6)/192$$

```
$EXECUTE          IBJOB
$ID    CHU    *305/65/020*3M$
$IBJOB
$IBFTC VER5
C*****SOLVING VAN DER POL'S EQUATION    VERSION 5
C*****TWO SUBROUTINES. COMMON STATEMENT. FORMAT VARIABLES
C*****FOURTH-ORDER RUNGE-KUTTA INTEGRATION
      COMMON X(50),P(50),CON(50),PAR(50),N,T
      DIMENSION KON(50)
      DIMENSION TITLE(24),INDEX(24),CONST(24)
      DIMENSION WPAR(24),HDR(24),OUT(24)
      READ(5,100) TITLE,INDEX,CONST,WPAR,HDR,OUT
  100 FORMAT (12A6)
C*****WRITE THE TITLE
      WRITE (6,TITLE)
C*****READ AND WRITE INDEX LIMITS
      READ(5,101) K,L,M,N
  101 FORMAT(8I10)
      WRITE(6,90)
   90 FORMAT(1H0,9X,12HINDEX LIMITS)
      WRITE(6,INDEX) K,L,M,N
C*****READ AND WRITE CONSTANTS
      READ(5,103) (CON(I),I=1,L)
      READ(5,101) (KON(I),I=1,K)
      WRITE (6,91)
   91 FORMAT(1H0,9X,9HCONSTANTS)
      WRITE(6,CONST) (CON(I),I=1,L),(KON(I),I=1,K)
C*****READ AND WRITE PARAMETERS
   10 READ(5,103) (PAR(I),I=1,M)
  103 FORMAT(8F10.0)
      WRITE (6,92)
   92 FORMAT(1H0,9X,10HPARAMETERS)
      WRITE (6,WPAR)    (PAR(I),I=1,M)
C*****READ INITIAL VALUES
      READ(5,103) (X(I),I=1,N)
C*****WRITE THE OUTPUT HEADINGS
      WRITE (6,HDR)
C*****SET PRINT COUNTER TO ONE
      KOUNT=1
C*****SET TIMER TO ZERO
      T=0.0
C*****BEGIN OF COMPUTATION
   20 KOUNT=KOUNT-1
C*****TEST FOR COUNTER BEING ZERO
      IF(KOUNT.EQ.0) GO TO 30
      GO TO 40
C*****PRINT RESULT
   30 WRITE(6,OUT) T,(X(I),I=1,N)
C*****RESET PRINT COUNTER
      KOUNT=KON(1)
C*****COMPUTING DERIVATIVE
   40 CALL DERV
C*****INTEGRATION
      CALL INTEGR
C*****TEST FOR RUN TERMINATION
      IF (T-CON(1)) 20,20,60
C*****PRINT THE RESULT OF THE LAST ITERATION
   60 WRITE(6,OUT) T,(X(I),I=1,N)
C*****SKIP TO THE TOP OF NEXT PAGE
```

Fig. 5.16 FORTRAN program for computing the solution of van der Pol's equation, version 5.

```
            WRITE (6,96)
     96 FORMAT(1H1)
            GO TO 10
            END
$IBFTC SUB1
            SUBROUTINE INTEGR
            COMMON X(50),P(50),CON(50),PAR(50),N,T
            DIMENSION XZ(50),XK(50,4)
            H = CON(2)
            DO 10 I=1,N
     10 XZ(I)=X(I)
            T=T+.5*H
            DO 20 I=1,N
            XK(I,1)=H*P(I)
     20 X(I)=XZ(I)+0.5*XK(I,1)
            CALL DERV
            DO 30 I=1,N
            XK(I,2)=H*P(I)
     30 X(I)=XZ(I)+0.5*XK(I,2)
            CALL DERV
            T=T+.5*H
            DO 40 I=1,N
            XK(I,3)=H*P(I)
     40 X(I)=XZ(I)+XK(I,3)
            CALL DERV
            DO 50 I=1,N
            XK(I,4)=H*P(I)
     50 X(I)=XZ(I)+(XK(I,1)+2.0*XK(I,2)+2.0*XK(I,3)+XK(I,4))/6.0
            RETURN
            END
$IBFTC SUB2
            SUBROUTINE DERV
            COMMON X(50),P(50),CON(50),PAR(50),N,T
            P(1)=X(2)
            P(2)=-PAR(1)*(X(1)*X(1)-1.0)*X(2)-PAR(2)*X(1)
            RETURN
            END
$DATA
(1H1,9X,34HSOLUTION OF VAN DER POL'S EQUATION)

(1H0,9X,4HK   =I6,10X,4HL   =I6//10X,4HM   =I6,10X,4HN   =I6)

(1H0,9X,4HMAX=F6.3,10X,4HH   =F6.3,10X,6HCOUNT=I3)

(1H0,9X,4HA   =F6.3,10X,4HB   =F6.3)

(1H0,9X,5HTIME ,15X,5HX    ,15X,5HDX   )

(1H ,8X,2(1PF14.7,6X),1PE14.7)
```

```
              1          2          2          2
3.0           0.001
              100
0.1           1.0
1.0           0.0
0.5           1.0
3.0           0.0
1.0           1.0
3.0           3.0
```

Fig. 5.16   (Continued)

As shown in Table 5.18, f is to be evaluated n times for n equal to 4 or less, but six times for n equal to 5. For this reason, computation for the Runge-Kutta method of fifth order may become excessive. The truncation error in the increment $(x_{n+1} - x_n)$ is of order h^3, h^4, h^5, and h^6 for the formulas of the second through fifth order, respectively.

The Runge-Kutta method is self-starting; this is an important advantage. This method may thus be used as a starter for methods which are not self-starting. However, error estimation after each step of integration by the Runge-Kutta method is tedious.

As an example, van der Pol's equation is selected again. This FORTRAN program, to be called version 5, is shown in Fig. 5.16. This version is essentially the same as version 4 except that subroutine INTEGR will be programmed with the fourth-order Runge-Kutta formula. Similar to the Euler integration, the inputs to subroutine INTEGR are x_i's and $\dot{x}_i$'s at t equal to nh, while the outputs are x_i's at t equal to $(n + 1)h$.

Table 5.19 shows the equivalence between variable names in Table 5.18 and those in subroutine INTEGR in Fig. 5.16. Subroutine INTEGR begins by defining a one-dimensional array XZ(50) for storing $(x_i)_n$ and a two-dimensional array XK(50,4) for storing the k_{ik}'s. As indicated in Table 5.18, X(I)'s initially represent $(x_i)_n$'s and finally $(x_i)_{n+1}$'s; they also represent some intermediate quantities during the execution of the subroutine. The fourth-order Runge-Kutta formula requires evaluation of function f four times. The first evaluation is initiated by the CALL DERV statement in the main program, which is located immediately before the CALL INTEGR statement. The three CALL DERV statements in subroutine INTEGR initiate the second, third, and fourth

Table 5.19   Equivalent variable names

Program variable†	Formula variable	Remark
XK(I,1)	k_1	
XK(I,2)	k_2	
XK(I,3)	k_3	
XK(I,4)	k_4	
XZ(I)	$(x_i)_n$	Inputs
X(I)‡	$(x_i)_{n+1}$	Outputs
P(I)	$(x_i)_n$	Inputs
H	h	Step size

† I = 1, 2, . . . , N, where N represents number of integrators.
‡ X(I) also temporarily stores $(x_i)_n$, $(x_i)_n + k_1/2$, $(x_i)_n + k_2/2$, $(x_i)_n + k_3$.

SOLUTION OF VAN DER POL'S EQUATION

INDEX LIMITS

K =   1   L =   2

M =   2   N =   2

CONSTANTS

MAX= 3.000   H = 0.001   COUNT=100

PARAMETERS

A = 0.100   B = 1.000

TIME	X	DX
0.	1.0000000E 00	0.
9.9999907E-02	9.9500371E-01	-9.9835857E-02
1.9999974E-01	9.8006425E-01	-1.9870857E-01
2.9999938E-01	9.5532352E-01	-2.9571581E-01
3.9999884E-01	9.2101043E-01	-3.9002180E-01
4.9999830E-01	8.7743430E-01	-4.8085290E-01
5.9999701E-01	8.2497901E-01	-5.6748911E-01
6.9999573E-01	7.6409818E-01	-6.4925361E-01
7.9999444E-01	6.9531150E-01	-7.2550051E-01
8.9999315E-01	6.1920217E-01	-7.9560366E-01
9.9999186E-01	5.3641534E-01	-8.5894692E-01
1.0999906E 00	4.4765785E-01	-9.1491797E-01
1.1999893E 00	3.5369742E-01	-9.6290600E-01
1.2999880E 00	2.5536262E-01	-1.0023050E 00
1.3999867E 00	1.5354224E-01	-1.0325224E 00
1.4999854E 00	4.9182900E-02	-1.0529942E 00
1.5999841E 00	-5.6714543E-02	-1.0632050E 00
1.6999829E 00	-1.6310117E-01	-1.0627132E 00
1.7999816E 00	-2.6888878E-01	-1.0511788E 00
1.8999803E 00	-3.7296139E-01	-1.0283925E 00
1.9999790E 00	-4.7418995E-01	-9.9430383E-01
2.0999777E 00	-5.7144906E-01	-9.4904355E-01
2.1999764E 00	-6.6363629E-01	-8.9293877E-01
2.2999751E 00	-7.4969204E-01	-8.2651949E-01
2.3999738E 00	-8.2861966E-01	-7.5051349E-01
2.4999726E 00	-8.9950458E-01	-6.6582952E-01
2.5999713E 00	-9.6153090E-01	-5.7353048E-01
2.6999700E 00	-1.0139953E 00	-4.7479798E-01
2.7999687E 00	-1.0563169E 00	-3.7089215E-01
2.8999674E 00	-1.0880430E 00	-2.6310933E-01
2.9999661E 00	-1.1088511E 00	-1.5274257E-01
3.0009661E 00	-1.1090033E 00	-1.5163014E-01

Fig. 5.17 Table output for the FORTRAN program in Fig. 5.16 (version 5).

evaluations.   Independent variable T in subroutine INTEGR is properly incremented before subroutine DERV is called each time.

The computed result is shown in Fig. 5.17.   By using the previous result from the MIMIC program as a reference, the result from version 5 is more accurate than the results from versions 1 through 4, where the simple Euler formula is used.

5.7.3 PREDICTOR–CORRECTOR FORMULAS AND VERSION 6

Let $x(t)$ be the calculated solution of a differential equation.   Then, we define

$$x_i = x(t_i) \qquad x_i' = \frac{dx}{dt}_{t=t_i}$$

Let $X(t)$ be the true solution.   Then we define

$$X^n = \frac{d^n X}{dt^n}$$

A predictor is a forward integration formula which predicts x_{i+1} from one or more preceding values of x_i', x_{i-1}', etc.   Table 5.20 shows Adams-Bashforth predictors of first through sixth order.   The first-order predictor in Table 5.20 is the previously used Euler formula.   This formula does not require any preceding value and is thus self-starting.   It does not require equal-integration step size.   In Table 5.20, the last terms on the right sides of these formulas are terms for error estimation which indicate a truncation error of the order of h^2 through h^7 for the first- through sixth-order formulas, respectively.   The predictor requires only one iteration per step; this gives an advantage in speed over the Runge-Kutta formulas.   Except for the first-order predictor, predictors are not self-starting; a self-starting formula is required to compute an adequate number of preceding values of x_{i-1}', etc., for the predictor to start.

A corrector also gives a value for x_{i+1} which is more accurate than that given by a predictor.   But a corrector requires the value of x_{i+1}' as well as preceding values of x_{i-1}', x_{i-2}', etc.   For this reason, a predictor is first chosen to calculate x_{i+1}, from which x_{i+1}' is then computed.   This x_{i+1}' is used in a corrector to give a more accurate x_{i+1}.   This more accurate x_{i+1} can be used again to compute x_{i+1}', which is then used again in the corrector for a still more accurate x_{i+1}.   Thus, a corrector is an iterative formula.   Each iteration requires one evaluation of the derivatives.

Table 5.21 shows Adams-Moulton correctors of first through sixth order.   The second-order corrector in Table 5.21 is known as the trapezoidal rule.   It is important that the chosen pair of predictor and corrector have the error terms of the same order as those in derivative.   Thus, a predictor in Table 5.20 should be paired with a corrector in Table

Table 5.20 Adams-Bashforth predictors†

1st order: $x_{n+1} = x_n + x'_n h - X^2(\tau)(h^2/2)$

2nd order: $x_{n+1} = x_n + (3x'_n - x'_{n-1})h/2 + X^3(\tau)(5h^3/12)$

3rd order: $x_{n+1} = x_n + (23x'_n - 16x'_{n-1} + 5x'_{n-2})h/12 - X^4(\tau)(9h^4/24)$

4th order: $x_{n+1} = x_n + (55x'_n - 59x'_{n-1} + 37x'_{n-2} - 9x'_{n-3})h/24 + X^5(\tau)(251h^5/720)$

5th order: $x_{n+1} = x_n + (1{,}901x'_n - 2{,}774x'_{n-1} + 2616x'_{n-2} - 1{,}274x'_{n-3} + 251x'_{n-4})h/720 - X^6(\tau)(425h^6/1{,}440)$

6th order: $x_{n+1} = x_n + (4{,}277x'_n - 7{,}923x'_{n-1} + 9{,}982x'_{n-2} - 7{,}298x'_{n-3} + 2{,}877x'_{n-4} - 475x'_{n-5})h/1{,}440 + X^7(\tau)(19{,}087h^7/60{,}480)$

† τ is a value of independent variable within a range of interest.

Table 5.21 Adams-Moulton correctors

1st order: $x_{n+1} = x_n + x'_{n+1}h + X^2(\tau)(h^2/2)$

2nd order: $x_{n+1} = x_n + (x'_{n+1} + x'_n)h/2 - X^3(\tau)(h^3/12)$

3rd order: $x_{n+1} = x_n + (5x'_{n+1} + 8x'_n - x'_{n-1})h/12 + X^4(\tau)(h^4/24)$

4th order: $x_{n+1} = x_n + (9x'_{n+1} + 19x'_n - 5x'_{n-1} + x'_{n-2})h/24 - X^5(\tau)(19h^5/720)$

5th order: $x_{n+1} = x_n + (251x'_{n+1} + 646x'_n - 264x'_{n-1} + 106x'_{n-2} - 19x'_{n-3})h/720 + X^6(\tau)(27h^6/1{,}440)$

6th order: $x_{n+1} = x_n + (475x'_{n+1} + 1{,}427x'_n - 798x'_{n-1} + 482x'_{n-2} - 173x'_{n-3} + 27x'_{n-4})h/1{,}440 - X^7(\tau)(863h^3/60{,}480)$

```
$EXECUTE         IBJOB
$ID    CHU    *305/65/020*3M$
$IBJOB
*IBFTC VER6
C*****SOLVING VAN DER POL'S EQUATION    VERSION 6
C*****TWO SUBROUTINES, COMMON STATEMENT, FORMAT VARIABLES.
C*****SECOND-ORDER PREDICTOR-CORRECTOR INTEGRATION
      COMMON X(50),P(50),CON(50),PAR(50),N,T
      DIMENSION KON(50)
      DIMENSION TITLE(24),INDEX(24),CONST(24)
      DIMENSION WPAR(24),HDR(24),OUT(24)
      READ(5,100) TITLE,INDEX,CONST,WPAR,HDR,OUT
  100 FORMAT (12A6)
C*****WRITE THE TITLE
      WRITE (6,TITLE)
C*****READ AND WRITE INDEX LIMITS
      READ(5,101) K,L,M,N
  101 FORMAT(8I10)
      WRITE(6,90)
   90 FORMAT(1H0,9X,12HINDEX LIMITS)
      WRITE(6,INDEX) K,L,M,N
C*****READ AND WRITE CONSTANTS
      READ(5,103) (CON(I),I=1,L)
      READ(5,101) (KON(I),I=1,K)
      WRITE (6,91)
   91 FORMAT(1H0,9X,9HCONSTANTS)
      WRITE(6,CONST) (CON(I),I=1,L),(KON(I),I=1,K)
C*****READ AND WRITE PARAMETERS
   10 READ(5,103) (PAR(I),I=1,M)
  103 FORMAT(8F10.0)
      WRITE (6,92)
   92 FORMAT(1H0,9X,10HPARAMETERS)
      WRITE (6,WPAR)     (PAR(I),I=1,M)
C*****READ INITIAL VALUES
      READ(5,103) (X(I),I=1,N)
C*****WRITE THE OUTPUT HEADINGS
      WRITE (6,HDR)
C*****SET PRINT COUNTER TO ONE
      KOUNT=1
C*****SET TIMER TO ZERO
      T=0.0
C*****BEGIN OF COMPUTATION
   20 KOUNT=KOUNT-1
C*****TEST FOR COUNTER BEING ZERO
      IF(KOUNT.EQ.0) GO TO 30
      GO TO 40
C*****PRINT RESULT
   30 WRITE(6,OUT) T,(X(I),I=1,N)
C*****RESET PRINT COUNTER
      KOUNT=KON(1)
C*****COMPUTING DERIVATIVES
   40 CALL DERV
C*****INTEGRATIONS
      CALL INTEGR
C*****TEST FOR RUN TERMINATIOM
      IF (T-CON(1)) 20,20,60
C*****PRINT THE RESULT OF THE LAST ITERATION
   60 WRITE(6,OUT) T,(X(I),I=1,N)
      WRITE (6,96)
```

Fig. 5.18 FORTRAN program for computing the solution of van der Pol's equation, version 6.

```
   96 FORMAT(1H1)
      GO TO 10
      END
$IBFTC SUB1
      SUBROUTINE INTEGR
      COMMON X(50),P(50),CON(50),PAR(50),N,T
      DIMENSION XPR(50),XCR(50),XOLD(50),P1(50),P2(50),XK(50,4)
      EQUIVALENCE (XPR(1),XK(1,1)),(XCR(1),XK(1,2)),(P2(1),XK(1,3))
      IF(T.GT.0.) GO TO 100
C*****FOURTH-ORDER RUNGE-KUTTA INTEGRATION FOR STARTING
C*****STORE CURRENT VALUES OF DEPENDENT VARIABLES AND DERIVATIVES
      H   = CON(2)
      DO 10 I=1,N
      P1(I)=P(I)
   10 XOLD(I)=X(I)
      T=T+.5*H
      DO 20 I=1,N
      XK(I,1)=H*P(I)
   20 X(I)=XOLD(I)+0.5*XK(I,1)
      CALL DERV
      DO 30 I=1,N
      XK(I,2)=H*P(I)
   30 X(I)=XOLD(I)+0.5*XK(I,2)
      CALL DERV
      T=T+.5*H
      DO 40 I=1,N
      XK(I,3)=H*P(I)
   40 X(I)=XOLD(I)+XK(I,3)
      CALL DERV
      DO 50 I=1,N
      XK(I,4)=H*P(I)
   50 X(I)=XOLD(I)+(XK(I,1)+2.0*XK(I,2)+2.0*XK(I,3)+XK(I,4))/6.0
      RETURN
C*****SECOND-ORDER PREDICTOR-CORRECTOR INTEGRATION
C*****STORE CURRENT VALUES OF DEPENDENT VARIABLES AND DERIVATIVES
  100 DO 110 I=1,N
      XOLD(I)=X(I)
  110 P2(I)=P(I)
      T=T+H
C*****PREDICTOR
      DO 130 I=1,N
      XPR(I)=XOLD(I)+H*(3.0*P2(I)-P1(I))/2.0
  130 X(I)=XPR(I)
C*****COMPUTE DERIVATIVES WITH PREDICTOR
      CALL DERV
C*****CORRECTOR
      DO 140 I=1,N
      XCR(I)=XOLD(I)+H*(P(I)+P2(I))/2.0
      X(I)=XCR(I)
  140 P1(I)=P2(I)
      RETURN
      END
```

Fig. 5.18 (Continued)

```
$IBFTC SUB2
      SUBROUTINE DERV
      COMMON X(50),P(50),CON(50),PAR(50),N,T
      P(1)=X(2)
      P(2)=-PAR(1)*(X(1)*X(1)-1.0)*X(2)-PAR(2)*X(1)
      RETURN
      END
      $DATA
      (1H1,9X,34HSOLUTION OF VAN DER POL'S EQUATION)

      (1H0,9X,4HK   =I6,10X,4HL   =I6//10X,4HM   =I6,10X,4HN   =I6)

      (1H0,9X,4HMAX=F6.3,10X,4HH   =F6.3,10X,6HCOUNT=I3)

      (1H0,9X,4HA   =F6.3,10X,4HB   =F6.3)

      (1H0,9X,5HTIME ,15X,5HX    ,15X,5HDX    )

      (1H ,8X,2(1PE14.7,6X),1PE14.7)
```

```
             1          2        2         2
3.0          0.001
             100
0.1          1.0
1.0          0.0
0.5          1.0
3.0          0.0
1.0          1.0
3.0          3.0
```

Fig. 5.18   (Continued)

5.21 of the same order.   Except the first-order pair, other predictor-corrector pairs require a constant-integration step size.   Whenever the step size is changed, restart is required.

The van der Pol equation is again chosen for solution by a pair of predictor-corrector formulas.   This FORTRAN program, to be called version 6, is shown in Fig. 5.18.   This version is the same as version 5 except for the subroutine INTEGR.

Subroutine INTEGR is programmed with the following second-order predictor and corrector taken from Tables 5.20 and 5.21:

Predictor: $x_{n+1} = x_n + \dfrac{(3x'_n - x'_{n-1})h}{2}$

Corrector: $x_{n+1} = x_n + \dfrac{(x'_{n+1} + x'_n)h}{2}$

Because the predictor-corrector cannot self-start, the previous Runge-Kutta subroutine is employed as a starter and incorporated in subroutine INTEGR in Fig. 5.18.   When subroutine INTEGR is called by the main program for the first time, a logical IF statement in subroutine INTEGR transfers to the execution of the Runge-Kutta part of subroutine INTEGR. When it is called at other times, the predictor-corrector part of subroutine

Table 5.22   Equivalent variable names

Program variable	Runge-Kutta variable	Predictor variable	Corrector variable
P(I)	x_0†	x_n	x_{n+1}
X(I)	x_1†	x_{n+1}†	x_{n+1}†
XPR(I)		x_{n+1}	
XCR(I)			x_{n+1}
XOLD(I)	x_0	x_n	x_n
P1(I)	x_0	x_{n-1}	x_n†
P2(I)		x_n	x_n
XK(I,1)	k_1		
XK(I,2)	k_2		
XK(I,3)	k_3		
XK(I,4)	k_4		

† Also temporarily stores some other variables.

INTEGR is executed. Notice the two RETURN statements in the subroutine.

Table 5.22 lists the names of the Runge-Kutta variables, predictor variables, and corrector variables represented by the names of the program variables. Since arrays XK(I,1), XK(I,2), and XK(I,3) are needed only during the evaluation of Runge-Kutta formulas, these arrays are shared during the evaluation of predictor and corrector by using them as arrays XPR(I), XCR(I), and P2(I), respectively. This sharing is specified by the following EQUIVALENCE statement (see Table 5.14):

EQUIVALENCE (XPR(1),XK(1,1)),(XCR(1),XK(1,2)),
(P2(1),XK(1,3))

The above also serves as an example to show how storage locations can be saved by using the EQUIVALENCE statement.

The computed result from the FORTRAN program in Fig. 5.18 is shown in Fig. 5.19. The numerical result is very close to that from version 5.

5.7.4   VERSION 7

As mentioned before, accuracy of simulation is affected by round-off error, which is due to insufficient digits of a computer word to represent the number in numerical calculation. An obvious way to reduce the round-off error is to use a computer with a longer word length. An alternative way is to use double-precision arithmetic.

FORTRAN allows constants, variables, functions, format specifications, and arithmetic in double precision. To exemplify the use of double-precision computation, the FORTRAN program in Fig. 5.16 (version 5)

SOLUTICN OF VAN DER POL'S EQUATION

INDEX LIMITS

K =   1   L =   2

M =   2   N =   2

CONSTANTS

MAX= 3.000   H = 0.001   COUNT=100

PARAMETERS

A = 0.100   B = 1.000

TIME	X	DX
0.	1.0000000E 00	0.
9.9999959E-02	9.9500371E-01	-9.9835852E-02
1.9999981E-01	9.8006425E-01	-1.9870856E-01
2.9999964E-01	9.5532352E-01	-2.9571579E-01
3.9999947E-01	9.2101043E-01	-3.9002178E-01
4.9999930E-01	8.7743431E-01	-4.8085288E-01
5.9999876E-01	8.2497902E-01	-5.6748909E-01
6.9999822E-01	7.6409820E-01	-6.4925358E-01
7.9999768E-01	6.9531153E-01	-7.2550049E-01
8.9999713E-01	6.1920220E-01	-7.9560363E-01
9.9999659E-01	5.3641538E-01	-8.5894688E-01
1.0999953E 00	4.4765789E-01	-9.1491793E-01
1.1999940E 00	3.5369746E-01	-9.6290596E-01
1.2999927E 00	2.5536266E-01	-1.0023050E 00
1.3999915E 00	1.5354229E-01	-1.0325223E 00
1.4999902E 00	4.9182967E-02	-1.0529942E 00
1.5999889E 00	-5.6714464E-02	-1.0632050E 00
1.6999876E 00	-1.6310108E-01	-1.0627132E 00
1.7999863E 00	-2.6888868E-01	-1.0511787E 00
1.8999850E 00	-3.7296127E-01	-1.0283925E 00
1.9999837E 00	-4.7418982E-01	-9.9430385E-01
2.0999824E 00	-5.7144892E-01	-9.4904358E-01
2.1999812E 00	-6.6363615E-01	-8.9293880E-01
2.2999799E 00	-7.4969190E-01	-8.2651953E-01
2.3999786E 00	-8.2861952E-01	-7.5051357E-01
2.4999773E 00	-8.9950444E-01	-6.6582962E-01
2.5999760E 00	-9.6153076E-01	-5.7353061E-01
2.6999747E 00	-1.0139952E 00	-4.7479814E-01
2.7999734E 00	-1.0563167E 00	-3.7089232E-01
2.8999721E 00	-1.0880429E 00	-2.6310951E-01
2.9999709E 00	-1.1088510E 00	-1.5274277E-01
3.0009708E 00	-1.1090032E 00	-1.5163034E-01

Fig. 5.19 Table output for the FORTRAN program in Fig. 5.18 (version 6).

is to be modified for double-precision computation; the modified program is to be called version 7.   In version 7, double precision should be provided in derivative computation and numerical integration.   Variables involved in these calculations should be declared double precision.   Thus, by the following TYPE statement, we declare

DOUBLE PRECISION X,P,PAR,T

in the main program and in subroutine DERV, and we declare

DOUBLE PRECISION X,P,PAR,T,XZ(50),XK(50,4),H

in subroutine INTEGR.   The dimensions of variables XZ and XK are declared in the above DOUBLE PRECISION statement; those of variables X, P, and PAR have been declared in a COMMON statement.

The input values of constants and parameters should be double-precision numbers.   Therefore, field specifications for these formats should be changed.   We have the following two READ statements with double-precision specifications and data:

```
      READ (5,103)    (PAR(I),I = 1,M)
      READ (5,103)    (X(I),I = 1,N)
  103 FORMAT(5D15.5)
      0.00001D04        0.00001D05
      0.00001D05        0.00000D01
```

The specification of the D field, as shown in Table 5.10, has the form of $Dw.d$ or $mDw.d$.   A double-precision constant is written with 10 or more significant decimal digits with a decimal point, or with a sequence of decimal digits with a decimal point followed by a decimal exponent which consists of letter D followed by a signed or unsigned integer constant as shown by the two examples above.

The printed output of the numerical result should also be in double precision.   We thus have the following WRITE statement and format data:

```
      WRITE (6,OUT) T,(X(I),I = 1,N)
(1H ,X,,2(1PD19.12,6X),1PD19.12)
```

The above data are for format variable OUT in the above WRITE statement.   Specification 1PD19.12 is for T, X(1), and X(2), and also serves as an example of the use of a scale factor for the D field.

In an arithmetic expression for double precision where operators $+$, $-$, $*$, and $/$ are involved, the numbers should normally be in double precision.   If there are real numbers mixed with double-precision numbers in the expression, the real numbers are first converted into double precision and the result is in double precision.   In the case of exponentiation,

```
$EXECUTE        IBJOB
$ID   CHU   *305/65/020*3M$
$IBJOB
$IBFTC VER7
C*****SOLVING VAN DER POL'S EQUATION   VERSION 7
C*****TWO SUBROUTINES. COMMON STATEMENTS. FORMAT VARIABLES.
C*****FOURTH-ORDER RUNGE-KUTTA INTEGRATION (DOUBLE PRECISION)
      COMMON X(50),P(50),CON(50),PAR(50),T,N
      DIMENSION KON(50)
      DIMENSION TITLE(24),INDEX(24),CONST(24)
      DIMENSION WPAR(24),HDR(24),OUT(24)
      DOUBLE PRECISION X,P,PAR,T
      READ(5,100) TITLE,INDEX,CONST,WPAR,HDR,OUT
  100 FORMAT (12A6)
C*****WRITE THE TITLE
      WRITE (6,TITLE)
C*****READ AND WRITE INDEX LIMITS
      READ(5,101) K,L,M,N
  101 FORMAT(8I10)
      WRITE(6,90)
   90 FORMAT(1H0,4X,12HINDEX LIMITS)
      WRITE(6,INDEX) K,L,M,N
C*****READ AND WRITE CONSTANTS
      READ(5,102) (CON(I),I=1,L)
      READ(5,101) (KON(I),I=1,K)
  102 FORMAT(8F10.0)
      WRITE (6,91)
   91 FORMAT(1H0,4X,9HCONSTANTS)
      WRITE(6,CONST) (CON(I),I=1,L),(KON(I),I=1,K)
C*****READ AND WRITE PARAMETERS
   10 READ(5,103) (PAR(I),I=1,M)
  103 FORMAT(5D15.5)
      WRITE (6,92)
   92 FORMAT(1H0,4X,10HPARAMETERS)
      WRITE (6,WPAR)    (PAR(I),I=1,M)
C*****READ INITIAL VALUES
      READ(5,103) (X(I),I=1,N)
C*****WRITE THE OUTPUT HEADINGS
      WRITE (6,HDR)
C*****SET PRINT COUNTER TO ONE
      KOUNT=1
C*****SET TIMER TO ZERO
      T=0.0
C*****BEGIN OF COMPUTATION
   20 KOUNT=KOUNT-1
C*****TEST FOR COUNTER BEING ZERO
      IF(KOUNT.EQ.0) GO TO 30
      GO TO 40
C*****PRINT RESULT
   30 WRITE(6,OUT) T,(X(I),I=1,N)
C*****RESET PRINT COUNTER
      KOUNT=KON(1)
C*****COMPUTING DERIVATIVES
   40 CALL DERV
C*****INTEGRATIONS
      CALL INTEGR
C*****TEST FOR TERMINATION
      IF (T-CON(1)) 20,20,60
```

Fig. 5.20 FORTRAN program for computing the solution of van der Pol's equation, version 7.

```
C*****PRINT THE RESULT OF THE LAST ITERATION
   60 WRITE(6,OUT) T,(X(I),I=1,N)
      WRITE (6,96)
   96 FORMAT(1H1)
      GO TO 10
      END
$IBFTC SUB1
      SUBROUTINE INTEGR
      COMMON X(50),P(50),CON(50),PAR(50),T,N
      DOUBLE PRECISION X,P,PAR,T,XZ(50),XK(50,4),H
      H = CON(2)
      DO 10 I=1,N
   10 XZ(I)=X(I)
      T=T+.5*H
      DO 20 I=1,N
      XK(I,1)=H*P(I)
   20 X(I)=XZ(I)+0.5*XK(I,1)
      CALL DERV
      DO 30 I=1,N
      XK(I,2)=H*P(I)
   30 X(I)=XZ(I)+0.5*XK(I,2)
      CALL DERV
      T=T+.5*H
      DO 40 I=1,N
      XK(I,3)=H*P(I)
   40 X(I)=XZ(I)+XK(I,3)
      CALL DERV
      DO 50 I=1,N
      XK(I,4)=H*P(I)
   50 X(I)=XZ(I)+(XK(I,1)+2.0*XK(I,2)+2.0*XK(I,3)+XK(I,4))/6.0
      RETURN
      END
$IBFTC SUB2
      SUBROUTINE DERV
      COMMON X(50),P(50),CON(50),PAR(50),T,N
      DOUBLE PRECISION X,P,PAR,T
      P(1)=X(2)
      P(2)=-PAR(1)*(X(1)*X(1)-1.0)*X(2)-PAR(2)*X(1)
      RETURN
      END
$DATA
(1H1,4X,34HSOLUTION OF VAN DER POL'S EQUATION)

(1H0,4X,4HK  =I6,15X,4HL  =I6// 5X,4HM  =I6,15X,4HN =I6)

(1H0,4X,4HMAX=F6.3,15X,4HH  =F6.3,15X,6HCOUNT=I3)

(1H0,4X,4HA  =F6.3,15X,4HB  =F6.3)

(1H0,4X,5HTIME ,20X,5HX   ,20X,5HDX   )

(1H ,3X,2(1PD19.12,6X),1PD19.12)


        1          2         2         2
2.0        0.001
       100
     0.00001D04       0.00001D05
     0.00001D05       0.00000D01
```

Fig. 5.20   (Continued)

the exponent can be an integer, a real number, or a double-precision number.

In a double-precision arithmetic statement, both sides of the statement should normally be double precision. If they are different, then a precision conversion will result. If the right side is a double-precision expression while the left side is not, then the expression is evaluated in double precision but the result is converted into single precision, and vice versa.

```
SOLUTION OF VAN DER POL'S EQUATION

INDEX LIMITS

K  =     1                    L  =     2

M  =     2                    N  =     2

CONSTANTS

MAX= 3.000               H  = 0.001                    COUNT=100

PARAMETERS

A  = 0.100                B  = 1.000

TIME                     X                        DX
0.                       1.0000000000000D 00      0.
1.000000003842D-01       9.950041153698D-01       -9.983590792731D-02
2.000000007683D-01       9.800649942075D-01       -1.987087549988D-01
3.000000011525D-01       9.553246179567D-01       -2.957162275094D-01
4.000000015367D-01       9.210118573798D-01       -3.900225196419D-01
5.000000019209D-01       8.774360024994D-01       -4.808539521320D-01
6.000000023050D-01       8.249809390160D-01       -5.674906473809D-01
7.000000026892D-01       7.641002959140D-01       -6.492556764965D-01
8.000000030734D-01       6.953137424348D-01       -7.255031763941D-01
9.000000034575D-01       6.192044624857D-01       -7.956069281021D-01
1.000000003842D 00       5.364176886320D-01       -8.589508141608D-01
1.100000004226D 00       4.476600418886D-01       -9.149224476321D-01
1.200000004610D 00       3.536993026073D-01       -9.629110898704D-01
1.300000004994D 00       2.553641372084D-01       -1.002310739715D 00
1.400000005378D 00       1.535432320334D-01       -1.032528966881D 00
1.500000005763D 00       4.918324757728D-02       -1.053001660845D 00
1.600000006147D 00       -5.671498657741D-02      -1.063213366485D 00
1.700000006531D 00       -1.631025542224D-01      -1.062722291785D 00
1.800000006915D 00       -2.688912075569D-01      -1.051188441179D 00
1.900000007299D 00       -3.729650044465D-01      -1.028402722447D 00
2.000000007683D 00       -4.741947967966D-01      -9.943143939016D-01
2.100000008068D 00       -5.714552608982D-01      -9.490539726431D-01
2.200000008452D 00       -6.636438739618D-01      -8.929488124428D-01
2.300000008836D 00       -7.497009825093D-01      -8.265290383854D-01
2.400000009220D 00       -8.286299170494D-01      -7.505223846202D-01
2.500000009604D 00       -8.995160177319D-01      -6.658376310282D-01
2.600000009988D 00       -9.615434688787D-01      -5.735376118982D-01
2.700000010373D 00       -1.014008999147D 00      -4.748039703631D-01
2.800000010757D 00       -1.056331770664D 00      -3.708967555443D-01
2.900000011141D 00       -1.088059118946D 00      -2.631245553680D-01
3.000000011525D 00       -1.088681690043D 00      -1.527440627889D-01
```

Fig. 5.21 Table output for the FORTRAN program in Fig. 5.20 (version 7).

FORTRAN also provides built-in functions in double precision. Examples are DABS, DMAX1, DMIN1, and DSIGN, which are, respectively, double-precision versions of ABS, AMAX1, AMIN1, and SIGN; the latter are shown in Table 5.12. FORTRAN also provides mathematical functions in double precision. Examples are DLOG, DSIN, DATAN, and DSQRT, which are, respectively, double-precision versions of ALOG, SIN, ATAN, and SQRT; these single-precision functions are shown in Table 5.13.

The FORTRAN program of version 7 is shown in Fig. 5.20. In comparing versions 5 and 7, the changes are rather few; they are essentially the statements and data described above. The computed result is shown in Fig. 5.21. In comparing the numerical results in Fig. 5.17 (version 5) and in Fig. 5.21, they agree to five decimal digits when T is equal to about 3. The difference between these two results is due to accumulation and propagation of round-off error.

In summarizing the numerical results of the seven versions, the result from version 7 is the most accurate, followed by version 5 and then version 6 (though the results from these two versions are very close), followed by version 4 and then by versions 1, 2, and 3. The results from versions 1, 2, and 3 are identical (as they should be) and the least accurate. The result from version 4 is very close to versions 1, 2, and 3.

PROBLEMS

5.1. Write FORTRAN programs to generate
    (a) A cycloid as described in Prob. 3.1
    (b) An epicycloid as described in Prob. 3.2
    (c) A hypocycloid as described in Prob. 3.3
    (d) A cardioid as described in Prob. 3.4

5.2. Write FORTRAN programs to find the magnitude and phase spectra for the transfer function
    (a) In Prob. 3.7   (b) In Prob. 3.8

5.3. Given the data

$$\zeta_x = -0.01 \qquad \omega_{nx} = 1 \qquad \zeta_y = -0.01 \qquad \omega_{ny} = 2$$

write a FORTRAN program to compute the solution of differential equations (3.13) by using a flowchart similar to that in Fig. 5.1 (version 1).

5.4. Pure-pursuit courses are described by Eqs. (3.57) and (3.58). Given the data in Table 3.5, write a FORTRAN program to compute a pure-pursuit course by using a flowchart similar to that in Fig. 5.5 (version 2).

5.5. A simple relay servo is described by Eqs. (3.72) and (3.74) and the bang-bang characteristic in Fig. 3.53a. Given the data in Table 3.6, write a FORTRAN program to find the trajectory in the phase plane by using a flowchart similar to that in Fig. 5.1 (version 1).

5.6. Write a FORTRAN program to compute the solution of the differential equations in Prob. 1.1. The FORTRAN program is to be similar to that in Fig. 5.8 (version 3).

5.7. Write a FORTRAN program to compute the solution of the differential equations in Prob. 1.2. The FORTRAN program is to be similar to that in Fig. 5.11 (version 4).

5.8. Write a FORTRAN program to compute the solution of the differential equations in Prob. 1.3. The FORTRAN program is to be similar to that in Fig. 5.16 (version 5).

5.9. Write a FORTRAN program to compute the solution of the nonlinear mass-spring system as described in Prob. 3.13. The FORTRAN program is to be similar to that

   (a) In Fig. 5.8 (version 3)
   (b) In Fig. 5.11 (version 4)
   (c) In Fig. 5.16 (version 5)
   (d) In Fig. 5.18 (version 6)
   (e) In Fig. 5.20 (version 7)
   (f) Compare the results from (a) through (e).

5.10. Repeat Prob. 5.4, except that the FORTRAN program is to be similar to that in Fig. 5.16 (version 5).

5.11. Repeat Prob. 5.5, except that the FORTRAN program is to be similar to that in Fig. 5.18 (version 6).

5.12. Write a FORTRAN program to compute the solution of the differential equation

   (a) In Prob. 4.9   (b) In Prob. 4.10
   (c) In Prob. 4.11   (d) In Prob. 4.12

5.13. Write a FORTRAN program to compute the solution of the partial differential equation

   (a) In Prob. 4.16   (b) In Prob. 4.17

REFERENCES

1. Kunz, K. S.: "Numerical Analysis," McGraw-Hill Book Company, New York, 1957.
2. Collatz, L.: "The Numerical Treatment of Differential Equations," 3d English ed., Springer-Verlag OHG, Berlin, 1960.
3. Henrici, P.: "Discrete Variable Methods in Ordinary Differential Equations," John Wiley & Sons, Inc., New York, 1962.
4. Ralston, A., and H. S. Wilf (eds.): "Mathematical Methods for Digital Computers," John Wiley & Sons, Inc., New York, 1962.
5. Southworth, R. W., and S. L. DeLeeuw: "Digital Computation and Numerical Methods," McGraw-Hill Book Company, New York, 1965.
6. Shanks, E. Baylis: "Formulas for Obtaining Solutions of Differential Equations by Evaluations of Functions," unpublished notes, Vanderbilt University, Nashville, Tenn., 1963.
7. Shanks, E. Baylis: Higher Order Approximations of Runge-Kutta Type, *NASA* TN D-2920, G. C. Marshall Space Flight Center, NASA, Huntsville, Ala., September, 1965.
8. Golden, J. T.: "Fortran IV Programming and Computing," Prentice-Hall, Inc., Englewood Cliffs, N.J., 1965.
9. Dimitry, D., and T. Mott, Jr.: "Introduction to Fortran IV Programming," Holt, Rinehart and Winston, Inc., New York, 1966.
10. Ralston, A.: "A First Course in Numerical Analysis," McGraw-Hill Book Company, New York, 1965.

11. Kuo, S. S.: "Numerical Methods and Computers," Addison-Wesley Publishing Company, Inc., Reading, Mass., 1965.
12. Organick, E. I.: "A Fortran IV Primer," Addison-Wesley Publishing Company, Inc., Reading, Mass., 1966.
13. Lee, John A. N.: "Numerical Analysis for Computers," Reinhold Publishing Corporation, New York, 1966.
14. Noble, B.: "Applications of Undergraduate Mathematics in Engineering," The Macmillan Company, New York, 1967.
15. James, M. L., G. M. Smith, and J. C. Wolford: "Applied Numerical Methods for Digital Computation with Fortran," International Textbook Company, Scranton, Pa., 1967.
16. McCracken, D. D.: "Fortran with Engineering Applications," John Wiley & Sons, Inc., New York, 1967.
17. David, P. J., and P. Rabinowitz: "Numerical Integration," Blaisdell Publishing Company, 1967.
18. Fortran IV Language, version 13, IBM 7090/7094 IBSYS Operating System, File No. 7090-25, Form C28-6390-3, IBM Corporation.

6

Logic and Construction of a Simulation Processor

A digital simulation processor is a specially prepared program which may perform many functions, including translation, sorting, simulation, integration, input-output handling, and provision of a library of special routines. A bird's-eye view of the MIMIC processor is shown in the flowchart of Fig. 1.3. It is important to understand in depth the logic and construction of the digital simulation processor, because this is equivalent to the understanding of functional operation and construction of analog and hybrid computers in the case of analog and hybrid simulations. However, the MIMIC processor, though much shorter than many other digital simulation processors, is still too lengthy to be presented here. Instead, a simplified version of the MIMIC processor, to be called the SIMIC processor, is presented in this chapter. This version, which consists of less than 500 cards, is a debugged, working digital simulation processor. The SIMIC processor consists of the programs in Figs. 6.4, 6.5, 6.6, 6.13, 6.16, 6.18, and 6.20. It can actually be used for simulation.

6.1 SIMIC

SIMIC is a simplified version of MIMIC specially prepared for educational purposes. The SIMIC language is a subset of the MIMIC language, and the SIMIC processor models the logic and programming techniques of the MIMIC processor. A SIMIC program is compatible with the MIMIC processor.

6.1.1 SIMIC LANGUAGE

The card format for the SIMIC is identical to that for the MIMIC, as shown in Table 2.2, except that there are no processor control cards. SIMIC follows the same rules for constants, parameters, and variables as those for the MIMIC. The reserved names are the same. It accepts the same MIMIC operators (Table 2.3) and follows the same precedence (Table 2.11). SIMIC functions, however, are limited to those in Table 6.1. There are no special functions; no hybrid functions; no plot, derivative, or implicit functions; and no mode control for the integration function. The argument of a function, when appropriate, can be an arithmetic expression. And nesting of functions is permitted. There is an adequate number of functions in Table 6.1 for simulating many models. And other functions can be added in the SIMIC processor.

There is no sorting in the SIMIC processor. Therefore, the statements of a SIMIC program must be properly ordered in sequence. To ensure a proper order, the CON, PAR, FIN, HDR, OUT, and END statements should have the following order:

1. CON statements
2. PAR statements
3. Properly ordered statements simulating the model
4. FIN statements
5. HDR statements
6. OUT statements
7. END statement
8. Data cards whose order follows that of CON and PAR statements

In addition, each variable name and each LCV name in a statement must satisfy one of the following conditions:

1. It is one of the reserved names T, DT, DTMAX, DTMIN, TRUE, FALSE, OR (blank).
2. It is the result name of an INT function.
3. It is a name defined by a CON or PAR statement.
4. It is a literal name.

Table 6.1 SIMIC functions

Function form	Function description	Code generated	
ABS(A)	R = |A|	CAL	A
		STO	R
ADD(A,B)	R = A+B	CLA	A
		FAD	B
		STO	R
AND(A,B)	R = TRUE if A = B = TRUE	CAL	A
		ANA	B
		SLW	R
ATN(A,B)	R = ARCTAN(A/B)	TSX	ATAN2, 4
		TXI	* + 4, 0, 2
	R is in radians	PZE	0, 0, ALKDR
		PZE	A
		PZE	B
		STO	R
CON(A,B,C,D,E,F)	Names constants	None	
COS(A)	R = COS(A)	TSX	COS, 4
		TXI	* + 3, 0, 1
	A is in radians	PZE	0, 0, ALKDR
		PZE	A
		STO	R
DIV(A,B)	R = A/B	CLA	A
		FDP	B
		STQ	R
END	End of program	TRA	FEXIT
EQL(A)	R = A	CLA	A
		STO	R
EXP(A)	R = EXP(A)	TSX	EXP, 4
		TXI	* + 3, 0, 1
		PZE	0, 0, ALKDR
		PZE	A
		STO	R
FIN(A,B)	Ends run if A > B	NZT	IFIN
		TRA	* + 6
		CLA	A
		FSB	B
		TZE	* + 2
		TMI	* + 2
		STL	IEND

Table 6.1   SIMIC functions (continued)

Function form	Function description	Code generated	
FSW(A,B,C,D)	R = B if A < 0	CLA	A
		LDQ	C
	R = C if A = 0	TZE	* + 4
		LDQ	B
	R = D if A > 0	TMI	* + 2
		LDQ	D
		STQ	R
HDR(A,B,C,D,E,F)	Outputs headers at T = 0	ZET	IHDR
		TSX	MIMHDR, 4
		TXI	* + 8, 0, 6
		PZE	0, 0, ALKDR
		PZE	A
		PZE	B
		. . .	
		PZE	F
INT(A,B)	$R = B + \int_0^\tau A\,dt$	CLA	A
		STO	R − 100
		CLA	B
		NZT	T
		STO	R
IOR(A,B)	R = TRUE if A = TRUE or if B = TRUE	CAL	A
		ORA	B
		SLW	R
LOG(A)	R = LOG(A)	TSX	ALOG, 4
		TXI	* + 3, 0, 1
	Natural logarithm	PZE	0, 0, ALKDR
		PZE	A
		STO	R
LSW(A,B,C)	R = B if A = TRUE	CLA	B
		NZT	A
	R = C if A = FALSE	CLA	C
		STO	R
MPY(A,B)	R = A * B	LDQ	A
		FMP	B
		STO	R
NEG(A)	R = −A	CLS	A
		STO	R
NOT(A)	R = TRUE if A = FALSE	STZ	R
		NZT	A
	R = FALSE if A = TRUE	STL	R

Table 6.1   SIMIC functions (continued)

Function form	Function description	Code generated	
OUT(A,B,C,D,E,F)	Outputs A, B, C, D, E, F every DT units of T	ZET	IOUT
		TSX	MIMOUT, 4
		TXI	* + 8, 0, 6
		PZE	0, 0, ALKDR
		PZE	A
		PZE	B
		. . .	
		PZE	F
PAR(A,B,C,D,E,F)	Names parameters A, B, C, D, E, F to be input for each run	ZET	IPAR
		TSX	MIMPAR, 4
		TXI	* + 8, 0, 6
		PZE	0, 0, ALKDR
		PZE	A
		PZE	B
		. . .	
		PZE	F
SIN(A)	R = SIN(A)	TSX	SIN, 4
		TXI	* + 3, 0, 1
	A is in radians	PZE	0, 0, ALKDR
		PZE	A
		STO	R
SQR	R = $\sqrt{A}$	TSX	SQRT, 4
		TXIQ	* + 3, 0, 1
		PZE	0, 0, ALKDR
		PZE	A
		STO	R
SUB(A,B)	R = A − B	CLA	A
		FSB	B
		STO	R

5. It is the result name of a preceding statement but not the result name of a succeeding statement. (This condition could occur for an LCV name.)

An example of a SIMIC program is shown in Fig. 6.1. This program is identical to the MIMIC program in Fig. 4.33, except that there are no PLO statements and that the condition for run termination and the data cards are different.

```
EXAMPLE        VAN DER POL'S EQUATION
*
NAME CONSTANTS AND PARAMETERS
*
                        CON(B)
                        PAR(A,X0,1DX0)
*
SOLVE EQUATIONS
*
        2DX        = A*1DX-A*1DX**X*X-B*X
        1DX        = INT(2DX,1DX0)
        X          = INT(1DX,X0)
*
FINISH STATEMENTS
*
                        FIN(T,3.0)
*
HEADERS
*
                        HDR(TIME,X,XDOT)
                        HDR
*
READOUT
*
                        OUT(T,X,XDOT)
*
END STATEMENT
*
                        END
1.
.1              1.              0.
.5              3.              0.
```

Fig. 6.1 SIMIC program for van der Pol's equation.

6.1.2 SIMIC PROCESSOR

As mentioned, two major simplifications of the SIMIC from the MIMIC are elimination of sorting and reduction of functions available. The SIMIC processor accepts the SIMIC program and generates an executable machine-language (of the 7090 family of computers) program in two phases, called compilation and assembly. These are followed by a third phase called execution, during which the generated machine-language program is executed to compute a solution to the given model.

As listed in Table 6.2, the SIMIC processor consists of an executive program and five subroutines; they are FORTRAN programs. In addition, there is a group of short MAP-coded functions. (MAP is an assembly language of the 7090 family of computers.) The FORTRAN subroutines are: MIMCO for compilation, MIMAS for assembly, MIMEX for execution, MIMIN for integration, and MIMIO for handling input

Table 6.2   Main and subprograms of SIMIC

Program	Deck name	Language	Number of cards†
Executive program	MMIC	FORTRAN	23
Subroutine MIMEX	MMEX	FORTRAN	28
MAP-coded functions	MMAP	MAP	43
Subroutine MIMCO	MMCO	FORTRAN	98
Subroutine MIMAS	MMAS	FORTRAN	190
Subroutine MIMIO	MMIO‡	FORTRAN	30
Subroutine MIMIN	MMIN	FORTRAN	44
			456

† Exclude comment cards.
‡ Entries MIMHDR, MIMPAR, and MIMOUT are in this subroutine.

and output.   Some of the MAP-coded functions are used to link the generated program with the integration and execution subroutines, while the others are used to ease coding for symbol manipulation during compilation and assembly.

The organization of the processor is shown in Fig. 6.2.   The executive program is the main program, which calls the compiler, assembler, and executor in turn.   The compiler reads the SIMIC program and translates it into a function-language (i.e., a block-oriented-language) program from which a machine-language program is generated by the assembler.   The executor executes the machine-language program and produces a solution.   The function-language program for the SIMIC program in Fig. 6.1 is shown in Table 6.3, and the symbol table which is fully developed during assembly is shown in Table 6.4.   During execution, the integration sub-

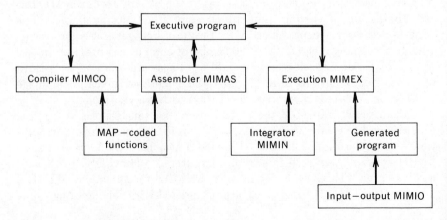

Fig. 6.2   Organization of the SIMIC processor.

Table 6.3   Contents of the BCD array

J	BCD(1,J)	BCD(2,J)	BCD(3,J)	BCD(4,J)	BCD(5,J)
1		CON	B		
2		PAR	A	XO	1DXO
3	(003)	MPY	A	1DX	
4	(004)	MPY	A	1DX	
5	(005)	MPY	(004)	X	
6	(006)	MPY	(005)	X	
7	(007)	SUB	(003)	(006)	
8	(008)	MPY	B	X	
9	2DX	SUB	(007)	(008)	
10	1DX	INT	2DX	1DXO	
11	X	INT	1DX	XO	
12		FIN	T	3.0	
13		HDR	TIME	X	XDOT
14		HDR			
15		OUT	T	X	1DX
16		END			

Table 6.4   Contents of the symbol table in the S array

I	S(I)
1	T
2	(blank)
3	DT
4	DTMAX
5	DTMIN
6	TRUE
7	FALSE
8	1DX
9	X
10	B
11	A
12	XO
13	1DXO
14	(003)
15	(004)
16	(005)
17	(006)
18	(007)
19	(008)
20	2DX
21	3.0
22	TIME
23	XDOT

routine and the machine-language program are called by the executor, and the input-output subroutine is called by the machine-language program.

6.2 EXECUTIVE PROGRAM

The executive program is the main program of the SIMIC processor. Its function is to sequence the three phases of compilation, assembly, and execution by calling subroutines MIMCO, MIMAS, and MIMEX, respectively. This is shown in the flowchart of Fig. 6.3.

The executive program is shown in Fig. 6.4. The two COMMON statements specify a COMMON data storage area which is referenced by the executive program and the subroutines. These statements specify the names of variables and arrays and the size of arrays. The storage functions of these variables and arrays are described in Table 6.5. Array R, which occupies 2,500 memory locations, stores the data of constants,

Table 6.5   Variables in the COMMON storage area

Name	Storage function
NEQ	A location storing the number of INT functions.
P(93)	An array of 93 locations storing the derivatives computed by the machine-language program.
R(2500)	An array of 2,500 locations (or data table) which store a numeric value for every constant, parameter, literal, and variable named by the user or by the compiler.
S(2500)	An array of 2,500 locations (or symbol table) which store alphameric names for all the values in the data table. The first seven names in S are reserved names. Next follow the names of the dependent variables, and then follow all other names.
FF(4000)	An array of 4,000 locations which store the machine-language program generated by the assembler.
BCD(10,900)	A two-dimension array of 10 by 900 locations which store the function-language program generated by the compiler.
IOUT	A location where a nonzero value indicates that there is output of computed results.
IPAR	A location where a nonzero value indicates that there is input of parameter data.
IHDR	A location where a nonzero value indicates that there is printing of headers.
IFIN	A location where a nonzero value requires a test of run termination condition.
IEND	A location where a nonzero value indicates that the run should be terminated.
NPAR	A location where a nonzero value indicates that more than one run is to be made.

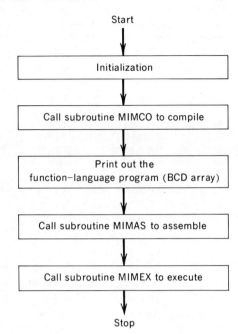

Fig. 6.3 Flowchart of the executive program of the SIMIC processor.

```
$IBFTC MMIC    XR7                                                  MMIC0000
C**** EXECUTIVE PROGRAM.                                            MMIC0001
      COMMON NEQ,P(93),R(2500),S(2500),FF(4000),BCD(10,900)         MMIC0002
      COMMON IOUT,IPAR,IHDR,IFIN,IEND,NPAR                          MMIC0003
      DIMENSION SIMAGE(7),RIMAGE(7)                                 MMIC0004
      DATA SIMAGE/1HT,1H ,2HDT,5HDTMAX,5HDTMIN,4HTRUE,5HFALSE/      MMIC0005
      DATA RIMAGE/0.,0.,.1,1000.,0.,0777777777777,0./              MMIC0006
C**** INITIALIZE.                                                   MMIC0007
      NPAR = 0                                                      MMIC0008
      NEQ = 0                                                       MMIC0009
      DO 10 K=1,7                                                   MMIC0010
      S(K) = SIMAGE(K)                                              MMIC0011
   10 R(K) = RIMAGE(K)                                              MMIC0012
C**** COMPILE.                                                      MMIC0013
      CALL MIMCO(I)                                                 MMIC0014
C**** WRITE COMPILED PROGRAM.                                       MMIC0015
      WRITE (6,30)                                                  MMIC0016
      WRITE (6,40)    (J,BCD(9,J),(BCD(K,J),K=1,8) ,J=1,I)          MMIC0017
      WRITE (6,20)                                                  MMIC0018
C**** ASSEMBLE.                                                     MMIC0019
      CALL MIMAS                                                    MMIC0020
C**** EXECUTE.                                                      MMIC0021
      CALL MIMEX                                                    MMIC0022
      STOP                                                          MMIC0023
   20 FORMAT (1H1)                                                  MMIC0024
   30 FORMAT(1H124X41H***FUNCTION-LANGUAGE PROGRAM GENERATED***//4X3HIFNMMIC0025
     1 3X3HLCV 5X6HRESULT 3X3HFTN 5X1HA 6X1HB 6X1HC 6X1HD 6X1HE 6X1HF//)MMIC0026
   40 FORMAT((I6,3XA6,3XA6,3XA3,3XA6,5(1XA6)))                      MMIC0027
      END                                                           MMIC0028
```

Fig. 6.4 Executive program of the SIMIC processor.

Table 6.6   Contents in the initial part of arrays R and S

S(i)	Contents	R(i)	Contents†
S(1)	T	R(1)	0
S(2)	"blank"	R(2)	0
S(3)	DT	R(3)	.1
S(4)	DTMAX	R(4)	1000
S(5)	DTMIN	R(5)	0
S(6)	TRUE	R(6)	777777777777
S(7)	FALSE	R(7)	0

† These decimal numbers are actually in the floating-point format of the 7090 family of computers, except the octal number in R(6), which is actually binary.

parameters, literals, and variables for the simulation. Array S, also occupying 2,500 locations, stores the symbolic names of the data in array R. The corresponding locations of arrays S and R form pairs. The BCD array stores the function-language program generated by the compiler. The FF array stores the machine-language program generated by the assembler. The P array, which has 93 locations, stores the values of up to 93 derivatives; these values are iteratively computed by the program in the FF array. The remaining variable names in Table 6.3 are indicators (they may also be called switches). Their usage will be described subsequently.

The DIMENSION statement specifies two arrays SIMAGE and RIMAGE. The two data statements specify the storing of six reserved names (T, DT, DTMAX, etc.) and a blank name in array SIMAGE, and of their numerical values in array RIMAGE.

Initialization of the executive program calls for setting indicators NPAR (when nonzero, it indicates more than one run) and NEQ (indicating the number of INT function) to zero and for storing the contents of SIMAGE and RIMAGE to the first seven locations of arrays S and R, respectively; the latter is illustrated in Table 6.6. The variable names in array S in Table 6.6 are left-justified, and the numbers in array R are actually in the floating-point format (of the 7090 family of computers) except that the octal number in R(6) is actually binary. Because of this initialization, the values of DT, DTMAX, and DTMIN are, respectively, 0.1, 1,000, and 0 if they are not specified. The executive program then calls subroutine MIMCO to compile a SIMIC program. After compilation, the BCD array in a tabular form together with the heading FUNC-TION-LANGUAGE PROGRAM GENERATED is printed. The executive program then calls subroutine MIMAS to assemble the BCD array into a machine-language program. After assembly, the executive program calls subroutine MIMEX for execution. After execution, the simulation is terminated.

6.3 MAP-CODED FUNCTIONS

A group of six special functions is employed during compilation and assembly. These functions are coded in MAP (Macro Assembly Language of the 7090 family of computers). Table 6.7 shows the entry names and functions of these MAP-coded functions. The accumulator referred to in Table 6.7 is a 36-bit register where, among other operations, arithmetic, shift, and logical operations are performed.

The use of these functions is now briefly described. The ADV(A) function is used during assembly to acquire the address of a variable for assembling it into a machine instruction. The OR(A,B) function is used by both compiler and assembler for assembling symbolic names during compilation and machine-language instructions during assembly. The ALS(A,N) and ARS(A,N) functions allow the shift of a variable placed in the accumulator N bit positions to left or right. These two functions are used by the compiler to pack characters into names and by the assembler in computing the numeric values of literal names. The F function first stores the linkage (contents of index register 4) and then transfers the control of program execution to the first location FF(1) of the machine-language program in array FF. The FEXIT function restores the contents of index register 4 and returns the control to the program which called F.

The MAP subprogram is shown in Fig. 6.5. Although the reader may not know Macro Assembly Language, this subprogram is provided to

Table 6.7   MAP-coded functions

Entry name	Function
ADV(A)	Place address of variable A in the accumulator.
ALS(A,N)	Place variable A in the accumulator and shift the contents of the accumulator N bit positions to the left. The result is left in the accumulator.
ARS(A,N)	Ditto, except shift to the right.
OR(A,B)	Perform logical OR operation on variables A and B, and leave the result in the accumulator.
F	Store system linkage and transfer to the machine-language program in array FF.
FEXIT	Return control to the calling program.

```
$IBMAP MMAP                                                                         MMAP0000
       ENTRY  ADV           SPECIFIES ADV AS AN ENTRY POINT.                        MMAP0001
       ENTRY  ALS           SPECIFIES ALS AS AN ENTRY POINT.                        MMAP0002
       ENTRY  ARS           SPECIFIES ARS AS AN ENTRY POINT.                        MMAP0003
       ENTRY  OR            SPECIFIES OR AS AN ENTRY POINT.                          MMAP0004
       ENTRY  F             SPECIFIES F AS AN ENTRY POINT.                           MMAP0005
       ENTRY  FEXIT         SPECIFIES FEXIT AS AN ENTRY POINT.                       MMAP0006
ADV    CLA    3,4           PLACES ARGUMENT ADDRESS IN ARITHMETIC AC.               MMAP0007
       TRA    1,4           RETURNS CONTROL TO CALLING PROGRAM.                      MMAP0008
ALS    CLA*   4,4           PLACES SHIFT COUNT IN ARITHMETIC AC.                     MMAP0009
       STA    *+2           STORES SHIFT COUNT IN SHIFT INSTRUCTION.                 MMAP0010
       LDQ*   3,4           PLACES ARGUMENT IN MQ.                                   MMAP0011
       LGL    0             SHIFTS ARGUMENT LEFT IN MQ.                              MMAP0012
       XCA                  PLACES RESULT IN ARITHMETIC AC.                          MMAP0013
       TRA    1,4           RETURNS CONTROL TO CALLING PROGRAM.                      MMAP0014
ARS    CLA*   4,4           PLACES SHIFT COUNT IN ARITHMETIC AC.                     MMAP0015
       STA    *+2           STORES SHIFT COUNT IN SHIFT INSTRUCTION.                 MMAP0016
       CAL*   3,4           PLACES ARGUMENT IN LOGICAL AC.                           MMAP0017
       ARS    0             SHIFTS ARGUMENT RIGHT IN LOGICAL AC.                     MMAP0018
       XCL                  PLACES RESULT IN MQ.                                     MMAP0019
       XCA                  PLACES RESULT IN ARITHMETIC AC.                          MMAP0020
       TRA    1,4           RETURNS CONTROL TO CALLING PROGRAM.                      MMAP0021
OR     CAL*   3,4           PLACES FIRST ARGUMENT IN LOGICAL AC.                     MMAP0022
       ORA*   4,4           ORS LOGICAL AC WITH SECOND ARGUMENT.                     MMAP0023
       XCL                  PLACES RESULT IN MQ.                                     MMAP0024
       XCA                  PLACES RESULT IN ARITHMETIC AC.                          MMAP0025
       TRA    1,4           RETURNS CONTROL TO CALLING PROGRAM.                      MMAP0026
F      SXA    SYSLOC,4      STORE CONTENTS OF INDEX REGISTER 4 IN                    MMAP0027
       SXA    LKDR,4          ADDRESS PORTIONS OF SYSTEM LOCATION                    MMAP0028
       SXA    FEXIT,4         SYSLOC, LINK DIRECTOR LKDR, AND FEXIT.                 MMAP0029
       CLA    FC1           STORE THE PROGRAM NAME **** AT LKDR + 1.                 MMAP0030
       STO    LKDR+1                                                                 MMAP0031
       TRA    FF            TRANSFERS CONTROL TO GENERATED PROGRAM FF.               MMAP0032
FC1    BCI    1, ****       CONTAINS PROGRAM NAME ****.                             MMAP0033
FEXIT  AXT    **,4          RESTORES CONTENTS OF INDEX REGISTER 4.                   MMAP0034
       TRA    1,4           RETURNS CONTROL TO PROGRAM CALLING F.                    MMAP0035
//     CONTRL //            DEFINES BLANK COMMON AS A CONTROL SECTION.               MMAP0036
NQPRS  COMMON 5094          SPECIFIES 5094 COMMON WORDS FOR NEQ, ETC.                MMAP0037
FF     COMMON 4000          SPECIFIES 4000 COMMON WORDS FOR FF.                      MMAP0038
BCD    COMMON 9000          SPECIFIES 9000 COMMON WORDS FOR BCD.                     MMAP0039
SWTCH  COMMON 6             SPECIFIES 6 COMMON WORDS FOR IOUT, ETC.                  MMAP0040
LKDR   COMMON 2             SPECIFIES 2 COMMON WORDS FOR LKDR.                       MMAP0041
       END                  SPECIFIES END OF MAP PROGRAMS.                           MMAP0042
```

Fig. 6.5 MAP-coded functions.

complete the SIMIC processor.   However, each line of the code in Fig.
6.5 is remarked, and these remarks give the reader some explanation.

6.4 COMPILATION

Compiler MIMCO reads the statements of a SIMIC program and translates them into a function-language program stored in the BCD array.
The format of the BCD array is shown in Table 6.8, where each row of
the array consists of a result name, a function name, an LCV name, up to
six operand names (or arguments) of the function, and an LCV name.
Each statement is decomposed into one or more functions (or columns).
An example of the BCD array is shown in Table 6.3, where there are 16
functions.   Quantities such as (003) and (004) are internal names generated during compilation.

The code of subroutine MIMCO is shown in Fig. 6.6, and a flow-

Table 6.8   Storage format of the BCD array

Location	Storage function
BCD(1,I)	Result name of ith entry
BCD(2,I)	Function name of ith entry
BCD(3,I)	Operand A of ith entry
BCD(4,I)	Operand B of ith entry
BCD(5,I)	Operand C of ith entry
BCD(6,I)	Operand D of ith entry
BCD(7,I)	Operand E of ith entry
BCD(8,I)	Operand F of ith entry
BCD(9,I)	LCV name of ith entry

chart in Fig. 6.7. The compilation employs three buffers: a 61-word buffer B, a one-word buffer CH (also called buffer ICH), and a 57-word buffer C (also called buffer IC). (Each word contains six characters, and each character contains six bits.) The data transfers among these buffers and to the BCD array, illustrated in Fig. 6.8, will be described subsequently. In addition to the variables in the COMMON area shown in Table 6.5, other variables in the MIMCO, including those in the DIMEN-

Table 6.9   Variables in subroutine MIMCO

Name	Storage function
B(61)	A 61-word input buffer.
IC(57)	A 57-word buffer storing a string.
C(57)	Equivalent to IC(57).
ICH	A one-word working buffer.
CH	Equivalent to ICH.
I	Index of the ith column of the BCD array.
JC	Index of buffer C.
JB	Index of buffer B.
JL	Location where the leftmost left parenthesis for the expression is stored. It indicates the beginning of a new string.
JLEFT	Pointer in buffer C which points the location of the innermost left parenthesis of the string.
JRIGHT	Pointer in buffer C which points two less than the location of the innermost right parenthesis of the string.
J	A local index used in many places.
JS	A local index.
FADD	Location storing the left-justified function name ADD. Similarly for others.

```
$IBFTC MMCO     XR7                                                       MMC00000
C**** COMPILER.                                                           MMC00001
      SUBROUTINE MIMCO(I)                                                 MMC00002
      DIMENSION B(61),IC(57),C(57)                                        MMC00003
      COMMON NEQ,P(93),R(2500),S(2500),FF(4000),BCD(10,900)               MMC00004
      EQUIVALENCE (CH,ICH), (C,IC)                                        MMC00005
C**** LEFT-JUSTIFIED BCD STORAGE EQUIVALENTS OF MIMIC FUNCTION NAMES.     MMC00006
      DATA FADD,FDIV,FEND,FEQL,FINT,FMPY,FNEG,FSUB/3HADD,3HDIV,3HEND,     MMC00007
     1     3HEQL,3HI'IT,3HMPY,3HNEG,3HSUB/,MASK,BLANK/5H(000),1H /        MMC00008
   10 FORMAT (A1,A6,A2,A6,A3,54A1,A6,A2)                                  MMC00009
   20 FORMAT(9XA1,A6,A2,A6,A3,54A1,A6,A2)                                 MMC00010
   30 FORMAT(1H1,27X35H***MIMIC SOURCE-LANGUAGE PROGRAM***,//)            MMC00011
C**** INITIALIZE.                                                         MMC00012
      WRITE(6,30)                                                         MMC00013
      I=0                                                                 MMC00014
C**** READ AND WRITE SOURCE-LANGUAGE PROGRAM.                             MMC00015
   40 READ (5,10) B                                                       MMC00016
      WRITE(6,20)B                                                        MMC00017
C**** IF NOT A COMMENTS CARD, PACK NAMES AND RIGHT-JUSTIFY SEPARATORS.    MMC00018
      IF (B(1).NE.BLANK) GO TO 40                                         MMC00019
      JC=57                                                               MMC00020
      JB=59                                                               MMC00021
   50 JC=JC-1                                                             MMC00022
      C(JC)=BLANK                                                         MMC00023
C**** TEST FOR SEPARATORS ()+-*/,.                                        MMC00024
   60 CH=ARS(B(JB),30)                                                    MMC00025
      IF((ICH.EQ.60).OR.(ICH.EQ.28).OR.(ICH.EQ.16).OR.(ICH.EQ.32).OR.     MMC00026
     1   (ICH.EQ.44).OR.(ICH.EQ.49).OR.(ICH.EQ.59)) GO TO 70             MMC00027
C**** IF CHARACTER IS NOT BLANK, PACK INTO NAME.                          MMC00028
      IF (ICH.NE.48) C(JC)=OR(ARS(C(JC),6),ALS(CH,30))                    MMC00029
      JB=JB-1                                                             MMC00030
      IF (JB-5) 80,80,60                                                  MMC00031
   70 IF (C(JC).NE.BLANK) JC=JC-1                                         MMC00032
      C(JC)=CH                                                            MMC00033
      JB=JB-1                                                             MMC00034
      IF (JB.GT.5) GO TO 50                                               MMC00035
C**** ENCLOSE STRING IN PARENTHESES.                                      MMC00036
   80 JL=JC-1                                                             MMC00037
      IC(JL)=60                                                           MMC00038
      IC(57)=28                                                           MMC00039
C**** TEST FOR (NAME).                                                    MMC00040
      IF (IC(JL+2).NE.28) GO TO 120                                       MMC00041
C**** INCREASE LOCATION, STORE RESULT AND LCV NAMES, BLANK OPERANDS.      MMC00042
      I=I+1                                                               MMC00043
      BCD(1,I)=B(4)                                                       MMC00044
      BCD(9,I)=B(2)                                                       MMC00045
      DO 90 J=3,8                                                         MMC00046
   90 BCD(J,I)=BLANK                                                      MMC00047
C**** IF RESULT NAME IS NOT BLANK, STORE EQL OPERATION, OPERAND.          MMC00048
      IF (B(4).NE.BLANK) BCD(2,I) = FEQL                                  MMC00049
      IF (B(4).NE.BLANK) BCD(3,I) = C(JL+1)                              MMC00050
C**** IF RESULT NAME IS BLANK, STORE GIVEN FUNCTION NAME.                 MMC00051
      IF (B(4).EQ.BLANK) BCD(2,I) = C(JL+1)                              MMC00052
C**** TEST FOR FUNCTION END.                                              MMC00053
      IF (BCD(2,I).EQ.FEND) RETURN                                        MMC00054
      GO TO 40                                                            MMC00055
C**** IF NO SEPARATOR PRECEDES PARENTHESES, REMOVE PARENTHESES.           MMC00056
  100 IF((IC(JLEFT-1)/64).NE.0) GO TO 160                                MMC00057
      IC(JLEFT+2)=IC(JLEFT+1)                                            MMC00058
      DO 110 K=JLEFT,55                                                   MMC00059
  110 IC(K)=IC(K+2)                                                      MMC00060
C**** FIND INNER PARENTHESIS PAIR.                                        MMC00061
  120 DO 130 J=JL,57                                                      MMC00062
```

Fig. 6.6 Subroutine MIMCO.

```
      IF(IC(J).EQ.28) GO TO 140                                    MMC00063
  130 IF(IC(J).EQ.60) JLEFT=J                                      MMC00064
  140 JRIGHT=J-2                                                   MMC00065
C**** TEST FOR (NAME).                                            MMC00066
  150 IF (JLEFT.GE.JRIGHT) GO TO 260                               MMC00067
C**** INCREASE LOCATOR, STORE RESULT, LCV, AND BLANK OPERAND NAMES. MMC00068
  160 I=I+1                                                        MMC00069
      BCD(1,I)=OR(4096*(4096*(I/100)+64*(MOD(I,100)/10)+MOD(I,10)),MASK)MMC00070
      BCD(9,I)=B(2)                                                MMC00071
      DO 170 JS=3,8                                                MMC00072
  170 BCD(JS,I)=BLANK                                              MMC00073
C**** TEST FOR * AND / AND + AND -.                               MMC00074
      DO 180 J=JLEFT,JRIGHT                                        MMC00075
      IF ((IC(J+2).EQ.44).OR.(IC(J+2).EQ.49)) GO TO 210           MMC00076
  180 IF ((IC(J).EQ.16).OR.(IC(J).EQ.32)) GO TO 240               MMC00077
C**** STORE FUNCTION AND OPERAND NAMES IN BCD, RESULT NAME IN C.  MMC00078
      BCD(2,I)=C(JLEFT-1)                                          MMC00079
      JS=3                                                         MMC00080
      DO 190 J=JLEFT,JRIGHT                                        MMC00081
      IF (IC(J+1).NE.59) BCD(JS,I)=C(J+1)                          MMC00082
  190 IF (IC(J+1).EQ.59) JS=JS+1                                   MMC00083
      C(JLEFT-1)=BCD(1,I)                                          MMC00084
C**** TEST FOR INTEGRATOR.                                        MMC00085
      IF (BCD(2,I).EQ.FINT) NEQ=NEQ+1                              MMC00086
      IF (BCD(2,I).EQ.FINT) S(NEQ+7)=BCD(1,I)                      MMC00087
C**** CLOSE STRING AND CONTINUE.                                  MMC00088
      DO 200 J=JRIGHT,54                                           MMC00089
      K=JLEFT+J-JRIGHT                                             MMC00090
  200 IC(K)=IC(J+3)                                                MMC00091
      GO TO 120                                                    MMC00092
C**** STORE OPERATION ADD OR SUB OR MPY OR DIV.                   MMC00093
  210 J=J+2                                                        MMC00094
      IF (IC(J).EQ.44) BCD(2,I) = FMPY                             MMC00095
      IF (IC(J).EQ.49) BCD(2,I) = FDIV                             MMC00096
  220 IF (IC(J).EQ.16) BCD(2,I) = FADD                             MMC00097
      IF (IC(J).EQ.32) BCD(2,I) = FSUB                             MMC00098
C**** STORE BINARY OPERAND NAMES IN BCD, RESULT NAME IN C.        MMC00099
      BCD(3,I)=C(J-1)                                              MMC00100
      BCD(4,I)=C(J+1)                                              MMC00101
      C(J-1)=BCD(1,I)                                              MMC00102
C**** CLOSE STRING AND CONTINUE.                                  MMC00103
      DO 230 K=J,55                                                MMC00104
  230 C(K)=C(K+2)                                                  MMC00105
      JRIGHT=JRIGHT-2                                              MMC00106
      GO TO 150                                                    MMC00107
C**** GENERATE OPERATION EQL OR NEG IF ( OR , PRECEDES + OR -.    MMC00108
  240 IF ((IC(J-1).NE.60).AND.(IC(J-1).NE.59)) GO TO 220          MMC00109
      IF (IC(J).EQ.16) BCD(2,I) = FEQL                             MMC00110
      IF (IC(J).EQ.32) BCD(2,I) = FNEG                             MMC00111
C**** STORE OPERAND NAME IN BCD, RESULT NAME IN C.                MMC00112
      BCD(3,I)=C(J+1)                                              MMC00113
      C(J)=BCD(1,I)                                                MMC00114
C**** CLOSE STRING AND CONTINUE.                                  MMC00115
      DO 250 K=J,55                                                MMC00116
  250 C(K+1)=C(K+2)                                                MMC00117
      JRIGHT=JRIGHT-1                                              MMC00118
      GO TO 150                                                    MMC00119
C**** IF LAST PARENTHESES, STORE GIVEN RESULT NAME IN LAST OPERATION. MMC00120
  260 IF(JLEFT.NE.JL) GO TO 100                                    MMC00121
      BCD(1,I)=B(4)                                                MMC00122
      IF (BCD(2,I).EQ.FINT) S(NEQ+7)=B(4)                          MMC00123
      GO TO 40                                                     MMC00124
      END                                                          MMC00125
```

Fig. 6.6 (Continued)

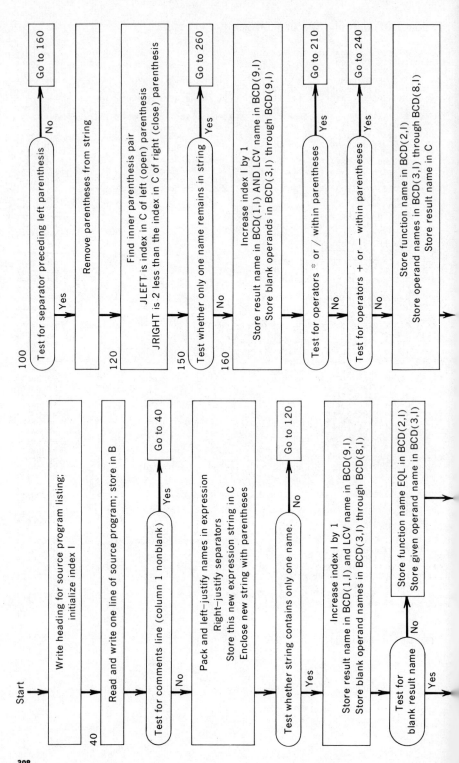

308

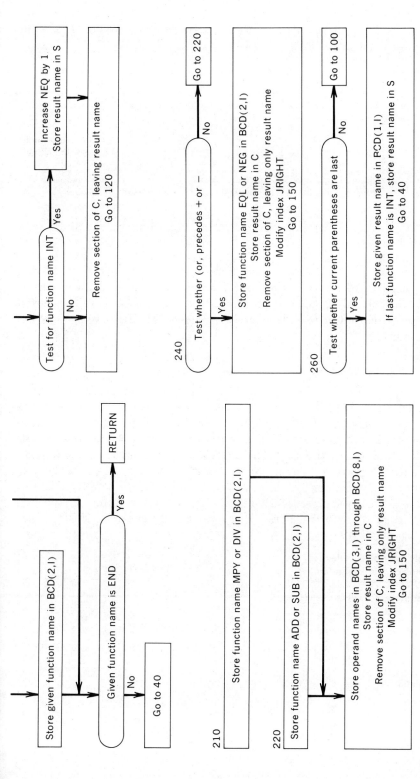

Fig. 6.7 Flowchart for subroutine MIMCO.

309

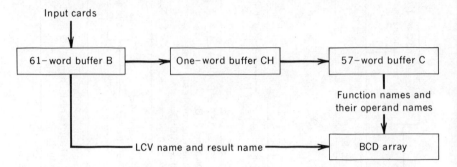

Fig. 6.8 Block diagram showing the use of three buffers for translating a SIMIC statement into one or more functions stored in the BCD array.

SION, EQUIVALENCE, and DATA statements, are listed and described in Table 6.9.   BCD codes for the operators and separators to be referred to by the subroutine (e.g., see cards 26, 27, and 29 in Fig. 6.6) are listed in Table 6.10.

6.4.1 READ INPUT CARDS

During initialization (cards 12 to 14 in Fig. 6.6), the compiler prints out the heading MIMIC SOURCE-LANGUAGE PROGRAM and sets index I of the BCD array to 0.   The first task of compilation (cards 15 to 19) is to read a card from the SIMIC program into buffer B and print out the statement as a reference.   The FORMAT statement with statement number 10 specifies a particular way that the 80 characters on the card be stored in the buffer B; this is illustrated in Fig. 6.9a, where each number inside buffer B represents a column number of the card.   In the first word B(1) is stored the character in column 1 of the card.   If B(1) is not

Table 6.10   BCD codes for operators and separators

Character	Decimal code
+	16
)	28
−	32
*	44
Blank	48
/	49
,	59
(	60

blank, the input card is a COMMENT statement (see Table 2.2) and the compiler proceeds to the next card. The LCV name (columns 2 to 7) is stored in the second word B(2). The third and fifth words are not used. The result name (columns 10 to 15) is stored in the fourth word. Because a fixed format is used, these names are readily located and identified.

However, the expression in a SIMIC statement (columns 19 to 72) is in a free format. The variable names, separators, and operators in the expression have to be located and identified. For this reason, the characters in columns 19 to 72 are stored individually in words B(6) to B(59) to be processed further.

As an example, the contents of buffer B after the statement

$$2DX = A*1DX - A*1DX*X*X - B*X$$

is read in are shown in Fig. 6.9b. The equal sign is provided for readability and is ignored during compilation.

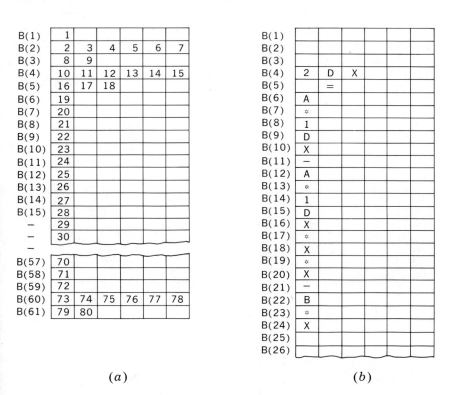

(a) (b)

Fig. 6.9 Storage of the characters on a statement card in the B buffer. (a) Locations of characters on a statement card in buffer B; (b) an example.

6.4.2 FORM A STRING IN BUFFER C

The second task of compilation is to obtain in buffer C a string which is formed from the expression of the INPUT statement. The variable names, operators, and separators in the expression can then be identified and located in the string. As an example, the string in buffer C shown in Fig. 6.10 is the result of packing the contents of the buffer B in Fig. 6.9b.

To obtain the string in buffer C, each word from words B(6) to B(59), beginning at B(59), is transferred to buffer CH. It is then determined whether the character in the word is a separator or an operator (those in Table 6.10 except blank). If it is, the word is right-justified and stored in buffer C, beginning at C(57). If it is not, the character must be a part of a variable name; it is then packed with the next character to form a name.

This task consists of the statements on cards 20 to 39 in Fig. 6.6. In these statements, JB and JC are the indices (or pointers) in buffers B and C, respectively. Notice that the MAP-coded functions of ALS(A,N), ARS(A,N), and OR(A,B) are used in manipulating and assembling the characters. After the string is ready in buffer C, the string is enclosed by a pair of parentheses. The right parenthesis is located at C(57) and the left parenthesis at C(JL), where JL is the pointer (see Fig. 6.10). It should be noted that this pair of parentheses is the outermost pair enclosing the string.

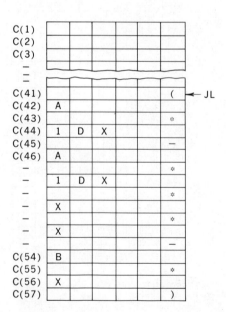

Fig. 6.10 An example of unpacking in the C buffer.

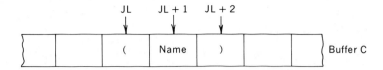

Fig. 6.11   Format of the name-only expression in buffer C.

6.4.3 NAME–ONLY EXPRESSION

At this point, the expression now enclosed by a pair of parentheses in buffer C is examined.   There is a special case where the enclosed expression contains only a name.   The name can be a function name such as (END) or a literal such as (3.1416).   Therefore, the third task of compilation (cards 40 to 55) is to test the name-only expression.   An unsuccessful test by the statement

IF   (IC(JL+2).NE.28)   GO TO 120

determines the case of a name-only expression.   Note, as shown in Fig. 6.11, that JL and JL+2 point, respectively, to the left and right parentheses, and JL+1 points to the name.   And the following DO loop blanks BCD(3,I) to BCD(8,I):

DO 90 J = 3, 8
90 BCD(J,I) = BLANK

If there is a result name, the name in the expression is a literal, and function name EQL is entered into BCD(2,I).   Otherwise, the name in JL+1 is entered into BCD(2,I).   Finally, BCD(2,I) is tested to see whether the function name is END.   If it is, compilation is completed and control is returned to the executive program.   If it is not, the compiler proceeds to read the next card.

6.4.4 FIND THE INNERMOST PAIR OF PARENTHESES

If the enclosed expression in buffer C is not a name-only expression, it can be an arithmetic expression, such as

(A*B+C+D)   or   (A*(B+C)+D)

a functional expression, such as

(FSW(T,B,C,D))

a nesting of functional expressions, such as

(FSW(SIN(T),B,C,D))

a functional expression with one or more arguments being an arithmetic expression, such as

(FSW(E*F,B,C,D))

or a combination of the last two cases, such as

(FSW(E*(F+G),B,C,SIN(T)))

Because of the precedence of parentheses, the compiler first finds an innermost pair of parentheses. This task (cards 61 to 67) is performed by a DO loop, where JLEFT and JRIGHT+2 point to the locations of the left and right parentheses, respectively. Notice that the string is scanned from left to right. The string enclosed by the innermost pair can be any of the following:

1. (A)
2. (A*B+C+D)
3. (T,B,C,D)
4. (E*F,B,C,D)

The statement

IF   (JLEFT.GE.JRIGHT)   GO TO 260

has three possible conditions, which are illustrated in Fig. 6.12.   When

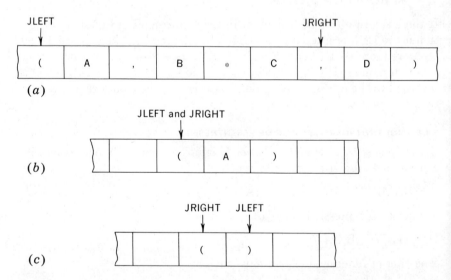

Fig. 6.12   Examples showing the three cases of the relative locations of JLEFT and JRIGHT in buffer C.   (*a*) JLEFT < JRIGHT; (*b*) JLEFT = JRIGHT; (*c*) JLEFT > JRIGHT.

JLEFT is less than JRIGHT, it is the above case 1, 3, or 4. When they are equal, it is the above case 1 of name-only string. (This case is different from the previous case of name-only expression, where the pair of parentheses must be the outermost pair.) The condition that JLEFT is greater than JRIGHT does not occur.

6.4.5 PROCESS ARITHMETIC EXPRESSION

If JLEFT is less than JRIGHT, the enclosed string contains an arithmetic expression with one or more arithmetic operators (case 2 above), a number of operand names separated by commas (case 3 above), or a combination of the two (case 4 above). In any case, processing of an arithmetic expression should be ahead of that of a functional expression.

This task of processing an arithmetic expression (cards 68 to 77 and 93 to 119) requires generating an internal variable name for use in the BCD array, providing precedence in the four arithmetic operators, distinguishing and handling operators $+$ and $-$ being binary or unary, storing operand names in BCD array, and closing up the string.

The internal variable name is chosen with the format of a three-decimal-digit number enclosed by a pair of parentheses, such as (001) and (105). Since column index I of the BCD array is unique, it can be used for this purpose, but it must be converted into a literal, as the number is used as a name. The following statement converts I as a number to a literal:

$$BCD(1,I) = OR(4096*(4096*(I/100) + 64*(MOD(I,100)/10) + MOD(I,10)),MASK)$$

In the above, multiplication of 64 and 4096 is to shift I (as a number) one- and two-character positions, respectively (six bits for one character). MOD(I,10) or MOD(I,100) is to keep the residue after I is divided by 10 or 100. Division I/100 is performed in integer arithmetic; only integral digits are retained. The mask provides the digits with a pair of parentheses. And the literal is assembled by the MAP-coded function OR.

The precedence of arithmetic operators is implemented by the following DO loop, which scans the characters of the string:

```
     DO 180 J = JLEFT, JRIGHT
        IF ((IC(J+2).EQ.44).OR.(IC(J+2).EQ.49))   GO TO 210
180  IF ((IC(J).EQ.16).OR.(IC(J).EQ.32))   GO TO 240
```

In the above, the search of operators * and / occurs ahead of that of operators $+$ and $-$. Furthermore, the index for searching operators * and / is J+2, while the index for searching operators $+$ and $-$ is J. The difference of 2 in the index is to provide a "look-ahead" for operators

* and /, as illustrated by the following arithmetic expressions:

A*B+C
A+B*C
A*B*C
A+B+C

If the operator is + or −, it is first determined whether the operation is unary or binary. A unary operator is distinguished by the presence of a comma or a left parenthesis preceding the operator, as shown below:

,+
,−
(+
(−

If the operator is unary, the function name is EQL or NEQ. If it is binary, the function name is ADD and SUB. For operators * and /, the function names are MPY and DIV.

The operand names are next stored in the BCD array by the following statements:

BCD(3,I) = C(J−1)
BCD(4,I) = C(J+1)

Let us define an arithmetic operation to be an arithmetic operator together with the associated one or two operands. Since the arithmetic operation is no longer needed in the string, the first of the locations now occupied by the arithmetic operation is replaced by the result name in BCD(1,I). This replacement in a FORTRAN statement is

C(J−1) = BCD(1,I)

And the character positions in buffer C left over by the arithmetic operation are closed up by the following DO loop:

DO 230 K=J,55
230 C(K) = C(K+2)

The pointer of the right parenthesis, JRIGHT, is accordingly changed by the statement

JRIGHT = JRIGHT−2

while the pointer of the left parenthesis, JLEFT, should remain unchanged.

The process of removing the arithmetic operation from the enclosed string continues one after another until all arithmetic operations in the same enclosed string are removed.

6.4.6 PROCESS FUNCTIONAL EXPRESSION

When all arithmetic operations in the string are removed, a test is made again to determine whether JLEFT is less than JRIGHT.   If it is, then the enclosed string now contains a functional expression.

This task (cards 78 to 92) simply stores the function name and operand names, enters the generated internal result name, removes the pair of parentheses, and closes up the locations left over by the functional expression.   In addition, the function name is tested to determine whether it is INT.   If it is, this name is entered into array S.   As shown previously, in the first seven locations in array S are stored the reserved names; therefore, the first available location in array S is 8, and the index for the S array becomes NEQ+7, where NEQ is initially set to 1.

When the functional expression in the string is removed, the next innermost pair of parentheses is searched, and whether JLEFT is less than JRIGHT is tested again.   If it is, the process of removing arithmetic operations and/or functional expressions continues until JLEFT is not less than JRIGHT.

6.4.7 PROCESS NAME–ONLY STRING

This task (cards 120 to 124 and 56 to 60) begins when it is found that JLEFT is equal to JRIGHT.   Under this condition, there is only a single name within the enclosed string, as shown in Fig. 6.12(b).   A test is made to determine whether the parentheses are the last pair.   If not, another test is made to determine whether a separator or an operator precedes the left parenthesis, such as

$$
\begin{array}{l}
\text{NAME(} \\
\quad\text{,(} \\
\quad\text{((} \\
\quad\text{+(} \\
\quad\text{−(} \\
\quad\text{*(} \\
\quad\text{/(}
\end{array}
$$

If a separator or an operator does not precede the left parenthesis, the present pair of parentheses is simply removed by closing up the string, and a next innermost pair of parentheses is searched.   If a separator or an operator does precede the left parenthesis, then it indicates that the pair of parentheses encloses operand names of a function.

If only a single name remains within the last pair of parentheses, the given result name B(4) is stored in the BCD array as the result name for

the last function.   If this function name is INT, this result name is also
stored in array S.   And the compiler proceeds to read in the next card.
The compiler processes one card after another until it reaches the END
statement.   At that time, as mentioned previously, the control is returned
to the executive program.

6.5 ASSEMBLY

Assembler MIMAS translates the function-language program in the BCD
array into a machine-language program and stores the latter in the FF
array.   Each column of the BCD array which contains one of the 25 functions in Table 6.1 is translated into a group of machine instructions; these
groups in MAP codes are also shown in Table 6.1.

Associated with the FF array are the symbol table and data table,
which are the S and R arrays, respectively.   After assembly, the symbol
table contains the names of all constants, parameters, literals, and variables; these names are referenced in the FF array.   And the data table
reserves the locations for the values of these constants, parameters,
literals, and variables.   When the program in the FF array is being executed, the required data are provided in the R array.

The assembler examines each function (i.e., column) of the BCD
array and carries out the following four tasks:

1. Determine the address for the names of the operands, result, and LCV
    associated with the function.
2. Store two instructions for an LCV test if the function is to be con-
    trolled by an LCV.
3. Generate a group of machine-language instructions for the function
    and store them in the FF array.
4. Increment index IF of the FF array to the proper value at which
    storage of the next group of machine-language instructions begins.

Subroutine MIMAS is shown in Fig. 6.13, and a flowchart is shown
in Fig. 6.14.   In addition to the variables in the COMMON area shown
in Table 6.5, additional variables in the MIMAS are listed and described
in Table 6.11.   In Fig. 6.13, one DATA statement provides the names of
25 functions in Table 6.1 for function identification during assembly.
Another DATA statement provides the operation codes of 22 machine
instructions also shown in Table 6.1; these instructions are all that are
needed in a generated machine-language program.   The EXTERNAL
statement identifies those subprogram names such as ALOG and
MIMHDR which are external to this subroutine.

During initialization (cards 28 to 32), the assembler left-justifies the

```
$IBFTC MMAS    XR7                                                          MMAS0000
C**** ASSEMBLER.                                                            MMAS0001
      SUBROUTINE MIMAS                                                      MMAS0002
      DIMENSION IM(8)                                                       MMAS0003
      COMMON NEQ,P(93),R(2500),S(2500),FF(4000),BCD(10,900)                 MMAS0004
      COMMON IOUT,IPAR,IHDR,IFIN,IEND,NPAR,LKDR,LKDR2                        MMAS0005
      EQUIVALENCE (AA,IAA),(AR,IAR),(CH,ICH),(AFF,IAFF)                      MMAS0006
      EQUIVALENCE(IRA,IM(1)),(IRB,IM(2)),(IRC,IM(3)),(IRD,IM(4)),            MMAS0007
     1          (IRE,IM(5)),(IRF,IM(6)),(IRCV,IM(7)),(IRR,IM(8))             MMAS0008
C**** LEFT-JUSTIFIED MIMIC FUNCTION NAMES.                                  MMAS0009
      DATA FABS,FADD,FAND,FATN,FCON,FCOS,FDIV,FEND,FEQL,FEXP,FFIN,FFSW,      MMAS0010
     1     FHDR,FINT,FIOR,FLOG,FLSW,FMPY,FNEG,FNOT,FOUT,FPAR,FSIN,FSQR,      MMAS0011
     2     FSUB/3HABS,3HADD,3HAND,3HATN,3HCON,3HCOS,3HDIV,3HEND,3HEQL,       MMAS0012
     3     3HEXP,3HFIN,3HFSW,3HHDR,3HINT,3HIOR,3HLOG,3HLSW,3HMPY,3HNEG,      MMAS0013
     4     3HNOT,3HOUT,3HPAR,3HSIN,3HSQR,3HSUB/                             MMAS0014
C**** OCTAL 7094 INSTRUCTIONS USED.                                         MMAS0015
      DATA BANA,BCAL,BCLA,BCLS,BFAD,BFDP,BFMP,BFSB,BLDQ,BNZT,BORA,BSTL,      MMAS0016
     1     BSTO,BSTQ,BSLW,BSTZ,BTMI,BTRA,BTSX4,BTXI,BTZE,BZET/               MMAS0017
     2     0432000000000,0450000000000,0050000000000,0050200000000,         MMAS0018
     3     0030000000000,0024100000000,0026000000000,0030200000000,         MMAS0019
     4     0056000000000,0452000000000,0450100000000,0462500000000,         MMAS0020
     5     0060100000000,0460000000000,0060200000000,0060000000000,         MMAS0021
     6     0412000000000,0002000000000,0007400400000,0100000000000,         MMAS0022
     7     0010000000000,0052000000000/                                     MMAS0023
C**** SUBPROGRAM NAMES USED AS EXTERNAL VARIABLES.                          MMAS0024
      EXTERNAL ALOG,ATAN2,COS,EXP,SIN,SQRT,MIMHDR,MIMOUT,MIMPAR,FEXIT       MMAS0025
C**** OTHER CONSTANTS USED.                                                 MMAS0026
      DATA D1,D2,D6,BLANK/01000000,02000000,06000000,1H /                   MMAS0027
C**** INITIALIZATION.                                                       MMAS0028
      ALKDR=ALS(ADV(LKDR),18)                                               MMAS0029
      IS=NEQ+7                                                              MMAS0030
      IBCD=0                                                                MMAS0031
      IF=1                                                                  MMAS0032
   10 IBCD=IBCD+1                                                           MMAS0033
      FCTN=BCD(2,IBCD)                                                      MMAS0034
C**** COMPUTE OPERAND AND RESULT STORAGE LOCATIONS.                         MMAS0035
      BCD(10,IBCD)=BCD(1,IBCD)                                              MMAS0036
      DO 40 I=3,10                                                          MMAS0037
C**** TEST FOR PREVIOUSLY STORED NAME.                                      MMAS0038
      DO 20 J=1,IS                                                          MMAS0039
   20 IF(BCD(I,IBCD).EQ.S(J)) GO TO 40                                      MMAS0040
C**** STORE NEW SYMBOL.                                                     MMAS0041
      J=IS+1                                                                MMAS0042
      IS=J                                                                  MMAS0043
      S(J)=BCD(I,IBCD)                                                      MMAS0044
      IF(I.GE.9) GO TO 40                                                   MMAS0045
C**** FLOAT LITERAL.                                                        MMAS0046
      LIT=0                                                                 MMAS0047
      P10=0.                                                                MMAS0048
      DO 30 IBI=1,6                                                         MMAS0049
      CH=ARS(ALS(BCD(I,IBCD),6*IBI-6),30)                                   MMAS0050
C**** TEST FOR DIGIT, SPACE, DECIMAL POINT.                                 MMAS0051
      IF(ICH.LT.10) LIT=10*LIT+ICH                                          MMAS0052
      IF(ICH.EQ.48) LIT=10*LIT                                              MMAS0053
   30 IF(ICH.EQ.27) P10=10.**IBI                                           MMAS0054
      R(J)=(P10*FLOAT(LIT))/1000000.                                        MMAS0055
   40 IM(I-2)=J                                                             MMAS0056
C**** STORE OPERAND AND RESULT STORAGE LOCATIONS.                           MMAS0057
C**** FUNCTION ADV COMPUTES RIGHT-JUSTIFIED ADDRESS OF A VARIABLE.          MMAS0058
      AA=ADV(R(IRA))                                                        MMAS0059
      AB=ADV(R(IRB))                                                        MMAS0060
      AC=ADV(R(IRC))                                                        MMAS0061
      AD=ADV(R(IRD))                                                        MMAS0062
      AE=ADV(R(IRE))                                                        MMAS0063
      AF=ADV(R(IRF))                                                        MMAS0064
      AR=ADV(R(IRR))                                                        MMAS0065
C**** TEST FOR CONTROL VARIABLE.                                            MMAS0066
      IF (BCD(9,IBCD).EQ.BLANK) GO TO 50                                    MMAS0067
      FF(IF)=OR(BNZT,ADV(R(IRCV)))                                          MMAS0068
      IBR=IF+1                                                              MMAS0069
      IF=IF+2                                                               MMAS0070
   50 AFF=ADV(FF(IF))                                                       MMAS0071
```

Fig. 6.13 Subroutine MIMAS.

```
C****  GENERATE MACHINE CODE FOR GIVEN OPERATION.                      MMAS0072
   60  IF (FCTN.NE.FABS) GO TO 80                                       MMAS0073
       FF(IF)=OR (BCAL,AA)                                              MMAS0074
   70  FF(IF+1)=OR(BSTO,AR)                                             MMAS0075
       GO TO 420                                                        MMAS0076
   80  IF (FCTN.NE.FADD) GO TO 110                                      MMAS0077
       FF(IF+1)=OR (BFAD,AB)                                            MMAS0078
   90  FF(IF)=OR(BCLA,AA)                                               MMAS0079
  100  FF(IF+2)=OR(BSTO,AR)                                             MMAS0080
       GO TO 410                                                        MMAS0081
  110  IF(FCTN.NE.FAND) GO TO 130                                       MMAS0082
       FF(IF+1)=OR(BANA,AB)                                             MMAS0083
  120  FF(IF)=OR(BCAL,AA)                                               MMAS0084
       FF(IF+2)=OR(BSLW,AR)                                             MMAS0085
       GO TO 410                                                        MMAS0086
  130  IF (FCTN.NE.FATN) GO TO 140                                      MMAS0087
       FF(IF)=OR(BTSX4,ADV(ATAN2))                                      MMAS0088
       FF(IF+1)=OR(OR(BTXI,D2),IAFF+5)                                  MMAS0089
       FF(IF+2)=OR(ALKDR,IBCD)                                          MMAS0090
       FF(IF+3)=AA                                                      MMAS0091
       FF(IF+4)=AB                                                      MMAS0092
       FF(IF+5)=OR(BSTO,AR)                                             MMAS0093
       GO TO 380                                                        MMAS0094
  140  IF (FCTN.NE.FCON) GO TO 150                                      MMAS0095
       CALL MIMPAR (R(IRA),R(IRB),R(IRC),R(IRD),R(IRE),R(IRF))          MMAS0096
       GO TO 10                                                         MMAS0097
  150  IF ((FCTN.NE.FCOS).AND.(FCTN.NE.FEXP).AND.(FCTN.NE.FLOG).AND.    MMAS0098
      1   (FCTN.NE.FSIN).AND.(FCTN.NE.FSQR)) GO TO 170                  MMAS0099
  160  IF(FCTN.EQ.FCOS) FF(IF)=OR(BTSX4,ADV(COS))                       MMAS0100
       IF(FCTN.EQ.FEXP) FF(IF)=OR(BTSX4,ADV(EXP))                       MMAS0101
       IF(FCTN.EQ.FLOG) FF(IF)=OR(BTSX4,ADV(ALOG))                      MMAS0102
       IF(FCTN.EQ.FSIN) FF(IF)=OR(BTSX4,ADV(SIN))                       MMAS0103
       IF(FCTN.EQ.FSQR) FF(IF)=OR(BTSX4,ADV(SQRT))                      MMAS0104
       FF(IF+1)=OR(OR(BTXI ,D1),IAFF+4)                                 MMAS0105
       FF(IF+2)=OR(ALKDR, IBCD)                                         MMAS0106
       FF(IF+3)=AA                                                      MMAS0107
       FF(IF+4)=OR(BSTO,AR)                                             MMAS0108
       GO TO 390                                                        MMAS0109
  170  IF(FCTN.NE.FDIV) GO TO 180                                       MMAS0110
       FF(IF)=OR (BCLA,AA)                                              MMAS0111
       FF(IF+1)=OR (BFDP,AB)                                            MMAS0112
       FF(IF+2)=OR (BSTQ,AR)                                            MMAS0113
       GO TO 410                                                        MMAS0114
  180  IF (FCTN.NE.FEND) GO TO 190                                      MMAS0115
       FF(IF)=OR(BTRA,ADV(FEXIT))                                       MMAS0116
       RETURN                                                           MMAS0117
  190  IF(FCTN.NE.FEQL) GO TO 200                                       MMAS0118
       FF(IF)=OR (BCLA,AA)                                              MMAS0119
       GO TO 70                                                         MMAS0120
  200  IF(FCTN.NE.FFIN) GO TO 210                                       MMAS0121
       FF(IF)=OR (BNZT,ADV(IFIN))                                       MMAS0122
       FF(IF+1)=OR (BTRA,IAFF+7)                                        MMAS0123
       FF(IF+2)=OR (BCLA,AA)                                            MMAS0124
       FF(IF+3)=OR (BFSB,AB)                                            MMAS0125
       FF(IF+4)=OR (BTZE,IAFF+6)                                        MMAS0126
       FF(IF+5)=OR (BTMI,IAFF+7)                                        MMAS0127
       FF(IF+6)=OR (BSTL,ADV(IFND))                                     MMAS0128
       GO TO 370                                                        MMAS0129
  210  IF(FCTN.NE.FFSW) GO TO 220                                       MMAS0130
       FF(IF)=OR (BCLA,AA)                                              MMAS0131
       FF(IF+1)=OR (BLDQ,AC)                                            MMAS0132
       FF(IF+2)=OR (BTZE,IAFF+6)                                        MMAS0133
       FF(IF+3)=OR (BLDQ,AB)                                            MMAS0134
       FF(IF+4)=OR (BTMI,IAFF+6)                                        MMAS0135
       FF(IF+5)=OR (BLDQ,AD)                                            MMAS0136
       FF(IF+6)=OR (BSTQ,AR)                                            MMAS0137
       GO TO 370                                                        MMAS0138
  220  IF(FCTN.NE.FHDR) GO TO 240                                       MMAS0139
       FF(IF)=OR(BZET,ADV(IHDR))                                        MMAS0140
       FF(IF+1)=OR(BTSX4,ADV(MIMHDR))                                   MMAS0141
  230  FF(IF+2)=OR(OR(BTXI,D6),IAFF+10)                                 MMAS0142
```

Fig. 6.13   (Continued)

```
      FF(IF+3)=OR(ALKDR,IBCD)                                      MMAS0143
      FF(IF+4)=AA                                                  MMAS0144
      FF(IF+5)=AB                                                  MMAS0145
      FF(IF+6)=AC                                                  MMAS0146
      FF(IF+7)=AD                                                  MMAS0147
      FF(IF+8)=AE                                                  MMAS0148
      FF(IF+9)=AF                                                  MMAS0149
      GO TO 360                                                    MMAS0150
  240 IF(FCTN.NE.FINT) GO TO 250                                   MMAS0151
      FF(IF)=OR(BCLA,AA)                                           MMAS0152
      FF(IF+1)=OR(BSTO,IAR-100)                                    MMAS0153
      FF(IF+2)=OR(BCLA,AB)                                         MMAS0154
      FF(IF+3)=OR(BNZT,ADV(R(1)))                                  MMAS0155
      FF(IF+4)=OR(BSTO,AR)                                         MMAS0156
      R(IRR)=.5                                                    MMAS0157
      GO TO 390                                                    MMAS0158
  250 IF (FCTN.NE.FIOR) GO TO 260                                  MMAS0159
      FF(IF+1)=OR(BORA,AB)                                         MMAS0160
      GO TO 120                                                    MMAS0161
  260 IF (FCTN.NE.FLSW) GO TO 270                                  MMAS0162
      FF(IF)=OR (BCLA,AB)                                          MMAS0163
      FF(IF+1)=OR (BNZT,AA)                                        MMAS0164
      FF(IF+2)=OR (BCLA,AC)                                        MMAS0165
      FF(IF+3)=OR (BSTO,AR)                                        MMAS0166
      GO TO 400                                                    MMAS0167
  270 IF(FCTN.NE.FMPY) GO TO 280                                   MMAS0168
      FF(IF)=OR (BLDQ,AA)                                          MMAS0169
      FF(IF+1)=OR (BFMP,AB)                                        MMAS0170
      GO TO 100                                                    MMAS0171
  280 IF(FCTN.NE.FNEG) GO TO 290                                   MMAS0172
      FF(IF)=OR (BCLS,AA)                                          MMAS0173
      GO TO 70                                                     MMAS0174
  290 IF (FCTN.NE.FNOT) GO TO 300                                  MMAS0175
      FF(IF)=OR(BSTZ,AR)                                           MMAS0176
      FF(IF+1)=OR (BNZT,AA)                                        MMAS0177
      FF(IF+2)=OR(BSTL,AR)                                         MMAS0178
      GO TO 410                                                    MMAS0179
  300 IF(FCTN.NE.FOUT) GO TO 310                                   MMAS0180
      FF(IF)=OR(BZFT,ADV(IOUT))                                    MMAS0181
      FF(IF+1)=OR(BTSX4,ADV(MIMOUT))                               MMAS0182
      GO TO 230                                                    MMAS0183
  310 IF (FCTN.NE.FPAR) GO TO 330                                  MMAS0184
      FF(IF+1)=OR(BTSX4,ADV(MIMPAR))                               MMAS0185
  320 FF(IF)=OR(BZET,ADV(IPAR))                                    MMAS0186
      NPAR=1                                                       MMAS0187
      GO TO 230                                                    MMAS0188
  330 IF(FCTN.NE.FSUB) GO TO 340                                   MMAS0189
      FF(IF+1)=OR (BFSB,AB)                                        MMAS0190
      GO TO 90                                                     MMAS0191
  340 WRITE (6,350) FCTN                                           MMAS0192
  350 FORMAT(18H ILLEGAL FUNCTION A3,8H IGNORED)                   MMAS0193
      GO TO 10                                                     MMAS0194
C**** ADVANCE CODE STORAGE LOCATION.                              MMAS0195
  360 IF=IF+3                                                      MMAS0196
  370 IF=IF+1                                                      MMAS0197
  380 IF=IF+1                                                      MMAS0198
  390 IF=IF+1                                                      MMAS0199
  400 IF=IF+1                                                      MMAS0200
  410 IF=IF+1                                                      MMAS0201
  420 IF=IF+2                                                      MMAS0202
      IF (BCD(9,IBCD).NE.BLANK) FF(IBR)=OR(BTRA,ADV(FF(IF)))       MMAS0203
      GO TO 10                                                     MMAS0204
      END                                                          MMAS0205
```

Fig. 6.13   (Continued)

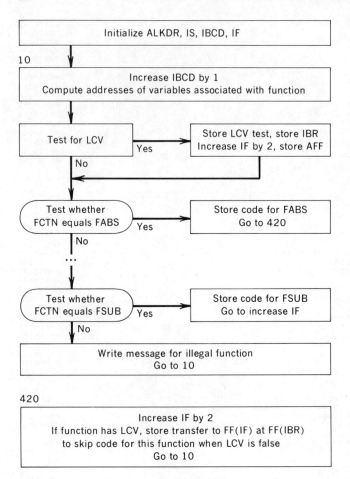

Fig. 6.14 Flowchart of subroutine MIMAS.

address of linkage director LKDR and stores it in location ALKDR. Index IS of the S array is set at $NEQ+7$; index IBCD of the BCD array is set to 0; and index IF of the FF array is set to 1.   The above-mentioned four tasks of assembly are described below.

6.5.1 ADDRESS DETERMINATION

The task of address determination (cards 33 to 65) begins by taking the function name in a column of the BCD array and storing it in location FCTN and by moving the result name in BCD(1,IBCD) to BCD(10,IBCD).   Each of the eight names (six operand names, one LCV name, and one result name) now located at BCD(3,IBCD) to BCD(10, IBCD) is tested to determine whether the name is in the symbol table.

If it is not, the name is entered in the S array. In either case, the index is stored in the IM array. If any of the six operand names is a literal, it is converted into a floating-point number (cards 46 to 55) after the values of LIT and P10 are obtained. This number is then stored in the R array by the following FORTRAN statement:

$$R(J) = (P10*FLOAT(LIT))/1000000.$$

where FLOAT is a FORTRAN built-in function. If the operand name is not a literal, there is no decimal point in the name, and the value so obtained becomes 0. Note that the indices obtained for array S are also the respective indices for the R array.

The address of a location in the R array is obtained by having its index as the argument of MAP-coded function ADV. For example, R(IRA) is a location in the R array with index of IRA. ADV(R(IRA))

Table 6.11 Variables in subroutine MIMAS

Name	Storage function
IBCD	Index of the current function (i.e., column) in the BCD array.
IBR	Index of the FF array at which the second instruction generated for an LCV is to be stored.
IF	Index of the FF array at which a generated code is stored.
IS	Index of the S array at which the current variable name is stored.
LKDR	A location storing a linkage director.
LKDR2	A location storing a linkage director.
ALKDR	A location storing the address of LKDR.
AA	A location storing the address of R(IRA). Similarly, AB, AC, etc., store the address of R(IRB), R(IRC), etc., respectively.
AR	A location storing the address of the result of the current function.
AFF	A location storing the first address of FF available for storing generated instructions.
IAFF	Equivalent to AFF.
FABS	A location storing the left-justified function name ADD. Similarly for other function names.
BANA	Location storing op-code of instruction ANA. Similarly for op-code of other instructions.
FCTN	A location storing the current function name.
D1	A location storing the constant for integer 1. Similarly, D2 and D6 for integers 2 and 6.
IM(8)	An array for storing the indices of arrays S and R at which operand, result, and LCV names of the current function in the BCD array are stored.
IRA	Equivalent to IM(1). Similarly for IRB, IRC, etc.

gives the address of the location of R(IRA); this address is then stored in AA. Other addresses are similarly found and stored in AB, AC, AD, AE, AF, and AR.

6.5.2 INSTRUCTIONS FOR THE LCV

The LCV makes a SIMIC statement conditional. A SIMIC statement is skipped and not executed if its LCV is FALSE (a value of zero). This task (cards 66 to 71 and 203) is to generate two instructions whenever there is an LCV in the statement.

To accomplish this task, the following two FORTRAN statements, in addition to others, are employed:

$$FF(IF) = OR(BNZT,ADV(R(IRCV)))$$
$$FF(IBR) = OR(BTRA,ADV(FF(IF)))$$

The first statement generates a machine instruction which tests whether the value of the LCV [the address of the LCV is ADV(R(IRCV))] is zero. If it is not zero, the next instruction is skipped. Otherwise, the next sequential instruction is taken. The second statement generates this next instruction, whose address has been temporarily stored at location IBR. This instruction merely transfers the control to the first instruction of the group of instructions for the next function.

The beginning address ADV(FF(IF)) of the next group of instructions is not known until the current function is assembled. Therefore, the above second statement is placed immediately after index IF is incremented.

6.5.3 GENERATION OF MACHINE-LANGUAGE CODE

This task is to identify the function name (now in FCTN) and to generate a group of machine instructions. The functions and their respective groups of machine instructions to be generated are both shown in Table 6.1. The addresses required in the machine instructions are now in AA, AB, AC, AD, AE, AF, and AR.

As an example, according to Table 6.1, the group of instructions to be generated for function DIV(A,B) is

```
CLA   A
FDP   B
STQ   R
```

where A, B, and R are available at AA, AB, and AR, respectively. The

FORTRAN statements to generate them are:

```
170 IF (FCTN.NE.FDIV)   GO TO 180
    FF(IF) = OR(BCLA,AA)
    FF(IF+1) = OR(BFDP,AB)
    FF(IF+2) = OR(BSTO,AR)
    GO TO 390
```

The above first statement is to identify function DIV, and the remaining three statements are to generate the three required instructions and to store them at locations IF, IF+1, and IF+2 in the FF array.

If the generated instructions of a function require the calling of a subprogram such as a FORTRAN subroutine (ALOG, ATAN2, COS, EXP, SIN, or SQRT) or an entry in subroutine MIMCO (MIMHDR, MIMOUT, or MIMPAR) or a MAP-coded function (FEXIT), a calling sequence is needed. As an example, according to Table 6.1, the group of instructions to be generated for function SIN(A) is

```
TSX   SIN,4
TXI   *+3,0,1
PZE   0,0,ALKDR
PZE   A
STO   R
```

where A and R are available at AA and AR, respectively. The FOR-TRAN statements to generate them are:

```
FF(IF) = OR(BTSX4,ADV(SIN))
FF(IF+1) = OR(OR(BTXI,D1),IAFF+4)
FF(IF+2) = OR(ALKDR,IBCD)
FF(IF+3) = AA
FF(IF+4) = OR(BSTO,AR)
```

where SIN is declared as an external variable, D1 gives integer 1, IAFF (or AFF) stores the first address of FF(IF) available for storing generated instructions, and ALKDR stores the address of linkage director LKDR. The first statement transfers control to subroutine SIN. The second statement provides the return address. The third statement sets up the linkage director for use in case of error. The fourth statement provides the address for fetching the operand, and the last statement gives the address for storing the result.

There are five indicators (which may be called switches), IOUT, IPAR, IHDR, IFIN, and IEND, which are shown in Table 6.5. When the indicator contains a nonzero value, it means to output the computed results in case the indicator is IOUT, to input the parameter data in case of IPAR, to print the heading in case of IHDR, to test run termination in case of IFIN, and to terminate a run in case of IEND.   For the FIN function, an instruction is generated to test indicator IFIN.   If IFIN is nonzero, the operands in the FIN statement are compared by subtracting the second operand from the first.   If the difference is positive or zero, this value is stored in IEND.   (IEND is initially set to zero.)   This value of IEND will be tested later during execution by subroutine MIMEX.   For functions HDR, OUT, and PAR, one instruction is generated to test respectively indicator IHDR, IOUT, or IPAR, and another instruction to transfer respectively to entry MIMHDR, MIMOUT, or MIMPAR if the indicator has a nonzero value.   There is another indicator NPAR, which indicates, when nonzero, more than one run.   This indicator is set to 1 during assembly if IPAR is found to have a nonzero value, and will be tested later during execution by subroutine MIMEX.

For function INT(A,B), instructions are generated to store the derivative (operand A) at the location whose address is 100 less than the address of the location for storing the result (a dependent variable).   This location for operand A is in the P array, and is illustrated in Fig. 6.15, where x_i's are dependent variables and $\dot{x}_i$'s are their derivatives.   The initial value (operand B) is stored at the location for x_i's in the R array at the time when the value of R(1) is equal to zero.

For function END, one instruction is generated.   This instruction transfers control to entry FEXIT, which returns the control to the program or subprogram that called entry F.

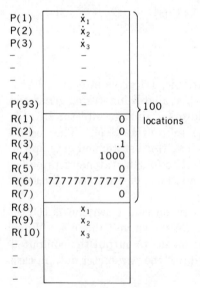

Fig. 6.15 An example showing the locations in arrays P and R where dependent variables x_i's and their derivatives $\dot{x}_i$'s are stored.

6.5.4 INCREMENT INDEX IF

Since the number of instructions generated for each function is different, the amount that index IF has to be incremented for each function is also different.   In subroutine MIMAS, the increment of index IF is centralized at the end of instruction generation.   In this way, only seven statements (cards 196 to 202) are needed for the incrementing.   After index IF is incremented, the assembler takes the next function from the BCD array and generates another group of instructions.   This process continues until it reaches function END.   At this time, subroutine MIMAS returns to the executive program.

6.6 EXECUTION

Execution involves the storage areas of array FF (assembled program), array S (symbol table), array R (data table), array P (derivative table), and six indicators (IOUT, IPAR, IHDR, IFIN, IEND, and NPAR). The functions of these storage areas are described in Table 6.5.   Sub-

```
$IBFTC MMEX    XR7                                            MMEX0000
C**** EXECUTION PROGRAM.                                      MMEX0001
      SUBROUTINE MIMEX                                        MMEX0002
      COMMON NEQ,P(93),R(2500),S(2500),FF(4000),BCD(10,900)   MMEX0003
      COMMON IOUT,IPAR,IHDR,IFIN,IEND,NPAR                    MMEX0004
C**** SET FOR READING INPUT DATA.                             MMEX0005
   10 IPAR=1                                                  MMEX0006
      IEND=0                                                  MMEX0007
      IOUT=0                                                  MMEX0008
      IFIN=0                                                  MMEX0009
      IHDR=0                                                  MMEX0010
      R(1)=0.                                                 MMEX0011
      CALL F                                                  MMEX0012
      IPAR=0                                                  MMEX0013
      CALL F                                                  MMEX0014
C**** SET FOR HEADING, OUTPUT, TESTING END OF RUN.            MMEX0015
      IHDR=1                                                  MMEX0016
   20 IFIN=1                                                  MMEX0017
      IOUT=1                                                  MMEX0018
      CALL F                                                  MMEX0019
      IHDR=0                                                  MMEX0020
      IFIN=0                                                  MMEX0021
      IOUT=0                                                  MMEX0022
C**** TEST FOR END OF RUN.                                    MMEX0023
      IF(IEND.NE.0) GO TO 30                                  MMEX0024
C**** INTEGRATE.                                              MMEX0025
      CALL MIMIN                                              MMEX0026
      GO TO 20                                                MMEX0027
C**** TEST FOR FURTHER RUNS.                                  MMEX0028
   30 WRITE(6,40)                                             MMEX0029
      IF(NPAR.NE.0) GO TO 10                                  MMEX0030
      STOP                                                    MMEX0031
   40 FORMAT(1H1)                                             MMEX0032
      END                                                     MMEX0033
```

Fig. 6.16 Subroutine MIMEX.

10

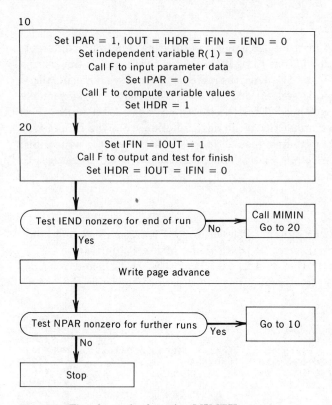

Fig. 6.17 Flowchart of subroutine MIMEX.

routine MIMEX is shown in Fig. 6.16, and a flowchart is shown in Fig. 6.17. The MIMEX executes the simulation by initiating or performing the following tasks:

1. To read parameter data as specified by the PAR statement. (The constant data are read during assembly. See card 96 of MIMAS.)
2. To compute initial derivatives of dependent variables.
3. To print the headings as specified by the HDR statements.
4. To print the computed results as specified by the OUT statements.
5. To test the condition for run termination.
6. To determine the end of a run.
7. To test whether there is a next run.
8. To call subroutine MIMIN.

The manner and the sequence in which these tasks are carried out are now described.

6.6.1 CALL F

CALL F is a FORTRAN statement to call the MAP-coded function F
(see Table 6.7), which essentially transfers control of program execution
to the assembled program in the FF array.   In the assembled program
are embedded five indicators IOUT, IPAR, IHDR, IFIN, and IEND.
By setting the proper values of these indicators, execution of the assembled
program carries out some of the above-mentioned tasks.

For example, if these five indicators are set to 0, except IPAR which
is set to 1, and followed by a CALL F statement, as shown below,

IOUT = 0
IPAR = 1
IHDR = 0
ITIN = 0
IEND = 0
CALL   F

execution of these statements causes the card reader to read the parameter
data into the R array.   If these indicators are all set to 0 and followed by
a CALL F statement, as shown below,

IOUT = 0
IPAR = 0
IHDR = 0
IFIN = 0
IEND = 0
CALL   F

execution of these statements causes the computer to compute the derivatives and store them in the P array (initial derivatives if this occurs at T
equal to 0).   If these indicators are set in the manner shown below and
followed by a CALL F statement,

IOUT = 1
IPAR = 0
IHDR = 1
IFIN = 1
IEND = 0
CALL   F

execution of these statements causes the printer to print out the headings,
to print out the computed results (initial values if this occurs at T equal
to 0), and to test the condition for run termination.

Execution of a CALL F statement always computes the derivatives
of the values stored at locations R(8) to R(NEQ) of the R array (where

they are the values of dependent variables), and then stores the computed values of derivatives in the P array. Therefore, derivatives are computed in each of the above examples. However, if the values of the dependent variables have not been changed, the computed values of derivatives will not change. (Integration by subroutine MIMIN will cause the values of dependent variables to change.) It is expedient to use the CALL F statement to perform various tasks after setting the indicators to proper values.

6.6.2 INITIALIZATION

Execution begins by setting $R(1)$ (that is, T) to 0. The indicators are set, and a CALL F statement is executed to read the parameter data. The indicators are then reset, and another CALL F statement is executed to compute initial derivatives. The indicators are again reset, and a third CALL F statement is executed to print out the headings and initial outputs as well as to test the condition for run termination. The indicators are finally set to 0 so that execution of the next CALL F statement (which will occur during subsequent execution of subroutine MIMIN) will compute derivatives. Computation of derivatives during integration is required by the method chosen for the numerical integration.

6.6.3 EXECUTION CYCLE

After initialization, execution is carried out in a loop, to be referred to here as the execution cycle. An execution cycle consists of two half-cycles. During the first half-cycle, the indicators are set and subroutine MIMIN is called to integrate numerically for a period of DT. During the second half-cycle, the indicators are reset and a CALL F statement is executed to compute derivatives. A test of indicator IEND is made at the completion of the execution cycle to determine whether the run is to be terminated. If it is not, another execution cycle is carried out, and this is followed by another test of indicator IEND. This process continues until indicator IEND signifies that the run is to be terminated.

When indicator IEND contains a nonzero (to be precise, a positive value), it indicates that the run is to be terminated. At this time, indicator NPAR is tested to determine whether the simulation has a next run. (NPAR is set to 1 during assembly when the PAR statement is being assembled.) If there is another run, subroutine MIMEX returns to input parameter values for the next run, and then to carry out another sequence of execution cycles until the run is terminated. This process continues until there are no more data cards. At this time, the end-of-file card of the input deck is reached and control of program execution is turned over to the operating system.

6.7 INTEGRATION

Subroutine MIMIN integrates the derivatives in the P array for a period of T (independent variable) equal to DT (print interval) and stores the results (dependent variables) in R(8) to R(NEQ). In addition to T and DT, there are two parameters, DTMAX and DTMIN, which are stored in R(4) and R(5), respectively. If the values of DT, DTMAX, and DTMIN are not specified, 0.1, 1,000, and 0 are taken, respectively.

During the integration period of DT, there may be many integration steps, each with a step size h. Subroutine MIMIN changes the step size automatically according to an error criterion by which the step size, after chosen initially, is either doubled or halved. This automatic change of step size is very significant because it practically eliminates time scaling of the simulation.

Subroutine MIMIN is shown in Fig. 6.18, and a flowchart is shown in Fig. 6.19. The variables of subroutine MIMIN are described in Table 6.12. Notice that, in Fig. 6.18, T is declared a double-precision variable and DOUBLE a logical variable.

6.7.1 INTEGRATION FORMULAS

Numerical integration in subroutine MIMIN employs the Adams-Bashforth second-order predictor and corrector, which have been shown

Table 6.12 Variables in subroutine MIMIN

Name	Storage function
DT	Print interval
DTMAX	Maximum integration step size
DTMIN	Minimum integration step size
T	Current value of independent variable t
TFINAL	Final value of t for an integration interval
TNEW	New value of t
NEQ	Number of INT functions
H	Integration step size h
POLD(93)	Derivative $\dot{y}_{n-1}$
P(93)	Derivative $\dot{y}_n$
PNEW(93)	Derivative $\dot{y}_{n+1}$
Y(93)	Dependent variable $\dot{y}_n$
YNEW(93)	Predicted $\dot{y}_{n+1}$ ($\dot{y}_{n+1,p}$) or corrected $\dot{y}_{n+1}$ ($\dot{y}_{n+1,c}$)
E	Approximate error of a dependent variable
RMAX	Largest approximate relative error of all dependent variables during an integrating step
DOUBLE	A logical variable which indicates whether current H is to be doubled

in Tables 5.20 and 5.21, respectively. The predictor from Table 5.20, after leaving out the error term, is

$$y_{n+1,p} = y_n + \frac{h(3\dot{y}_n - \dot{y}_{n-1})}{2} \tag{6.1}$$

and the corresponding FORTRAN statement in subroutine MIMIN is

$$YNEW(I) = Y(I) + H*(3.*P(I) - POLD(I))/2.$$

```
$IBFTC MMIN      XR7                                              MMIN0000
C**** INTEGRATION SUBROUTINE.                                     MMIN0001
      SUBROUTINE MIMIN                                            MMIN0002
      DIMENSION Y(93),P(93),POLD(93)                              MMIN0003
      COMMON NEQ,PNEW(93),TNEW,BLANK,DT,DTMAX,DTMIN,TRUE,FALSE,YNEW(93) MMIN0004
      LOGICAL DOUBLE                                              MMIN0005
      DOUBLE PRECISION T                                          MMIN0006
C**** INITIALIZE.                                                 MMIN0007
      TFINAL = TNEW + DT                                          MMIN0008
   10 H = AMIN1 (DTMAX, TFINAL - TNEW)                            MMIN0009
      T = TNEW                                                    MMIN0010
      DO 20 I=1,NEQ                                               MMIN0011
      Y(I) = YNEW(I)                                              MMIN0012
      P(I) = PNEW(I)                                              MMIN0013
   20 POLD(I) = PNEW(I)                                           MMIN0014
C**** PREDICT NEW POINT.                                          MMIN0015
   30 TNEW = T + H                                                MMIN0016
      DO 40 I=1,NEQ                                               MMIN0017
   40 YNEW(I) = Y(I) + H*(3.*P(I) - POLD(I))/2.                   MMIN0018
C**** CORRECT NEW POINT AND COMPUTE MAXIMUM RELATIVE ERROR.       MMIN0019
      CALL F                                                      MMIN0020
      RMAX = 0.                                                   MMIN0021
      DO 50 I=1,NEQ                                               MMIN0022
      YNEW(I) = Y(I) + H*(P(I) + PNEW(I))/2.                      MMIN0023
      E = H*(PNEW(I) - 2.*P(I) + POLD(I))/12.                     MMIN0024
   50 RMAX = AMAX1 (RMAX,ABS(E/YNEW(I)))                          MMIN0025
C**** TEST FOR INTERVAL HALVING.                                  MMIN0026
      IF ((RMAX.GT.5.E-6).AND.(H.GT.DTMIN)) GO TO 70              MMIN0027
C**** TEST FOR TIME TO RETURN.                                    MMIN0028
      IF (TNEW.GE.TFINAL) RETURN                                  MMIN0029
C**** COMPUTE CORRECTED DERIVATIVE.                               MMIN0030
      CALL F                                                      MMIN0031
C**** COMPUTE LOGICAL VARIABLE DOUBLE.                            MMIN0032
      DOUBLE = (RMAX.LE..625E-6).AND.(2.*H.LE.DTMAX).AND.         MMIN0033
     1          ((TNEW+2.*H).LE.TFINAL)                           MMIN0034
C**** TEST FOR RETURN OVERSHOOT.                                  MMIN0035
      IF ((TNEW+H).GT.TFINAL) GO TO 10                            MMIN0036
C**** ADVANCE TO COMPUTE NEW POINT.                               MMIN0037
      T = T + H                                                   MMIN0038
      IF (DOUBLE) H = 2.*H                                        MMIN0039
      DO 60 I=1,NEQ                                               MMIN0040
      Y(I) = YNEW(I)                                              MMIN0041
      IF (.NOT.DOUBLE) POLD(I) = P(I)                             MMIN0042
   60 P(I) = PNEW(I)                                              MMIN0043
      GO TO 30                                                    MMIN0044
C**** HALVE THE INTERVAL.                                         MMIN0045
   70 DO 80 I=1,NEQ                                               MMIN0046
   80 YNEW(I) = Y(I) - H*(3.*P(I) + POLD(I))/8.                   MMIN0047
      H = H/2.                                                    MMIN0048
      TNEW = T - H                                                MMIN0049
      CALL F                                                      MMIN0050
      DO 90 I=1,NEQ                                               MMIN0051
   90 POLD(I) = PNEW(I)                                           MMIN0052
      GO TO 30                                                    MMIN0053
      END                                                         MMIN0054
```

Fig. 6.18 Subroutine MIMIN.

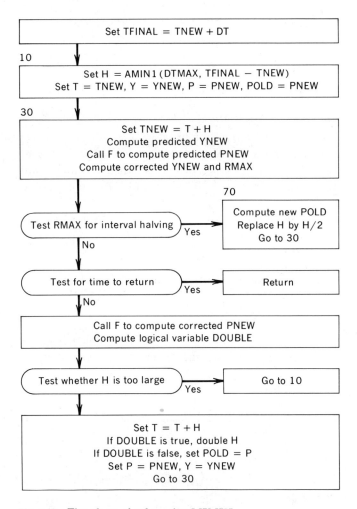

Fig. 6.19 Flowchart of subroutine MIMIN.

The corrector from Table 5.21, after leaving out the error term, is

$$y_{n+1,c} = y_n + \frac{h(\dot{y}_{n+1} + \dot{y}_n)}{2} \tag{6.2}$$

and the corresponding FORTRAN statement is

    YNEW(I) = Y(I) + H*(P(I) + PNEW(I))/2.

where index I ranges from 1 to NEQ.   It is obvious that y_n, y_{n+1}, $\dot{y}_{n-1}$, $\dot{y}_n$, and $\dot{y}_{n+1}$ are represented, respectively, by Y , YNEW, POLD, P, and PNEW.

In subroutine MIMIN, the initial value of $\dot{y}_{n-1}$ at the beginning of an integration interval is made equal to $\dot{y}_n$. In this case, Eq. (6.1) becomes

$$y_{n+1,p} = y_n + h\dot{y}_n \tag{6.3}$$

which is the first-order predictor shown in Table 5.20.

6.7.2 ERROR ESTIMATION

The automatic change of integration step size requires a measure of error so that increase or decrease of step size can be determined. This measure here is a quantity $R_{\max}$, which is called the maximum relative error for an integration step. The formula for computing $R_{\max}$ is derived below.

The predictor with the error term from Table 5.20 is

$$y_{n+1} = y_{n+1,p} + \frac{5h^3\dddot{y}}{12} \tag{6.4}$$

and the corrector with the error term from Table 5.21 is

$$y_{n+1} = y_{n+1,c} - \frac{h^3\dddot{y}}{12} \tag{6.5}$$

where $\dddot{y}$ is the third derivative. The magnitude of the error for the step, e, is approximately, assuming that $\dddot{y}$ is constant during the step,

$$e = |y_{n+1} - y_{n+1,c}| = \left| \frac{h^3\dddot{y}}{12} \right| \tag{6.6}$$

If y_{n+1} in Eqs. (6.4) and (6.5) is eliminated, we obtain

$$\left| \frac{h^3\dddot{y}}{12} \right| = \left| \frac{y_{n+1,c} - y_{n+1,p}}{6} \right| \tag{6.7}$$

By combining Eqs. (6.1), (6.2), (6.6), and (6.7), we have the magnitude of error e,

$$e = \left| \frac{(\dot{y}_{n+1} - 2\dot{y}_n + \dot{y}_{n-1})h}{12} \right| \tag{6.8}$$

The corresponding FORTRAN statement is

    E = (PNEW(I) − 2.*P(I) + POLD(I))*H/12.

where I ranges from 1 to NEQ. Since this error depends on the actual magnitude of the dependent variable, it is better to use a relative error, which is defined as $e/y_{n+1,c}$ or E/YNEW. It is necessary to find the relative errors of all dependent variables from which the maximum is chosen. This maximum is $R_{\max}$ and is obtained from the following FORTRAN statement:

    RMAX = AMAX1(RMAX,ABS(E/YNEW(I)))

where AMAX1 is a FORTRAN built-in function.   The range of R_{max} that has been chosen for use in establishing the error criterion is

$$0.625 \times 10^{-6} < R_{max} \leq 5 \times 10^{-6} \tag{6.9}$$

6.7.3 STEP SIZE OF INTEGRATION

Step size is the interval h in the integration formulas.   When subroutine MIMIN is called to integrate, the integration is limited to an interval specified by print interval DT.   During this integration interval, the MIMIN makes as many steps of integration as possible.   The selection of step size has several considerations.   First is the method of choosing the initial step size.   Then, the ratio DT/H may not be an integer. Furthermore, H is allowed to be neither larger than DTMAX nor smaller than DTMIN.

There are three variables which represent the independent variable t: T, TNEW, and TFINAL.   The value of t at the start of an integration interval is stored in TNEW.   The integration interval is DT.   Therefore, the value of t at the end of an integration interval should be, in a FORTRAN statement,

   TFINAL = TNEW + DT

The initial step size is selected from the smaller of the two quantities DTMAX and TFINAL-TNEW.   Expressed by a FORTRAN statement, this is

   H = AMINI(DTMAX, TFINAL-TNEW)

where AMINI is a FORTRAN function to select a minimum.   Note that (TFINAL-TNEW) at this time is not necessarily equal to DT because of possible round-off error which may occur during the subtraction.

Before incrementing t to a new t, it is necessary to keep the current t, because the latter is needed in case the step size is to be halved.   The current t is stored in T.   In a FORTRAN statement, we have

   T = TNEW

The FORTRAN statement for incrementing t now is

   TNEW = T + H

To halve the step size and to decrease t, the FORTRAN statements are

   H = H/2.
   TNEW = T − H

To double the step size and to increase t, the FORTRAN statements are

   T = T + H
   TNEW = T + H

There are several reasons that ratio DT/H may not be an integer. DT may not be a multiple of H. The change of H is subject to restrictions on DTMAX and DTMIN which can be arbitrarily chosen by the user. Round-off error occurs at every step of arithmetic operation. This problem is handled in the following manner. Before t is incremented, the following "overshoot" test, stated in a FORTRAN statement, is made:

$$\text{IF ((TNEW+H).GT.TFINAL)} \qquad (6.10)$$

If (TNEW+H) is greater than TFINAL, t is incremented. If it is not, a new step size is chosen by the following FORTRAN statement:

$$\text{H = AMINI(DTMAX, TFINAL-TNEW)}$$

which has been shown previously. Choosing the difference between TFINAL and TNEW as a step size ensures termination of an integration interval at the specified time. And the use of double-precision arithmetic for computing t reduces the round-off error in t.

6.7.4 AUTOMATIC CHANGE OF STEP SIZE

Automatic change of step size requires error criteria to determine when the step size should be halved, doubled, or not changed. In subroutine MIMIN, there are four important tests which occur according to the sequence presented below.

After new values of dependent variables are calculated by the integration formulas, R_{max} is computed. Step size is to be halved if the following error criterion is met:

$$R_{max} > 5 \times 10^{-6} \qquad \text{and} \qquad H > \text{DTMIN} \qquad (6.11)$$

In a FORTRAN statement, the test is

$$\text{IF ((RMAX.GT.5.E}-6\text{).AND.(H.GT.DTMIN))}$$

If there is no need of halving the step size, the following test is made to determine whether integration should be terminated, and the MIMIN returns to the MIMEX:

$$\text{IF (TNEW.GE.TFINAL) RETURN}$$

If integration is to be continued, the previously mentioned overshoot test (6.10) is made here. If (TNEW+H) exceeds TFINAL, then H is set equal to (TFINAL-TNEW), and H and POLD are set equal to PNEW. If there is no overshoot, then the values of Y, T, and P are replaced by the values of (T+H), YNEW, and PNEW. Step size of integration should be doubled if the following error criterion is met:

$$R_{max} \leq 0.625 \times 10^{-6} \qquad \text{and} \qquad 2H \leq \text{DTMAX} \qquad \text{and}$$
$$\text{(TFINAL+2H)} \leq \text{TFINAL} \qquad (6.12)$$

In FORTRAN statements, the test is

DOUBLE = (RMAX.LE..625E − 6).AND.(2.*H.LE.DTMAX)

.AND.((TNEW + 2.*H).LE.TFINAL)

IF (DOUBLE)   H = 2.*H

If the logical value of DOUBLE is FALSE, then the size for the next integration step remains unchanged.

If halving the step size is called for, $\dot{y}_{n-\frac{1}{2}}$ (that is, the derivative lies between $\dot{y}_{n-1}$ and $\dot{y}_n$) is required. To obtain this derivative, $y_{n-\frac{1}{2}}$ is first computed by the following formula:

$$y_{n-\frac{1}{2}} = y_n - \frac{(3\dot{y}_n + \dot{y}_{n-1})h}{8} \tag{6.13}$$

Derivative $\dot{y}_{n-\frac{1}{2}}$ is then computed by the execution of a CALL F statement with the above value of $y_{n-\frac{1}{2}}$.

6.8 INPUT–OUTPUT

Subroutine MIMIO inputs data for variables names in CON and PAR statements, outputs headings specified by HDR statements, and outputs computed values for operands named in OUT statements. The MIMIO is called by the assembler when the latter encounters a CON statement during assembly, and by the assembled program when the latter reaches an HDR, OUT, or PAR function during execution.

Subroutine MIMIO is shown in Fig. 6.20. There are three entries: MIMHDR, MIMPAR, and MIMOUT. Entry MIMHDR is called by an HDR function, entry MIMPAR by either a CON or a PAR function, and entry MIMOUT by an OUT function. Statements for entry MIMOUT follow those for entry MIMPAR; in this way, input data from CON and PAR functions will be printed out.

6.8.1 ENTRY MIMHDR

Entry MIMHDR(A,B,C,D,E,F) prints variable names A, . . . , F, but not the values of A, . . . , F. These symbolic names are stored in the symbol table (array S), while the values are in the data table (array R). The corresponding name and value are thus 2,500 locations apart. To print out symbolic names of these variables, the following statements are used:

WRITE (6,20)   A(2501),C(2501),D(2501),E(2501),F(2501)

20 FORMAT(6(11X,A6,3X))

These names are printed out in 20-column width as specified by the FORMAT statement.

```
$IBFTC MMIO    XR7.                                              MMIO0000
C**** INPUT-OUTPUT.                                              MMIO0001
      SUBROUTINE MMIO(A,B,C,D,F,F)                               MMIO0002
      COMMON NEQ,P(93),R(2500),S(2500),FF(4000),BCD(10,900)      MMIO0003
      COMMON IOUT,IPAR,IHDR,IFIN,IFND,NPAR                       MMIO0004
      DIMENSION A(1),B(1),C(1),D(1),F(1),F(1),FMT(8)             MMIO0005
      DATA OE205/6H,F20.5/,OBL/1H /,O14XA6/6H,14XA6/             MMIO0006
      DATA FMT(1)/6H(1P    /,FMT(8)/6H)      /                   MMIO0007
      ENTRY MIMHDR (A,B,C,D,E,F)                                 MMIO0008
      WRITE (6,20) A(2501),B(2501),C(2501),D(2501),E(2501),F(2501)  MMIO0009
      RETURN                                                     MMIO0010
      ENTRY MIMPAR (A,B,C,D,F,F)                                 MMIO0011
      READ (5,30) A,B,C,D,E,F                                    MMIO0012
      WRITE (6,40)                                               MMIO0013
      WRITE (6,20) A(2501),B(2501),C(2501),D(2501),E(2501),F(2501)  MMIO0014
      ENTRY MIMOUT (A,B,C,D,E,F)                                 MMIO0015
      DO 10 I=2,7                                                MMIO0016
   10 FMT(I) = OE205                                             MMIO0017
      R(2)=OBL                                                   MMIO0018
      IF (A.EQ.OBL) FMT(2)=O14XA6                                MMIO0019
      IF (B.EQ.OBL) FMT(3)=O14XA6                                MMIO0020
      IF (C.EQ.OBL) FMT(4)=O14XA6                                MMIO0021
      IF (D.EQ.OBL) FMT(5)=O14XA6                                MMIO0022
      IF (E.EQ.OBL) FMT(6)=O14XA6                                MMIO0023
      IF (F.EQ.OBL) FMT(7)=O14XA6                                MMIO0024
      WRITE(6,FMT) A,B,C,D,E,F                                   MMIO0025
      RETURN                                                     MMIO0026
   20 FORMAT(6(11X,A6,3X))                                       MMIO0027
   30 FORMAT(6F12.4)                                             MMIO0028
   40 FORMAT(/)                                                  MMIO0029
      END                                                        MMIO0030
```

Fig. 6.20 Subroutine MIMIO.

6.8.2 ENTRY MIMOUT

Entry MIMOUT(A,B,C,D,E,F) prints out the values of variables A, . . . , F. If any one of the six arguments does not appear, the corresponding space for the variable in the printed line should be left blank. This is achieved by using a variable format. The FORTRAN statements

```
      DIMENSION  FMT(8)
      DATA FMT(1)/6H(1P        /,FMT(8)/6H)          /
      DATA OE205/6H,E20.5/
      DO 10    I = 2, 7
   10 FMT(I) = OE205
      WRITE (6,FMT) A,B,C,D,E,F
```

print the values of variables A, . . . , F according to the following format:

(1P   ,E20.5,E20.5,E20.5,E20.5,E20.5,E20.5)

In Fig. 6.20, an IF statement is used to insert a blank in the location of the FMT array whenever the respective argument does not appear in the CALL statement.

6.8.3 ENTRY MIMPAR

Entry MIMPAR(A,B,C,D,E,F) reads values of A, . . . , F on a data card. These arguments are specified by a CON or a PAR statement.

The data card has a format of six fields, each of 12 columns for a decimal number in the fixed-point format.   Entry MIMPAR also prints out variable names A, . . . , F and their values.   An identical FORTRAN statement is used to print out variable names, and the statements in MIMOUT are used to print out the values.

6.9 AN EXAMPLE

An example is presented here to illustrate the results of compilation and assembly by the SIMIC processor.   Consider the following simple model,

$$\frac{dy}{dt} = \begin{cases} y & \text{for } y < e \\ e & \text{for } y \geq e \end{cases} \tag{6.14}$$

where e is a constant of 2.71828.

The SIMIC program for this model is shown in Fig. 6.21.   There are two logical control variables YLTE and YGEE which control DYDT equal to Y or to EXP(1.).   YLTE is TRUE only when $Y - EXP(1.)$ is less than 0.   YGEE is set equal to the logical complement (or NOT) of YLTE; thus, YGEE is TRUE when YLTE is FALSE.   The computation terminates when T exceeds 2.   Values of T and Y are to be printed out.

The SIMIC program is translated into a function-language program by the compiler and stored in the BCD array.   The function-language program is shown in Table 6.13.   There are 12 functions.   The function-language program is next assembled into a machine-language program. The symbol and data tables after assembly is completed are shown in Table 6.14.   The symbol table shows all the constants, parameters, literals, variables (either chosen by the user or generated internally during compilation), and reserved names of the SIMIC program.   Notice that the names of the constants are the values themselves.   The symbolic

LCV	Result		Expression
	DT	=	.1
	YLTE	=	FSW (Y − EXP (1.), TRUE, FALSE, FALSE)
	YGEE	=	NOT (YLTE)
YLTE	DYDT	=	Y
YGEE	DYDT	=	EXP (1.)
	Y	=	INT (DYDT, 1.)
			FIN (T, 2.)
			HDR T, Y)
			OUT (T, Y)
			END

Fig. 6.21 An example of the SIMIC program.

Table 6.13 Contents of the BCD array

J	BCD(1,J)	BCD(2,J)	BCD(3,J)	BCD(4,J)	BCD(5,J)	BCD(6,J)	BCD(9,J)
1	DT	EQL	.1				
2	(002)	EXP	1.				
3	(003)	SUB	Y	(002)			
4	YLTE	FSW	(003)	TRUE	FALSE	FALSE	
5	YGEE	NOT	YLTE				
6	DYDT	EQL	Y				YLTE
7	DYDT	EXP	1.				YGEE
8	Y	INT	DYDT	1.			
9		FIN	T	2.			
10		HDR	T	Y			
11		OUT	T	Y			
12		END					

equivalent of the machine-language program generated during assembly and stored in the FF array is shown in Table 6.15, where there are 12 groups of instructions for the 12 functions in Table 6.13. The machine-language program will next be executed under the control of subroutine MIMEX, which in turn will call subroutines MIMIN and MIMIO. A tabulated result will become available at the end of execution.

Table 6.14 Contents of the S and R arrays

I	S(I)	R(I)	Where occurs
1	T	0.	Subroutine MIMEX
2	(blank)	0.	Executive program
3	DT	.1	Generated program
4	DTMAX	1000.	Executive program
5	DTMIN	0.	Executive program
6	TRUE	$\neq 0.$	Executive program
7	FALSE	0.	Executive program
8	Y	1.	Generated program
9	.1	.1	Subroutine MIMAS
10	1.	1.	Subroutine MIMAS
11	(002)	e	Generated program
12	(003)	1. − e	Generated program
13	YLTE	$\neq 0.$	Generated program
14	YGEE	0.	Generated program
15	DYDT	1.	Generated program
16	2.	2.	Subroutine MIMAS

Table 6.15 Contents of the FF array

I	Contents of FF(I)		Explanation
1	CLA	L(.1)	Store DT = .1.
2	STO	DT	
3	TSX	EXP, 4	Store (002) = EXP (1.).
4	TXI	* + 3, 0, 1	
5	PZE	0, 0, ALKDR	
6	PZE	L(1.)	
7	STO	(002)	
8	CLA	Y	Store (003) = Y − (002).
9	FSB	(002)	
10	STO	(003)	
11	CLA	(003)	Store YLTE = FALSE if (003) = 0.
12	LDQ	FALSE	
13	TZE	* + 4	
14	LDQ	TRUE	Store YLTE = TRUE if (003) < 0.
15	TMI	* + 2	
16	LDQ	FALSE	Store YLTE = FALSE if (003) > 0.
17	STQ	YLTE	
18	STZ	YGEE	Store YGEE = FALSE (zero).
19	NZT	YLTE	Skip if YLTE = TRUE (nonzero).
20	STL	YGEE	Store YGEE = TRUE (nonzero).
21	NZT	YLTE	Skip transfer if YLTE = TRUE.
22	TRA	* + 3	Transfer if YLTE = FALSE.
23	CLA	Y	Store DYDT = Y.
24	STO	DYDT	
25	NZT	YGEE	Skip transfer if YGEE = TRUE.
26	TRA	* + 6	Transfer if YGEE = FALSE.
27	TSX	EXP, 4	Store DYDT = EXP(1.).
28	TXI	* + 3, 0, 1	
29	PZE	0, 0, ALKDR	
30	PZE	L(1.)	
31	STO	DYDT	
32	CLA	DYDT	Store DYDT in P(1).
33	STO	P	
34	CLA	L(1.)	Store Y = 1 if T = 0.
35	NZT	T	
36	STO	Y	
37	NZT	IFIN	Skip transfer if IFIN $\neq$ 0.

Table 6.15   Contents of the FF array (continued)

I	Contents of $FF(I)$		Explanation
38	TRA	* + 6	Transfer if IFIN = 0.
39	CLA	T	Test T − 2.
40	FSB	L(2.)	
41	TZE	* + 2	Store IEND $\neq$ 0 if (T − 2.) = 0.
42	TMI	* + 2	Transfer if (T − 2.) < 0.
43	STL	IEND	Store IEND $\neq$ 0 if (T − 2) $\geq$ 0.
44	ZET	IHDR	Skip if IHDR = 0.
45	TSX	MIMHDR, 4	Output headers T, Y.
46	TXI	* + 8, 0, 6	
47	PZE	0, 0, ALKDR	
48	PZE	T	
49	PZE	Y	
50	PZE		
51	PZE		
52	PZE		
53	PZE		
54	ZET	IOUT	Skip if IOUT = 0.
55	TSX	MIMOUT, 4	Output T, Y.
56	TXI	* + 8, 0, 6	
57	PZE	0, 0, ALKDR	
58	PZE	T	
59	PZE	Y	
60	PZE		
61	PZE		
62	PZE		
63	PZE		
64	TRA	FEXIT	Transfer to return control.

PROBLEMS

6.1. Write a SIMIC program for computing the solution of the differential equations
      (a) In Prob. 1.3   (b) In Prob. 3.13

6.2. To what extent has the symbol table been completed after compilation but before assembly?

6.3. How is the precedence in an arithmetic expression implemented in the MIMCO? The expression may contain one or more pairs of parentheses.

6.4. Given the following values of I, show what numerical names are generated by the statement on card 70 in the MIMCO:
      (a) 3.15   (b) 3015

6.5. It is possible to omit buffer C and use only buffer B. Omit buffer C and modify the statements in subroutine MIMCO accordingly.

6.6 Simplify subroutine MIMCO by not allowing arithmetic expressions which may contain one or more pairs of parentheses.

6.7. Simplify subroutine MIMCO by not allowing parentheses in a statement except the pair associated with the function name.

6.8. Simplify subroutine MIMCO by not allowing nesting of functions. Arithmetic expressions which may contain one or more pairs of parentheses are allowed.

6.9. If subscripted variables are permitted, what changes have to be made in the SIMIC language and processor?

6.10. Explain step by step which one of the quantities can be converted into a floating-point number by the statements on cards 46 to 55 of subroutine MIMAS.

    (a) 3.1416   (b) GEORGE   (c) 8921

6.11. Where are indicators IOUT, IPAR, IHDR, IFIN, IEND, NPAR, and NEW initialized?

6.12. If an illegal function occurs in a SIMIC program, what happens during compilation and during assembly?

6.13. What has to be added and changed in the assembler if each of the following functions is to be added?

    (a) Dead-space function
    (b) Implicit function
    (c) CFN and PFN functions

6.14. For the differential equations in Prob. 1.1:

    (a) Write a SIMIC program.
    (b) Translate it into a function-language program.
    (c) Translate the function-language program into a machine-language program.
    (d) Show the contents of the S and R arrays just before the MIMIN is called during execution.

6.15. Repeat Prob. 6.14 for the differential equations in Prob. 1.2.

6.16. What has to be changed in subroutine MIMIN if the statement DTMAX = DTMIN is allowed to mean that step size of integration remains constant?

6.17. Write a subroutine using the fourth-order Runge-Kutta integration formula with a fixed step size of integration to replace the MIMIN.

6.18. Repeat Prob. 6.17 but with automatic change of step size.

6.19. Write a subroutine using the fourth-order Adams-Bashforth predictor and corrector with a fixed step size to replace the MIMIN.

6.20. Repeat Prob. 6.19 but with automatic change of step size.

6.21. If a discontinuity occurs during an integration interval, is it desirable to terminate the interval at the discontinuity and start integration once again? What has to be changed in the MIMIN to provide this feature?

6.22. Which value (positive, zero, or negative) in indicator IEND indicates that the run be terminated? What are the FORTRAN statements in the SIMIC processor to substantiate the choice?

6.23. Draw a flowchart for sorting the functions in the BCD array after compilation into a proper sequence, as described in Sec. 6.1. This sorting can be accomplished by interchanging the columns of the BCD array or by defining a new array into which the sorted sequence of functions can be stored as it is developed.

6.24. Write a sorting subroutine for the flowchart in Prob. 6.23.

REFERENCES

1. Fortran IV Language, version 13, IBM 7090/7094 IBSYS Operating System, File No. 7090-25, Form C28-6390-3, IBM Corporation.
2. Macro Assembly Program (MAP) Language, version 13, IBM 7090/7094 IBSYS Operating System, Form C28-6392-0, IBM Corporation.
3. IBM 7094 Principles of Operation, Form A22-6703-4, IBM Corporation.

7
Simulation by DSL/90 Programming

DSL derives its name from Digital Simulation Language, which was developed by the IBM Corporation. There are several versions of DSL: DSL/90, DSL/40, DSL/1130, DSL/1180, DSL/44, DSL/360, System/360 CSMP, and 1130 CSMP. These are different implementations of one language for different computers with different objectives.

The development of DSL by IBM was initiated in 1964. The first implementation was for the IBM 7090 family of computers. In July, 1965, the program, called DSL/90-00, was distributed through SHARE. It was categorized as a type 3 program by IBM (this means that the responsibility for program errors and maintenance lies solely with the authors). The development of DSL/90 was contributed mostly by W. M. Syn and D. G. Wyman.

Since July, 1965, DSL/90 has gone through two modifications, DSL/90-01 and DSL/90-02. DSL/90-01 was extended to become DSL/40 for the IBM 7040 computer, and was also used as the basis for System/360 CSMP (Continuous System Modeling Program). System/

360 CSMP is a type 2 program by IBM (which means that IBM assumes responsibility for correcting any program errors). DSL/90-02 was used for implementations of DSL/1130, DSL/1800, and DSL/44 for the IBM computers 1130, 1800, and System/360 model 44, respectively. DSL/ 90-02 was also used for implementing DSL/360, which is distributed through SHARE as a type 3 program, early 1968.

System/360 CSMP is an implementation of DSL to some of the IBM System/360 computers. Because it is a type 2 program, its release is subject to stricter test and documentation requirements. System/360 CSMP is written in FORTRAN E and requires a FORTRAN E compiler, but it may be modified to execute under a FORTRAN G or H compiler (FORTRAN E, F, and H are System/360 versions of FORTRAN IV). However, DSL/360 will become available, again as a type 3 program, for those System/360 computers which have a FORTRAN F or H compiler.

This chapter presents digital analog and hybrid simulations by DSL/90 programming. Unlike the MIMIC, DSL (or CSMP) does not have a logical control variable in its statements, but it permits intermixing of FORTRAN statements with DSL (or CSMP) statements; this extends some FORTRAN capability to DSL (or CSMP) programming. It also permits incorporation of a DSL or CSMP program into a FORTRAN program; this extends DSL (or CSMP) capability to FORTRAN programming. These features make DSL and CSMP a powerful language for digital hybrid simulation; but for an effective use of DSL and CSMP, one needs to know FORTRAN programming. Another difference between the MIMIC and DSL (or CSMP) is the translation. A DSL (or CSMP) program is translated into a FORTRAN program by the DSL (or CSMP) processor. A MIMIC program is translated into a machine-language program by the MIMIC processor. Because of this difference, the processing time of a DSL (or CSMP) program may be significantly more than that of a MIMIC program.

7.2 BASIC LANGUAGE ELEMENTS

A DSL/90 program consists of a sequence of statements. The statements are composed of basic language elements of constants, variables, operators, expressions, and functions. Here we present all these language elements except the functions, which will be presented in the next section.

7.2.1 CONSTANTS

Constants are unchanging quantities expressed in numeric form. There are two types of constants: integer and real. An integer constant is a whole number with 1 to 11 decimal digits without a decimal point. The magnitude of an integer must be less than 3.436×10^{10}, approximately.

Examples are 3, -45, $+8500$. A real constant is a floating-point number. It may be written in a fixed-point format, which consists of one to nine significant decimal digits with a decimal point; examples are 21., 0.0, $+.203$, -8.006789. Or it may be written in a floating-point format, which is a real constant in a fixed-point format followed by letter E and a signed or unsigned integer; examples are $5.2E - 3$, $-.546E4$. The magnitude of a real constant must be either 0 or between the approximate limits of 10^{38} and 10^{-38}. Constants used as integrator initial conditions or macro arguments are restricted to a total of 12 characters.

7.2.2 VARIABLE NAMES

Variable names (or simply variables) are symbolic representations of quantities whose values vary during a run. A variable name contains from one to six alphameric characters (i.e., numeric 0 through 9 or alphabetic A through Z), the first of which must be alphabetic. A variable name must not contain embedded blanks or any others of the character set such as $+$, $/$, etc. A variable name cannot be a word reserved by the DSL/90 processor. Examples of valid variable names are K1, ERROR, XDOT, and X0; examples of invalid names are 1D2X, 123, $C - 3$, and B*A (the first two are valid in MIMIC).

   All variables are normally regarded as floating-point numbers (i.e., real). Functions defined by the user must be named according to the above rule for variable names. Subscripted variable names are allowed to reference one-dimensional tables. The subscript must be an integer or an integer name, and is enclosed in a pair of parentheses immediately following the variable name.

   As will be shown, an integer variable must be specified by an INTGER statement. A subscripted variable cannot be used to the left of an equal sign except between a pair of PROCED and ENDPRO statements or after a NOSORT statement. If so used, the variable name appears in a STORAG statement. Arguments of a MACRO definition and of a PROCED function, as well as any variable to the left of an equal sign in a MACRO definition, cannot be dimensioned.

7.2.3 RESERVED NAMES

There are two types of variables: system variables and simulation variables. Simulation variables are created by the user in modeling his problem, while system variables carry a special meaning to the DSL/90 processor. The names for the system variables are reserved names and should not be used by the user in his program. The following six reserved names occur most often and should be memorized.

1. *TIME* This name represents the current value of simulation time, which is the independent variable of the simulation.

2. _DELT_   This name specifies step size of the independent variable during integration.
3. _DELMIN_   This name specifies the minimum allowable step size. It is $(10^{-8} \cdot \text{TIME})$ if not specified.
4. _DELMAX_   This name specifies the maximum allowable step size. It is 10^{37} if not specified.
5. _FINTIM_   This name specifies the maximum simulation time of the independent variable TIME in seconds. When TIME reaches this value, the simulation is terminated by the processor.
6. _CLKTIM_   This name specifies the maximum actual clock time of the computer, in seconds, for the entire simulation run. It is not used if not specified. When the computer time reaches this value, the simulation ends.

In addition to the above names, there are many function names (shown in Tables 7.3 through 7.8) and about 50 subroutine names of the DSL/90 processor. All these are reserved names. Since a user is unlikely to choose these subroutine names, they are not shown. Should such a use occur unknowingly, an error message will appear.

7.2.4 OPERATORS AND EXPRESSIONS

Operators denote arithmetical and other operations. The DSL/90 operators are shown in Table 7.1. There are five mathematical operators: addition, subtraction, multiplication, division, and exponentiation, whose precedence is shown in Table 7.2.

An expression is a string of functions, variables, and constants connected by mathematical operators. Examples of expressions are:

1. A+B−C/D
2. C*(D/100.)
3. SQRT(X**2+Y**2)

Table 7.1   DSL/90 operators

Symbol	Operation
+	Addition
−	Subtraction
*	Multiplication
/	Division
**	Exponentiation
(	Grouping
)	Grouping
=	Equal/replacement

Table 7.2 Precedence of operations

Operation	Precedence
Function evaluation	1 (highest)
**	2
*, 1 ∧	3
+, −	4
=	5 (lowest)

7.3 FUNCTIONS

Functions or blocks are the building blocks of the DSL/90.   Each block can perform a more complex mathematical operation than an arithmetical operator.   Examples of the functions are:

1. INTGRL(IC,X)
2. AFGEN(F,X)
3. COS(Y)
4. BLOCK(X,Y,Z)

There are three types of functions.   Those provided by the DSL/90 are called built-in functions, such as examples 1 and 2.   Those available in the FORTRAN processor are called FORTRAN functions, such as example 3.   Those supplied by the user are called user-supplied functions, such as example 4.

7.3.1 BUILT-IN FUNCTIONS

The DSL/90 processor provides a large number of operational elements that are similar to corresponding analog-computer elements.   These elements are called built-in functions (or built-in blocks).   A DSL/90 program is essentially prepared by interconnecting these blocks according to the model to be simulated.   This programming is analogous to the use of patch cords on an analog computer to interconnect the electronic operational elements.

The built-in functions may be divided into five groups: linear functions, nonlinear functions, function generators, switching functions, and special functions.

7.3.1.1 Linear functions

The names, general forms, function descriptions, and Laplace transforms of eight linear functions are shown in Table 7.3.   In Table 7.3, block INTGRL indicates centralized integration; its arguments are IC and X.   X can be a constant, a constant name, a

Table 7.3 Linear functions

Name	General form	Function	Laplace transform
Integrator	$Y = INTGRL(IC,X)$ $Y(0) = IC$	$Y = \int_0^t X\,dt + IC$	$\dfrac{1}{S}$
Mode-controlled integrator	$Y = MODINT(IC,P_1,P_2,X)$	$Y = \begin{cases} \int_0^t X\,dt + IC & P_1=1,\ P_2=0 \\ IC & P_1=0,\ P_2=1 \\ \text{Last output} & P_1=0,\ P_2=0 \end{cases}$	$\dfrac{1}{S}$
First-order system (real pole)	$Y = REALPL(IC,P,X)$ $Y(0) = IC$	$P\dot{Y} + Y = X$	$\dfrac{1}{PS+1}$
Lead-lag	$Y = LEDLAG(IC,P_1,P_2,X)$ $IC = \dfrac{P_1 X(0) - P_2 Y(0)}{P_1 - P_2}$	$P_2 \dot{Y} + Y = P_1 \dot{X} + X$	$\dfrac{P_1 S + 1}{P_2 S + 1}$
Second-order system (complex pole)	$Y = CMPXPL(IC_1,IC_2,P_1,P_2,X)$ $Y(0) = IC_1$ $\dot{Y}(0) = IC_2$	$\ddot{Y} + 2P_1 P_2 \dot{Y} + P_2^2 Y = X$	$\dfrac{1}{S^2 + 2P_1 P_2 S + P_2^2}$
Derivative	$Y = DERIV(IC,X)$ $Y(0) = IC$	$Y = \dfrac{dx}{dTIME}$ $\dfrac{dx}{dt}$ quadratic interpolation	S
Dead time (delay)	$Y = DELAY(N,P,X)$ $P = $ Total delay time $N = $ No. of storage points (≥ 10)	$\begin{aligned} Y(t) &= X(t-P) & t \geq P \\ Y &= 0 & t < P \end{aligned}$	e^{-PS}
Zero-order hold	$Y = ZHOLD(P,X)$ $Y(0) = 0$	$Y = \begin{cases} X & P=1 \\ \text{Last output} & P=0 \end{cases}$	$\dfrac{1}{S}(1 - e^{-st})$

variable name, or an expression. If X is a variable name or if IC is a constant name, the name must be unique for each INTGRL block. IC cannot be an expression but must be a constant or a constant name. Block MODINT is used in conjunction with logical variables and logical functions (see Table 7.7); its arguments P_1 and P_2 are logical quantities (see Table 7.7). Blocks REALPL, LEDLAG, and CMPXPL are used in simulating feedback control systems. In block DERIV, TIME is the independent variable, X the dependent variable, and IC the initial value of derivative dX/d(TIME). Argument P of block DELAY specifies the total delay desired, argument N (a positive integer equal to 10 or larger) is the number of locations reserved for storage, and X is the input variable. Both blocks DERIV and DELAY will be discussed later. Block ZHOLD is a sample-hold block. When argument P is 1, output Y is equal to input X. When P is 0, Y remains unchanged.

7.3.1.2 Nonlinear functions The names, general forms, function descriptions, and characteristics of four nonlinear blocks are shown in Table 7.4. Blocks LIMIT, QNTZR, DEADSP, and HSTRSS are commonly used in simulating feedback control systems. Arguments P_1 and P_2 in block LIMIT are the limits. Argument P in block QNTZR is the step size

Table 7.4 Nonlinear functions

Name	General form	Function	Characteristic
Limiter	$Y = LIMIT(P_1, P_2, X)$	$Y = \begin{cases} P_1 & X < P_1 \\ P_2 & X > P_2 \\ X & P_1 \leq X \leq P_2 \end{cases}$	
Quantizer	$Y = QNTZR(P, X)$	$Y = kP \quad (k-\tfrac{1}{2})P < X < (k+\tfrac{1}{2})P$ $k = 0, \pm 1, \pm 2, \pm 3$	
Dead space	$Y = DEADSP(P_1, P_2, X)$	$Y = \begin{cases} 0 & P_1 \leq X \leq P_2 \\ X - P_2 & X > P_2 \\ X - P_1 & X < P_1 \end{cases}$	
Hysteresis loop	$Y = HSTRSS(IC, P_1, P_2, X)$ $Y(0) = IC$	$Y = \begin{cases} X - P_2 & (X - X_{n-1}) > 0 \text{ AND } (X - P_2) \geq Y_{n-1} \\ X - P_1 & (X - X_{n-1}) < 0 \text{ AND } (X - P_1) \geq Y_{n-1} \end{cases}$ Otherwise, $Y = $ last output	

Table 7.5 Function generators

Name	General form	Function	Characteristic
Arbitrary linear function generator	$Y = \text{AFGEN(FUNCT,X)}$	$Y = \begin{cases} \text{FUNCT}(X) & X_0 \le X \le X_n \\ \text{FUNCT}(X_0) & X < X_0 \\ \text{FUNCT}(X_n) & X > X_n \end{cases}$	
Arbitrary non-linear function generator	$Y = \text{NLFGEN(FUNCT,X)}$	$Y = \begin{cases} \text{FUNCT}(X) & X_0 \le X \le X_n \\ \text{FUNCT}(X_0) & X < X_0 \\ \text{FUNCT}(X_n) & X > X_n \end{cases}$	
Step-function generator	$Y = \text{STEP}(P)$	$Y = \begin{cases} 0 & t < P \\ 1 & t \ge P \end{cases}$	
Ramp-function generator	$Y = \text{RAMP}(P)$	$Y = \begin{cases} 0 & t < P \\ t - P & t \ge P \end{cases}$	
Impulse generator	$Y = \text{IMPULS}(P_1,P_2)$	$Y = \begin{cases} 0 & t < P_1 \\ 1 & (t-P_1) = kP_2 \\ 0 & (t-P_1) \ne kP_2 \end{cases}$ $k = 0,1,2,3,\ldots$	
Pulse generator	$Y = \text{PULSE}(P,X)$ $P = \text{trigger}$ $X = \text{pulse width}$	$Y = \begin{cases} 0 & \text{Initial} \\ 1 & T_k \le t < (T_k + X) \\ 0 & \text{Otherwise} \end{cases}$ $k = 1,2,3,\ldots$	

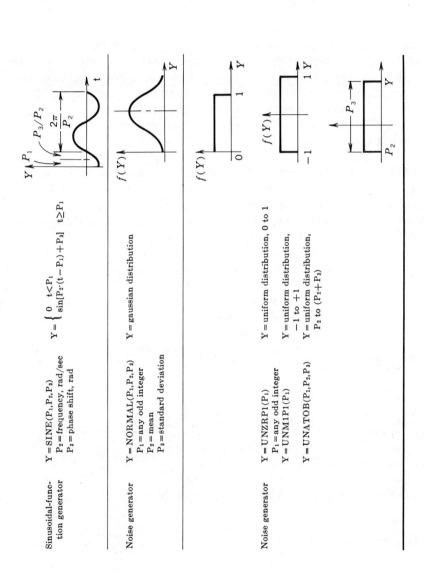

Sinusoidal-func-
tion generator

$Y = SINE(P_1,P_2,P_3)$
$P_2 = $ frequency, rad/sec
$P_3 = $ phase shift, rad

$$Y = \begin{cases} 0 & t < P_1 \\ \sin[P_2 \cdot (t - P_1) + P_3] & t \geq P_1 \end{cases}$$

Noise generator

$Y = NORMAL(P_1,P_2,P_3)$
$P_1 = $ any odd integer
$P_2 = $ mean
$P_3 = $ standard deviation

$Y = $ gaussian distribution

Noise generator

$Y = UNZRP1(P_1)$
$P_1 = $ any odd integer
$Y = UNM1P1(P_1)$

$Y = UNATOB(P_1,P_2,P_3)$

$Y = $ uniform distribution, 0 to 1

$Y = $ uniform distribution,
-1 to $+1$
$Y = $ uniform distribution,
P_2 to $(P_2 + P_3)$

in X.   Arguments P_1 and P_2 are the amount of dead space in the positive and negative directions of the X axis.   In Table 7.4, quantities X_{n-1} and Y_{n-1} in the description of block HSTRSS refer to the last values of X and Y, respectively.

7.3.1.3   Function generators   There are nine function generators in the DSL/90: two arbitrary function generators (one with linear and the other with nonlinear interpolation); a step-function, a ramp-function, and a sinusoidal-function generator; a pulse and an impulse generator; and two noise generators (one with normal and the other with uniform distribution).   The names, general forms, function descriptions, and characteristics of these generators are shown in Table 7.5.

7.3.1.4   Switching functions   Switching functions are decision-making blocks.   There are four switching functions in the DSL/90.   The function switch is a three-way switch; the output Y is equal to input X_1, X_2, or X_3 when input P is less than, equal to, or greater than 0, respectively. The input switch is a two-way switch; the output Y is equal to X_1 when input P is less than 0 and is equal to X_2 when P is equal to or greater than 0.   The output switch has two outputs.   Output Y_1 is equal to input X when input P is less than 0 and is equal to 0 when P is equal to or larger than 0.   The output of the comparator Y has only two values, 0 and 1; Y is equal to 0 when input X_1 is less than input X_2 and is equal to 1 when X_1 is equal to or larger than X_2.   The names, general forms, and function descriptions of these four switching functions are shown in Table 7.6.

Table 7.6   Switching functions

Name	General form	Function
Function switch	$Y = FCNSW(P,X_1,X_2,X_3)$	$Y = \begin{cases} X_1 & P < 0 \\ X_2 & P = 0 \\ X_3 & P > 0 \end{cases}$
Input switch (relay)	$Y = INSW(P,X_1,X_2)$	$Y = \begin{cases} X_1 & P < 0 \\ X_2 & P \geq 0 \end{cases}$
Output switch	$Y_1, Y_2 = OUTSW(P,X)$	$Y_1 = X,\ Y_2 = 0 \qquad P < 0$ $Y_1 = 0,\ Y_2 = X \qquad P \geq 0$
Comparator	$Y = COMPAR(X_1,X_2)$	$Y = \begin{cases} 0, & X_1 < X_2 \\ 1, & X_1 \geq X_2 \end{cases}$

Table 7.7   Special functions

Name	General form	Function
Implicit function	$Y = IMPL(IC,ERROR,FUNCT)$	$Y = \begin{cases} IC & t = 0 \text{ first} \\ & \text{entry} \\ FUNCT(Y) & t \geq 0 \end{cases}$ $Y = FUNCT(Y) \leq (ERROR \cdot \lvert Y \rvert$
Logical functions	$Y = AND(X_1,X_2)$ $Y = OR(X_1,X_2)$ $Y = COMPL(X_1)$ $Y = BOOL(X_1)$	Logical intersection of X_1 and X_2 Logical union of X_1 and X_2 Logical 1's complement of X_1 Logical 36-bit argument from signed 36-bit argument
RST flip-flop	$Y = RST(P_1,P_2,P_3)$	$Y = P_3$ at $t = 0$ $Y(t) = P_1 \cup (P_2' \cap Y)$ $P_2' = $ Complement of P_2
Locate symbol	$K = LOOK(X)$	$K =$ index or memory address of variable X
Dump	$Y = DEBUG(N,T)$ $N =$ Positive integer	Dump current values and symbols for all model variables for N iterations starting at time T

7.3.1.5   Special functions   The names, general forms, and function descriptions of special functions are shown in Table 7.7.   The implicit-function block IMPL(IC,ERROR,FUNCT) finds the real root of equation $f(y) = 0$, which must be expressed in the form $y = F(y)$.   Argument IC is the first value of y which the user must provide.   Argument FUNCT is the function $F(y)$.   The computation of the root requires some iterative methods, and the ERROR specifies the maximum error permitted.   This function will be discussed later.

There are four logical functions: AND, OR, COMPL, and BOOL. These four functions are the built-in FORTRAN functions.   (They are thus limited to the IBM IBSYS version 13 only.)   Arguments X_1 and X_2 are binary words of 36 bits.

Block $RST(P_1,P_2,P_3)$ is an RST flip-flop for storing a bit.   There are three inputs: P_1, P_2, and P_3.   Both inputs and outputs of this block can have only the value of 0 or 1.   Only one of the three inputs can be 1 at one time.   When P_1 is 1, the flip-flop is set to store 0.   When P_2 is 1, it is set to store 1.   When P_3 is 1, the stored value is complemented. Output Y is the value stored in the flip-flop.

The locate symbol function $K = LOOK(X)$ allows the user to find the index (or memory location) of a variable in the magnetic-core memory. Dump function $Y = DEBUG(N,T)$ is helpful to the user in the early stage of problem checkout. These two functions will be described later in this chapter.

7.3.2 FORTRAN FUNCTIONS

All standard functions available from the FORTRAN IV library may be used in the DSL/90 program; some are listed in Table 7.8. Examples of their use are shown below:

$$INTGRL(0.,(SIN(TIME)-B*XDOT-K*X)/M)$$
$$INTGRL(IC,INTGRL(290.,$$
$$-2.*FK1*(X/SQRT(X**2+H**2))/M1))$$

In the above, FORTRAN functions SIN and SQRT are used, as well as the built-in function INTGRL. Note that some inputs of INTGRL functions are expressions; by using the expressions, multiple inputs for these functions indirectly become possible. Furthermore, the output of one function is used directly as the input of another function (nesting); this allows compact statements.

7.3.3 USER–SUPPLIED FUNCTIONS

There are occasions when special functions are required to simulate blocks or elements. These functions are programmed by the user as subroutines either in FORTRAN or in MAP language. Once these functions are defined, the user can then use them in a manner like the other DSL/90 functions. More special functions will be discussed later.

Table 7.8   FORTRAN built-in functions

Name	Purpose	Definition
ABS	Absolute value	$|arg|$
ALOG	Natural logarithm	$\log_e(arg)$
ALOG10	Common logarithm	$\log_{10}(arg)$
AMAX1	Choosing largest value	$\max(arg_1, arg_2, \ldots)$
AMIN1	Choosing smallest value	$\min(arg_1, arg_2, \ldots)$
AMOD	Remainder	$arg - (arg_1/arg_2) \cdot arg_2$†
ATAN	Arctangent	$\arctan(arg)$
COS	Trigonometric cosine	$\cos(arg)$
EXP	Exponential	e^{arg}
SIGN	Sign of arg_2 times $|arg_1|$	$\text{sign}(arg_2) \cdot |arg_1|$
SIN	Trigonometric sine	$\sin(arg)$
SQRT	Square root	$\sqrt{arg}$

† Only the integral part of the term within parentheses is used.

As an example, consider the modeling of a nonlinear stepwise quantization with characteristics shown in Table 7.4. If this function were not available, it would be difficult to construct from the DSL/90 and FORTRAN functions. However, the following FORTRAN subprogram defines function QNTZR with the required quantization characteristic:

```
FUNCTION QNTZR(P,XIN)
QNT = AINT(0.5+ABS(XIN)/P)
QNTZR = SIGN(P*QNT,XIN)
RETURN
END
```

where P is the parameter of quantum step size. It is the only parameter supplied to the QNTZR function. The value of P is entered into the simulation program in exactly the same way as other DSL/90 parameters (i.e., by a PARAM statement, as will be described). Note that the above functions AINT (for truncation into a whole real number) and SIGN (for transfer of sign of the second argument to the first argument) are standard subroutines of the FORTRAN library.

The above FORTRAN subprogram for the quantizer may be entered into the simulation program in three ways: (1) it can be entered directly with the data cards for the simulation run; (2) it may be compiled independently, and the resulting machine-language deck (binary deck) is then added to the data deck; or (3) this function may be added to the permanent DSL/90 library by simply loading it on the library tape. In fact, this was the case with the QNTZR function when it was found to be sufficiently useful to warrant a place in the DSL/90 library.

7.4 CODING A DSL/90 PROGRAM

Before the statements which make up a DSL/90 program are described, simulation of a simple system is presented as an introduction to DSL/90 statements.

7.4.1 SYSTEM DESCRIPTION

Consider the classical mass-damper-spring system, which can be described by the following linear differential equation:

$$M\ddot{x} + B\dot{x} + Kx = \sin{(t)} \tag{7.1}$$

where M = mass
  B = damping coefficient
  K = spring constant

The forcing function of the system is a sinusoidal function of time t. In addition, we have the following two equations:

$$\dot{x} = \int \ddot{x}\, dt + \dot{x}(0)$$
$$x = \int \dot{x}\, dt + x(0) \tag{7.2}$$

where $\dot{x}(0)$ and $x(0)$ are initial conditions with the following values:

$$\dot{x}(0) = 0 \qquad x(0) = A$$

7.4.2 DSL/90 PROGRAM

The above equations can be represented by a block diagram such as the one shown in Fig. 7.1. A DSL/90 program, describing the block diagram, may consist of the following statements:

```
FCN     = SIN(TIME)
MULT1   = −B*XDOT
MULT2   = −K*X
MX2DOT  = FCN+MULT1+MULT2
X2DOT   = MX2DOT/M
XDOT    = INTGRL(0.,X2DOT)
X       = INTGRL(A,XDOT)
```

A DSL/90 program may also be obtained directly from Eqs. (7.1) and

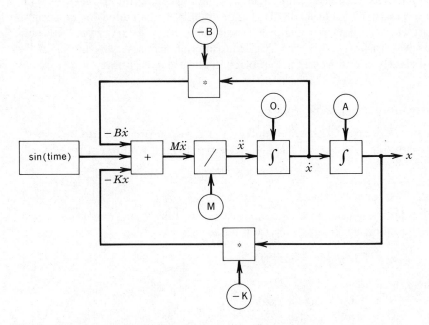

Fig. 7.1 Block diagram for the mass-damper-spring system.

(7.2), as shown below.

XDOT = INTGRL(O.,(SIN(TIME) − B*XDOT − K*X)/M)
X = INTGRL(A,XDOT)

In the above statements, SIN is a FORTRAN function, and INTGRL is a built-in function. The other expressions use the arithmetic operators of addition, subtraction, multiplication, and division. All the statements for the above two programs are called *connection statements*, as they serve the purpose of connecting these blocks.

To complete programming of this problem, the following *data statements* and *control statements* are needed for the execution of the DSL/90 program. No *pseudo-operation statement* is needed here. All these statements have a label in Columns 1 to 6:

TITLE   DSL/90 PROGRAM FOR MASS-SPRING-
            DAMPER SYSTEM
INCON   A = 20.
CONTRL   FINTIM = 5., DELT = .005
INTEG   MILNE
PARAM   M = 10., B = 2.5, K = 8.6
PRINT   .1,X,XDOT
PREPAR   .01,X,XDOT
GRAPH   8.,6.,TIME,X,XDOT
LABEL   MASS-SPRING-DAMPER SYSTEM 9/15/67
END
STOP

Any of the above three types of statements are called *labeled statements*.

In the above program, the first line is a data output statement which specifies the title in the print output. The second line is a data input statement which specifies the value of the initial condition A to be 20 (the other initial condition has been specified to be 0). The third and fourth statements are control statements. The third statement specifies the integration step size to be 0.005 sec, and the computation is to be terminated when TIME (the independent variable) is equal to 5 sec. The fourth statement specifies the use of MILNE integration subroutine. The fifth statement is a data input statement, specifying the values of the parameters M, B, and K. The next four statements are all data output statements. The sixth statement specifies the print interval and the values of the quantities to be printed out. Both X and XDOT are to be printed in increments of 0.1 sec. The seventh and eighth statements specify a plot where both X and XDOT are plotted vs. TIME in increments of 0.01 sec and the plot is an 8- by 6-in. graph. The ninth statement specifies that the graph be labeled with MASS-SPRING-DAMPER

```
      BLOCK DATA
      COMMON/SYMBLS/NCINTG,NCSYMB,SYMB(  15)
      COMMON/KEYS/NALARM,KPCINT,Y(17)
      COMMON/CURVAL/C(8LCC)
      DIMENSION LC(8LCC)
      EQUIVALENCE (LC,C)
      DATA KPCINT/  16/,NCINTG/  2/,NCSYMB/  15/,  SYMB(1)/  90HTIME
     1DELT   DELMINFINTIMCLKTIMDELMAXXDCT  X        ZZCCO3ZZ00O5ZZ0CC2A
     1M       B       K
     1 /
      DATA C( 11)/C.           /
      END




      SUBROUTINE UPDATE
      COMMON/CURVAL/TIME   ,DELT   ,DELMIN,FINTIM,CLKTIM,DELMAX
     1 ,XDCT  ,X     ,ZZCCO3,ZZCCO5,ZZCCC2,A      ,M      ,B      ,K
      REAL          M
     1 ,K      ,INTGRL
C     XDCT  =INTGRL(ZZCCC2,ZZOOC3)
C     X     =INTGRL(A,XDCT)
      ZZCCO3=(SIN(TIME)-B*XDCT-K*X)/M
      ZZCCC5 =   XDCT
      RETURN
      END


***DSL/90 PROGRAM FOR MASS-SPRING-DAMPER SYSTEM
```

TIME	X	XDUT
0.	2.0000E 01	0.
1.000E-01	1.9915E 01	-1.6957E 0C
2.000E-01	1.9663E 01	-3.3343E 0C
3.000E-01	1.9250E 01	-4.9030E 0C
4.000E-01	1.8685E 01	-6.3305E 0C
5.000E-01	1.7975E 01	-7.7062E 0C
6.000E-01	1.7131E 01	-9.0904E 0C
7.000E-01	1.6163E 01	-1.0265E 01
8.000E-01	1.5032E 01	-1.1332E 01
9.000E-01	1.3901E 01	-1.2276E 01
1.000E 00	1.2631E 01	-1.3092E 01
1.100E 00	1.1286E 01	-1.3776E 01
1.200E 00	9.8803E 00	-1.4326E 01
1.300E 00	8.4258E 00	-1.4740E 01
1.400E 00	6.9367E 00	-1.5019E 01
1.500E 00	5.4265E 00	-1.5163E 01
1.600E 00	3.9084E 00	-1.5175E 01
1.700E 00	2.3957E 00	-1.5058E 01
1.800E 00	9.0096E-01	-1.4916E 01
1.900E 00	-5.6356E-01	-1.4455E 01
2.000E 00	-1.9862E 00	-1.3980E 01
2.100E 00	-3.3560E 00	-1.3398E 01
2.200E 00	-4.6626E 00	-1.2718E 01
2.300E 00	-5.8966E 00	-1.1947E 01
2.400E 00	-7.0493E 00	-1.1095E 01
2.500E 00	-8.1131E 00	-1.0170E 01

Fig. 7.2 Translated subprogram and table output of the mass-damper-spring simulation.

SYSTEM 9/15/67.   The STOP statement specifies the end of a job.   A job consists of one or more runs, each terminated by one END statement.

7.4.3 RESULT

When the DSL/90 processor accepts a DSL/90 program, it first translates the connection statements into a BLOCK DATA subprogram and a subroutine UPDATE; these are shown in Fig. 7.2.   It then simulates the translated subprograms and prints the result, which is also shown in Fig. 7.2.   Notice that the result is titled according to the TITLE statement. The headings of TIME, X, and XDOT, as well at the print interval of 0.1, are due to the PRINT statement.   Only a part of the printed result is shown in Fig. 7.2, though the computation continues until TIME is 5.

7.5 STATEMENTS

As has been shown, a DSL/90 program consists of a series of statements. The basic elements of statements are the previously described constants, variables, operators, expressions, and functions.   There are five types of statements: comment, connection, data, control, and pseudo-operation statements.   A comment statement is characterized by an asterisk in column 1.   Comment statements are for program readability; they are reprinted and then ignored by the DSL/90 processor.   Connection statements describe the relations among the inputs and outputs of the functions; they constitute the body of a simulation.   Data statements assign numerical values to the parameters, constants, initial conditions, and table entries as well as provide data for titles and labels and specify print outputs and plots.   Control statements specify execution control, program control, and run control (such as run time and integration step size). Pseudo-operation statements offer additional facilities such as procedure-block and macro generation.   The data, control, and pseudo-operation statements have the same format (a label in columns 1 to 6 and the statement proper in columns 7 to 72); they are called *labeled statements*.   A list of all labeled statements, together with examples, is shown in Table 7.9 for quick reference.

7.5.1 CONNECTION STATEMENTS

A connection statement specifies a function and its inputs and outputs (usually one output), as well as initial conditions and parameters, if any. The general form is

$$\begin{bmatrix} \text{Statement} \\ \text{number} \end{bmatrix} [\text{outputs}] = \begin{matrix} \text{function} \\ \text{name} \end{matrix} \left(\begin{bmatrix} \text{init.} \\ \text{cond.} \end{bmatrix}, [\text{parameters}], [\text{inputs}] \right)$$

The initial conditions and parameters can be variables or constants; they

Table 7.9   DSL/90 labeled statements

Label (Cols. 1–6)	*Examples of data or specifications (Cols. 7–72)*

Input data statements:

PARAM	H = 125., ERROR = 1.E − 4
CONST	K1 = 4550., K2 = 25300., M2 = 45.28, M3 = 20
INCON	XO = 0., Y3DOTO = 0., Y30 = 0.
AFGEN	FOFY3 = 0., 8.33, 30., 4., 60., 1.6, 120., 5.2, . . .
NLFGEN	F = 0., 85.5, 5., 144.5, 9., 1.5E3, 12.9, 2.4EO3
STORAG	IC(2), PAR(10)
TABLE	IC(1) = 2.0, IC(2) = 0., PAR(1) = 4., PAR(2–10) = 9*1.5

Output data statements:

TITLE	DSL/90 PROGRAM FOR VAN DER POL'S EQUATION
PRINT	.1, X, XDOT, DELT
PREPAR	.05, X, XDOT, ANGLE
GRAPH	8., 6., TIME, X, XDOT
LABEL	AIRCRAFT ARRESTING GEAR SYSTEM SIMULATION
RANGE	X, XDOT, DELT
PRPLOT	

Control statements:

CONTRL	FINTIM = 5., DELT = .005, DELMIN = 1.5E − 8, CLKTIM = 100.
FINISH	Y = 30., X = − 60.
INTEG	RKS
RELERR	X = 1.E − 4, XDOT = 1.E − 5
ABSERR	X = 1.E − 3, XDOT = 1.E − 4
CONTIN	
RESET	GRAPH, PREPAR
END	
STOP	

Pseudo-operation statements:

RENAME	TIME = DISPL, DELT = DELTX
INTGER	COUNT, K
MEMORY	INT(4), FUNC(25)
HISTRY	DEL(50), PUL(100)
DECK	
NOCENT†	
NOSORT	
D	DIMENSION P(3,2)
SORT	
PROCED	FD = FCNY3(Y3, Y3DOT)
ENDPRO	
MACRO	OUT = REALPR(IC, TAU, GAIN, INPUT)
ENDMAC	

† Deleted in DSL/90-02.

exist in the above form only when applicable.   Normally, there is no statement number.   When there is, it is for cross reference and is used only when appropriate FORTRAN statements, such as the GO TO statement, are employed under certain allowed conditions, as will be shown.   The inputs can be expressions, so that nesting is permitted.   FORTRAN arithmetic statements employing operators $+$, $-$, $*$, $/$, and $**$ (and left and right parentheses) are also permitted.   The card format for connection statements is shown in Table 7.10.

The following are examples of connection statements:

$$
\begin{aligned}
4 \quad & X = A + B - C*D/E \\
& Y = SQRT(X**2 + H**2) \\
20 \quad & Z = INTGRL(Y0, INTGRL(0., Y2DOT))
\end{aligned}
$$

The first example illustrates a simple FORTRAN statement; the second shows an arithmetic expression as the input of a SQRT function; and the third shows initial condition Y0 and the input of an INTGRL function, where the input is another INTGRL function (i.e., nesting).   Numbers 4 and 20 are statement numbers.   In short, a connection statement specifies one or more operations, the data to be operated on, and the data which represent the results.

7.5.2 DATA STATEMENTS

There are two types of data statements: input statements and output statements.   The input statements assign numeric values to the parameters, constants, initial conditions, and table entries.   The output statements provide data for titles and labels and specify printouts, plots, etc.

Table 7.10   Card format for connection statements

Column	Description
2–5	A statement number may be written here except within a MACRO. Blanks and leading zeros are ignored in these columns. For a multiple-card statement, a statement number may be written for the first card only.
6	This column must be either blank or zero; otherwise, it is a continuation card. A statement may be continued on as many as 10 cards. Any card concluded with three consecutive decimal points is considered to be followed by a continuation card.
7–72	The connection statement proper is written here. All blanks are ignored in these columns.
73–80	These columns are not processed by the DSL/90 processor. They may be used for identification.

A data statement consists of a label which specifies the particular input or output statement in columns 1 to 6. The label must be left-adjusted in the six columns. The actual specification of input or output is in columns 7 to 72. Data are specified in a free form and blanks are ignored. A data statement may be continued on as many cards as required, limited only by the total storage allocated for the data statements (namely, 200 statements). Any card concluded with three consecutive decimal points is considered to be followed by a continuation card, and continuation may begin anywhere in columns 1 to 72. Some examples of data statements are shown in Table 7.9.

7.5.2.1 Input data statements   There are seven input data statements; their labels and some examples are shown in Table 7.9.

(a) *PARAM*   This statement assigns the values to variable names chosen as parameters. Values of parameters may be changed for each run. To specify a value N for the name of a parameter A, the form A = N is used for each parameter. Blanks are ignored. Commas are used to separate the specifications. Any number of variables and their specified values may appear on a card or on continuation cards.

(b) *CONST*   This statement assigns values to variable names chosen as constants; otherwise, it is the same as the PARAM. Values of constants remain unchanged for runs.

(c) *INCON*   This statement assigns values to variable names chosen as initial conditions; otherwise, it is the same as the PARAM.

(d) *AFGEN and NLFGEN*   AFGEN (arbitrary function generator) and NLFGEN (nonlinear function generator) are tables to represent an arbitrary function $Y = f(X)$. The values of the table are referenced by using the chosen name of the table with a subscript as the argument. The first value and alternating values thereafter are those of the independent variable and must be presented in order of algebraically increasing values. Increments may be of unequal size. Each of these must be followed by its corresponding coordinate value. This list of values may be extended to continuation cards, but it ends when a number is not followed by a comma. There is no specific restriction on the number of function generators in a simulation or the number of points per function.

(e) *AFGEN OVRLAY and NLFGEN OVRLAY*   This is an option of AFGEN and NLFGEN which is used to conserve memory by replacing the previous table of the same function name with a new table of values. This overlay feature can be used only if the overlaying table does not contain more values than the previous table defined without overlay.

The identifier, OVRLAY, should appear only on the first card; it should be separated from the AFGEN or NLFGEN label by at least one blank, and from the function name by a comma.

(*f*) *STORAG*   This statement allows the user to specify those variable names which are subscripted.   The number within the parentheses represents the maximum number of storage locations needed to contain data for the corresponding variable.   Data are entered into these areas by use of a TABLE statement.

(*g*) *TABLE*   This statement allows blocks of data to be transferred to the subroutine UPDATE in tabular form by assigning values to the subscripted variables declared in a STORAG statement.   By this statement, table values are converted and substituted for the current values of the corresponding dimensioned variables according to the specified index or consecutive indices.   An example is shown below:

Column   1–6   7–72
          STORAG IC(2), PAR(10)
          TABLE   IC(1) = 2.0, IC(2) = 0.0, PAR(1) = 4.,
                                              PAR(2–10) = 9*1.5

The first statement assigns a total of 12 locations (2 for the array IC and 10 for PAR).   The second statement illustrates the manner in which numeric values are entered into these reserved locations.   The form K*N is used to cause K repeats of the number N.

This statement makes it possible to eliminate the need for a lengthy subroutine-argument string.   Consider the following statement:

YOUT = SPEC(IC,PAR,XINPUT)

The names IC and PAR will be replaced by the DSL/90 processor with the addresses of the first locations of the arrays IC and PAR, respectively. Obviously, when programming his subroutine SPEC, the user must realize that the first two arguments in SPEC are location points to his arrays. His subroutine in FORTRAN could begin with the following:

FUNCTION SPEC(LOGIC, LOCPAR, XIN)
COMMON/CURVAL/C(1)
I = LOGIC
J = LOCPAR

CURVAL is the name of a labeled COMMON area where the current values of all variables are stored, and I and J are indices referencing the first initial conditions IC and parameter values PAR.

The TABLE statement changes one or more points in an AFGEN or an NLFGEN array in the subsequent run without having to reenter all the points.   For example, the AFGEN statement

    AFGEN   CV = -1.0, .5, 0.0, .7, .8, 2.9, 1.2, 4.4, . . .
             2.5, 3.6, 3.0, 3.2
             .
             .
             .
    END
    TABLE   CV(3$-$4) = 0.1, .6, CV(7) = 1.25
             .
             .
             .
    END

defines an arbitrary function with six pairs of points.   For a subsequent
run, the TABLE statement is used to change the values of the pair of
points of (0.0, .7) to (0.1, .6) and the values of (1.2, 4.4) to (1.25, 4.4).

The combination of STORAG and TABLE statements enables a
user to define and store data in a one-dimensional array which can then
be used by a user-defined MACRO or a user-defined subroutine.   As an
example, the statements

    STORAG   P1(3), P2(3)
    TABLE   P1(1 $-$ 3) = 1.0, 2.0, 3.0, P2(1) = 4.5,
                                          P2(2–3) = 2*6.0
    MACRO   ANS = POLY(C,X)
              ANS = C(1)*X*X + C(2)*X + C(3)
    ENDMAC
              A1 = POLY(P1, A2)
              A2 = POLY(P2, TIME)

show a user-defined MACRO called POLY which evaluates the polynomial of $ax^2 + bx + c$.   These statements also show how the STORAG
and TABLE statements provide the values of the coefficients of the polynomial when the MACRO POLY is called.

7.5.2.2 Output data statements   There are seven output data statements; their labels and some examples are shown in Table 7.9.   Note that
only one PRINT, PREPAR, and RANGE statement is recognized per
program.

As shown below, plots can be made by using PREPAR, GRAPH,
and LABEL statements.   However, if a run ends prematurely because
of errors, all the accumulated points will be plotted before the next run
is made.   This is not the case if, for some reason such as exceeding the
maximum time, a run is terminated by the operator.   To obtain a graph-

ical output in case the maximum run time is exceeded, the CLKTIM option should be used. CLKTIM specifies the total time in seconds for a DSL/90 program; and as soon as the run time exceeds the value of CLKTIM, the processing is terminated. If CLKTIM is not specified by the user, this termination is ignored. Also, if an installation does not have a clock in the core memory, the CLKTIM feature cannot be used.

(a) *TITLE* This statement allows the user to specify in columns 7 to 72 a heading to be printed at the top of each page of a printed output. Successive cards are printed in sequence for a maximum of five cards; in this case, label TITLE must also appear in columns 1 to 6 on all successive cards.

(b) *PRINT* This statement specifies variables whose values are to be printed. The first field is interpreted as the print increment for all the variables in the PRINT statement. The remaining field contains variable names whose values are printed at each interval during the simulation. If variables are specified, it automatically means the printout of the independent variable TIME. Variable names are also printed out as headings.

There are two fixed formats for print outputs: one in column form, which has variable-name headings at the top of each column; and the other in equation form, which has variable-name headings on the left side of an equal sign. The column form is for printout where there are less than 10 dependent variables. Otherwise, the equation form is used. In this case, a maximum of 50 variables may be printed per run.

(c) *PREPAR* This statement allows the user to specify a plot for off-line plotting with TIME as the independent variable. The label PREPAR should appear only on the first PREPAR card if more than one is required. The first field specifies the plot increment, and the remaining fields specify the variable names which are the dependent variables of the plot.

(d) *GRAPH* This statement allows the user to specify a graph more flexible than the PREPAR statement, but it must be used in conjunction with the PREPAR card to request for plots. In the first two fields are specified the numerical values of the horizontal and vertical axis-lengths in inches. If the lengths are unspecified (two consecutive commas must be used before the independent variable), they will be set at 12 and 8 in., respectively. In the remaining fields variable names are specified; the first variable name is the independent variable plotted along the horizontal axis, and the remaining names are dependent variables. Variable names are printed adjacent to the axes. A maximum of 10 dependent variables may be plotted on the same graph, each with its own axis. Only 50 variables may be plotted per run, and these may be distributed on as many as 10 graphs. Five types of lines are used in succession on any one graph: solid, dashed, dotted, center, and phantom. Any variable appearing on a GRAPH statement must have appeared first on the PREPAR statement. Consecutive GRAPH statements cause additional plots.

One or more families of curves with different values of a parameter computed from several consecutive runs can be plotted on one set of axes. For example, consider the following statements:

```
CONTRL      FINTIM = 5.0
PARAM       C = 1.0
PREPAR      .05,X,Y,Z
GRAPH       ,,TIME,Y
END
PARAM       C = 1.2
RESET       GRAPH
END
PARAM       C = 1.4
END
PARAM       C = 1.6
GRAPH       ,,TIME,X,Y
LABEL       FAMILIES X AND Y FOR C = 1.2, 1.4 AND 1.6
GRAPH       8.,8.,X,Z
LABEL       PHASE PLANE FOR C = 1.2, 1.4 AND 1.6
END
```

The first run will produce a standard-size (8.0 by 6.0 in.) plot of Y against time for the case where parameter $C = 1.0$. In the next three runs, as C varies from 1.2 to 1.6, the program will save the computed values of X, Y, and Z. Note carefully that the points from the first run ($C = 1.0$) are destroyed once a GRAPH card appears. Since GRAPH requests are cumulative, the RESET GRAPH card in run 2 is necessary to cancel the GRAPH request in run 1. (Otherwise that request remains effective for each subsequent run.) Now the first GRAPH card in run 4 will produce two families of three curves each (X versus time and Y versus time), and the other GRAPH request will plot a family of three curves (Z versus X).

(e) *LABEL* This statement allows the user to label the graph below the horizontal axis when the label proper is specified in columns 7 to 72. A LABEL statement should follow immediately the GRAPH statement whose graph is to be labeled. A LABEL statement remains effective for successive runs. If it is no longer needed, it should be nullified by a RESET statement.

(f) *RANGE* This statement allows the user to specify the variable names for which the minimum and maximum values obtained by them during the simulation are printed at the end of the run. These values are collected at the integration interval, not at the print interval. The initial time at which these values are attained is also recorded.

(g) *PRPLOT* This statement allows the user to specify printer plots in addition to or in lieu of digital plots. These plots must have TIME as the independent variable. This statement can have the following format:

Column 1   7–72
     PRPLOT
     PRPLOT ONLY

The printer and digital plot routines use the same PREPAR, GRAPH, and LABEL statements. One other restriction is that the printer plotter will not plot a family of curves; instead, the curves will be plotted in succession. After a PRPLOT or PRPLOT ONLY statement is used, the printer-plot request may be canceled by specifying PRPLOT on a RESET statement.

7.5.3 CONTROL STATEMENTS

Control statements allow the user to specify certain options during execution, to set conditions for termination of a run, and to reset conditions for successive runs. They have the same card format as that of data statements. The labels of control statements and some examples are shown in Table 7.9. There are nine statements, as described below.

(a) *CONTRL* This statement specifies the values of DELT, FINTIM, DELMAX, DELMIN, and CLKTIM. The value of FINTIM must be specified. The value of DELMIN is $(10^{-8} \cdot \text{TIME})$ if not specified. The clock time is not used if CLKTIM is not specified.

(b) *FINISH* In addition to being terminated at a specific time as specified by the values of FINTIM and CLKTIM, a run may also be terminated when any dependent variable specified by this statement reaches a specified value. For example, the FINISH statement

FINISH   ALT = 0., X = 5000.

means that the run will be terminated if ALT reaches 0 or X reaches 5,000 before the specified value of FINTIM or CLKTIM has been reached. There should be only one FINISH statement per run.

(c) *INTEG* This statement selects one of a number of centralized integration subroutines for the simulation. Table 7.11 shows the avail-

Table 7.11   Available integration subroutines

Name	Method
RKS	Fourth-order Runge-Kutta with variable integration interval to keep the difference between the integrated values and Simpson-rule checks within prescribed limits.
RKSFX	Fourth-order Runge-Kutta with fixed interval.
SIMP	Simpson's rule integration with fixed interval.
MILNE	Variable-step, fifth-order, predictor-corrector integration method by Milne.
TRAPZ	Trapezoidal integration.
RECT	Rectangular integration.
CENTRL	A dummy subroutine that may be easily replaced by a user-supplied centralized integration subroutine if desired. (Remove the $IBLDR CENTRL card in the deck setup.)

able integration subroutines.   Subroutines RKS and MILNE are of vary-ing step; subroutines RKSFX, RECT, SIMP, and TRAPZ are of fixed step; and subroutine CENTRL is a dummy subroutine for incorporating a user-defined integration subroutine if the user so chooses.

The fixed-step integration subroutines expect an initial step size of DELT to be specified.   Once DELT is given, this value is retained until another DELT value is specified.   If no DELT is given, DELT is set to 0.01*FINTIM.   The variable-step integration subroutines do not require a starting value of DELT.   MILNE is completely self-starting, but RKS will use an initial DELT value if one is supplied.   However, neither MILNE nor RKS will destroy any given DELT.

The user is allowed to change the value of DELT during a run. This can be done for all the integration subroutines except MILNE, which is a predictor-corrector requiring past history points.   For example,

```
          .
          .
          .

INTEG      RECT
CONTRL     DELT = .01,FINTIM = 1.5
END
CONTIN
CONTRL     DELT = .005,FINTIM = 2.0
END
STOP
```

The first run, using rectangular integration with a step size of .01, will terminate at time $t = 1.5$.   The run will be continued from $t = 1.5$ to $t = 2.0$ with a step size of .005.

(d) *RELERR*   This statement allows the user to specify a relative error bound for integrator outputs for use by the RKS or MILNE integration subroutine to control error.   If none is specified, the error is set at 0.00001.   If one or more errors are specified, then the last error specified is applied to all integrators that are not specified.

(e) *ABSERR*   This statement is similar to the RELERR statement except that an absolute error is specified.   If none is specified, the error is set to 0.0001.

(f) *CONTIN*   When a run is completed and the next run can be specified to begin without resetting the initial conditions of the integrators and/or the initial value of the independent variable, this statement allows the user to specify that the program continues from the point at which the previous run ended.   Output specifications such as integration interval, integration error bounds, and parameter values can be altered.

The use of a CONTIN statement allows graph points to be accumulated over two or more runs.   For example, the statements

.

.

.

```
CONTRL      FINTIM = 5.0
PREPAR      .05,Y,Z
END
CONTIN
CONTRL      FINTIM = 10.0
PREPAR      .1,Y,Z
GRAPH       ,,TIME,Y,Z
END
```

.

.

.

cause 100 points to be collected from $t = 0$ to $t = 5.0$ and 50 more points from $t = 5.0$ to $t = 10.0$.   The GRAPH card produces a 150-point graph of Y and Z versus time.

(g) *RESET*   This statement allows the user to change data and control of the simulation for successive runs.   When labels PRINT, PREPAR, RANGE, FINISH, LABEL, and/or GRAPH are specified in this statement, the statements with these labels in the DSL/90 program are nullified for successive runs.   When labels RELERR and

ABSERR are specified in a RESET statement, these errors are reset to their original values.   When labels CONST and/or PARAM are specified in a RESET statement, all values are set to zero except those used within the INTGRL block.   If columns 7 to 72 of a RESET statement are left blank, it is the same as specifying labels PRINT, PREPAR, GRAPH, and RANGE.   With label GRAPH on a RESET statement, reset the label on the GRAPH statement is implied; but the reverse is not true.   The values of the variables on a STORAG statement cannot be set to zero by a RESET statement.

(*h*) *END*   This statement indicates the end of a DSL/90 program for a particular simulation run (not the end of a DSL/90 program) and permits the simulation to accept new data and control statements for the next run, which is automatically initiated at the conclusion of the preceding run.   The END statement resets the independent variable (i.e., TIME) to zero and resets the initial conditions of the integrators.

(*i*) *STOP*   This statement indicates the final end of a DSL/90 program.   It must follow the last END statement when there are multiple runs of the simulation.

7.5.4 PSEUDO–OPERATION STATEMENTS

The pseudo-operation statements specify how the connection, data, and control statements are to be translated by the DSL/90 processor, and how FORTRAN statements may be intermixed.   The card format is the same as that of data statements.   The labels of these statements and their examples are shown in Table 7.9.   There are 13 pseudo-operation statements, as described below.

(*a*) *RENAME*   This statement allows the user to change the names of five reserved names (TIME, DELT, DELMAX, DELMIN, and FINTIM).   The substitute names should then be used in the connection statements of the user's DSL/90 program, and they will appear on all the outputs.   No more than one card may be used with the RENAME statement.   The RENAME statement in Table 7.9 gives the reserved names TIME and DELT new names of DISPL and DELTX, respectively.

(*b*) *INTGER*   This statement allows the user to declare a list of variables as integers within the UPDATE subroutine, and can then (and only then) be used as such in connection statements and/or FORTRAN statements.

(*c*) *MEMORY/HISTRY*   Certain DSL/90 functions such as INTGRL and DELAY require storage area (i.e., locations in the magnetic-core memory). Such functions are called memory functions or history functions. Functions CMPXPL, DERIV, HSTRSS, INTGRL, MODINT, and REALPL are examples of memory functions, while functions DELAY, LEDLAG, IMPULS, PULSE, RST, and ZHOLD are examples of history functions. Memory functions require the specification of initial values for their storage areas, while history functions do not. This distinction applies not only to the DSL/90 built-in functions but to user-defined functions as well.

The DSL/90 processor provides a sorting subroutine to sequence the statements of a DSL/90 program into a proper order for execution. One or more statements may form a closed loop. If such a loop does not include a memory function or an implicit function whether the loop contains a history function or not, execution of such a loop cannot be carried out, and the sort subroutine will flag down with a message of "undefined implicit loops."

The storage areas for the built-in memory and history functions are reserved by the DSL/90 system, but the storage area for a user-defined memory or history function is specified by a MEMORY or a HISTRY statement, respectively. Examples for these two statements are:

```
MEMORY   INT(4), PASS(2)
HISTRY   DAY(3), CASA(10)
```

Either statement identifies memory or history functions and specifies the number of storage locations by a numerical subscript, as shown above. This number should be the total number of past inputs and outputs that are required each time the function is executed in a simulation run.

As an example, consider memory function FUNCT, which is a FORTRAN subroutine defined by the user as below:

```
FUNCTION FUNCT(K,YIC,PARAM,X)
COMMON/MEMRY/C(1)
COMMON/CURVAL/TIME
I = K
IF(TIME)4,4,5
4 C(I+1) = YIC
GO TO 6
5 C(I+1) = F(X,C(I),C(I+1),PARAM,TIME)
6 C(I) = X
FUNCT = C(I+1)
RETURN
END
```

Assume that this function requires one input and one output to be stored for each use. The MEMORY and connection statements for this block are shown below:

> MEMORY FUNCT(2)
> $Y = FUNCT(IC,PARAM,X)$

The MEMORY statement informs the DSL/90 translator how many storage locations are required for each use, and the translator assigns storage in the labeled COMMON/MEMRY/ and inserts the index (say 25) of the assigned location as the first subprogram argument

> $Y = FUNCT(25,IC,PARAM,X)$

The next assignment of storage area for another memory function allocates the location at an index of 27.

(*d*) *DECK* This statement causes the translated object decks (binary) of DATA and UPDATE to be punched. It does not produce source decks for these subroutines. The translated decks can be compiled and executed by using a FORTRAN-compile load-and-go procedure without going through the translation again. Note that the data and control statements are not included in the translated deck. These statements must be provided as a separate data set to be read during execution. An object deck can be obtained by compiling the translated deck, and then used with the above-mentioned data set.

(*e*) *NOCENT* This statement allows the user to specify that centralized integration is not to be used for the simulation. Instead, the translator sequences the statements in such a way that INTGRL functions become the last and then cause a transfer to the user's subroutine INTGRL during execution. Note that INTGRL must be specified as a memory function if noncentralized integration and sorting are used together. (This option is removed for DSL/90-02.)

(*f*) *NOSORT/SORT* The NOSORT and SORT statements allow the user to identify groups of statements in a DSL/90 program not to be sorted (i.e., to be kept in the original order). A NOSORT statement must precede the group of statements, and a SORT statement must follow it. Groups of statements that are separated by an unsorted group are sorted separately.

As an example, the following statements are a part of a DSL/90 program where the NOSORT statement allows FORTRAN DO loops and subscripted variables. As shown below, a FORTRAN WRITE statement is permitted after a NOSORT statement. POLY is a user-supplied FORTRAN subroutine.

```
        NOSORT
        STORAG   P1(3), P2(3)
        TABLE    P1(1-3) = 1.,2.,3.
        INTGER   GO, I
        PARAM    GO = 1
                 GO TO (1, 2), GO
            1    GO = 2
                 DO 5 I=1, 2
            5    P2(I) = P1(I) + 1.0
                 P2(3) = 2.0*P1(3)
                 WRITE (6, 10) (P2(J), J=1, 3)
           10    FORMAT (1 HO, 3E20.5)
            2    CONTINUE
                 A = POLY (P2, P1(3)+TIME)

                    .
                    .
                    .

        END
        STOP
        $IBFTC   POLY
                 FUNCTION POLY(K,X)
                 COMMON/CURVAL/C(2)
                 POLY = C(K)*X*X+C(K+1)*X+C(K+2)
                 RETURN
                 END
```

As shown in the above example, the subscripted variables may be used after a NOSORT statement, but not the DSL/90 PRINT statement to print out the values of the subscripted variables. One may either use a FORTRAN WRITE statement or set the subscripted variable equal to a new undimensioned variable. The following is an example showing the use of a FORTRAN WRITE statement to print the values of a subscripted variable P:

```
                    .
                    .
                    .

        D        DIMENSION P(3, 2)
        INTGER   I
        NOSORT
                 DO   10   I=1, 3
           10    P(I, 1) = I
                 P(1, 2) = P(1,1) + 9.0
                 P(2, 2) = SQRT (P(1,2))
                 P(3, 2) = P(2,2)/4.0
                 WRITE (6, 20) ((P(J,K), J=1,3), K=1,2)
           20    FORMAT (1HO, 10E13.4)
```

```
    SORT
              A = P(3, 2)*B
              B = P(1, 2)+P(2, 2)
    PRINT     .2, A, B
              .

              .

              .
```

(g) *D statement* When there is a D in column 1 of a statement, as shown above, this statement is not processed. The D is removed and the statement is transferred as it is to the UPDATE subroutine. This statement thus allows the user to insert FORTRAN specification statements such as DIMENSION, TYPE, and DATA into the UPDATE subroutine. Only 10 D statements are permitted in one DSL/90 program. Continuation cards for D statements must be nonzero in column 6.

(h) *PROCED/ENDPRO* DSL/90 is a nonprocedural language because execution of a DSL/90 program does not depend on the order of the statements. In contrast, FORTRAN is a procedural language since execution of a FORTRAN program does depend on the statement order. The PROCED and ENDPRO statements are used to inform the translator to allow a section of FORTRAN statements in a DSL/90 program. Such a section may be called a procedural block. An example of defining a procedural block is shown below:

```
Column 1-6        7-72
    PROCED  VALUE = BLOCKA(TRIG,IN)
            IF(TRIG)1,1,2
        1   VALUE = LIMIT(PAR1,PAR2,IN)
            GO TO 3
        2   VALUE = IN+TRIG
        3   CONTINUE
    ENDPRO
```

As shown above, the labels PROCED and ENDPRO are punched in columns 1 to 6; they designate the beginning and the end of a procedural block. Inputs (TRIG and IN in this example) and outputs (VALUE in this example) must be specified in the PROCED statement. The procedural block will be sorted as a whole relative to the remaining DSL/90 statements. In other words, the order of statements within the procedural block remains unchanged. Any DSL/90 or FORTRAN statement, except MACRO, may be used within PROCED. In the above, LIMIT is a DSL/90 built-in function. If an entire program is procedural, as in a FORTRAN program, or if a section is not to be sorted in relation to the others, the NOSORT option should be used instead of PROCED. This pair of statements ensures proper sequencing whether statements are DSL/90 or FORTRAN and whether centralized integration is used or not. There is no limit to the number of inputs or outputs that can be specified. (For more than one output, separate variables with commas.)

(*i*) *MACRO/ENDMAC* The statements MACRO and ENDMAC define a macro. A macro is a repeatable procedural block with parameter variations. As an example, consider the following macro definition:

```
Column 1-6        7-72
     MACRO    OUT = FILTER(V1,V2,K,IN)
              V1  = (IN−V2)/K
              V2  = INTGRL(0.,V1)
              OUT = V2+0.5*V1
     ENDMAC
```

The name of the macro, in this case FILTER, must be unique. OUT is the output name and V1, V2, K, and IN are input names; they all are dummy symbols which will be replaced by the actual names or literals when the macro is used. MACRO function names cannot appear as a term in an expression.

When the above macro is used, it appears in a connection statement, as below:

```
LINE1 = FILTER(A1,A2,1.5,XIN)
```

The above statement causes the generation of the statements

```
A1 = (XIN−A2)/1.5
A2 = INTGRL(0.,A1)
LINE1 = A2+0.5*A1
```

to replace the above calling statement. (This is known as generation of in-line code.) As is the case with the procedural block, these statements are sequenced as a single block; LINE1 is the output, and A1, A2, and XIN are inputs. The statements within the block are not sorted. Both DSL/90 and FORTRAN statements, except a PROCED or MACRO statement, may appear within a macro. However, statement numbers cannot be used in a macro, and a macro cannot be used as a term in an expression.

The built-in functions of real pole (REALPL), lead lag (LEDLAG), complex pole (CMPXPL), and mode-controlled integration (MODINT) are built-in macros in the DSL/90 processor. In-line code is generated for each use of these blocks with corresponding parameter substitutions.

7.6 SIMULATION EXAMPLES

With the syntax of the DSL/90 language described, four examples to
illustrate simulations by DSL/90 programming are now presented.
These simulations have all been shown before, as they were examples of
MIMIC programming. Nevertheless, they are chosen here so that the
programs by these two languages can be compared. As will be noticed
from the comparison, the connection statements of the DSL/90 programs
are very similar to MIMIC statements, except that the latter have a
logical control variable field. The functions of the logical control variable as well as the input and output statements in MIMIC are taken over
in DSL/90 by the DSL/90 labeled statements.

7.6.1 CONTROL CARDS

Control cards represent a system language by which the user communicates with the computer system. As an example, a listing of the control
cards for accepting a DSL/90 program for batch processing is shown in
Fig. 7.3. These cards are explained in the Appendix.

```
$JOB              UOM COMPUTER SCIENCE CENTER ****A****  JOB NUMBER 123400   DSL/90  0
$IBSYS                                                                        DSL/90  1
$*      MOUNT CSC-928 ON A5, RING OUT.                                        DSL/90  2
$*      SCRATCH ON B5 AND B6.                                                 DSL/90  3
$PAUSE                                                                        DSL/90  4
$ATTACH           B5                                                          DSL/90  5
$AS              SYSLB4                                                       DSL/90  6
$ATTACH          B6                                                           DSL/90  7
$AS              SYSUT6                                                       DSL/90  8
$REWIND          SYSUT6                                                       DSL/90  9
$REWIND          SYSCK1                                                       DSL/9010
$EXECUTE         IBJOB                                                        DSL/9011
$ID      CHU     *305/65/020*5MS     DSL/90                                   DSL/9012
$IBJOB           MAP,FIOCS                                                    DSL/9013
$IBEDIT          SYSCK1,SRCH                                                  DSL/9014
$IBLDR .GETID                                                                 DSL/9015
$IBLDR CKSTOP                                                                 DSL/9016
$IBLDR CONTIN                                                                 DSL/9017
$IBLDR FINISH                                                                 DSL/9018
$IBLDR INTEG                                                                  DSL/9019
$IBLDR JIGSAW                                                                 DSL/9020
$IBLDR NAME                                                                   DSL/9021
$IBLDR OUTIN                                                                  DSL/9022
$IBLDR OUTPUT                                                                 DSL/9023
$IBLDR RDWRMX                                                                 DSL/9024
$IBLDR SCAN                                                                   DSL/9025
$IBLDR SORT                                                                   DSL/9026
$IBLDR STORE                                                                  DSL/9027
$IBLDR TRANSL                                                                 DSL/9028
$IBLDR XMSG1                                                                  DSL/9029
$IBEDIT                                                                       DSL/9030
$DATA                                                                         DSL/9031
$IBEDIT          SYSCK1,SRCH                                                  DSL/9032
$IBLDR MAIN                                                                   DSL/9033
$IBLDR CENTRL                                                                 DSL/9034
$IBEDIT                                                                       DSL/9035
```

Fig. 7.3 A listing of DSL/90 control cards.

```
TITLE  ***DSL/90 PROGRAM FOR VAN DER POLS EQUATION
       XDOT=INTGRL(XDOTO,A*XDOT*(1.-X*X)-B*X)
       X=INTGRL(YO*XDOT)
CONTRL FINTIM=5.,DELT=.1
INTEG  RKS
PARAM  A=.1
CONST  B=1.
INCON  XO=1.,XDOTO=C.
PRINT  .1,X,YDOT
END
"
INTEG  MILNE
END
"
PARAM  A=.5
INCON  XO=3.
INTEG  RKS
END
*
PARAM  A=1.
INCON  XDOTO=3.
INTEG  RKS
END
*
STOP
```

Fig. 7.4 DSL/90 program for computing the solution of van der Pol's equation.

7.6.2 VAN DER POL'S EQUATION

The first example is to compute the solution of van der Pol's equation. The MIMIC program was shown in Fig. 4.33, and the DSL/90 program is shown in Fig. 7.4. As shown in Fig. 7.4, there are two connection statements which represent the equation, and four sets of labeled statements for four simulation runs. Each set is terminated by an END statement.

The first run calls for Runge-Kutta integration and specifies only an initial step size of 0.1, as the Runge-Kutta integration subroutine changes the step size to meet the error criterion. Constant B, parameter A, and initial conditions XO and XDOTO are also specified. Print output of X and XDOT versus TIME is specified with a print interval of 0.1.

The second run is identical to the first except that Milne's integration subroutine is specified. The third run specifies again the Runge-Kutta integration subroutine and different values of A and XP. The last run is identical to the third run except that different values of A and XDOTO are specified. The program must be and is ended by a STOP statement.

As mentioned previously, a DSL/90 program consists of two job segments. The execution of the first segment produces a FORTRAN

```
$IBSYS
$*       MOUNT CSC-928 ON A5, RING OUT.
$PAUSE
$ATTACH          B5                                              DSL/90 5
$AS              SYSLB4                                          DSL/90 6
$EXECUTE         IPJOB
$ID     CHU      *305/65/020*5M$    DSL/90              54650100000000
$IBJOB           GO,FIOCS,MAP
$IEDIT           SYSCK1,SRCH                                     DSL/9031
$IBLDR MAIN                                                      DSL/9032
$IBLDR CENTRL                                                    DSL/9033
$IEDIT                                                           DSL/9034
$IBFTC DATA      NODECK
       BLOCK DATA
       COMMON/SYMBLS/NOINTG,NOSYMB,SYMB(  14)
       COMMON/KEYS/NALARM,KPOINT,Y(17)
       COMMON/CURVAL/C(8000)
       DIMENSION LC(8000)
       EQUIVALENCE (LC,C)
       DATA KPOINT/  15/,NOINTG/  2/,NOSYMB/  14/,   SYMB(1)/   84HTIME
      1DELT   DELMINFINTIMCLKTIMDELMAXXDOT  X       ZZ0002ZZ0004XDOTO XO
      1A      B
      1 /
       END
$IBFTC UPDAT     NOLIST,NOREF,NODECK
       SUBROUTINE UPDATE
       COMMON/CURVAL/TIME  ,DELT  ,DELMIN,FINTIM,CLKTIM,DELMAX
      1 ,XDOT  ,X      ,ZZ0002,ZZ0004,XDOTO ,XO      ,A      ,B
       REAL        INTGRL
C      XDOT  =INTGRL(XDOTO,ZZ0002)
C      X     =INTGRL(XO,XDOT)
       ZZ0002=A*XDOT*(1.-X*X)-B*X
       ZZ0004 =   XDOT
       RETURN
       END
$IEDIT           SYSCK1,SRCH
$IBLDR ALPHA
$IBLDR ANGLE
$IBLDR ANN4
$IBLDR AXIS4
$IBLDR BYTER
$IBJOB CLOK2
$IBLDR DASH
$IBLDR DEBUG
$IBLDR F
$IBLDR INITLZ
$IBLDR INTRAN
$IBLDR LOOK
$IBLDR LWIDTH
$IBLDR MILNE
$IBLDR NMBER4
$IBLDR NUMER
$IBLDR PLOT4
$IBLDR PLOTR
$IBLDR RECT
$IBLDR RKS
$IBLDR SCALE4
$IBLDR SIMP
$IBLDR SIMUL
$IBLDR SYMBL4
$IBLDR TRAPZ
$IEDIT
'
```

Fig. 7.5 Magnetic-tape output from the translation phase of DSL/90 processing for the program in Fig. 7.4.

```
TITLE ***DSL/90 PROGRAM FOR VAN DER POLS EQUATION
CONTRL FINTIM=5.,DELT=.1
INTEG RKS
PARAM A=.1
CONST B=1.
INCON XO=1.,XDOTO=0.
PRINT .1,X,XDOT
END
INTEG MILNE
END
PARAM A=.5
INCON XO=3.
INTEG RKS
END
PARAM A=1.
INCON XDOTO=3.
INTEG RKS
END
STOP
'
$IBSYS
$SWITCH           SYSIN1,SYSUT6
'
$JOB
$IBSYS
$RESTORE
```

Fig. 7.5   (Continued)

program, which is the second job segment.   This FORTRAN program
for van der Pol's equation is shown in Fig. 7.5.   Explanation of this
program is also given in the Appendix.   The translated subprograms in
Fig. 7.5 and the table output are shown in Fig. 7.6.

7.6.3 BESSEL FUNCTIONS OF THE FIRST KIND

The second example is generation of Bessel functions of the first kind.
The MIMIC program was shown in Fig. 4.23, and the DSL/90 program
is shown in Fig. 7.7.   Both programs are prepared from Eqs. (4.66).
However, the manner in which the term $iJ_i(t)/t$ is programmed is different.   In the DSL/90 program, a procedural block is employed by using
a pair of PROCED and ENDPRO statements for each of the four such
required terms.   Notice that inputs (J1 and TIME) and output (KO)
must be specified in the PROCED statement.   Each block contains four
FORTRAN statements and will be sorted as a whole.   There are two
runs.   The first run specifies Runge-Kutta subroutine and termination
at TIME equal to 10.   The print interval is .1, and values of simulation
variables J0, J1, J2, J3, and J4 are to be printed.   The second run is
identical to the first except for the use of the MILNE integration subroutine.   These two runs offer a case for comparing the results of two
different integration subroutines.   An initial part of the result is shown
in Fig. 7.8.

```
BLOCK DATA
COMMON/SYMBLS/NOINTG,NCSYMB,SYMB(  14)
COMMON/KEYS/NALARM,KPCINT,Y(17)
COMMON/CURVAL/C(8000)
DIMENSION LC(8000)
EQUIVALENCE (LC,C)
DATA KPCINT/  15/,NOINTG/  2/,NCSYMB/  14/,   SYMB(1)/   84HTIME
1DELT   DELMINFINTIMCLKTIMDELMAXXDOT    X       ZZ0002ZZ0004XDOTO XO
1A     B
1 /
 END


SUBROUTINE UPDATE
COMMON/CURVAL/TIME   ,DELT   ,DELMIN,FINTIM,CLKTIM,DELMAX
1 ,XDOT  ,X      ,ZZ0002,ZZ0004,XDOTO ,XO     ,A      ,B
REAL      INTGRL
C  XDOT  =INTGRL(XDOTO,ZZ0002)
C  X     =INTGRL(XO,XDOT)
ZZ0002=A*XDOT*(1.-X*X)-B*X
ZZ0004  =    XDOT
RETURN
END



***CSL/SC PROGRAM FCR VAN DER POLS EQUATION

  TIME         X           XDOT
  C.         1.0000E CC  C.
  1.000E-01  9.9502E-01 -9.9836E-02
  2.000E-01  9.8006E-01 -1.9571E-01
  3.000E-01  9.5532E-01 -2.9572E-01
  4.000E-01  9.2101E-01 -3.9002E-01
  5.000E-01  8.7744E-01 -4.8085E-01
  6.000E-01  8.2493E-01 -5.6749E-01
  7.000E-01  7.6410E-01 -6.4926E-01
  8.000E-01  6.9531E-01 -7.2550E-01
  9.000E-01  6.1920E-01 -7.9561E-01
  1.000E CC  5.3642E-01 -8.5895E-01
  1.100E CC  4.4766E-01 -9.1492E-01
  1.200E CC  3.5270E-01 -9.6291E-01
  1.300E CC  2.5536E-01 -1.0023E CC
  1.400E CC  1.5354E-01 -1.0325E CC
  1.500E CC  4.9183E-02 -1.0530E CC
  1.600E CC -5.6715E-02 -1.0632E CC
  1.700E CC -1.6310E-01 -1.0627E CC
  1.800E CC -2.6889E-01 -1.0512E CC
  1.900E CC -3.7297E-01 -1.0284E CC
  2.000E CC -4.7419E-01 -9.9431E-01
  2.100E CC -5.7146E-01 -9.4905E-01
  2.200E CC -6.6364E-01 -8.9295E-01
  2.300E CC -7.4970E-01 -8.2653E-01
  2.400E CC -8.2863E-01 -7.5052E-01
  2.500E CC -8.9952E-01 -6.6584E-01
```

Fig. 7.6 Translated subprogram and table output from the program in Fig. 7.4.

```
TITLE ***DSL/90 PROGRAM FOR GENERATION OF BESSEL FUNCTIONS
      J0=INTGRL(1.0,-J1)
      J1=INTGRL(0.,J0-K0)
      J2=INTGRL(0.,J1-K1)
      J3=INTGRL(0.,J2-K2)
      J4=INTGRL(0.,J3-K3)
PROCED K0=BL0(J1,TIME)
      K0=J1
      IF(TIME.EQ.0.) GO TO 1
      K0=J1/TIME
    1 CONTINUE
ENDPRO
*
PROCED K1=BL1(J2,TIME)
      K1=J2
      IF(TIME.EQ.0.) GO TO 2
      K1=2.*J2/TIME
    2 CONTINUE
ENDPRO
*
PROCED K2=BL2(J3,TIME)
      K2=J3
      IF(TIME.EQ.0.) GO TO 3
      K2=3.*J3/TIME
    3 CONTINUE
ENDPRO
*
PROCED K3=BL3(J4,TIME)
      K3=J4
      IF(TIME.EQ.0.) GO TO 4
      K3=4.*J4/TIME
    4 CONTINUE
ENDPRO
*
CONTRL FINTIM=10.,DELT=.1
PRINT .1,J0,J1,J2,J3,J4
INTEG RKS
END
*
INTEG MILNE
END
*
STOP
```

Fig. 7.7 DSL/90 program for generating Bessel functions of the first kind.

7.6.4 A PARTIAL DIFFERENTIAL EQUATION

The third example is the solution of one-dimensional heat flow. The MIMIC program is shown in Fig. 4.40; the DSL/90 program is shown in Fig. 7.9. Both are programmed from Eqs. (4.116).

These two programs are very similar except for the manner in which the values of initial conditions are specified. As shown in Fig. 7.9, the

```
***DSL/90 PROGRAM FOR GENERATION OF BESSEL FUNCTIONS
```

TIME	J0	J1	J2	J3	J4
0.	1.0000E 00	0.	0.	0.	0.
1.000E-01	9.9750E-01	4.9938E-02	1.2493E-03	2.0785E-05	2.5963E-07
2.000E-01	9.9002E-01	9.9501E-02	4.9848E-03	1.6596E-04	4.1478E-06
3.000E-01	9.7763E-01	1.4932E-01	1.1167E-02	5.5919E-04	2.0984E-05
4.000E-01	9.6040E-01	1.9603E-01	1.9735E-02	1.3200E-03	6.6121E-05
5.000E-01	9.3847E-01	2.4227E-01	3.0605E-02	2.5637E-03	1.6072E-04
6.000E-01	9.1200E-01	2.8670E-01	4.3665E-02	4.3996E-03	3.3146E-04
7.000E-01	8.8120E-01	3.2900E-01	5.8787E-02	6.9296E-03	6.1009E-04
8.000E-01	8.4629E-01	3.6884E-01	7.5818E-02	1.0247E-02	1.0330E-03
9.000E-01	8.0752E-01	4.0595E-01	9.4586E-02	1.4434E-02	1.6405E-03
1.000E 00	7.6520E-01	4.4005E-01	1.1490E-01	1.9563E-02	2.4766E-03

Fig. 7.8 Table output from the program in Fig. 7.7.

```
TITLE ***DSL/90 PROGRAM FOR A PARTIAL DIFF. EQUATION
*
      DELTAX = L/20.
      Z      = K/(C*P*DELTAX*DELTAX)
*
      T0  = 0.
      T1  = INTGRL(IC1,    Z*(T2 -2.*T1 +T0 ))
      T2  = INTGRL(IC2,    Z*(T3 -2.*T2 +T1 ))
      T3  = INTGRL(IC3,    Z*(T4 -2.*T3 +T2 ))
      T4  = INTGRL(IC4,    Z*(T5 -2.*T4 +T3 ))
      T5  = INTGRL(IC5,    Z*(T6 -2.*T5 +T4 ))
*
      T6  = INTGRL(IC6,    Z*(T7 -2.*T6 +T5 ))
      T7  = INTGRL(IC7,    Z*(T8 -2.*T7 +T6 ))
      T8  = INTGRL(IC8,    Z*(T9 -2.*T8 +T7 ))
      T9  = INTGRL(IC9,    Z*(T10-2.*T9 +T8 ))
      T10 = INTGRL(IC10,   Z*(T11-2.*T10+T9 ))
*
      T11 = INTGRL(IC11,   Z*(T12-2.*T11+T10))
      T12 = INTGRL(IC12,   Z*(T13-2.*T12+T11))
      T13 = INTGRL(IC13,   Z*(T14-2.*T13+T12))
      T14 = INTGRL(IC14,   Z*(T15-2.*T14+T13))
      T15 = INTGRL(IC15,   Z*(T16-2.*T15+T14))
*
      T16 = INTGRL(IC16,   Z*(T17-2.*T16+T15))
      T17 = INTGRL(IC17,   Z*(T18-2.*T17+T16))
      T18 = INTGRL(IC18,   Z*(T19-2.*T18+T17))
      T19 = INTGRL(IC19,   Z*(T20-2.*T19+T18))
      T20 = 0.
*
CONST L=1.,K=2.4,C=0.2,P=150.
INCON IC1 =100.,IC2 =100.,IC3 =100.,IC4 =100.,IC5 =100.,IC6 =100.,,...
      IC7 =100.,IC8 =100.,IC9 =100.,IC10=100.,IC11=100.,IC12=100.,,...
      IC13=100.,IC14=100.,IC15=100.,IC16=100.,IC17=100.,IC18=100.,,...
      IC19=100.
CONTRL FINTIM=5.
INTEG RKS
PRINT .1,T,T2,T4,T6,T8,T10
END
STOP
```

Fig. 7.9 DSL/90 program for computing the solution of a one-dimensional heat-flow equation.

```
***DSL/90 PROGRAM FOR A PARTIAL DIFF. EQUATION
```

TIME	T2	T4	T6	T8	T10
0.	1.0000E 02	1.0000E 02	1.0000E 02	1.0000E 02	1.000.E 02
1.000E-01	5.7183E 01	8.8247E 01	9.7901E 01	9.9745E 01	9.9956E 01
2.000E-01	4.2471E 01	7.3598E 01	9.0434E 01	9.7166E 01	9.8768E 01
3.000E-01	3.5243E 01	6.3849E 01	8.2655E 01	9.2383E 01	9.5261E 01
4.000E-01	3.0732E 01	5.6927E 01	7.5783E 01	8.6671E 01	9.0167E 01
5.000E-01	2.7511E 01	5.1577E 01	6.9714E 01	8.0745E 01	8.4416E 01
6.000E-01	2.4986E 01	4.7152E 01	6.4265E 01	7.4946E 01	7.8561E 01
7.000E-01	2.2873E 01	4.3322E 01	5.9313E 01	6.9426E 01	7.2878F 01
8.000E-01	2.1031E 01	3.9912E 01	5.4777E 01	6.4245E 01	6.7491E 01
9.000E-01	1.9384E 01	3.6824E 01	5.0606E 01	5.9416F 01	6.2444E 01
1.000E 00	1.7888E 01	3.4002E 01	4.6761E 01	5.4934E 01	5.7746E 01

Fig. 7.10 Table output from the program in Fig. 7.9.

name of the initial conditions for each INTGRL function must be different, even though the values of these initial conditions are the same. For this reason, an INCON statement with three continuation cards is required. The initial part of the table output is shown in Fig. 7.10.

7.6.5 A SATELLITE ROLL-AXIS CONTROL SYSTEM

The fourth example is the previously discussed satellite roll-axis control system. The MIMIC program is shown in Fig. 3.76, and the DSL/90 program is shown in Fig. 7.11. Both are programmed from the block diagram in Fig. 3.75.

This example shows the use of LEDLAG and LIMIT functions. It also demonstrates a user-defined MACRO for a transfer function as well as a NOSORT block of FORTRAN statements in simulating the friction torque. The arguments of the MACRO calls cannot be expressions. A DELMIN of .0001 is specified, as there exist sharp changes in the characteristics of some elements in the system. Note that input XC is arc-seconds, and the conversion factor (CONV1*3600.) converts it into radians. The initial part of the table output is shown in Fig. 7.12.

7.7 DSL/90 PROCESSOR

A DSL/90 program is processed by the DSL/90 processor, which is written in FORTRAN IV. This section presents some information about this processor which may be helpful to the user in preparing and debugging a DSL/90 program.

7.7.1 PROCESSOR ORGANIZATION

The DSL/90 processor for the IBM 7090/7094 computers operates under the standard IBSYS control with three additional tape drives (a DSL/90 processor tape, a plot output tape, and a scratch tape). The processor

```
TITLE ***DSL/90 PROGRAM FOR A SATELLITE ROLL AXIS CONTROL SYSTEM
*
MACRO OUT = REALPO(IC,TAU,GAIN,INPUT)
      OUT = INTGRL(IC,(GAIN*INPUT-OUT)/TAU)
ENDMAC
******RATE INTEGRATING GYRO
      XE       = (XC/(CONV1*3600.)-X)
      Y        = REALPO(0.,T1,K1,XE)
******AMPLIFIER-DEMODULATOR
      Z        = REALPO(0.,T2,K2,Y)
******COMPENSATION NETWORK-AMPLIFIER
      P        = ALPHA*T3
      Q        = K3*Z
      V        = LEDLAG(0.,P,T3,Q)
******TORQUE MOTOR
      TM       = LIMIT(-1.,+1.,V)
******FRICTION TORQUE
NOSORT
      IF ((XDOT.EQ.0.).AND.(ABS(TM).LE.TS).AND.(TM.GE.0.)) GO TO 90
      IF ((XDOT.EQ.0.).AND.(ABS(TM).LE.TS).AND.(TM.LT.0.)) GO TO 80
      IF ((XDOT.EQ.0.).AND.(ABS(TM).GT.TS).AND.(TM.GE.0.)) GO TO 70
      IF ((XDOT.EQ.0.).AND.(ABS(TM).GT.TS).AND.(TM.LT.0.)) GO TO 60
      IF ((XDOT.NE.0.).AND.(ABS(TM).GT.TC).AND.(TM.GE.0.)) GO TO 50
      IF ((XDOT.NE.0.).AND.(ABS(TM).GT.TC).AND.(TM.LT.0.)) GO TO 40
      IF ((XDOT.NE.0.).AND.(ABS(TM).LE.TC).AND.(TM.GE.0.)) GO TO 90
      IF ((XDOT.NE.0.).AND.(ABS(TM).LE.TC).AND.(TM.LT.0.)) GO TO 80
   40 TF=-TC
      GO TO 100
   50 TF=+TC
      GO TO 100
   60 TF=-TS
      GO TO 100
   70 TF=+TS
      GO TO 100
   80 TF=-TM
      GO TO 100
   90 TF=+TM
  100 CONTINUE
SORT
******AVAILABLE TORQUE
      TA       = TM-TF
******SATELLITE DYNAMICS
      XDOT     = INTGRL(0.,TA/I)
      X        = INTGRL(0.,XDOT)
******UNITS CONVERSION
******X  IS IN RADIANS, 1DX  IS IN RADIANS PER SEC
******XX IS IN ARC-SEC, 1DXX IS IN ARC-SEC PER SEC
      XX       = X   *CONV1*3600.
      XXDOT    = XDOT*CONV1*3600.
CONST CONV1=57.2957795,I=200.,T1=.006,T2=.01,T3=.0555,...
      ALPHA=10.,TC=.1,TS=.2,K1=15.,K2=1000.,K3=.1
PARAM XC=1800.
CONTRL FINTIM=6.,DELT=.1,DELMIN=1.0E-4
INTEG RKS
PRINT .1,XF,XX,V,TM,TA,Y,Z
END
STOP
```

Fig. 7.11 DSL/90 program for simulating a satellite control system.

***DSL/90 PROGRAM FOR A SATELLITE ROLL AXIS CONTROL SYSTEM

TIME	XE	XX	V	TM	TA	Y	Z
0.	8.7266E-03	0.	0.	0.	0.	0.	0.
1.000E-01	8.7045E-03	4.5726E 00	3.9497E 01	1.0000E 00	9.0000E-01	1.3060E-01	1.3065E 02
2.000E-01	8.6373E-03	1.8427E 01	1.6925E 01	1.0000E 00	9.0000E-01	1.2964E-01	1.2975E 02
3.000E-01	8.5251E-03	4.1563E 01	1.2774E 01	1.0000E 00	9.0000E-01	1.2800E-01	1.2819E 02
4.000E-01	8.3680E-03	7.3981E 01	1.1608E 01	1.0000E 00	9.0000E-01	1.2568E-01	1.2594E 02
5.000E-01	8.1658E-03	1.1568E 02	1.0879E 01	1.0000E 00	9.0000E-01	1.2269E-01	1.2301E 02
6.000E-01	7.9186E-03	1.6666E 02	1.0165E 01	1.0000E 00	9.0000E-01	1.1902E-01	1.1941E 02
7.000E-01	7.6265E-03	2.2693E 02	9.3977E 00	1.0000E 00	9.0000E-01	1.1468E-01	1.1514E 02
8.000E-01	7.2893E-03	2.9647E 02	8.5653E 00	1.0000E 00	9.0000E-01	1.0966E-01	1.1019E 02
9.000E-01	6.9071E-03	3.7530E 02	7.6656E 00	1.0000E 00	9.0000E-01	1.0397E-01	1.0457E 02
1.000E 00	6.4800E-03	4.6341E 02	6.6982E 00	1.0000E 00	9.0000E-01	9.7602E-02	9.8265E 01

Fig. 7.12   Table output from the program in Fig. 7.11.

performs two independent functions in two phases: DSL/90 language translation during the first phase and model simulation during the second phase. Each function is a separate program, but the processor executes these two programs continuously in a single pass.

During the first phase, the DSL/90 translator converts the DSL/90 statements into a series of internal tables. The DSL/90 SORT subroutine may be executed optionally after the translation in order to establish the proper sequence for the DSL/90 statements. Finally, the processor outputs on a library tape (SYSUT6) two FORTRAN IV programs followed by the user-supplied binary and source programs, if any. Appropriate IBSYS control statements are inserted both to make the translated program appear as a standard job and to load the portions of the DSL/90 simulator that are necessary for the second phase. The normal IBSYS input tape (SYSIN1) and output tape (SYSUT6) are switched, and the DSL/90 program returns to IBSYS for the second phase.

During the second phase, the FORTRAN programs generated or loaded during the translation are compiled. Next, all simulator programs and those DSL/90 functions which will be used in the simulation are loaded. Then, the actual simulation takes place. The DSL/90 simulator translates the data and control statements of the DSL/90 program, sets up the parameters and run control, and then executes alternately the compiled program and the integration subroutine to achieve the simulation. PLOT and PRINT outputs are taken at preselected intervals. If plotting is required at the end of a run, the PLOT data collected during the run are input, scaled, and output in a special format for an IBM 1627 plotter. The program then returns to the simulator for another run. The execution of the program ends when a STOP card appears.

7.7.2 PROGRAM CHECKOUT

As programming aids, the DSL/90 processor provides diagnostic messages and subroutine DEBUG for tracing the simulation, as presented below.

7.7.2.1 Diagnostic messages When errors are encountered during the translation and simulation of a DSL/90 program, diagnostic messages are printed out. Some examples of these errors are shown below:

1. Output variable name not unique
2. Same output and input variable names in one block
3. Reuse of dummy MACRO names
4. Control variable name not a system variable name
5. Parameter value not an input
6. Output variable not specified

When an error does not destroy the validity of a simulation or is not wholly discernible in the translation, a "warning only" message is printed. If the processing of a DSL/90 program is halted at the end of translation, some examples of diagnostic messages are as follows:

1. Incorrect statement format
2. Invalid data card type (columns 1–6)
3. Failure of integration or implicit function to meet error criterion
4. Unspecified algebraic loop
5. Misspelled subroutine name
6. RELERR specification on other than an integrator output name

7.7.2.2 Subroutine DEBUG One effective approach for simulation checkout in digital analog simulation is to trace the values of simulation variables for each iteration. A few iterations are usually sufficient to detect programming errors. In DSL/90, this is provided by subroutine DEBUG, a subroutine of the DSL/90 processor.

As an example of the subroutine DEBUG, consider the following statement:

$$Z = DEBUG(N,T)$$

The above statement will cause the values of all simulation variables, including system variables and parameters, to be printed out for N successive iterations beginning at independent variable TIME equal to T. Z is any dummy name and should not be used again to represent a simulation variable. N must be a positive integer. Any number of DEBUG statements may be used in one DSL/90 program.

7.7.3 SORTING

Sorting is sequencing the statements of a DSL/90 program into a proper order for execution. The program is sorted on the following rule: A statement is properly sequenced if all its inputs are available either as input parameters or initial conditions or as previously computed values in the current iteration cycle. Outputs of integration blocks and user-defined MEMORY blocks are known because their initial values are given. The run is halted if an algebraic loop without the use of function IMPL is found. The result of sorting is a properly organized FORTRAN IV program.

In sorting, each loop involving integrators is sorted independently of all others. For example, the first loop ends with the first integrator and includes all statements involving the variables necessary to calculate the integrator input value. This also applies to MEMORY blocks, except that they are sorted within the integrator or other MEMORY block loops if they are needed to compute a previous input value.

By using the SORT and NOSORT statements, the user may sort only sections of his program. For example, an early NOSORT section in the program may be used for initializing the run or computing parameter values required only once for the program. A central NOSORT section may be used to test the run response for the purpose of switching portions of the program into or out of the simulation to decrease the run time or alter the information flow. The FORTRAN-computed GO TO statement may be used to branch a program to different statement sequences within a NOSORT section. The control variable may be computed or input on a PARAM statement, but it must be declared as an integer; an example is shown below:

> INTGER KEY
> > GO TO(1,2,3),KEY

7.7.4 PROGRAM RESTRICTIONS

How large a simulation program can the DSL/90 processor handle? In general, this is limited by the sizes of the tables in the translator. These tables are set up to store variable names. If these tables are exceeded, errors will occur. This and other restrictions on DSL/90 programs are listed in Table 7.12.

If a DSL/90 program reaches the maximum of a certain table, this difficulty can usually be removed by modifying the program. For example, if the SORT table exceeds its maximum, a sequence of statements which appears several times may be placed in a NOSORT section to remove it from the sort. If the maximum of 500 output variable names is reached, statements may be combined or nested to reduce the number of variable names. Consider the following three statements:

> A1 = B1 + SIN(B2)
> A2 = BLK1(A1)
> A3 = BLK2(A2,B1)

Table 7.12   DSL/90 programming restrictions

Item	Maximum
1. TYPE statements	10
2. Data statements	200
3. Output variable names (including names generated by DSL/90 as in MACROS)	500
4. Input variable names (includes parameters)	1,500
5. Integrators and statements with memory blocks	300
6. Parameter names	400
7. User-supplied memory blocks (unique)	25
8. Tables (STORAG variables)	25
9. Connection statements (including those generated by DSL/90)	600†
10. Simulator data storage (includes the current value of model variables, function and error tables, central integration history, and subscripted variable data storage)	8,000
11. Print output variables	50
12. Plot output variables	50
13. Graphs (independent)	10
14. Range variables	50
15. Finish specifications (not FINTIM or CLKTIM)	10

† Blanks are not considered in CONNECTION statements except for INTGRL, PROCED, and MACRO; therefore the average statement length is assumed to be about 48 characters, starting from column 1.

The first and third statements have two inputs and one output, and the second statement has one input and one output. Thus, a total of eight memory locations are required. If the statements are rewritten as

$$A3 = BLK2(BLK1(B1+SIN(B2)),B1)$$

only three locations are needed. Maximum size and utilization of each table are listed by the translator at the end of the translation phase.

7.7.5 INTEGRATION FUNCTION

Function INTGRL(IC,X), where X is the integrand and IC the initial condition, specifies the integration of X by means of centralized integration. With centralized integration, the derivative and integration routines are separated and executed alternately during each iteration cycle. An INTEG statement is required to select a particular integration subroutine. Available integration subroutines are listed in Table 7.11. Integration formulas from which these integration subroutines are programmed are listed below.

7.7.5.1 Integration function

(a) *Rectangular*

$$x_{n+1} = x_n + h \cdot x_n' \tag{7.3}$$

(b) *Trapezoidal*   Rectangular predictor to advance integrator output values:

$$x_{n+1} = x_n + h \cdot x_n' \tag{7.4}$$

Trapezoidal integration:

$$x_{n+1} = x_n + \frac{(x_n' + x_{n+1}')h}{2} \tag{7.5}$$

(c) *Simpson's rule*

$$x_{n+1} = x_n + \frac{(x_n' + 4x_{n+1/2}' + x_{n+1}')h}{6} \tag{7.6}$$

(d) *Runge-Kutta (fourth order)*

$$x_{n+1} = x_n + \frac{k_1 + 2k_2 + 2k_3 + k_4}{6} \tag{7.7}$$

$$k_1 = h \cdot f(t, x_n)$$

$$k_2 = h \cdot f\left(t_n + \frac{h}{2}, \ x_n + \frac{k_1}{2}\right)$$

$$k_3 = h \cdot f\left(t_n + \frac{h}{2}, \ x_n + \frac{k_2}{2}\right) \tag{7.8}$$

$$k_4 = h \cdot f(t_n + h, \ x_n + k_3)$$

(e) *Milne fifth-order predictor-corrector*
Predictor:

$$x_{n+1}^p = x_{n-1} + \frac{(8x_n' - 5x_{n-1}' + 4x_{n-2}' - x_{n-3}')h}{3} \tag{7.9}$$

Corrector:

$$x_{n+1}^c = \frac{x_n + 7x_{n-1}}{8} + \frac{(65x_{n+1}' + 243x_n' + 51x_{n-1}' + x_{n-2}')h}{192} \tag{7.10}$$

$$x_{n+1} = 0.96116x_{n+1}^c + 0.03884x_{n+1}^p \tag{7.11}$$

The integration interval (or step size) of the above predictor-corrector and Runge-Kutta subroutines varies automatically to a specified error criterion.   This factor allows the integration subroutine to take a larger or smaller step depending on the rate of change of one or more variables.   A different error bound may be specified for each integral and, by using CONTIN statements, for each portion of the simulation.

7.7.5.2 RELERR and ABSERR for MILNE and RKS routines For each integrator output, a user may specify values for the two system variables, RELERR and ABSERR, which are used to provide error control for varying steps in MILNE and RKS. The inequalities used to vary DELT are

(a) *For MILNE*

$$\left| \frac{x^c - x^p}{x^c} \right| \leq 4R \qquad \text{if } |x^c| > 1$$

$$|x^c - x^p| \leq 4R \qquad \text{if } |x^c| \leq 1 \qquad\qquad (7.12)$$

where x^p and x^c are the values computed from the MILNE predictor and corrector formulas, respectively, and R is the given value of RELERR. Note that MILNE does not use ABSERR.

(b) *For RKS*

$$|x_{n+1} - x_{\text{Simpson}}| \leq A + R - |x_{n+1}| \qquad\qquad (7.13)$$

where x_{n+1} is the value computed from RKS, and x_{Simpson} is that from Simpson's rule. R and A are the values of RELERR and ABSERR, respectively.

If RELERR and ABSERR are not specified by the user, they are assigned the values 10^{-5} and 10^{-4}, respectively. These values can be relaxed to obtain a better run time at the expense of accuracy of the result.

All data items entered into a DSL/90 program are not destroyed until subsequent replacement. This holds for RELERR and ABSERR. Once RELERR and ABSERR values have been specified, they can be replaced by reading in new values, or reset to 10^{-5} and 10^{-4}, respectively, by use of a RESET statement.

7.7.5.3 DELMAX and DELMIN for MILNE and RKS subroutines System variables DELMAX and DELMIN are provided for use with the MILNE and RKS integration subroutines. The value of DELMAX provides the upper bound for DELT, while that of DELMIN provides the lower bound. DELT will not be permitted to exceed DELMAX at any time during the run. On the other hand, if DELT has to be made smaller than DELMIN in order to satisfy specified error criterion, the simulation run will be terminated with an error message showing the value of DELT and the first offending integrator output variable. The job will continue with the next run, if any. If DELMAX and DELMIN are not specified by the user, they are assigned the values 10^{37} and $(10^{-8} \cdot \text{TIME})$, respectively. DELMAX, like DELMIN, is specified on a CONTRL statement.

As an example, consider the following statements:

```
INTEG    RKS
CONTRL   FINTIM = 2.0
END
CONTIN
CONTRL   FINTIM = 3.0,DELT = .001,DELMAX = .001
END
CONTIN
CONTRL   DELMAX = 100.0,FINTIM = 4.0
END
STOP
```

The first run ends at TIME equal to 2. The execution is continued during the second run, which ends at TIME equal to 3. However, DELT in the second run is given a value of .001 and, since DELMAX is given the same value, DELT will not be allowed to exceed .001. The execution is again continued with the third run, which ends at TIME equal to 4. During this last run, DELMAX is set to 100; this removes the previous constraint on DELT.

7.7.6 DERIVATIVE FUNCTION

Function $Y = \mathrm{DERIV}(\mathrm{IC},\mathrm{X})$ specifies derivative Y equal to dX/dt, where IC is the initial value of dX/dt. This function is approximated from a second-order Lagrange interpolation formula. The derivative at X equal to X_j is computed from the following polynomial:

$$Y_j = \prod_{k=0}^{2} (t_j - t_k) \sum_{k=0}^{2} \frac{X_k}{(t_j - t_k) \cdot \prod_{n=0}^{2} (t_k - t_n)} + \sum_{k=0}^{2} \frac{X_j}{t_j - t_k}$$

$$(k \neq j, n) \quad (7.14)$$

For example, when $j = 2$, we have

$$Y_2 = (t_2 - t_0)(t_2 - t_1)\left[\frac{X_0}{(t_2 - t_0)(t_0 - t_1)(t_0 - t_2)} \right.$$
$$\left. + \frac{X_1}{(t_2 - t_1)(t_1 - t_0)(t_1 - t_2)} \right] + \frac{X_2}{t_2 - t_0} + \frac{X_2}{t_2 - t_1} \quad (7.15)$$

7.7.7 NONLINEAR FUNCTION GENERATOR

Nonlinear function generator $Y = \mathrm{NLFGEN}(\mathrm{F},\mathrm{X})$ specifies

$$Y = \begin{cases} F(X) & \text{for } X_0 \leq X \leq X_n \\ F(X_0) & \text{for } X < X_0 \\ F(X_n) & \text{for } X > X_n \end{cases}$$

Function $F(X)$ is approximated by the following second-order Lagrange interpolation formula:

$$F(X) = Y_0 L_0{}^2(X) + Y_1 L_1{}^2(X) + Y_2 L_2{}^2(X) \qquad (7.16)$$

where

$$L_j{}^2(X) = \frac{\displaystyle\prod_{k=0}^{2} (X - X_k)}{(X - X_j) \cdot \displaystyle\prod_{k=0}^{2} (k \neq j)(X_j - X_k)} \qquad (7.17)$$

As an example, we have, for j equal to 1,

$$L_1{}^2(X) = \frac{(X - X_0)(X - X_1)(X - X_2)}{(X - X_1)(X_1 - X_0)(X_1 - X_2)} = \frac{(X - X_0)(X - X_2)}{(X_1 - X_0)(X_1 - X_2)} \qquad (7.18)$$

7.7.8 IMPLICIT FUNCTION

Function Y = IMPL(IC,ERROR,F) is provided for the solution of an implicit equation $f(y) = 0$, where IC is the starting value of y, F is equal to $f(y) + y$, and ERROR is the maximum relative error permitted.

This function is programmed by using the direct iteration method developed by Wegstein [1]. If there is no convergence in solving the equation after 100 iterations, this function produces a dump of all simulation variables, and identifies the loop wherein nonconvergence occurred. For example, the error message

***IMPLICIT LOOP 26 FAILED . . . DEBUG OUTPUT
FOLLOWS***

indicates nonconvergence of an implicit loop. To find out which loop, refer to the listing of the UPDATE subroutine. The loop with number 26 as its first argument is the one.

The user-supplied starting value (that is, IC as shown above) is used to begin the first series of iteration. For the succeeding series of iterations, the previously convergent solution is used as the starting value.

A statement number cannot be used with this function because the DSL/90 translator automatically tags the first and last statements of the implicit loop with internally generated numbers. These numbers for the IMPL function are generated in pairs beginning with 300001 and can be referenced for branching to an implicit loop.

As an example, consider the following implicit equation:

$$y = \frac{C(e^y - 1)}{e^y} \qquad (7.19)$$

where C is a constant.   This equation can be expressed by the following DSL/90 statements:

    Y = IMPL(Y0,ERROR,F)
    A = EXP(Y)
    F = C*(A−1.0)/A

The DSL/90 translator automatically generates the following statements:

    30001Y = IMPL(Y0,ERROR,F)
          IF(NALARM.LE.0)GO TO 30002
          A   = EXP(Y)
          F   = C*(A − 1.0)/A
    30002 CONTINUE

Three new statements are added to the ones written by the user.   The first time the IMPL subroutine is entered, NALARM is set to 1, and Y is given the initial guess Y0.   After each calculation of $f(y)$, the program returns to the IMPL subroutine, where the convergence criterion is tested. If the criterion is satisfied, NALARM is set equal to zero, and y assumes the most recently calculated value of $f(y)$.   If the convergence criterion is not satisfied, the iteration continues.   NALARM is set negative if convergence fails.   The error criterion is as follows:

$$\left| \frac{Y_{n+1} - Y_n}{Y_{n+1}} \right| \leq \text{ERROR} \qquad |Y_{n+1}| > 1$$
$$| Y_{n+1} - Y_n | \leq \text{ERROR} \qquad |Y_{n+1}| \leq 1 \tag{7.20}$$

7.7.9 DELAY FUNCTION

Function $Y = \text{DELAY}(N,P,X)$ produces an output Y which is the input delayed by an amount of P.   N is the number of storage locations that must be reserved in the memory, and it must be a positive integer of 10 or larger.   It is desirable to choose such an N that P/N is equal to DELT or larger.   DELT, however, varies in the variable-step integration subroutines MILNE and RKS, but it will not exceed the print or plot interval.   In this case, if DEL be the smaller of the print and plot intervals, the choice of N may be guided by the following relation:

$$10 \leq N \leq P/DEL$$

The delay is initialized at the first entry into the subroutine.   Therefore, it is permissible to switch an input into a DELAY function when TIME is larger than 0.

7.8 USER'S OPTIONS IN DSL/90 SIMULATION

The DSL/90 processor is written in FORTRAN IV and organized into functional subroutines. A user may use a DSL/90 program as a subprogram to be called by a FORTRAN main program, and may define functions for his DSL/90 program. These and other options in DSL/90 simulation are presented here.

7.8.1 DATA STORAGE

DSL/90 uses dynamic storage allocation (not in the translation phase). Storage areas in the core memory are assigned at execution time to tables, integrators, simulation variables, etc., according to the actual needs. Standard DSL/90 functions and FORTRAN functions are loaded only if used. Dynamic allocation storage leaves more space available in the core memory for the user's program because routines and tables not required do not take up the storage. (An alternative is to assign fixed areas to these tasks and functions; this gives no flexibility.)

If a user needs a storage area for a special purpose, he may have to know the area where the data are stored. This area is described by the following labeled COMMON statements:

```
COMMON/CURVAL/C(1)
COMMON/SYMBLS/NOINTG,NOSYMB,SYMB(1)
COMMON/KEYS/NALARM,KPOINT
COMMON/HMAX/H,KEEP
```

The labeled COMMON/CURVAL/ contains the current value of all DSL simulation and systems variables and function tables. The appearance of COMMON/CURVAL/X(1) in any subroutine makes X equivalent to C in the UPDATE subroutine. This gives the user access to the current values of all his variables. All the variable names in these COMMON statements are explained in Table 7.13.

7.8.2 LOCATING DSL/90 VARIABLES

Access to a specific variable in the COMMON/CURVAL/ area is to be achieved by a subroutine LOOK. This function allows the user to find the index of a variable in /CURVAL/. As an example, this function may be used in a subroutine that is executed with a simulation run in the following manner:

```
COMMON/CURVAL/X(1)
DATA XDOT/6HXDOT   /,NAME/3HFCN/
K = LOOK(XDOT)
N = LOOK(NAME)
```

Table 7.13   Descriptions of the names in COMMON statements

Name	Description
C(1)	First entry of a COMMON area which stores the values of all simulation variables, system variables, and function tables.
NOINTG	Number of integrators.
NOSYMB	Number of variable names (or symbols).
SYMB(1)	First entry of a table of names.
NALARM	When negative, the implicit function does not converge; when zero, it converges; when positive, it is computing the implicit function.
KPOINT	Index in /CURVAL/ which indicates the first entry available to the user. A user may advance KPOINT to give himself working storage.
KEEP	A value of 1, 0, or −1 which is set by the variable-step integration subroutine if the computation is for the next, past, or present value. Subroutines such as DERIV and DELAY must use KEEP to signify that the value is to be retained, disregarded, or used to replace the value of the last iteration.
H	Integration step size.

Any reference to $X(K)$ is a reference to the current value of the variable XDOT.

In the above example, the data for function generators are stored. Assume that the variable FCN is used as a function name on an AFGEN or an NLFGEN statement. Then, N is an index to locate in X [that is, $X(N)$] the value of the first independent variable from a table of consecutive pairs of values, and $X(N-1)$ contains the value for the last independent variable in the table. Since X is considered "real," the following statements are also required:

```
DIMENSION KX(1)
EQUIVALENCE (X,KX)
```

The first variables to appear in /CURVAL/ are TIME, DELT, DELMIN, FINTIM, and two other systems variables. If INTGRL is used, these systems variables are followed consecutively by integrator outputs, inputs, and initial conditions. To use TIME, the following statement is added:

```
EQUIVALENCE (X(1),TIME)
```

7.8.3 MAIN CONTROL ROUTINE

A user may define a main control routine in FORTRAN from which simulation subroutines can be called. Thus, a DSL/90 program can be incorporated into a FORTRAN program. In using this feature, the $IBLDR MAIN control card (i.e., the thirty-third card in Fig. 7.3) must be removed, and the user's main control routine substituted. The built-in main control routine appears as follows:

```
$IBFTC MAIN        DECK,LIST
       COMMON/CURVAL/C(1)
       CALL INITLZ
     3 CALL INTRAN
       CALL SIMUL
       GO TO 3
       END
```

In the above COMMON/CURVAL/ statement, C(1) should be specified because a previous program sets the maximum dimensions. Subroutine INITLZ initializes variables in the COMMON statements required to start a run. Subroutine INTRAN translates DSL/90 labeled statements and executes the required function in preparing for a simulation run. Subroutine SIMUL is the primary control program for the execution of the simulation. This control program essentially alternates between the execution of subroutine UPDATE, which computes derivatives, and the execution of a selected centralized integration routine, which integrates at specified TIME intervals and outputs at preselected TIME intervals. In the above main control routine, the loop is to test the current run and to establish initial conditions for the next run.

7.8.4 INTEGRATION SUBROUTINE

The user may provide his own integration subroutine. In this case, the $IBLDR CENTRL card (i.e., the thirty-fourth card in Fig. 7.3) is removed from the control cards, and the user's subroutine substitutes the dummy library subroutine CENTRL.

The calling sequence is CENTRL(NOINT,X,Y,WORK), where NOINT is the number of integrators, X and Y are locations of integrator inputs and outputs, and WORK is the area for retaining input and output histories. If any centralized integration scheme is used, area WORK is allocated as 17 times the number of integrators. Initial conditions are set prior to the first entry to subroutine UPDATE.

A NOCENT statement allows the central integration to be disregarded even though function INTGRL is used. In this case, subroutine UPDATE is called twice by the simulator with TIME equal to zero to

set initial conditions; then the simulation is executed with subroutine
UPDATE only.   If there is integration, an integration subroutine must
be provided, and the name of the subroutine must be specified on a
MEMORY statement.

7.8.5 IMPLICIT FUNCTION

The user may provide his own implicit function block, which should be
named IMPLCT.   The translator handles this replacement block exactly
as it handles IMPL.   The user is expected to set NALARM (see Table
7.13) based on his own convergence criterion.   Implicit blocks are treated
as MEMORY blocks with five available history elements.   The following
statements appear in IMPLCT:

REAL FUNCTION IMPLCT(N, FIRST, ERROR, FUNCT)
COMMON/KEYS/NALARM/CURVAL/TIME/MEMRY/C(1)

7.8.6 USER–SUPPLIED FUNCTIONS

Over fifty DSL/90 simulation functions (or blocks) are provided, either
by special subroutines or by existing FORTRAN routines.   If the user
requires a block that is unavailable in the library, he may define his own
block by following the FORTRAN specifications and add it to the library,
and may then use this block just as any other block.

If this particular block contains multiple outputs, the FORTRAN
subroutine form must be used.   In this case, the output arguments, as
called out in the DSL/90 connection statements, appear in their same
sequence but on the right-hand side of the subroutine argument string.
As an example,

Y1,Y2 = FLIP(RESET,TRIG)

The above statement is programmed by the user as a FORTRAN subroutine with an input argument string as follows:

SUBROUTINE FLIP(RESET,TRIG,Y1,Y2)

One caution is that the block INTGRL cannot appear as an input argument for a multiple-output block.

At execution time, all user-supplied subprograms are placed directly
behind the STOP card.   These subprograms may be an intermix of source
language decks and binary decks from previous compilations.   Binary
decks may be added to the DSL library by loading them behind the main
control routine on the library tape, and by including a $IBLDR card in
the control cards.

MEMORY blocks (i.e., blocks contain initial condition and history)
require special consideration.   With each use of the block, a unique stor-

age area must be assigned for history, and the initial values of history at
TIME = 0 must be set by the user (the derivative subroutine UPDATE
is executed twice at TIME = 0).   Since a MEMORY block, like an integrator, is a starting point of a closed loop, this block must be identified
to the SORT routine.   Note that in a feedback loop a time lag is created,
regardless of the block sequence.   Either a predictor formula may be
inserted within one block of the loop, as is the case with INTGRL, or a
special block may be added to advance an output.

7.9   ADDITIONAL EXAMPLES

Three additional examples are provided in this section.   These examples
are to show the user-supplied FORTRAN subroutine and the user-
supplied main control routine.

7.9.1   AIRCRAFT–ARRESTING GEAR SYSTEM DESIGN

The first example is the previous simulation of an aircraft-arresting gear
system.   The MIMIC program is shown in Fig. 3.34, and the DSL/90
program is shown in Fig. 7.13.   Both are programmed from equations
(3.38) through (3.45).

This DSL/90 program shows the use of INSW, RELERR, ABSERR,
AFGEN, RANGE, RESET, and CONTIN statements.   It also shows a
procedural block for selecting variable FD, an implicit function (IMPL)
in solving for variable THETA.   In addition, it shows a user-supplied,
multiple-output FORTRAN subroutine RESOLV.

Four runs are specified, as there are four END statements.   The
first run is terminated at TIME equal to 8 using the variable-step MILNE
integration subroutine.   Ranges of six variables are required and specified.   Output is printed at intervals of 0.1, and variables Y3DOT, X,
and XDOT are plotted vs. TIME on a single 8- by 6-in. graph with
points at intervals of 0.05.   The relative error on all equations is set at
0.00001.

The second run is the same as the first run except that one initial
condition, termination TIME, and the variables to be printed out are
changed.

The third run continues from the last computed values of the second
run as specified by the CONTIN statement.   It cancels plotting, changes
the variables for print output and the print interval, and sets additional
termination conditions on a FINISH statement.

The fourth run specifies a new title and changes to Runge-Kutta
integration subroutine.   It cancels the termination conditions on the
FINISH statement, the relative error criterion, and the request for vari-

```
TITLE ***DSL/90 PROGRAM FOR AIRCRAFT ARRESTING GEAR SYSTEM DESIGN
      SQR1=SQRT(X**2+H**2)
      Y23=Y2-Y3
      FK2=INSW(Y23,0.0,K2*Y23)
      Y12=SQR1-H-2.0*Y2
      FK1=INSW(Y12,0.0,K1*Y12)
PROCED FD=FCNY3(Y3,Y3DOT)
      IF(Y3)5,4,4
   4  FD=AFGEN(FOFY3,Y3)*Y3DOT**2
      GO TO 6
   5  FD=20.*Y3DOT**2
   6  CONTINUE
ENDPRO
      XDOT = INTGRL(XDOT0,-2.*FK1*(X/SQR1)/M1)
      X=INTGRL(X0,XDOT)
      Y3DOT = INTGRL(Y3DOT0,(FK2-FD)/M3)
      Y3=INTGRL(Y30,Y3DOT)
      Y2 = INTGRL(0.0,INTGRL(Y2DOT0,(2.0*FK1-FK2)/M2))
      THETA = IMPL(THETA0,ERROR,FOFTH)
      SINTH*COSTH=RESOLV(THETA)
      R=H*COSTH+X*SINTH
      FOFTH=(X*COSTH-H*SINTH+R*THETA)/R
PARAM H=125., THETA0=0.0, ERROR=1.B-4
CONST K1 = 4550.   , K2=25300., M1=1400., M2=45.28, M3=20.
INCON X0=0.0, Y3DOT0=0.0, Y30=0.0, Y2DOT0=0.0, XDOT0=290.
AFGEN FOFY3=   0. , 8.33, 30. ,  4. , 60. , 1.6,120. , 5.2,150., 5.2,....
            180. , 6.6 ,210. ,  8.3,240. , 10.7,270. ,16. ,282.,21. ,....
            294. ,28.  ,306. , 41. ,312. , 50. ,324. ,90.,999.,90.
INTEG MILNE
RELERR    XDOT=.00001
CONTRL DELT=0.002, DELMIN=1.0E-10, FINTIM=8.0
RANGE     X,XDOT,Y3,Y3DOT,Y2,DELT
PRINT     0.1,Y3,Y2,X,THETA,DELT
PREPAR    .05,X,XDOT,ANGLE,Y2,Y3,Y3DOT
GRAPH     8.,6.,TIME,Y3DOT,X,XDOT
LABEL     AIRCRAFT ARRESTING GEAR SYSTEM
END
*
INCON XDOT0=200.
CONTRL     FINTIM=6.0
PRINT     0.1,     Y3DOT,Y3,Y12,FD,FK2,FK1,SQR1,XDOT,X,DELT,THETA
END
*
CONTIN
RESET     GRAPH,PRLPAR
CONTRL    FINTIM=10.
PRINT     0.5,    X,XDOT,Y3,Y3DOT,Y2,DELT
FINISH    XDOT=9.5,THETA=1.427
END
*
TITLE AIRCRAFT ARRESTING GEAR SYSTEM DESIGN-RUN4 (RUNGE-KUTTA)
INTEG     RKS
RESET     FINISH, RELERR, RANGE
RELERR    XDOT=1.E-5
ABSERR       XDOT=1.E-4
CONTRL    DELT=0.005, CLKTIM=100.
END
*
STOP,
$IBFTC RESOLV    DECK
      SUBROUTINE RESOLV(THETA,SINE,COSINE)
SINE=SIN(THETA)
COSINE=COS(THETA)
RETURN
END
```

Fig. 7.13 DSL/90 program for simulating aircraft-arresting gear system.

able ranges.   It sets new relative and absolute error criteria as well as a clock time such that the run halts when the total run time reaches 100 sec.

The final part of the first run is shown in Fig. 7.14, where are also shown the maxima and minima of six variables (prescribed by a RANGE statement) as well as the times at which these maxima and minima occur.   In addition, the simulation time and the graph preparation time are shown.   An initial part of the second run is shown in Fig. 7.15; it is tabulated in equation form.

7.9.2   PILOT-EJECTION SIMULATION

The second example is simulation of the pilot-ejection system which has been shown previously.   The MIMIC program was shown in Fig.

```
***DSL/90 PROGRAM FOR AIRCRAFT ARRESTING GEAR SYSTEM DESIGN

    TIME          Y3              Y2              X             THETA            DELT
  5.500E 00    3.6642E 02     3.6652E 02      8.4914E 02     1.4246E 00     2.5000E-02
  5.600E 00    3.6694E 02     3.6703E 02      8.5016E 02     1.4248E 00     1.2500E-02
  5.700E 00    3.6744E 02     3.6753E 02      8.5116E 02     1.4250E 00     1.2500E-02
  5.800E 00    3.6793E 02     3.6802E 02      8.5215E 02     1.4251E 00     2.5000E-02
  5.900E 00    3.6842E 02     3.6850E 02      8.5313E 02     1.4253E 00     2.5000E-02
  6.000E 00    3.6890E 02     3.6898E 02      8.5409E 02     1.4255E 00     2.5000E-02
  6.100E 00    3.6937E 02     3.6945E 02      8.5503E 02     1.4256E 00     2.5000E-02
  6.200E 00    3.6984E 02     3.6992E 02      8.5596E 02     1.4258E 00     2.5000E-02
  6.300E 00    3.7030E 02     3.7037E 02      8.5688E 02     1.4259E 00     2.5000E-02
  6.400E 00    3.7075E 02     3.7082E 02      8.5778E 02     1.4261E 00     1.2500E-02
  6.500E 00    3.7120E 02     3.7127E 02      8.5867E 02     1.4262E 00     2.5000E-02
  6.600E 00    3.7164E 02     3.7171E 02      8.5955E 02     1.4264E 00     2.5000E-02
  6.700E 00    3.7207E 02     3.7214E 02      8.6042E 02     1.4265E 00     2.5000E-02
  6.800E 00    3.7250E 02     3.7256E 02      8.6128E 02     1.4267E 00     2.5000E-02
  6.900E 00    3.7292E 02     3.7298E 02      8.6212E 02     1.4268E 00     2.5000E-02
  7.000E 00    3.7334E 02     3.7340E 02      8.6296E 02     1.4269E 00     2.5000E-02
  7.100E 00    3.7375E 02     3.7381E 02      8.6378E 02     1.4271E 00     2.5000E-02
  7.200E 00    3.7416E 02     3.7421E 02      8.6460E 02     1.4272E 00     2.5000E-02
  7.300E 00    3.7456E 02     3.7461E 02      8.6540E 02     1.4273E 00     1.2500E-02
  7.400E 00    3.7495E 02     3.7501E 02      8.6619E 02     1.4275E 00     2.5000E-02
  7.500E 00    3.7534E 02     3.7540E 02      8.6698E 02     1.4276E 00     2.5000E-02
  7.600E 00    3.7573E 02     3.7578E 02      8.6775E 02     1.4277E 00     2.5000E-02
  7.700E 00    3.7611E 02     3.7616E 02      8.6851E 02     1.4279E 00     2.5000E-02
  7.800E 00    3.7649E 02     3.7654E 02      8.6927E 02     1.4280E 00     2.5000E-02
  7.900E 00    3.7686E 02     3.7691E 02      8.7002E 02     1.4281E 00     1.2500E-02
  8.000E 00    3.7723E 02     3.7728E 02      8.7076E 02     1.4282E 00     1.2500E-02
```

VARIABLE	MINIMUM	TIME	MAXIMUM	TIME
X	0.	0.	8.7076E 02	8.0000E 00
XDOT	7.3473E 00	8.0000E 00	2.9000E 02	0.
Y3	0.	0.	3.7723E 02	8.0000E 00
Y3DOT	0.	0.	1.3241E 02	7.5000E-01
Y2	0.	0.	3.7728E 02	8.0000E 00
DELT	1.5625E-03	3.0500E 00	2.5000E-02	1.1500E 00

DSL/90 SIMULATION TIME =   1.226 SECONDS

GRAPH PREPARATION TIME =   0.420 SECONDS

Fig. 7.14   Table output from the program in Fig. 7.13.

```
***DSL/90 PROGRAM FCR AIRCRAFT ARRESTING GEAR SYSTEM DFSIGN
TIME  =  0.            Y3DOT =  0.        Y3   =  0.          Y12  = -0.        FD   =  0.
                       FK1   = -0.        SQR1 =  1.2500E 02  XDOT =  2.0000E 02  A    =  0.
                       THETA = -0.

TIME  =  1.0000E-01    Y3DOT =  3.9520E 00  Y3   =  7.5966E-02  Y12  =  1.1843E 00  FD   =  1.2993E 02
                       FK1   =  5.3887E 03  SQR1 =  1.2659E 02  XDOT =  1.9997E 02  X    =  1.9999E 01
                       THETA =  1.5865E-01

TIME  =  2.0000E-01    Y3DOT =  2.6804E 01  Y3   =  1.5807E 00  Y12  =  2.2793E 00  FD   =  5.8206E 03
                       FK1   =  1.0371E 04  SQR1 =  1.3124E 02  XDOT =  1.9967E 02  X    =  3.9984E 01
                       THETA =  3.0959E-01

TIME  =  3.0000E-01    Y3DOT =  4.2944E 01  Y3   =  5.1772E 00  Y12  =  2.0284E 00  FD   =  1.3984E 04
                       FK1   =  9.2292E 03  SQR1 =  1.3862E 02  XDOT =  1.9915E 02  X    =  5.9926E 01
                       THETA =  4.4704E-01
```

Fig. 7.15 Table output from the program in Fig. 7.13.

3.29, and the DSL/90 program is shown in Fig. 7.16. This example shows the use of a user-supplied main control routine.

In this pilot-ejection simulation, initial values of velocity V and angle θ $[V(0)$ and $\theta(0)]$ have to be computed for use in the simulation. This is done in the DSL/90 program by providing a main control routine which is a FORTRAN program. As shown in Fig. 7.16, the main control routine starts at the $IBFTC card. It first finds the locations of $V(0)$ and $\theta(0)$ and V_a in the COMMON area labeled CURVAL, which begins at C(1). After some simple calculations, the main control routine calls subroutine INITLZ to initialize the variables in the COMMON area. It then calls subroutine INTRAN, which translates the labeled statements of the first run in the DSL/90 program. Initial values $V(0)$ and $\theta(0)$ are next calculated. It then calls subroutine SIMUL, which is the primary control program to execute the simulation. When the execution of the first run is completed by subroutine SIMUL, it calls subroutine INTRAN again to translate the labeled statements for the second run. This process continues until all the runs specified in the DSL/90 program are completed.

The preparation of the main control routine in FORTRAN in a DSL/90 program makes the DSL/90 program become essentially a FORTRAN program which calls the subprograms translated from the DSL/90 program proper. This is particularly so if the main control program is much larger than the DSL/90 program proper, as is the third example.

It should be noted that, when a main control routine is used, the thirty-third $IBLDR MAIN card in Fig. 7.3 should be removed, as the main control routine from the DSL/90 processor is no longer required.

The DSL/90 program in Fig. 7.16 has labeled statements for four runs. The initial parts of the first run are shown in Fig. 7.17. Note the printed message that simulation is halted at $X = -6.5027E+01$.

```
TITLE ***DSL/90 PROGRAM FOR PILOT EJECTION SIMULATION
      X=INTGRL(0.,V*COS(TH)-VA)
      Y=INTGRL(0.,V*SIN(TH))
      V1=-D/M-G*SIN(TH)
      Y2=Y-Y1
      VDOT=INSW(Y2,0.,V1)
      V=INTGRL(VO,VDOT)
      TH1=-G*COS(TH)/V
      THDOT=INSW(Y2,0.,TH1)
      TH=INTGRL(THO,THDOT)
      D=.5*RHO*CD*S*V*V
PARAM VA=900.,RHO=2.3769E-3
CONST G=32.2,M=7.,CD=1.,S=10.,Y1=4.
CONTRL FINTIM=4.,DELT=.05
FINISH Y=30.,X=-60.
PRINT .05,VDOT,V,TH,X,Y
INTEG RKS
END
*
INTEG MILNE
CONTRL FINTIM=4.,DELT=.05
FINISH Y=30.,X=-60.
PRINT .05,VDOT,V,TH,X,Y
END
*
PARAM VA=500.,RHO=2.3769E-3
INTEG RKS
CONTRL FINTIM=4.,DELT=.05
FINISH Y=30.,X=-60.
PRINT .05,VDOT,V,TH,X,Y
END
*
INTEG MILNE
CONTRL FINTIM=4.,DELT=.05
FINISH Y=30.,X=-60.
PRINT .05,VDOT,V,TH,X,Y
END
*
STOP
$IBFTC MAIN      DECK,LIST
      COMMON/CURVAL/C(1)
      DATA VA/6HVA     /,THO/6HTHO     /,VO/6HVO
      KVA=LOOK(VA)
      KTHO=LOOK(THO)
      KVO=LOOK(VO)
      VE=40.
      THE=15./57.3
      A1=VE*SIN(THE)
      A2=VE*COS(THE)
      CALL INITLZ
    1 CALL INTRAN
      C(KVO)=SQRT((C(KVA)-A1)**2+A2**2)
      C(KTHO)=ATAN(A2/(C(KVA)-A1))
      CALL SIMUL
      GO TO 1
      END
```

Fig. 7.16 DSL/90 program for the pilot-ejection simulation.

***DSL/90 PROGRAM FOR PILOT EJECTION SIMULATION

TIME	VOUT	V	TH	X	Y
0.	0.	5.J04JF 02	4.3403E-02	0.	0.
5.000E-02	0.	5.9049E 02	4.3403F-02	-5.1760F-01	1.9319E 00
1.000F-01	0.	8.9049E 02	4.3403E-02	-1.03529 00	3.8637F 00
1.500E-01	-1.1765E 03	8.3196E 02	4.1604E-02	-2.7410L 00	5.7013F 00
2.000E-01	-1.0263E 03	7.7702E 02	3.9662F-02	-7.7811E 00	7.3361E 00
2.500E-01	-9.0318E 02	7.2869E 02	3.7523E-02	-1.5187E 01	8.7386E 00
3.000E-01	-8.0093E 02	6.8635E 02	3.5248E-02	-2.4951E 01	1.0076E 01
3.500F-01	-7.1509F 02	6.4851E 02	3.2835E-02	-3.6517F 01	1.1212E 01
4.000E-01	-6.4234E 02	6.1463E 02	3.0265E-02	-4.9369E 01	1.2206E 01
4.500E-01	-5.8013E 02	5.8410E 02	2.7598E-02	-6.5027E 01	1.3076E 01

SIMULATION HALTED, X   = -6.5027E 01

DSL/90 SIMULATION TIME =   0.087 SECONDS

Fig. 7.17 Table output from the program in Fig. 7.16.

7.9.3 PARAMETER OPTIMIZATION USING BINARY SEARCH METHOD

The third example shows optimization of a parameter of a simple feed-back control system [10]; the block diagram of the control system is shown in Fig. 7.18, where feedback gain α is the parameter to be optimized.

Output $c(t)$ of the control system in Fig. 7.18 can be expressed by the following differential equation:

$$\ddot{c} + K_2\alpha\dot{c} + K_1K_2c = K_1K_2r(t) \tag{7.21}$$

where $r(t)$ is the input, and K_1 and K_2 are two constants of the system. Let the difference between $r(t)$ and $c(t)$ be called $e(t)$, or

$$e(t) = r(t) - c(t) \tag{7.22}$$

If the performance criterion is to minimize the mean-square error of the response, we then compute the following integral q:

$$q(\alpha) = \int_0^t e^2(t)\, dt \tag{7.23}$$

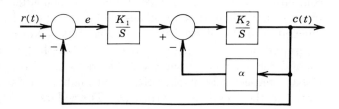

Fig. 7.18 Block diagram of a feedback control system.

An optimizing algorithm has been developed [2] which makes use of the binary search method. The maximum and minimum values of α's ($\alpha_{\max}$ and $\alpha_{\min}$), initial value of α (α_1), and increment in α ($\Delta\alpha$) are first established or estimated. The algorithm obtains two values of q_i and q_{i-1} from two values of α_i and α_{i-1} and then determines whether the difference ($q_i - q_{i-1}$) is positive, zero, or negative. If the difference is positive, a new α_i and a new $\alpha_{\max}$ are obtained, as below:

$$\alpha_i = \frac{\alpha_{i-1} + \alpha_{\max}}{2}$$

$$\alpha_{\max} = \alpha_{i-1}$$

If the difference is negative, a new α_i and a new $\alpha_{\min}$ are obtained, as below:

$$\alpha_i = \frac{\alpha_{i-1} + \alpha_{\min}}{2}$$

$$\alpha_{\min} = \alpha_{i-1}$$

If the difference is zero, the optimization is terminated. When the difference is positive or negative, two values of q_i and q_{i+1} are again obtained from the new α_i and α_{i+1}. This process continues until the following condition is met:

$$|q_{i+1} - q_i| < \Delta q$$

where Δq is the specified maximum difference. It has been shown that the optimum value of α for this system is

$$\alpha_{\mathrm{opt}} = \sqrt{\frac{K_1}{K_2}}$$

For K_1 and K_2 equal to 2 and 4, respectively, we have

$$\alpha_{\mathrm{opt}} = 0.707107$$

Computation of Eqs. (7.21) through (7.23) is programmed in the DSL/90 language; this part is analogous to that performed by an analog computer. The optimizing algorithm is implemented by the main control routine; this part is analogous to digital logic. This arrangement is illustrated in the block diagram of Fig. 7.19. Notice that the "analog computer" receives an α and delivers a q, while the "digital logic" receives a q and delivers an α. These α and q are to be referred as C(KALP) and C(KQ), respectively, in the subsequent main control routine, as they are stored in the locations of array C. The values of KQ and KALP are obtained by the LOOK functions. The initial part of the main control

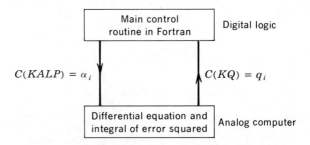

Fig. 7.19 Block diagram of a hybrid simulation by DSL/90 programming.

routine appears as below:

```
COMMON/CURVAL/C(1)
DIMENSION ALPHA(30), QA(30)
KQ = LOOK(Q)
KALP = LOOK(ALP)
```

Arrays ALPHA and QA in the above DIMENSION statement store the successive values of α and q, respectively.

Equations (7.21) through (7.23) can be expressed by the following DSL/90 connection statements:

```
CDOT = INTGRL(0.,KL2*(R − C) − K2*ALP*CDOT)
C = INTGRL(0.,CDOT)
E = R − C
Q = INTGRL(0.,E*E)
```

Table 7.14 Equivalent symbols

Equation	Program	Value or remark
K_1	K1	2
K_2	K2	4
$K_1 K_2$	K12	8
r	R	$u(t)$, input
c	C	Output
α	ALP	Parameter
e	E	Error
q	Q	Integral of e^2
Δq	DELQ	0.0000001
$\Delta \alpha$	DELA	0.0001
α_{max}	ALPMAX	1.
α_{min}	ALPMIN	0.
α_1	ALPHA(1)[8]	0.5

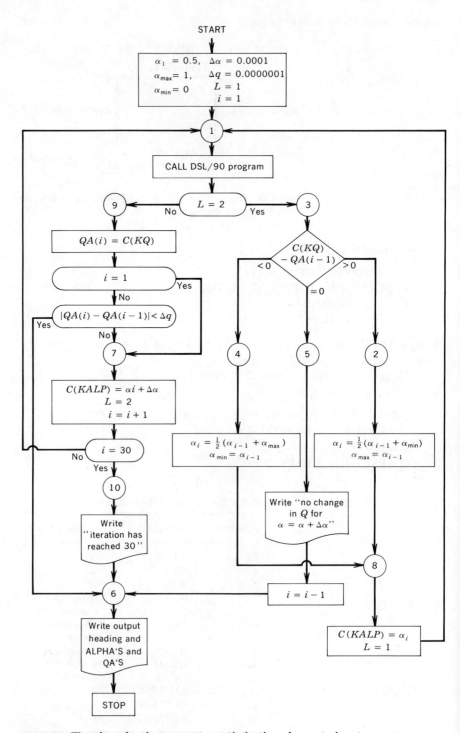

Fig. 7.20 Flowchart for the parameter optimization of a control system.

```
TITLE **DSL/90 PROGRAM FOR PARAMETER OPTIMIZATION
      CDOT=INTGRL(0.,K12*(1.-C)-K2*ALP*CDOT)
      C=INTGRL(0.,CDOT)
      E=1.-C
      Q=INTGRL(0.,E*E)
CONST K2=4.,K12=8.
CONTRL DELT=.1,FINTIM=10.
PRINT 1.,C,Q,ALP
END
STOP
$IBFTC MAIN
      COMMON/CURVAL/C(1)
      DIMENSION ALPHA(30),QA(30),INDEX(30)
      DATA Q       /6HQ       /,ALP   /6HALP     /
  100 FORMAT(1H ,38H THERE IS NO CHANGE IN Q FOR ALPHA+DELA)
  101 FORMAT(1H ,29H THE ITERATION HAS REACHED 30)
  102 FORMAT(1H ,10X,5HINDEX,3X,5HALPHA,12X,1HQ/)
  103 FORMAT(1H ,10X,I5,2F12.8)
      KQ=LOOK(Q)
      KALP=LOOK(ALP)
C        INITILIZATION OF PARAMETERS
      ALPHA(1)=.5
      ALPMAX = 1.0
      ALPMIN = 0.0
      C(KALP)=ALPHA(1)
      DELA=.001
      DELQ=1.0E-7
      I=1
      INDEX(I)=I
      L=1
      CALL INITLZ
      CALL INTRAN
    1 CALL SIMUL
      GO TO (9,3), L
    9 QA(I)   =C(KQ)
      IF(I.EQ.1) GO TO 7
C        TEST FOR CONVERGENCE
      IF (ABS(QA(I)-QA(I-1)).LT.DELQ) GO TO 6
    7 C(KALP)=ALPHA(I)+DELA
      L=2
      I=I+1
      INDEX(I)=I
      IF(I.EQ.30) GO TO 10
      GO TO 1
C        TEST FOR DIRECTION OF CHANGE IN ALPHA
    3 IF(C(KQ)-QA(I-1)) 4,5,2
    4 ALPHA(I)=.5*(ALPHA(I-1)+ALPMAX)
      ALPMIN   =ALPHA(I-1)
      GO TO 8
    2 ALPHA(I)=.5*(ALPHA(I-1)+ALPMIN)
      ALPMAX   =ALPHA(I-1)
    8 C(KALP)=ALPHA(I)
      L=1
      GO TO 1
    5 WRITE(6,100)
      GO TO 6
   10 WRITE(6,101)
    6 WRITE(6,102)
      WRITE(6,103) (INDEX(J),ALPHA(J),QA(J),J=1,I)
      STOP
      END
```

Fig. 7.21 DSL/90 program for the parameter optimization of a control system.

Figure 7.20 is a flowchart showing the optimizing algorithm. Index i is the pointer of arrays ALPHA and QA. The block labeled inside with "call DSL/90 PROGRAM" means the computation of Eqs. (7.21) through (7.23). There is a switch L with two values, 1 and 2. When L is equal to 1, α is incremented by $\Delta\alpha$. When L is equal to 2, a new α is established after the comparison $C(KQ) - QA(i-1)$, which means $(q_i - q_{i-1})$. Notice that one of two successive values of α_i and α_{i+1} is obtained when L is 2 and the other when L is 1. The optimization can also be terminated when there are 30 iterations.

Values of constants and input for an optimization are chosen and shown in Table 7.14. The DSL/90 program, together with the main control routine, is shown in Fig. 7.21. The DSL/90 program proper is relatively short. Equivalent symbols are shown in Table 7.14; the translated subprograms are shown in Fig. 7.22; the result is shown in Fig. 7.23. In the lower part of Fig. 7.23, there are eight values of α, which means eight tries; these values form a sequence produced from a binary search. There are 16 computations of Q; Fig. 7.23 shows the result of the second computation of Q for each try. The final value of α is 0.70703125, which is

```
BLOCK DATA
COMMON/SYMBLS/NOINTG,NOSYMB,SYMB(   19)
COMMON/KEYS/NALARM,KPOINT,Y(17)
COMMON/CURVAL/C(8000)
DIMENSION LC(8000)
EQUIVALENCE (LC,C)
DATA KPOINT/   20/,NOINTG/   3/,NOSYMB/   19/,     SYMB(1)/   114HTIME
1DELT   DELMINFINTIMCLKTIMDELMAXCDOT   C       Q         ZZ0003ZZ0009ZZ0008
1ZZ0002ZZ0005ZZ0007K2     K12     ALP     E
1 /
DATA C( 13)/0.           /
DATA C( 14)/0.           /
DATA C( 15)/0.           /
END




SUBROUTINE UPDATE
COMMON/CURVAL/TIME   ,DELT   ,DELMIN,FINTIM,CLKTIM,DELMAX
1 ,CDOT   ,C       ,Q       ,ZZ0003,ZZ0009,ZZ0008,ZZ0002,ZZ0005,ZZ0007
1 ,K2     ,K12     ,ALP     ,E
REAL       K2
1 ,K12     ,INTGRL
C   CDOT   =INTGRL(ZZ0002,ZZ0003)
C   C      =INTGRL(ZZ0005,CDOT )
E=1.-C
ZZ0003=E*E
C   Q      =INTGRL(ZZ0007,ZZ0008)
ZZ0008=K12*(1.-C)-K2*ALP*CDOT
ZZ0009 =   CDOT
RETURN
END
```

Fig. 7.22 Translated subprograms from the program in Fig. 7.21.

```
***DSL/90 PROGRAM FOR PARAMETER OPTIMIZATION

  TIME          C             Q             ALP
  0.            0.            0.            7.0713E-01
  1.000E 00     1.0976E 00    3.3833E-01    7.0713E-01
  2.000E 00     1.0226E 00    3.5311E-01    7.0713E-01
  3.000E 00     9.8581E-01    3.5352E-01    7.0713E-01
  4.000E 00     1.0040E 00    3.5355E-01    7.0713E-01
  5.000E 00     9.9934E-01    3.5355E-01    7.0713E-01
  6.000E 00     1.0000E 00    3.5355E-01    7.0713E-01
  7.000E 00     9.9997E-01    3.5355E-01    7.0713E-01
  8.000E 00     9.9994E-01    3.5355E-01    7.0713E-01
  9.000E 00     9.9998E-01    3.5355E-01    7.0713E-01
  1.000E 01     1.0000E 00    3.5355E-01    7.0713E-01

DSL/90 SIMULATION TIME =    0.031 SECONDS

THERE IS NO CHANGE IN Q FOR ALPHA+DELA
         INDEX    ALPHA           Q
           1    0.50000000    0.37500135
           2    0.75000000    0.35416549
           3    0.62500000    0.35624934
           4    0.68750000    0.35369216
           5    0.71875000    0.35359944
           6    0.70312500    0.35355806
           7    0.71093750    0.35355750
           8    0.70703125    0.35355239
```

Fig. 7.23 Table output from the program in Fig. 7.21.

close to the α_{opt} of 0.707107.   A closer result can be obtained by using
smaller values of $\Delta\alpha$ and Δq.

REFERENCES

1. Wegstein, J.: "Accelerating Convergence of Iterative Processes," National Bureau
   of Standards, Washington, D.C.
2. Mitchell, B. A.: "A Hybrid/Analog-Digital One-Parameter Optimizer," ACL
   Memo No. 69, Department of Electrical Engineering, University of Arizona,
   April, 1963.
3. Hurley, J. R., and J. J. Skiles: DYSAC: A Digital Simulated Analog Computer,
   Proc. Spring Joint Computer Conf., 1963, pp. 69–82.
4. Brennan, R. D., and R. N. Lineberger: A Survey of Digital Simulation: Digital
   Analog Simulator Programs, *Simulation*, vol. 3, no. 6, pp. 22–36, December,
   1964.
5. Syn, W. M., and D. G. Wyman: DSL/90 Digital Simulation Language User's
   Guide, *Rept. San José* TR 02.355, IBM Corporation, San José, Calif., July 1,
   1965.
6. Syn, W. M., and D. G. Wyman: DSL/90 Digital Simulation Language Systems
   Guide, IBM Corporation, San José, Calif., July 15, 1965.
7. Clancy, J. J., and M. S. Fineberg: Digital Simulation Languages: A Critique and
   Guide, *Proc. Fall Joint Computer Conf.*, vol. 27, pp. 22–36, 1965.

8. Syn, W. M., and R. N. Lineberger: DSL/90: A Digital Simulation Program for Continuous System Modeling, *Proc. Spring Joint Computer Conf.*, 1966, pp. 165–187.
9. Syn, W. M.: DSL/90 User's Guide Supplement, Notes, IBM Corporation, San José, Calif., Nov. 11, 1966.
10. Bloom, H. M.: "Problem Solving by Digital-Analog Simulation," thesis for master of science, Department of Electrical Engineering, University of Maryland, July, 1967.
11. Dost, M. H., and R. R. Barber: Simulation of Electron Beam Control Systems Using DSL/90, *Simulation*, November, 1967, pp. 237–247.

Appendix

Control Cards for the DSL/90 Program

The listing in Fig. 7.3 consists of 36 control cards for accepting a DSL/90 program by one of the computer systems at the University of Maryland. These control cards are rather similar to other computer systems accepting DSL/90 programs. Since an understanding of the control cards helps the user to use the computer system more effectively, these cards are explained below.

The zeroth card (DSL/90 0 in columns 73 to 80) is a $JOB card, which is the first card in each job deck and indicates the job number (123400 in this example). When this card is read, the control is turned over to the IBSYS monitor of the IBSYS operating system. The $IBSYS card defines the beginning of a job segment for the IBSYS monitor. When this first card is read, the system supervisor of the IBSYS monitor reads and processes the subsequent control cards. The next two $* cards are comment cards, which cause no action except that the comments are printed out by an on-line printer. One comment requests the operator to mount tape No. CSC-928 (SYSCK1) on tape station A5 with the ring out, and the other notifies him that the tapes on stations B5 and B6 are

413

scratch tapes. The fourth, or $PAUSE, card causes the printer to print out the contents of this card to serve as a message. It also turns on a red light and then causes the computer to stop. When the operator has mounted the requested tape, he pushes a START button and the computer resumes operation.

The fifth and sixth cards, which form a pair, cause tape station B5 to be logically attached to the computer and then assigned as a system unit for plot tape SYSLB4. Similarly, the seventh and eighth cards cause tape station B6 to be logically attached and assigned as a system unit for output tape SYSUT6 (on which the translated subprograms are to be written). The ninth and tenth, or $REWIND, cards cause tapes SYSCK1 and SYSUT6 to be rewound.

The eleventh, or $EXECUTE, card contains the name IBJOB. This card signals the beginning of a job segment. (A DSL/90 program actually consists of two job segments. The first is to generate two FORTRAN subprograms, and the second is to carry out the simulation.) When this card is read by the system supervisor, it passes control to the IBJOB processor. The twelfth, or $ID, card gives identification of the user, project number, and options such as limit on execution time of the program and limit on number of pages. The thirteenth, or $IBJOB, card initiates the IBJOB processor and registers the requests for various options. This card requests the printout of a core storage map and loading of the FIOCS package specially for FORTRAN IV object program. The fourteenth, or $IEDIT, card causes reading of the DSL/90 processor tape SYSCK1 on station A5 and searching of the first file for the subprograms with the deck names on the subsequent control cards.

Each of the next 15 ($IBLDR) cards causes the loader to load the decks with the deck names specified on these cards from the tape SYSCK1. Name .GETID on the fifteenth card is an entry name of a subprogram to generate an ID card with a job number, as a job number is required for the second job segment. Subroutine CKSTOR locates a six-character word in a table and adds the word to the table if it is not found. Subroutine CONTIN looks for continuation marks (three successive dots anywhere in columns 1 to 72), which indicate that the statement is to be continued on the next card. Subroutine FINISH checks, after the last DSL/90 statement is processed, for the presence of any centralized integration or NOSORT requests and records elapsed run time, and then calls the subroutines SORT, OUTPUT, and SWTAPE. (SWTAPE is an entry of a MAP subprogram OUTIN which closes input and output files, rewinds the output tape SYSUT6, and switches tapes SYSIN1 and SYSUT6.) Subroutine INTEG translates a DSL/90 statement containing an INTGRL block or blocks. JIGSAW is the deck name of a MAP subprogram which unpacks words into characters and vice versa, converts

BCD integers into binary and vice versa, etc. Subroutine NAME generates a unique BCD variable name. OUTIN is the deck name of a MAP subprogram for general input-output purposes. Subroutine OUTPUT generates an IBSYS job on the tape SYSUT6. Subroutine RDWRMX transfers a binary deck to a tape unit or transfers a FORTRAN or MAP source deck to certain tape units. Subroutine SCAN scans an array in the COMMON statements (each word of the array contains a single right-justified character with leading zeros), groups numbers and variable names between operator pairs, and repacks them into six-character BCD words left-justified with trailing blanks. Subroutine SORT sequences the translated FORTRAN IV statements so that values of variables used in each statement have been computed in the current iteration cycle or are constants. Subroutine STORE transfers data from one array to another. TRANSL is the name of the main program which converts a DSL/90 program into a FORTRAN subroutine. Subroutine XMSG1 contains all diagnostic messages.

The thirtieth is a $IEDIT card, which together with the fourteenth $IEDIT card, causes the computer to go to the input tape SYSIN1 where the DSL/90 program is stored. The thirty-first is a $DATA card that requests the loader to load the program from tape SYSIN1; thus, the thirty-second through thirty-fifth cards are regarded as data, but these cards become a part of the control cards of the second job segment. The thirty-second card, like the fourteenth, causes the computer to go to tape SYSCK1 and to search the first file for the decks with names MAIN and CENTRL. The thirty-third and thirty-fourth cards cause the loader to load these two subprograms, and the thirty-fifth card causes the computer to go back to tape SYSIN1.

Subroutine MAIN is the main program of the DSL/90 simulator, which calls subroutine INITLZ to initialize the run, then cycles through subroutines INTRAN and SIMUL once for each simulation run. Subroutine INITLZ is used once per simulation run to initialize variables in the COMMON statements. Subroutine INTRAN is used to translate DSL/90 labeled statements and execute the required operations on the data for a simulation run. Subroutine SIMUL is the control program for the execution of the simulation. Subroutine CENTRL is a dummy routine which may be replaced by the user at execution time to accomplish centralized integration.

When a DSL/90 program is processed, a FORTRAN program is generated and stored on tape SYSUT6 during the first, or translation, phase. This FORTRAN program is then processed during the next, or simulation, phase. Figure 7.5, which is printed out from tape SYSUT6, shows the FORTRAN program for van der Pol's equation. The first four cards in Fig. 7.5 were generated during the first phase. Generation

of the $ID card was due to the fifteenth card in Fig. 7.3.   The next four
control cards were the thirty-second through thirty-fifth cards in Fig. 7.3.
The subsequent 12 cards give the translated BLOCK DATA segment
with deck name DATA (as illustrated in Fig. 7.2), and the next 11 cards
give the translated subroutine UPDATE (also illustrated in Fig. 7.2)
with deck name DPDAT.   Twenty-seven control cards follow subroutine
UPDATE.   The two $IEDIT cards, similar to those in Fig. 7.3, cause
the computer to read the DSL/90 processor tape SYSCK1 and to search
the first file for subroutine decks and later to go to the input tape SYSUT6.
The remaining 25 $IBLDR cards cause the loader to load 25 subroutines
with the deck names specified on these cards from tape SYSCK1.   An
end-of-file card follows these 27 control cards.

   The above 25 subroutines are loaded for the simulation run.
Briefly, subroutines ANGLE, ANN4, AXIS4, DASH, LWIDTH,
NMBER4, PLOT4, PLOTR, SCALE4, and SYMBL4 are those required
for plotting.   Subroutines INITLZ, INTRAN, and SIMUL have previously been described.   Subroutines MILNE, RKS, SIMP, RECT, and
TRAPZ are centralized integration subroutines.   Subroutine LOOK
is described in Sec. 7.8.2.   Subroutine ALPHA selects the next alphameric name from each entry of an input data statement.   BYTER
is a MAP subprogram for format conversions.   Subroutine CLOK2 is
also a MAP subprogram for clock-time calculation.   Subroutine F is for
data transfer.   Subroutine NUMER selects the next numeric field from
each entry of an input data statement and converts it to a floating-point
or an integer binary number.

   Following the 27 control cards are the 19 labeled statements of the
DSL/90 program for van der Pol's equation; this is followed by an end-
of-file card.   At this point, execution of the FORTRAN program is completed; the following three control cards appear:

    $IBSYS
    $SWITCH   SYSIN1,SYSUT6
    end-of-file card

The above $IBSYS card causes the IBJOB processor to return to the
IBSYS monitor, which recognizes the subsequent $SWITCH card.   The
$SWITCH card causes the two tapes logically interchanged so that
SYSIN1 becomes the input tape and the IBSYS continues to read other
jobs on SYSIN1.   Finally, there are the following three control cards:

    $JOB
    $IBSYS
    $RESTORE

These three cards are provided in the case of a "core dump."   A core dump (usually 50 memory words at each side of the memory location where the difficulty arises) occurs when the time or output exceeds its limit, the operator intervenes due to an improper halt of the computer, or the like. When such a core dump occurs, the IBJOB processor hunts for the next $JOB card. When it is found, the IBJOB processor turns its control to the IBSYS monitor. The subsequent $IBSYS card recognizes the next $RESTORE card, which causes a "cold start" of the system.

Index

This book was set in Modern by The Maple Press Company, and printed on permanent paper and bound by The Maple Press Company. The designer was Richard Paul Kluga; the drawings were done by B. Handelman Associates, Inc. The editors were John T. Maloney and J. W. Maisel. Peter D. Guilmette supervised the production.